Action Learning

Action Learning

History and Evolution

Edited By

Yury Boshyk
Chairman, Global Executive Learning Network, and the annual Global Forum on Executive Development and Business Driven Action Learning

and

Robert L. Dilworth
Associate Professor Emeritus, Virginia Commonwealth University

First published 2010 by
PALGRAVE MACMILLAN

Palgrave Macmillan in the UK is an imprint of Macmillan Publishers Limited,
registered in England, company number 785998, of Houndmills, Basingstoke,
Hampshire RG21 6XS.

Palgrave Macmillan in the US is a division of St Martin's Press LLC,
175 Fifth Avenue, New York, NY 10010.

Palgrave Macmillan is the global academic imprint of the above companies
and has companies and representatives throughout the world.

Palgrave® and Macmillan® are registered trademarks in the United States,
the United Kingdom, Europe and other countries.

ISBN: 978–0–230–57640–7 hardback

This book is printed on paper suitable for recycling and made from fully
managed and sustained forest sources. Logging, pulping and manufacturing
processes are expected to conform to the environmental regulations of the
country of origin.

A catalogue record for this book is available from the British Library.

A catalog record for this book is available from the Library of Congress.

10 9 8 7 6 5 4 3 2 1
19 18 17 16 15 14 13 12 11 10

Printed and bound in Great Britain by
CPI Antony Rowe, Chippenham and Eastbourne

Contents

Preface

Shortly before the final submission of the manuscripts for both volumes my co-editor, Robert L. (Lex) Dilworth, passed away on June, 6, 2009. My sense of loss is still beyond adequate expression. We made a wonderful and deeply intellectually enriching journey together, even though we knew that there was much still to do to trace and understand the history, evolution and applications of action learning worldwide, and the story of its principal pioneer, Reg Revans. We both started our examination from different perspectives: he from having worked with Reg Revans and I from a non-traditional (Organizational Development-influenced) approach, learned from over 20 years of practice in the business world. Nevertheless, in our mutual exploration of the history and evolution of action learning, he found a renewed respect for Reg Revans and traditional action learning, and I, a new-found respect for the theory and practice of traditional action learning and its founder.

Lex was an inspirational partner and mentor. He was always ready to help, to share his knowledge and experience: a true "partner in adversity". Many people around the world feel the same and are very grateful for his generosity, unstinting assistance and encouragement. One manifestation of this respect was a Special Tribute paid to Lex at the 14th annual Global Forum on Executive Development and Action Learning – a community of practice – of which he and his wife Doris were valued members. A special award in his honor – The Robert L. (Lex) Dilworth Award for Outstanding Achievement in the Field of Executive Development and Action Learning was launched. In this way we shall maintain his memory, his contributions, and his values and commitment. Volume two of our co-edited work – *Action Learning and Its Applications* – is dedicated to Lex. His long-time collaborator, Professor Verna J. Willis, co-author with Lex of a seminal book on action learning, has written a memorial and biography of Lex in that volume for which we would like to thank her. To Doris, we express our deeply felt sympathy for her loss, and we hope she realizes that she will always be a special and warmly welcomed member of the Global Forum community.

YURY BOSHYK

Acknowledgments

Many contributed to the development of this book, but no one more importantly than Reg Revans himself. His "voice" is evident throughout, and much of it is not based on third party recall. What is stated frequently comes from personal conversations and correspondence with Revans. A number of the authors knew him and spent considerable time with him. Dilworth met him in 1991, was captivated by his concepts and deep insights, and went on to become a colleague and friend. Yury Boshyk never met Reg but, after the intensity of research on this book, feels that he knows Revans first hand.

Other important contributors included David Botham, Albert Barker, Alan Mumford, Verna Willis, Mike Pedler, and Donna Vick, all of whom personally knew Revans and provided important perspectives. Albert Barker and David Botham each spent a great deal of time with Revans. Barker was especially close to Revans in seeing to his needs, particularly after his wife Norah died.

David Botham was Revans' choice to become the Director of the Revans Centre when it was dedicated in 1995. Donna Vick was the first Revans Scholar, receiving a full scholarship to pursue her doctorate at the Revans Centre for Action Learning and Research at the University of Salford, and Revans became her mentor. She then joined the faculty.

Others who supported the development of action learning in critical ways and are no longer with us also are reflected in this book, including Lord Butterfield of Stechford, Professor John Morris, Nelson Coghill, and Janet Craig – Revans' close collaborator, friend and personal archivist for many years, and others.

For assisance in the research, as well as some of the people already mentioned, we and David Bellon would like to thank Roger Talpaert, Dirk Deschoolmeester, Daniel Deveusser, Leopold Vansina, Dirk Symoens, Luc Drieghe, Roland Van Dierdonck, Kenneth Bertrams and Liliana Petrella. From the U.K., we would like to thank Albert Barker, David Botham, Catherine Guelbert, Jean Lawrence, Alan Mumford, Pat Wright, Ian Hall, Jan Hall, Chavi Chi-yun Chen, Pavlo Smoliy, David Pearce; in France, Claire Meneveau, Chantal Fleuret and Leonie Chouard; in Germany, Otmar Donnenberg, Wolfgang Braun, Klaus Bodel and Karl-Georg Degenhardt; in Sweden, Åke Reinholdsson, Pia Anderberg, and Lennart Rohlin; in the U.S., Verna Willis, Donna Vick,

Lucinda Gibson-Myers, Lars Cederholm, Isabel Rimanoczy, Noel Tichy, John Johns, and Donald Sadoway. Thanks also to our publisher Stephen Rutt and Paul Milner for their understanding. To Nadia and Doris for their insight and support.

Revans influenced many people in his lifetime, and had over six hundred active correspondents around the world. He generously contributed of his time, rarely receiving any kind of stipend. To him, the development of action learning was a calling, no less compelling than that of a theologian. He saw action learning as more than an approach or technique. To him, it was a vehicle that could help provide a healthy balance in society, create more positive relationships and a deeper sense of fulfillment between employers and employees, and help understanding and peace among and between nations. These views undoubtedly came from his strong Quaker roots.

In sum, there are many people who have contributed to this book and to the development of action learning, but the major acknowledgement goes to Reg and his lifetime of service to action learning and humanitarian endeavors. He stands as our guiding light. Thanks also to our publisher Stephen Rutt and Paul Miner for their understanding and to the team at Newgen for their excellent editorial and typesetting services.

Contributors

Albert Barker (prof.albertbarker@tiscali.co.uk) studied philosophy before joining a U.S. multinational. He then became Chairman/CEO of a small engineering group, growing concerned about management and education standards. He also worked in the voluntary sector, on corporate rescues, and later led a research project in thermodynamics. He traveled the world working at board level with household-name multinationals. A Fellow of the British Institute of Management, in the 1980s concerns about management training brought him into contact with Reg Revans. They soon became close friends, researching, writing and working together until Revans' death in 2003. Latterly – and after Revans ceased writing himself – Albert helped with correspondence and represented Revans at various conferences. Albert Barker's interests are Applied Economics and Cybernetics. He contributes to an international economics journal, assisting on its editorial board. He practices, researches and writes about action learning.

David Bellon (david.bellon1@telenet.be) is passionate about supply chain organizations and has been working in the logistics industry since 1994 in various management roles, presently with DHL. Holding an MBA from Flanders Business School with the Kellogg School of Management in Chicago, he has been specializing in Lean and Six Sigma methodologies and all aspects related to Change Management in organizations. Through a leadership development program involving business driven action learning, he came to know Yury Boshyk. Based in Brussels, he was requested to do research on the Belgian Experiment led by Reg Revans in the 1960s. This led to interviews with former participants in that experiment, as well as research using archival materials related to Reginald Revans' ten-year stay in Belgium. David is also owner of Take (Training and Knowledge Expansion), a private consulting firm providing services on Business Performance Improvements and related concepts within various types of organizations and companies.

Yury Boshyk (yury@gel-net.com) is Chairman of the Global Executive Learning Network, a worldwide association of professionals involved for many years in assisting multinationals and organizations in the design and implementation of executive and management programs especially involving business driven action learning. The Network also researches, analyzes and publishes on global trends that affect companies and countries. Since 1996, Yury has been helping organize an annual Global Forum on Executive Development and Business Driven Action Learning, a worldwide "community of practice", and is presently its chairman. He lectures widely and works in cooperation with a number of institutions. His most recent article was on "Developing Global Executives: Today and Tomorrow" in *The 2009 Pfeiffer Annual: Leadership Development.* He is the editor of several books on action learning: *Business Driven Action Learning: Global best practices* (2000) and *Action Learning Worldwide: Experiences of leadership and organizational development* (2002), both published by Palgrave Macmillan and St Martin's Press. In 2010, two books on action learning, which he co-edited with Robert L. Dilworth, will be released by Palgrave Macmillan*: Action Learning: History and Evolution,* and *Action Learning and its Applications.* Formerly, he was Professor of Strategy, Geopolitics and the International Business Environment at IMD in Lausanne, Switzerland and the Theseus Institute in France. He completed his doctorate at the University of Oxford, and his Master's Degree at the London School of Economics.

David Botham (revansinstitute@binternet.com) is renowned for his work in the field of action learning. He was the first Director of the Revans' Centre for Action Learning and Research at the University of Salford when the Centre was dedicated on 2 December, 1995. A long-time associate of Revans, the "father of action learning", Botham had been Revans' personal choice to head the Centre. Botham has had a widely diversified career, spending time in both the "hard" and "soft" sciences. He established the first Further Education School of Art and Design based on action learning principles, at Central Manchester College for Further Education. Professor Botham is well known in the Health Service in the UK for developing and implementing many action learning programs for the Service and its top leaders and managers. Botham became interested in behavioral science while he worked for Her Majesty's Prisons in England from 1973–1990, counseling violent and hardened criminals. His interests and expertise in the behavioral sciences eventually led him into the field of management. Botham has done work around the world to expand knowledge of action learning, including the United States, Sweden, South Africa and Romania.

Robert L. (Lex) Dilworth was a retired U.S. Army brigadier general, with more than 31 years active service. He served as the 54th Adjutant General of the Army (TAG), a position dating back to 1775. He was also an Associate Professor Emeritus at Virginia Commonwealth University, Richmond, Virginia. Since 1991, when he became a colleague, collaborator and friend of Reg Revans, Lex has spent much of his time writing, researching and lecturing on the subject of action learning. This has included work in the UK, Australia and Romania. His book, with Verna Willis of Georgia State University, *Action Learning: Images and pathways*, was published in 2003. In 2008, his book, with Shlomo Maital of the Technion Institute of Management in Israel, *Fogs of War and Peace: A midstream analysis of World War III*, was published by Praeger Security International. Dilworth earned his doctorate at Columbia University and has Master's degrees from Columbia University, University of Oklahoma, and the United States Army's Command and General Staff College. He has also attended advanced management programs at Harvard, University, University of Michigan, and Northwestern University. He was a graduate of the Industrial College of the Armed forces.

Part 1

Action Learning: History and Foundations

1
Explaining Traditional Action Learning: Concepts and Beliefs

Robert L. Dilworth

Introduction

This chapter is designed to provide a thorough examination of traditional action learning, and the concepts and beliefs of its principal pioneer and founder, Reg Revans. As such, it is "pure" Revans – what he really believed and practiced. The chapter also shows how these roots of action learning have been adulterated, diluted and contradicted by later interpretations of how action learning should be practiced. Some profess alignment with what Revans believed, and then do something else that can be quite different.

Revans never intended for all applications of action learning to be carbon copies of his beliefs. That was not his intent, but he did hope that certain basic ingredients would be present, without regard to the design used. They include true empowerment of learners; minimum interference in the process by external expert facilitators; use of real problems that are of genuine difficulty and urgency; getting people out of their comfort zones by having them operate in unfamiliar settings and deal with unfamiliar problems; and reflecting throughout on these experiences and the assumptions behind their actions, including their implementation of solutions to the real problem addressed. Few of these precepts seem to carry much weight today in the way action learning is practiced. In some cases, the "learning coach" has been made the center of what happens. Revans believed, as most adult educators believe, that the learner is the center of the process. To him, action learning is democracy at work, letting the action learners largely self-govern what strategies and approaches they will use to diagnose what is happening and achieve a clear view of the problem.

3

Understanding action learning's principal pioneer

The "father" of action learning, Reg Revans, began as a physicist, before making his mark as an economist and educator. He was a revolutionary thinker, a person who could be abrasive and was, by nature, a maverick. He encountered much resistance along the way from those who were ensconced in traditional ways of viewing things and could see him as a threat. Revans would often say, "Unless your ideas are ridiculed by experts, they are worth nothing."

Revans never lacked the willingness to stand up for his beliefs, even if it could work against his professional success. Having been appointed as a Professor of Industrial Administration at what is now the University of Manchester in England, he ended up walking away. It seems to have been a mutual agreement. He did not want to stay and they did not encourage him to remain on the faculty. His ideas had clashed sharply with the ideas of more traditional academics. He was never driven by a desire for personal wealth. He lived an extremely Spartan existence, eating sparingly and spending little on himself, aside from book purchases. His eating habits could be a concern for family and friends. What he valued were ideas and making a difference. Action learning became his passion, and he viewed it as a promising avenue for opening up meaningful dialogue and promoting world peace. He was a Quaker, had a pacifist point of view, and abhorred world conflict and weapons of mass destruction. While he realized that he had special intellectual gifts, he was also a man of genuine humility, who believed in serving others rather than self. However, that does not mean he was short on ego. He had a healthy regard for his accomplishments and liked to have them recognized.

Revans lived to see his ideas widely adopted, but not without some continuing resistance. Certain of his precepts, especially those related to experiential learning, can receive particularly strong resistance because they seem so counter-intuitive (e.g., having learners tackle problem areas that they know little or nothing about, with the expectation that they will diagnose the problem, arrive at a solution, and have an uncommon learning experience in the process). As stated elsewhere in this book, the growth of action learning did not bring a great deal of acclaim to Revans, and some of his most basic and important precepts fell from view. One finds people citing him and his work, perceiving it as something significant, but without really having a clear idea of how he fits into the scheme of things. This book sets out to counter this shortfall and place Revans' beliefs in full view.

The world has, of course, moved on since Revans originally cited his beliefs more than a half century ago, and there can be expressions of action learning today that can represent an advance on Revans' thinking in some areas. For example, he did not consider simulations a form of action learning because they are not real problems. However, it now seems to be true that simulations, especially the highly sophisticated ones used in the military today, can be very real and can trigger the same kind of anxieties among the participants as crises in real life. This is true because they portray scenarios that could occur, and for which we must be prepared. Similarly powerful simulations can be used in the medical profession – dealing with possible life and death situations, and how to be ready to respond to them. Technology is changing, the way organizations are structured is changing, and the strong infusion of globalization alters the environment in which we live even further. But the fact remains that the very core precepts that Revans articulated are still valid, and we can learn from them, whether they are applied in totally real situations, or in simulations that can replicate life situations in almost every detail. The problem is that these core precepts are not always well-known. These core concepts and beliefs will now be outlined.

The commentary that follows will draw heavily on a number of private discussions between Revans and the author, as well as Revans' published and unpublished writing.

Basic precepts

Revans' experienced a clash of philosophies between his own beliefs and those who had a tendency to overcomplicate action learning as a process, as if no concept can be of value unless it is accompanied by a well-defined, even elaborate, framework. He would sometimes equate this with what he called the "MBA Mentality". Reg viewed action learning as "natural", flowing from the way people like to be treated and to relate to one another. It is fundamentally a straightforward and simple concept. He would even say that it represented a return to a childlike state – one where we are free to explore, be spontaneous, operate in a trusting environment, engage in open dialogue, and satisfy our curiosity. The importance of spontaneity was a theme he often emphasized. He considered spontaneity as a derivative of an environment devoid of pretense and bureaucratic encrustation, where even playfulness is allowed. There needs to be a significant degree of empowerment. Revans believed that this freedom to explore and reason is the foundation upon which action learning rests.

Verna Willis, in writing about spontaneity and self-organizing in action learning, states,

> It does not take high drama to show us spontaneity at work. We marvel when spontaneous gifts or praise are given, or when something suddenly crystallizes in our thinking. If we watch children at play with their impromptu "let's pretend" and their engagement in dialogue improvised to fit their scenarios, we can see naive, protypical effects of spontaneity. We witness a natural flow among the playmates that seems to fuel imaginative behavior and to satisfy deep longing to help each other make sense of the world around them, or alternatively, to create a world that might be. (Willis 2005, p. 162)

In addressing the naturalness of spontaneity and importance of action, rather than being so deliberate that the moment is lost, Revans says this:

> Theory is sometimes "preparatory action"; getting ready to do something. But many people in order to do something need to be confronted with the situation in which they have to do it. The billiard player needs to have his cue poised over the table to work out his next stroke, analyzing the situation with his arms and shoulder as he could not analyze with a pencil and paper; the batman thinks, in the moment of striking the ball, with his muscles and his bat, not in terms of abstract concepts and particle dynamics; the stone mason and the sculptor design the figure with their mallets and chisels as they go along; even the lawyer drawing up a complicated contract must allow the pen to "form his ideas for him", as it runs over the paper. And, at a much less specialized level, there are many people, old as well as young, who must hold audible conversations with themselves, to decide upon their next move. (1958, p. 65)

Revans refused to define action learning, preferring to describe it in terms of what it is not. He believed that to try and define it would artificially constrain it. He wanted to avoid giving simplistic cookbook or technique illustrations. He did not feel that action learning should be about puzzles, textbooks, lectures, case studies, fabricated issues or, as already mentioned, simulations. But Revans did come close to a definition of action learning in his book the *ABC of Action Learning*:

> Action learning is to make useful progress on the treatment of problems/opportunities where no "solution" can possibly exist

already because different managers, all honest, experienced, and wise, will advocate different courses of action in accordance with their different value systems, their past experiences and their different hopes for the future. (1983, p. 28)

Others have addressed the subtlety of action learning, among them Marvin Weisbord, who says this about action learning:

Few concepts have ever been so simple or so powerful. Yet this roadmap is not the kind you buy in Rand McNally. There are no visual keys for cities, airports or interchanges, no measuring scales in miles or kilometers. Indeed, our perceptions of the terrain keep changing as we involve more people and learn more about each situation. (2004, p. 203)

We will now turn to Revans' basic precepts of action learning.

Precept 1: When the velocity of change exceeds the velocity of learning, we are in trouble

Revans would often use a simple line graph tied to time to describe the accelerating speed of transport and information flows. He would start with Christopher Columbus, pointing out that it took him 45 days to make the Atlantic crossing to Wallops Island, his first landfall in the New World. He would compare that with a flight he took on a Concord between London and New York of only four hours.

The speed with which information is generated, distributed and analyzed has an even larger impact. He would make the point that, when the velocity of change exceeds the velocity of learning, you are in trouble – whether as an individual or as an organization. Therefore, the challenge is to accelerate the rate of learning to anticipate and match the rate of change. In other words, you achieve a state of dynamic equilibrium, or homeostasis, where the velocity of learning is in balance with, or even ahead of, the velocity of change. When it falls out of balance, you can experience disequilibrium, disorientation, organizational run-down, or personal failure because of inability to keep pace with the challenges being faced.

This balance between the velocity of change and the velocity of learning, which was so central to Revans' conception – as the impetus for moving away from traditional instructional methods and towards more experiential ones based on real problems – receives very limited attention in the literature related to action learning. That is a glaring omission.

We will now turn to Revans' formulation for accelerating the velocity of learning to keep pace with the velocity of change.

Precept 2: L = P + Q as a way to accelerate learning

Revans suggests that we need to turn the "normal" process of learning on its head. In his Learning Equation, the L stands for "Learning", the P for "Programmed Instruction" (the typical classroom or text book exercise) and Q for "Questioning Insight" (i.e., question-driven inquiry). It is the Q factor that makes action learning so different. That is where you begin. He believed that, in this age of global turbulence and rapid change, we need to shift much more emphasis to the Q and assign less to the P.

Rather than start with the P, as we have usually been programmed to do in both classrooms and our work life, action learning begins with the Q – the asking of questions – rather than immediately rushing to discuss possible solution sets. Why did Revans list the P before the Q in his equation? Revans told the author that it was done for a very simple reason. He was a mathematician and scientist, and the P always comes before Q in mathematical equations. He could not bring himself to reverse the two in written form for that reason, but he always emphasized that you must start with the Q and not the P.

Michael Marquardt, in addressing Revans' Learning Equation, apparently takes the sequencing of the P before the Q literally, seemingly not really understanding the full import of what Revans is suggesting:

> The action learning model starts with *programmed knowledge* (i.e., knowledge in current use, in books, in one's mind, in the organization's memory, lectures, case studies, etc.). To this base is added the process of *questioning*, which offers access to what is not yet known, and *reflection*, which involves recalling, thinking about, pulling apart, making sense, and trying to understand. Hence the formula $L = P + Q + R$, where L = learning, P = programmed knowledge, Q = questioning, and R = reflection. (1999, p. 29)

You cannot get farther removed from Revans' conception than this. Marquardt would have you start, based on his interpretation of the Learning Equation, at the opposite end from Revans. What Revans believed is that to start with P is a fundamentally flawed construct. You do not want to be mired in the past, but start with the here and now. Then, you look at the P, and you are likely to find that if you had started with the P it would have dragged you off course. That is the thrust of what Revans tells us over and over again in his writings of more than 50 years. Revans is not arguing that you discard P. You will obviously need parts of it, and might even need to create new knowledge (P) when the questioning process (Q) reveals that there are gaps in the available knowledge, or it is flawed.

To dramatize this, Revans liked to cite a major problem that was addressed during his Belgian Project (discussed in Chapter 5). It involved a problem that had existed for a long time in one of the largest companies in Belgium. Task force after task force, and consultant group after consultant group, had failed to solve the problem. A person unfamiliar with the steel industry ended up getting to the root of the problem. The key was asking fresh questions of a number of people – the Q factor in Revans' Learning Equation. That is where he started. By contrast, the earlier failed efforts had all started with the P, focusing on the production processes, since that had been the source of most other problems in the past. In the end, the problem was found to relate to the manner in which the company determined compensation of its workers. The experts had been looking in all the wrong places.

Alan Mumford, in an address to the EFMD Annual Conference on the subject of Action Learning, also makes some adjustments to Revans' Learning Equation:

> There has been an argument in the Action Learning world as to whether "Q" on its own can be effective. Revans' equation implies not, though his occasional diatribes about the content of "P" suggests a low importance for it. In my view "P" and "Q" must go together for effective learning, but I think the original Revans' equation does not satisfactorily express it. My revised version, using the same definitions, is: $Q+P+Q=L$. The significance here is…that we must start with "Q". That is the process through which appropriate "P" is determined. In some cases in the action learning literature, clearly inappropriate "P" has been provided at the beginning of the process. (1994)

Mumford has it right on several points here, including the need to start with the "Q". His modification of the Learning Equation also makes some sense, in that it lists the "Q" twice, as coming first and then after the "P", dramatizing the point that Questioning Insight ("Q") occurs throughout the process. When he states that Revans inferred "P" to be of a low significance, he is less on the mark. Revans did not throw the "P" out with the bath water. He realized its significance – after all, he was a scientist at heart. What he did debunk was assigning "P" the first priority of importance. That violated his conception.

To summarize this point, there are at least two good reasons for starting with Questioning Insight/Inquiry ("Q").

1. When we start with questions rather than solutions, we can find that the available "P" does not fit with what we need. If we had started by looking at the "P" first, such as documentation related to earlier solutions to similar problems, we would not necessarily have discovered this lack of fit. All of the "P" has one thing in common; it relates to the past. Therefore, in a fast-changing world it can lead you off course in terms of the current realities; and
2. We can also discover, as a result of starting with the "Q" factor, that no "P" exists for what we need to know. It might have to be created.

The "Q" factor can help us determine what "P" – or, at least, what part of it – is either valid or invalid. You can find that most of the available "P" is off-center with what is needed. Revans suggested a place to start, in terms of basic questions that can help you begin progressively to understand all the dimensions of the problem. He called it "System Alpha". There are three basic lead questions from which many others can then be derived:

1. What is happening?
2. What ought to be happening?
3. How do we make it happen?

The first two questions can lead to a gap analysis. In determining how to arrive at where you want to be, you then examine what it takes to close – or, at least, narrow – the gap. That, in turn, then opens up solution avenues and helps identify possible solution sets.

You will hear arguments that action learning is somehow "soft" in terms of analysis. That is not true. The questioning process can be highly disciplined. System Alpha leads to what Revans calls "System Beta". It is the logical follow-on, once you have run the causes of the problem to earth through the questioning process. System Beta includes:

• fact-finding and assumption-testing procedures to check and double-check what is being learned

- field research, data collection and interpretation, and other discovery methods
- survey and/or observation, trial hypothesis or theory, experiment (test), audit (evaluation), and review
- Ratification or rejection of results.

Here, you see evidence of Revans' grounding in the Scientific Discipline and Physics. While he wanted the learners to explore and demonstrate spontaneity, that did not mean being illogical in what they presented, in the end, as findings and recommendations. He looked for rigor. He also recognized that action learning is both an art and a science.

Finally, Revans believed that the action learning process could lead to what he called "System Gamma", where we come to better understand ourselves and the organizations in which we work:

> The learning process of the manager, and the corresponding change in the system he is trying to influence, is thus a symbiosis – here called System Gamma. It is suggested by the interaction between the managerial reporting channels and the manager's practical experience. The key element in this symbiosis is the ability of the manager to listen, and to change his behavior upon understanding what is said.
>
> This demands personal maturity and the resignation of defensive attitudes thrown up around the fortress of the self-image. (1982a, p. 347)

Revans' expressed views, in this case, edges us in the direction of what is known today as "organization development" (OD) in terms of strategies for changing mindsets and organizational behavior. Some have even termed action learning the premier OD strategy.

The symbiosis that Revans relates to his System Gamma occurs through the process of reflection, which also flows out of Questioning Insight ("Q") but, in this case, self-questioning. Revans was interested in deep self-questioning, what Jack Mezirow of Columbia University would refer to as both critical reflection and transformative learning. It involves more than asking the question "Why?" It entails looking for the "why" behind the "why", and then the "why" behind that "why". This means driving deep enough through self-inquiry that underlying assumptions, some even acquired in early childhood, that determine the way we think and problem solve can be brought to light and examined. Some of these assumptions that we develop in the course of a

lifetime can be buried in our subconscious. Having been brought to
the surface for examination through the process of critical reflection,
the assumptions that are now clearly dysfunctional can be jettisoned or
modified. It also allows us to develop new and more functional assumptions to govern our thought processes. Revans saw the action learning
and reflection process as an instrument for unlocking such changes
and, for that reason, he saw it as a way to promote collaboration among
the world's people and even help bring about world peace.

When you consider Revans' System Alpha, Beta and Gamma formulations with regard to action learning, you can see once again a hint
of the scientist in him, including the terminology and discussion of
Alpha, Beta and Gamma systems. When the author asked him how he
came up with the Gamma designation in one instance, he responded
that he did it for no particular reason. However, the similarity here
is striking between his scientific leanings and this action learning
typology.

Reflection and the questioning self-inquiry that drives it occur
throughout the action learning process, from start to finish. Some
reflection occurs as action is occurring, and some occurs at the end as
we look back and reflect on what has occurred. Donald A. Schön, in his
book *Educating the Reflective Practitioner*, says:

> We may reflect *on* action, thinking back on what we have done in
> order to discover how our knowing-in-action may have contributed
> to an unexpected outcome. We may do so after the fact, in tranquil-
> ity, or we may pause in the midst of action to make what Hannah
> Arendt calls a "stop-and-think". (1987, p. 26)

Reg believed, as Donald Schön does, that reflection occurs across the
entire spectrum. It is not a discrete phase. The learning that is harvested
comes from the process of reflection, with the actions and the real prob-
lem/project serving as the catalyst. This stands in stark contrast to the
conception of Marquardt, in his aforementioned interpretation of the
learning equation (L=P+Q+R (for reflection), as he states it. Here, he
takes great license with Revans' learning equation in adding the R.
That was not a part of Revans' Learning Equation, and for good reason.
Whereas Marquardt lists the reflective component as the "caboose" in
the process – the tail-end element – Revans saw it as a factor throughout
the process. This is very similar to the way Donald Schön viewed the
process of reflection, even though not speaking in an action learning
context.

Precept 3: The problem or issue to be addressed by the action learning set/team is always real

1. The problem is never fabricated. Pursuing artificial problem solving does not mobilize the full energies of those involved. There is no inherent risk present or authentic sense of urgency;
2. The problem needs to be real, somewhat urgent, and even daunting. Revans frequently stated that the best problems to tackle were the insoluble ones. It shows his faith in the action learning process;
3. Puzzles and case studies are not appropriate to his idea of action learning. Puzzles and case studies may stimulate your intellect but can be tangential to reality, and case studies are rooted in the past, not in the present;
4. The *real* problem is the "learning engine" – that is, what drives the energies of the group.

"Realness" is, of course, relative. The problem to be pursued can be real and yet, at the same time, rather mundane and free of risk. That was clearly not what Revans had in mind. He saw the stress of a difficult challenge – even one that could bring the enterprise to its knees if not solved – as what he was looking for. The stress and the realization that something truly important is being undertaken is what "powers" the learning experience and makes it much different that the ordinary "training" event.

The selection of truly difficult and complex problems can be more the exception than the rule. Allowing the employees to operate in ways that permit freedom and empowerment to problem-solve can be threatening to top management and human resource (HR) professionals. They can view it as an erosion of their authority and influence – even job-threatening. If you are a manager responsible for the unsolved problem to be addressed, you can be less than enthusiastic about having a team of employees, who you might view as novices, solve a problem that you had unsuccessfully struggled with. These counter-forces, rooted in human psychology, end up putting tight wraps around many action learning initiatives. The rule of the day can be: "Keep it safe and controlled. We want no rocking of the boat."

Precept 4: There are three basic forms of an action learning set/team

Revans' choice of words was "set" but, in modern day parlance, "team" is the better term to use, and we do so throughout this book, except when using quotes that employ the term. This avoids confusion and the inference that a set is somehow distinctive from a team, which it is not.

There are three forms of action learning team. Two of them are used often and one is not commonly used. Everyone in the team can pursue a joint problem, or individual members can pursue their own designated problem – either one they determine for themselves or have assigned to them. The third form was used by Revans as part of a major program in Belgium (discussed in Chapter 5). Here is an overview of the three forms:

One common joint problem: Everyone in the action learning team is dealing with one common joint problem. Because this is true, they must pool their knowledge and talents to diagnose the problem (System Alpha), and then develop the research, analysis, solution alternatives and recommendations (System Beta). Revans liked this joint form of problem-solving because it created a situation where the participants were "partners in adversity". The action learning team either sinks or swims together. This particular model is usually characterized by a strong bonding effect among team members. They have been brought together to take on a major problem, and they quickly come to understand that the only way they can deliver the result or meet the goal is through team effort and mutual collaboration.

The teamwork integral to this model can be a hurdle for some team members –at least, initially. They can state that they have never worked in a team before and do not like being in a team environment: the fact that most usually become adept at working in teams through the process represents a major learning yield in and of itself. It also promotes leadership development, because working in teams is of key significance to running successful organizations and businesses.

Everyone brings one (EBO): In this form, every team member brings his or her own problem to the table. This can be an effective learning approach, but it also has some notable downsides, which advocates tend to overlook:

- Problems brought to the team by its members tend to be highly uneven in their difficulty. Since individual team members want to be successful, there is an inclination to make safe picks – nothing that creates personal risks, interferes with a regular work routine, or raises eyebrows in any way;
- Members of the action learning team might listen politely to the problems and updates presented by other team members, but they are not usually vested in them. They are someone else's concern. Therefore,

the bonding effect among team members tends to be significantly less than that associated with a common joint problem team;

- Rather than let the team dialogue flow naturally, as occurs with a common joint problem team, the EBO-driven team has to ensure that each team member has "air time" to discuss their problem. The usual individual update reports alone can consume the time. While the team itself can impose time discipline, so all have a chance to be heard, it is also dealt with through the interventions of a learning coach. There is less spontaneity in this kind of team environment. The meetings can become orchestrated by design or tightly regulated by the learning coach.

The Belgian model: In the 1960s, Revans guided a major action learning experiment in Belgium. This program was intended to help improve the country's economic performance. It involved a consortium of the five universities in Belgium and a number of its principal industries. Senior executives in about half of the cases were exchanged between industries. A number of action learning teams were established, usually with five members each. Each individual team member was assigned an individual problem of considerable magnitude. On the surface, it would seem to be a regular EBO-type team. However, there was an interesting variation on this model. In the case of Belgium, each member of the team had a problem from an industry far removed from his own expertise. An executive from one of the largest banks in Belgium, for example, ended up being assigned a problem in Belgium's largest steel company. He ended up identifying the primary causal factor, something no one in the company, or its external consultants, had considered. I will explain the reason for assigning people to solve problems beyond their expertise in addressing Precept 6.

There was also another interesting aspect of the modeling that Revans used in Belgium. The senior executive in the problem identification and solution team would, after the nature of the problem had been well established, help "seed" a common joint action learning team in the client organization to implement the solutions. Therefore, two kinds of action learning teams were used in each case, one to identify the problem and the other to help implement a solution.

The size of an action learning team is usually limited to four to six individuals in order to facilitate intra-team communication. When you get much beyond that number, communication can become snarled and cliques can form within the team. The author knows of no one who practices action learning who prescribes any team size consisting of more than eight members. Revans believed, from his own experience, that teams of five were ideal.

In terms of practise, especially in academia, the "everyone bring one" (EBO) model seems to be the usual preference. For example, George Washington University (Marquardt's program) uses the EBO approach. The Revans Centre for Action Learning and Research (created in 1995 at the University of Salford in England under David Botham's leadership) uses the EBO model. That is rather interesting, because Revans, for whom the Centre is named, had an obvious preference for one common joint problem. He would often refer to "partners in adversity", calling attention to the difficulty of the task, and that all team members were in it together, a case of sink or swim. This tends to be much less true in an EBO team. Two universities that went with the "one common joint problem" model, dealing with problems of great complexity, were Virginia Commonwealth University (Robert L. Dilworth) and Georgia State University (Verna J. Willis).

Precept 5: The familiar versus the unfamiliar

Revans suggests that there are two kinds of problem and two kinds of setting/environment that we encounter in our lives. Figure 1.1 presents the way he depicted it. It is sometimes referred to as the "Four Square" Model. The examples listed in each quadrant are all from Revans' work and will be explained.

Familiar problem and/or setting: This is what we commonly experience in our own work environment. It can be the natural team of which we are a part in the workplace. In Japan, it can take the form of a "quality circle", such as a small team working to improve quality on an assembly line. Revans often cited this example, sometimes referring to these situations as "questioning circles".

Unfamiliar problem and/or setting: Revans believed that much could be learned when operating in an unfamiliar setting and dealing with an unfamiliar problem. That carries us beyond our "comfort zone" and requires that we ask "fresh questions", because the old questions and assumptions we commonly call upon are unlikely to be fully applicable. It would be like a dentist trying to ask his or her usual questions in dealing with a problem related to shipbuilding or complex informational systems.

The framework shown in Figure 1.1 displays the four combinations/variants involved, together with examples. What follows is an explanation of each quadrant.

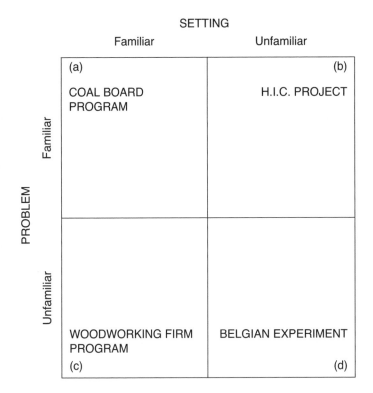

SETTING

Figure 1.1   The 'Four Square' Model

Quadrant (a)

The familiar problem and familiar setting: This is where we can find ourselves in most work situations.

The National Coal Board example given in that quadrant relates to work that Revans did in the collieries (coal mines) in England. He spent a significant amount of time working with teams of miners underground at the coalface. He found that, when the miners were allowed to design their own work methods and determine priorities, as opposed to being driven by dictates from management, production was greatly elevated. This reinforced Revans' beliefs about the value of action learning as a modality for solving problems and improving performance. It led him to coin the term "small is dutiful". He was, in effect, espousing the same basic principle articulated by E.F. Schumacher (1972). Essentially, small work teams, empowered to act, could score major advances over larger teams that were more tightly controlled and managed. The safety record in the mines was also significantly improved.

The importance of smallness in terms of team size was critical to Revans, hence his view that action learning teams should be limited to five or six members. In an article, Revans addresses the importance of organizational size:

> It has been known from the earliest times that the management of enterprises employing large numbers of men may demand the solution of problems quite unknown in the management of smaller groups. If the magnitude of managerial problems could be measured, as temperature or distance is measured, on a linear scale, the management problems of the industrial unit employing a thousand men would turn out to be greater than ten times those of a unit employing a hundred, and much greater than a hundred times those of a unit employing ten … Nor for all our telephones and speaker systems, have we gone much farther than Aristotle, who said, "The largest unit of men capable of effective action was a crowd that could be addressed by the voice of one man". (1956, p. 303)

The philosophy of Schumacher and Revans was well ahead of its time. Today, we find it in the emphasis large organizations place on operating as if they were smaller than they actually are, becoming "flatter", with fewer hierarchical layers, and using small teams (increasingly represented by action learning teams) to deal with complex problem-solving, promote leadership development, become closer to the customer, and increase competitive advantage.

The Mining Association example used here was, according to Revans, his first reference to what came to be called action learning. He was referring to an article he wrote,in which he states that this occurred in 1945 and was contained in a report on the future of the British coal mining industry issued by the Mining Association of Great Britain (1982b, p. 64). In the article, Revans had proposed the establishment of a staff college for the industry, "at which field managers would be encouraged to learn with and from each other using the group review to find solutions to their immediate problems".

Learning from and with each other was a theme often repeated by Revans throughout his life.

Quadrant (b)

Familiar problem in an unfamiliar setting: For the purposes of example, the Hospital Internal Communication Project (HIC) is listed. This study had medical staff from one hospital go to another hospital setting. The problem might be similar, but they were operating in a different corporate culture. The study, led by Revans, involved the 10 largest hospitals in London (1982a, pp. 245–79). Each had some common problems – namely, a very high turnover rate for nurses (as high as 67 percent), high mortality rates, long hospital stays, and demoralized staffs.

Professionals from one hospital were sent from their own hospital to one with which they were unfamiliar. They found the environment quite different, even though they were both related to hospitals. When medical professionals were sent from hospital A to hospital B, they could also find that they were operating in a different part of the hospital and specialty area than they were accustomed in their own hospital.

The author identifies with this, because he had several action learning teams work with two large hospitals in the Manchester area of England scheduled for merger in 1994. Revans was personally involved with this action learning project. In this case, only two of 32 participants, across five action learning teams, had any background in health care or administration of hospitals. However, they discovered that the cultures at the two hospitals were quite different, and that consolidating the management structures would not be easily achieved. I doubt that employees at the two hospitals could see the magnitude of the problem they faced. It took outsiders to signal that they were facing more of a challenge than they had anticipated. This might well have been what participants encountered during the HIC Project, despite the fact that they were going from one hospital setting to another. The corporate culture would have tended to be somewhat different from the one they were familiar with in their own hospital. Statistics were maintained on what happened at the hospitals in the experimental group during the HIC Project, as compared with hospitals in what constituted a control group not subject to the action learning intervention. It became clear that some positive results emerged. Turnover of nurses went down, the mortality rate went down, length of hospital stays was reduced, staff morale improved, and staff attrition dropped (it had been as high as 67 percent among nurses). While they were not major improvements for the most part, they were clearly gains. What drove these advances? It was found that the problem stemmed from lack of effective communication. Physicians did not talk to nurses, physicians did not talk to one another, and physicians and nurses did not adequately communicate with patients or their family members. When the communication blockages were identified and sorted out, things started to improve.

Revans was a physicist, and much of what he did can be traced back to his grounding in that science. He saw the connection in the case of hospitals, and it is reflected in an article he wrote:

> Physics is essentially the study of the ultimate structure of the observable world; as such it is interested in continuous fields and discrete entities, or at what can be represented as continuous fields and discrete entities. It has also become intensely interested in the nature and validity of human observation. To some extent these ideas have a parallel in the study of social institutions, in which individual persons, considered as discrete entities, come under the influence of social forces to which they respond. In the hospital the individuals may be surgeons or nurses, or patients; the forces may be the professional etiquette of the surgeon, the collective wage contract with the porter, the traditional myth of bedside routine enveloping the student nurse, the financial control exercised by the hospital budgets, and so forth. (1990, p. 108)

In this expression by Revans, we can also see similarities with what the renowned social scientist Kurt Lewin had to say when, in 1948, he wrote about his Topological Map, using the family unit to show the kind of interactions between the various actors involved in the process. (Lewin 2004, p. 79);

Quadrant (c)

Unfamiliar problem in a familiar setting: The example provided on the woodworking firm is covered in Revans (1983, p. 20). It concerned five directors of a large woodworking firm that was threatened with closure due to its uncompetitive factory costs. "Each director worked part time on a major problem in some other department…thereby starting the examination and treatment of unfamiliar problems in familiar settings – since all stayed in their own firm." Revans reports that the collective effort of all five directors, each working with an unfamiliar problem, led to a reduction of factory costs by 30 percent, enabled the main flow line to be reduced by two thirds its previous length, and preserved a thousand jobs that had been under notice only twelve months before.

Quadrant (d)

Unfamiliar problem in an unfamiliar setting: The example used here is the Belgian experiment, discussed earlier. Each of the executives was operating in an environment they were entirely unfamiliar with, and dealing with a problem they knew nothing about. In addition, the executives were working with the individuals in the action learning team that they had not worked with closely before. It was new ground for them, even though they were all well-seasoned businessmen.

The importance of placing people in unfamiliar environments to stimulate learning, get people out of their usual "sandbox", and inspire fresh questions is one of the lost dimensions of Revans. It receives little or no emphasis, and yet it was fundamental to Revans, an important driver of the outcomes he sought.

There is an incongruity, a dilemma of sorts, resident in the use of people unfamiliar with a problem. By definition, they will not have the necessary expertise to implement what they recommend. They will be limited, essentially, to diagnosis. To Revans, this was acceptable, because, for him, the bigger fish to fry was the coming to grips with what was generating the problem, as well as some thoughts on how to fix it. That was best done by using people who could distinguish between the forest and the trees. Those who had the expertise – who had not solved the problem to begin with – would tend to be bound up in paradigms and expert terminology that essentially blocked them from seeing what was really happening. Unbounded by past knowledge of the problem or area of expertise, those unfamiliar with it could view things through fresh eyes and ask "fresh questions" that the experts would have been unlikely to ask. That can create breakthroughs.

Some take a strong opposing position, believing that the action learning team must implement what they recommend – and they will not budge from that position. Here is what Alan Mumford has to say on the subject, in referring to this continuing area of debate (Note: When Mumford talks about "location", he is referring to which of the four quadrants is involved, such as "Unfamiliar problem" and "Unfamiliar setting"):

> This concerns the associated issues of the location for the action learning project or problem, and the likelihood of implementation ... The Belgian projects were all unfamiliar tasks in unfamiliar environments, and this has been an acceptable, and in some cases, desired form of Action Learning since. There is a paradox here, because of course Revans' original work in, for example, the Coal Board and Health Service were of familiar projects in familiar settings. Implementation becomes an issue where individuals are essentially carrying out consultancy assignments. Where learners recommend actions to others rather than being responsible for eventual implementation

themselves. Mumford argues that the Action Learning experience is fundamentally different. (1998, pp.: 376–7)

Mumford misses two subtleties here. The Belgian project, while involving business executives operating outside their expertise to diagnose a problem, also dealt with implementation. As the diagnosis came together, a team within the client organization in the enterprise owning the problem was formed to deal with implementation. The Fellow, Revans' term for those in the diagnosis team, began working with and seeding that team. Revans understood issues of "buy in" and worked to have a "circle of welcome" in the client organization to deal with the transition from problem diagnosis to solution implementation. He also had a clear design for who should be on the implementation team when formed. *Revans wanted three types of people represented – **those who care** (want the solution arrived at to work), **those who can** (have the power to make things happen), and **those who know** (have the expertise).*

On the "Health Service" (which is actually the Hospital Internal Communications (HIC) Project that involved exchange of medical professionals among the 10 major hospitals in the 1960s), Mumford mislabels it, in referring to a familiar setting. It was familiar to the medical professionals as a hospital setting, but it was not their hospital setting. It was a different corporate culture. That is why Revans engineered the exchanges!

So, how does one resolve this apparent dilemma? In a sense, you cannot have it both ways – having those without expertise diagnose a problem and then expecting them to have the expertise to implement the solutions. In logic, there are two ways to deal with the horns of a dilemma. You either break one of the horns, or you escape between the horns. You do not want to break or discount either horn in this case. The solution seems to lie in escaping between the horns, because you need diagnosis (that is really Priority Number 1, because if you cannot diagnose the problem, you cannot treat it) and you also need implementation. The answer is probably in having a receptive host – as was true with the various projects in Belgium – ready to deal with the implementation once the diagnosis is made. Anyone who has had experience working with action learning teams that are dealing with an unfamiliar problem, an unfamiliar setting, and even unfamiliar colleagues, understands the energy that is released, and it can lead to breakthroughs that could not otherwise have been realized. The author has experience with over 30 action learning teams operating in the unfamiliar–unfamiliar mode, and can attest to the fact that Revans had it right.

A case of an at least oblique connection with Revans' emphasis on the unfamiliar and the need to get people out of their normal venues is cited in O'Neil and Marsick (2007). They make reference to programs inaugurated by the Management in the Lund (MiL) Institute in Sweden:

> A hallmark of MiL's approach has been experiences that jolt people outside of their typical ways of understanding the world. Arts, sports, outdoor treks, or adventure training can be central to MiL's programs, as are journeys to other countries where the unexpected is turned into fertile territory for the questioning of one's values, beliefs and ways of working. (*ibid.*, p. 4)

The University of Michigan action learning initiatives, led by Noel Tichy, have for years included programs featuring travel to foreign countries as a way of opening up new thinking.

Revans would not have been entirely comfortable with these approaches, because to him they were "fabrications", and he wanted it to be entirely real. He would single out "adventure training", for example, as what he did *not* have in mind. To him it was in the same category as games, puzzles and simulations. However, it can serve to remove a person from his or her comfort zone.

Precept 6: No designated leader

There are differences of view about leadership of action learning teams. Revans was clear on the subject. He believed all mantles of authority should be left at the door when entering an action learning "set". He was entirely egalitarian in this regard. He viewed the team as an assembly of equals, with no team member enjoying any special authority over the others.

The leadership dimension is one that gets contested. It often ends up centering on how intrusive the role of the team advisor/learning coach should be. In its most pronounced expression, the facilitator can almost be tantamount to the leader of the team. Revans minced no words about the role of the facilitator. He felt that the facilitator (the term he preferred) had a definite role in "jump-starting" the process but that, as the work of the team went forward, the team members themselves were their own best facilitators, and the external facilitator should stand back unless asked to participate. Nothing irritated Revans more than excessive and controlling forms of facilitation. He would refer to facilitators in such situations as "silly taters".

The Revans viewpoint on use of "learning coaches" is at sharp odds with the approach used in the Action Reflection Learning (ARL) school of thought and the World Institute of Action Learning (WIAL), Marquardt's consultancy. Revans saw no need for "expert facilitators". The ARL model, on the other hand, calls for expert facilitation. The ARL approach grew out of the work of the MiL Institute, Sweden, beginning in 1977, and a group called the Leadership in International Management (LiM), which included Victoria Marsick in the early years. It also espouses the ARL principles. How does the Revans' approach to facilitation differ from the ARL model? Here is the way the difference can be described by those practicing the ARL approach:

> Expert facilitation is not recommended by others for different reasons. Revans's advocates decry coaches who, by inserting their own expertise into the process, can "steal the learning" of participants. In our experience, learning coaches help hold the space for learning. But they are more successful in their role when they resist taking on expert facilitation roles that participants themselves should take. The more that participants do it on their own, in this argument, the more likely that participants will fully internalize the learning and be better able to transfer that learning back on their jobs. Raelin points out that "ignorance (of subject matter expertise) implies a need to ask difficult questions that participants might find useful in framing the problem". (O'Neil and Marsick 2007, pp. 74–5)

There are several interesting things one can glean from this quotation, beginning with what Raelin suggests. What he is saying, in effect, is that the participants need a "crutch" from subject matter experts (i.e., expert facilitators) in order to frame the problem properly. In other words, you need someone who holds the "P" to help you over those hard bumps at the outset. That is a backwards remove from the point where Revans begins. Reference is made to learning coaches holding the space for learning. In other words, "We can't trust them to do that on their own." What this translates to in practise is a learning coach "protecting" this "learning space" by frequently intervening and doing "push backs" to keep the teams "on track". *If* (and, as pointed out, it is not always true) the team is pursuing a truly challenging problem, such interference by a learning coach can be seen as meddlesome, disruptive, and even infuriating to team members. The author has seen facilitators/learning coaches ejected by the team on three occasions. In terms of robbing participants of the learning experience by expert facilitation, Revans would absolutely support that view, and he spoke on it many times.

Marquardt has stated that the learning coach has "absolute authority" over the action learning team. There is only one obvious reason for dictating absolute control: you obviously do not trust the action learning process to work without somewhat tight orchestration of what happens by an external facilitator. In Revans' view, you take care to set up the process properly at the front end – "jump-starting" the process – and then step back and let the process work. As is true of ARL, Marquardt places the learning coach at the center of things. Revans has the learner at the centre. That is a huge difference in perspective.

What can be intriguing is how practitioners can talk about the need for empowerment in the action learning process, and even quote Revans, and then move forward with an authoritative and controlling model.

The author once went with Revans to a U.S. Department of Defense college for high-level executives in the Washington area. The faculty sat in a circle with us. They were about to launch a leadership curriculum using action learning and were looking for insights that we could provide, even though they already had one action learning program up and running. Their plan called for spending two full weeks orienting the executives on leadership before getting them started on projects. That seemed like overkill to Revans. That was not jump-starting an action learning program. It was rolling out a large quantity of "P" to senior executives who held some of the most challenging leadership positions in the U.S. Department of Defense. They did not need a basic course in leadership! Revans told them to eliminate most of that front end, letting executives get right into the issues they were to examine and "learn from and with each other". In other words, he said throw the real problem at them and let them have at it. Up-front hand-holding and teaching executives how to do what they already know when they had been doing that daily in extremely challenging leadership environments simply did not pass the common sense test with Revans.

Precept 7: Action needs to be balanced by reflection

While action is important, it needs to be balanced with critical reflection. *The true learning comes from the reflective component.*

Revans said this about reflection:

> It may well be that the set that most forcibly expresses the Aristotelian idea of which action learning is a modern example; the set has

been deliberately contrived so that managerial reflection can play upon the action of yesterday and anticipate the action of tomorrow, reminding its members that when tomorrow arrives, with its call to do something, that very doing must itself remember not only yesterday's reflection, but that reflection as it must be modified by the here- and-now dispositions of the moment making up the present – dispositions that could have been but imperfectly imagined during yesterday's set exchanges. (1983, p. 52)

The act of reflection is a skill, and it does not come easily in the Western culture, with its focus on action and immediate problem-solving. The exigencies of the moment can displace any inclination to step back and reflect on what is occurring or has occurred. To drive deeper and more critical reflection is an even more difficult skill to master, yet that is the realm where strategic thought resides. This leads to an argument that the ARL advocates would make – you need the expert facilitator to tweak the process regularly and promote reflection. However, inherent in that argument is the supposition that it takes frequent interventions by an expert facilitator to move people to reflect. As much importance as he assigned to reflection, Revans did not believe that.

Mumford, who is also on the side of expert facilitation, advocates some collateral techniques that others of us have found useful. One involves use of a "learning log" to capture reflection. Mumford also advocates what he calls "Type 2 Learning", which encourages the learner to reflect on what has occurred in the recent past (retrospective) and how it can influence the immediate future (a prospective view). However, as we have pointed out before (Dilworth, 2005), there is more than one way to induce critical reflection.

Conclusion

If there is "magic" in action learning, here are some of the key ingredients as expressed by Revans in his writings and public utterances:

1. *Asking fresh questions*: This becomes a natural occurrence when people are separated from what they know – and free to explore without the constant interference of external facilitators;
2. *Unfreezing underlying assumptions*: Since there are few old assumptions that seem applicable (when you are on unfamiliar ground), the person turns to fresh questions and, out of that, discovers that some of the assumptions long held to be true do not hold up well under

examination. Therefore, you end up constructing some new assumptions and testing them;

3. *Creating new connections and mental models*: This becomes possible when you move beyond the constraints imposed by assumptions and ways of thinking that are not relevant to the task at hand; and

4. *Rebalancing "P" and "Q"*: One outcome of the process is a new framework for "P" that is held to be valid. Some "P" is jettisoned, other "P" is created, and some "P" is either modified or validated. What drives this are the new forms of questions that emerge, and they evolve as the action learning process progresses.

In addressing a conference on Educating Cities in Gothenburg, Sweden, with Paolo Freire, the Brazilian educator, and others when he was 85-years-old, Revans said what, in essence, represents a good encapsulation of what he believed and what he held dear:

> I have struggled to explain that true understanding comes only after valid action verifies what one has been taught. The most simple fact, how one is able to mouth what one has just been told, is not evidence that one can start building on it whether or not for helping others. For, in trying to use what I have "learned", I must first know myself. And after arguing for decades with the experts, I see our need to recognize, more openly and more honestly, not ignorance alone, but also our pretentiousness. The Book of Genesis told the world and many independent sources warned as well, that rings of artful dodgers marketing their formulae for Paradise will bring Mankind to final devastation. Those now seriously worried about the trouble into which major towns are moving should see themselves as "comrades in adversity"; like the crews on any sinking vessels. It is among themselves, with and from each other, that they must settle what to do. We may well call this "citizen self-education", since all must educate themselves. (1992)

What has been outlined here are the philosophy, concepts and beliefs as expressed by Reginald W. Revans, action learning's principal pioneer.

References

Arendt, H. (1978) *The Life of the Mind, Volume I, Thinking* (San Diego: Harcourt Brace Jovanovich).

Cullotta, K. A. (2008) "The Parent-Teacher Gains a New Participant", *New York Times*, 27 December.

Davies, B., Principal of Willetton Senior High School in Western Australia, Personal letter addressed to Revans on 5 June 1991.

Dilworth, R. and Willis, V. (2005) *Action Learning: Images and Pathways* (Malabar, FL: Krieger Publishing).

Dilworth, R. (2005) "Creating Opportunities for Reflection in Action Learning: Nine Important Avenues", in S. Reddy and A. Barker (eds.), *Genuine Action Learning: Following the Spirit of Revans* (Hyderabad, India: ICFAI University Press), pp. 88–113.

Lewin, Kurt (2004) "Lewin: The Practical Theorist", in M. R Weisbord (1987) *Productive Workplaces: Organizing and Managing for Dignity, Meaning, and Community* (San Francisco: Jossey-Bass), pp. 70–87

Marquardt, M. J. (1999) *Action Learning in Action: Transforming Problems and People for World-Class Organizational Learning* (Palo Alto: Davies-Black).

Mumford, A. (1998) "Appendix 2: A Review of the Literature", in M. Pedler (ed.), *Action Learning in Practice* (London: Gower), pp. 373–92.

Mumford, A. (1994) "Action Learning – The Best Answer for Business Driven Management Development?", Presentation Seminar at the EFMD Annual Conference: The Special MiL Event, 8–10 June, Klippan, Sweden.

O'Neil, J. and Marsick, V. (2007) *Understanding Action Learning* (New York: American Management Association).

Raelin, J. (1993) "Persean Ethic: Consistency of Belief and Actions in Managerial Practice", *Human Relations*, 46(5), pp. 55–62.

Revans, R. W. (1992) Keynote address at the Conference on Educating Cities, Proceedings, November 25–7 1992 (Gothenburg, Sweden).

Revans, R. W. (1990) "The Hospital as a Human System", *Behavioral Science Journal*, 35(2), pp. 108–14.

Revans, R. W. (1983) *ABC of Action Learning* (Bromley, Kent: Chartwell-Bratt).

Revans, R. W. (1982a) *The Origins and Growth of Action Learning* (Bromley, Kent: Chartwell-Bratt).

Revans, R. W. (1982b) "What is Action Learning?", *Journal of Management Development*, 1(3), pp. 64–75.

Revans, R. W. (1958) "Theory and Practice: A Study of Technical Knowledge", *Researches and Studies*, 18, July, University of Leeds Institute of Education.

Revans, R. W. (1956) "Industrial Morale Size of Unit", *Political Quarterly*, 27(3), pp. 303–11.

Schön, D. (1987) *Educating the Reflective Practitioner* (San Francisco: Jossey-Bass).

Schumacher, E. F. (1972) *Small is Beautiful* (London: Blond & Briggs).

Weisbord, M. (2004) *Productive Workplaces Revisited* (San Francisco: Jossey-Bass).

Willis, V. J. (2005) "Spontaniety and Self-Organizing in Action Learning", in S. Reddy and A. Barker, *Genuine Action Learning: Following the Spirit of Revans* (Hyderabad: ICFAL University Press), pp. 155–82.

2

Remembering Reg Revans: Action Learning's Principal Pioneer

Albert E. Barker

This historical sketch of the life of Reg Revans, my close friend and colleague for many years, is based on innumerable conversations with him, input from his family and friends, and access to his personal records. Reg eschewed biographies and other forms of personal recognition but, in his later years, he became more receptive to providing me with information on which a profile of his life could be based.

I am honored to have been his friend. Like others he was closely associated with, he gave of himself freely. Each of us learned much from him. His life was marked by generosity and he had little regard for money or materialistic things. When he visited organizations to advise them on action learning, he almost never asked a fee. At the most, he usually received only a small honorarium and transportation expenses. He lived a simple Spartan existence and ate sparingly. It was discovered years after he had worked in Belgium, gaining a pension entitlement, that he had never claimed it. In 1994, as preparations advanced for an Action Learning and Mutual Collaboration Congress at Heathrow in England, Reg learned that several Eastern Europeans did not have the money to attend. He quietly came up with the money from his meager savings.

His interest was in making the world a better place and promoting the kind of dialogue that could advance understanding. Action learning was his instrument for doing this. One of his most common statements in beginning a conversation was, "All the world is discovering action learning".

In 1998, I prepared a more abbreviated profile on Reg's life as part of a special issue of the *Performance Improvement Quarterly* on action learning. However, what appears in this book chapter is far and away the most comprehensive statement on Revans' life in print.

Early years

Reginald William Revans was born on May 14, 1907 in the town of Portsmouth, a shipping and naval center on the south coast of England. Within a year or so, his father's occupation as a marine surveyor took the family north to live at Grafton Street, Claughton, in Birkenhead.[1] Revans mother (who held strong beliefs) made a practice of engaging in voluntary work. In fact, she helped out at the local hospital when there was no significant national health care provision. In 1910, when Revans was three-years-old, Florence Nightingale died. A memorial service was held which his mother, along with nurses whom he knew, all attended. Reg remembered them all being dressed in black for the occasion.

When Revans was about five-years-old, the family moved to 38 Foxbourne Road, Ballam, London. Reg attended the local Church of England primary school while his father carried out his duties as "His Majesty's Principal Surveyor of Mercantile Shipping" – he was highly involved in the inquiry into the *Titanic* Disaster. Revans remembers a procession of seafaring visitors to the family home. Some of the visitors, sailors and their families alike, were barefooted, so poorly were seamen paid in those days. As a teenager, he later asked his father to tell him the most important lesson he learned from the tragedy of the *Titanic*. His father took several days to consider the question and then responded: "We must learn the distinction between cleverness and wisdom". Even in his nineties, Revans still insisted that his father's answer to this probing question was one of the most important incidents of his life. Certainly, we see the young Revans already asking "Why?" type questions (associated with the quest for *understanding*) instead of the more common "What?" type questions (seeking basic *knowledge*).

At the age of eleven, the time came to consider secondary education. Both family and teachers alike were delighted and confident that young Reg would pass the entrance exam to one of London's most prestigious colleges – The Christ's Hospital School. However, Revans argued strongly against this. Reg had discovered that the traditional uniform at this school included yellow socks and a frock coat. There was no way he was going to walk the streets of London dressed like that. Despite his more than token resistance, he was firmly taken to the school to sit the required tests. Eventually, the results of the entrance exams came out, and for the first (and only) time in his life, he was adjudged to have failed the exam. So objectionable did Reg find yellow socks and a frock coat that he had simply written his name at the top of the page and nothing else whatever! This determination to stick to his views on a matter of principle was later to show itself more than once during his life. And so it was that Revans went to Battersea Grammar School instead.

From an early age, Revans showed a great affection for music and his mother remarked on his particular affection for the symphonies of Brahms; Revans told her how he was fascinated by the elegant simplicity of the melodic themes. He was interested in art too; indeed, he was so frequent a visitor to the local gallery (in London) that he was allowed not only to view those works on display, but also – as a teenager – to handle the paintings being kept in storage down in the vaults. Later, he took up painting and his work includes a portrait of his second wife Norah. The Revans' archives contain a number of his sketches, but most of the canvasses have been dispersed over the years. Neither was the teenage Revans a recluse nor nonparticipative child, for he engaged healthily in sports and, soon, his remarkable athletic prowess also began to assert itself. It was probably not surprising that he passed the entrance exams for both Oxford and Cambridge Universities.

When Revans subsequently attended an interview at Oxford, his idea was to study chemistry. The interviewing tutor, satisfied with his applicant's answers, asked one final question; "And what do you intend to do after Oxford has awarded you a fine degree in chemistry, young Revans?" Revans' innocent answer surprised the don; "I want to become a portrait artist!", he said – a reply which terminated the proceedings to the sound of application papers being torn up in disgust at what the tutor considered would be a waste of an excellent Oxford degree. Revans learned this worldly lesson well, for some years later – when invited to become a postgraduate researcher at Emmanuel College, Cambridge – Revans made no mention whatsoever of his interest in painting portraits.

Student years

On leaving Battersea Grammar School, Revans went to study at University College, London (1925–1928). Again, his talent and determination were noticed, not least when he soon started to get bored and insisted (against the wishes of his tutor, Professor Porter) on taking his physics finals after only two years instead of the normal three.

Not only did he pass his degree exams, but also won the prize as best student – not only for physics, but in the whole university (the Lord Rayleigh Prize). Paradoxically, he then spent a third year (1928) at University College – but now helping a hard-pressed professor with his research program. His athletic endeavors also continued apace.

As a result of World War I, Germany was banned from participating in the Olympic Games. Athletes from other countries decided to lobby against this and, in 1927, a party was assembled to visit Hannover where the International Olympic committee had its headquarters. Revans was a member of the delegation, and told friends of an event that had taken place during that visit. In the very hall where they were sitting at that time, Brahms had been a soloist at the world premier performance of his first piano concerto. At the end the first movement, the audience had taunted one of Germany's greatest composers. He was derided and ridiculed, shouted at and sneered at, and told to stop playing such rubbish forthwith. Revans told the assembly in Hanover that only when one is being lampooned and scoffed at by self-appointed "experts" can one be sure that one is offering something of any true worth. Later in life, he reminds us of others who have occasioned the same lesson. Revans was only 20-years-old when he addressed this august gathering. His declaration at this assembly had relevance throughout his life. He encountered frequent resistance to his views, but never wavered in his beliefs.

Revans was awarded the Sudbury–Hardiman Research Studentship at Emmanuel College, Cambridge, and from 1929 to 1930 undertook postgraduate research for his doctorate there. His intellectual gifts and hard work, as well as his athletic talents, won him the unusual distinction of a double blue – recognizing both academic and sporting achievements. Apart from his athletic endeavors and continued interest in art, he found time to play the trumpet and meet John Maynard Keynes. He also met with other twentieth-century giants, including Russell, Whitehead, Wittgenstein, Eddington, Bohr, and Einstein. Revans was now ensconced at Emmanuel College researching his doctoral thesis as the last doctoral student of J. J. Thomson, father of the electron. Revans also worked in the Cavendish Laboratory, where Rutherford became the new head of the laboratory when Thomson retired from this post in 1919. He went on become the Master of Trinity College. While Reg was at the laboratory, Rutherford was busy splitting the atom, James Chadwick discovered the neutron (1932) and Patrick M. S. Blackett pursued operational research (he was later to win the Nobel Prize in physics in 1948).

Other postgraduate activities

Those who have ever followed an intense individual athletic pursuit, or who have stood alone against another in a boxing ring, will know that the struggle they face also includes a battle to discover themselves and, in these circumstances, there is nowhere to hide from the truth; this process, too, was one that Reg was discovering during those Cambridge days and which was later recognized as part of the process he came to call "System Gamma".

Athletic meetings took him to inter-varsity tournaments in the U.K., Europe, and America – where he participated with the joint Oxford–Cambridge team against the Ivy League Universities, and for the Empire against the U.S.. Athletics persistently occupied him and he maintained his Olympic standards, specializing in the long jump and the triple jump. His Cambridge long jump record stood for over 30 years (1929–1962).

As a physicist, Revans was fascinated by the question of how the sun produced such prodigious amounts of energy on a continuing basis. He calculated that there was enough energy produced from one square centimeter of the sun's surface to power the biggest ship across the Atlantic – and the sun was 800,000 miles in diameter. Indeed, decades later our science fiction writers speak of spaceships using ion drives and solar winds as their source of power to explore the universe. (They would have to harvest energy since they could not carry a sufficient amount from launch.)

In 1930, a Commonwealth Fund Fellow award was granted, entitling Revans to study at any American university of his choice. He had already seen the halls of Yale and Harvard and, instead, he chose Michigan. It was here that he became friendly with Raul Wallenberg of the Swedish banking family – a man who went on to save thousands of Jewish lives during World War II by granting them Swedish passports, but only to disappear himself behind Soviet lines in 1945 under rather mysterious circumstances at the close of hostilities. (It was only admitted recently that he died in their custody). During his time in the USA, Revans took the opportunity to travel extensively around America, for the most part in his Ford open tourer, with fuel at 3 cents a gallon. He came to love the land and its remarkable people.

Seeds of action learning

While Revans was at the Cavendish Laboratory at Cambridge, there were 30 to 40 people there. More than a dozen of them were current or "about-to-be" Nobel Laureates; probably the greatest assembly of brains at one time in one place that the world has ever known. Some of the notions that later became action learning were undoubtedly formed during his two spells at Cambridge.

When Rutherford took over from Thomson as head of the Cavendish, he instituted a pattern of regular meetings; every other week there would be a general meeting at which a talk would be given by one of the researchers – each person "volunteering" in turn. Rutherford's guidance was, "Bring me each week something we all believe – but which can't be true".[2]

Every other Wednesday, at 4:00 pm, the researchers – each engaged in their own project – would meet together to discuss progress or lack of it. Some 15 or 20 out of the 30 assigned to the Laboratory would turn up – but not necessarily the same people each week. The spirit was one of struggle with the unknown, the bartering of ignorance, the quest to uncover another layer of particle physics only to find themselves presented with even greater mysteries. One afternoon in 1932, following a session by Chadwick, Revans recalls Rutherford saying: "Well, gentlemen, what has impressed me the most these last few hours is the extent of my own ignorance; what does yours look like to you?"[3]

What Revans later called "Q" (Questioning Insight) was present and provided by all. At the same time "P" (text book knowledge, established learning) was also present in copious amounts. The result was "L" – pivotal new learning which provided the basis for further "P". While Revans did not see the process at the time as the Learning Equation (something he arrived at later), what he appears to have been most impressed with was the spirit of the group and the personal changes that their struggles at the frontiers of science and knowledge were invoking. Not the least among them was the presence of a humility which enabled them to recognize the boundaries of their own understanding, and the appreciation that, until this was accepted, no further genuine progress could be made (what Revans came to call "Gamma"). For what they had to confront, above all else, was not their individual brilliance and understanding but their ignorance! This spiritual quality – both displayed by and generated among those intellectual giants – is quite contrary to the modern ethos of academic certitude and management consultant infallibility.

While what Winston Churchill later called "the gathering storm" began to assemble across Europe, Revans continued his work at the Cavendish Laboratory (1932–1935). Already, some were beginning to ask questions about the moral implications which might arise from the abuse of the new knowledge in the field of particle physics. It was between 1932 and 1935 that Revans met, and was impressed by, both Canon Collins and Bertrand Russell. He recalled the severe reservations of a Canadian from Montreal named Ferdinand Terroux, who also worried about the morality of the direction of physics research.[4] It was not until 1945 that Einstein lamented, saying – "If only I had known I should have become a watchmaker" (referring to use of the atomic bomb at Hiroshima, Japan).[5]

As their individual work progressed at the Cavendish, the interest displayed by government departments grew, particularly those concerned with military matters. The use of what might be made of their particle research became a disturbing factor at the Cavendish. In 1935, somewhat disenchanted and worried about the nature of the primary interest that the Cavendish research was now attracting, Revans left the Laboratory to become the Deputy Chief Education Officer for the County Council of Essex. It was now that his thoughts began to focus upon the learning process.

War clouds over Europe

By the 1930s, the East End of London had long-suffered from overcrowding and its elderly buildings were now neither healthy to live in nor otherwise suitable for modern needs. A new town was called for and this became "Dagenham"; it was located eastwards along the northern bank of the Thames. Large companies were attracted and its most famous industrial employer was the Ford Motor Company. When Revans arrived to take up his post as Deputy Chief Education Officer, Dagenham came within his area of responsibility. The planners had overlooked a few basic infrastructural needs, such as schools. Revans found himself facing the urgent task of establishing a number of large new schools.

During this short prewar period, Revans was approached by a colleague who had responsibility for the health needs of Essex. His problem centered on the shortage of nurses. They were being lost at a high rate during their training period. What was the problem in educating nurses that produced such a high rate of attrition? Revans was approached for solutions based on his responsibility for education services. This was another key point in Revans' life, for it was where he came in contact with problems of health care – an area that occupied much of his efforts over succeeding decades. Revans set out to investigate the cause of attrition. He soon encountered a culture that did not encourage the young trainees.

The idea that 18–20-year-old girls could possibly contribute to how a hospital ward might be organized and patients better cared for was simply ludicrous in the eyes of their "superiors". Revans recalled (usually with some anger) how they were referred to as "ignorant young sluts". Such then, was the ethos which drove the resultant paper, written in the form of a memorandum to the Essex Education Committee in 1938, and it led him to deal with the issue in a manner which establishes it as the first work in the field of what came to be known later as "Action Learning".[6]

Other seeds of later learning were also beginning to emerge, including the conviction that "Unless those trying to run an organization – like Ford Motor Company – understand that they only know their problems if they understand *what the workers* are thinking" will progress be possible.[7] However, Revans' words were not well received. The following year, the storm clouds broke and the war was finally unleashed across the whole of Europe.

Management by fire

Now in his early thirties, Revans was placed in charge of Emergency Services for the East End of London. This was to be his debut in the field of practical "here-and-now" management. There was no theory he could fall back on when dealing with Hitler's blitz on London (and the East End saw the worst of it). "That which we must learn to do we learn to do by doing", said Aristotle and this was eminently true for Revans at the time. It was practical, urgent, crisis management of the most intense character with death, destruction, air raids, incendiary driven fire storms and daily bombing.

Everything was a problem. Manpower was short and not physically the best (all the fittest young men had been called to arms). Equipment was scarce, severe usage brought problems of reliability, water mains burst and water supplies were cut off, gas mains breached and burned insatiably, electricity was missing or jury-rigged, buildings were reduced to dangerous shells, bodies were found and others "disappeared", rats became a health hazard, teams worked nonstop shifts, injuries brought even more crew shortages, some streets no longer existed and others were impassable. Food was short and, for most of the time, the infrastructure was wrecked. Revans even lost his car and all his clothes when it was hit by a bomb. He took it personally and never drove again.

> Those who see Revans as an academic – a guru of management theory – should dwell for a while upon this period of his life where he crammed more practical crisis management experience into those war years than many people encounter in the whole of their lives.

Revans was a practitioner of management in the most demanding and dire circumstances. Revans would say, practicing management and learning about management are one and the same thing.[8]

Coal Board

As the end of the war approached, plans were in hand to restructure much of British Industry. The coal mining industry was to be nationalized (1947), bringing about 1000 separate collieries into a single entity employing about a 700,000 people. Revans was chosen to be responsible for education and training, and he produced a plan for these activities in October 1945.[9] Revans' reaction, and it was typical of him, was to draw on his still persisting physical fitness and to proceed north to Durham; there he spent a number of weeks working down in the mines at the coalface with rough and robust miners well-educated in the harsh facts of mining operations. Not for Revans the modern practice of assuming expertise about something one has never done oneself!

It was during this coalface interlude that another important observation emerged for Revans amongst these perspiring miners, who were highly reliant on each other for their safety and successful team work. He saw a spirit that reminded him of that which had prevailed at the Cavendish Laboratory amongst Nobel Laureates in the 1930s. It was another clue that contributed to the ideas that became action learning.

Revans was convinced that colliery managers would learn more from each other than from prefabricated theories concocted by absentee management consultants who have neither never heard the chorus of miners' boots – nor ever been down in a mine. He championed a Staff College to be staffed by colliery managers. He researched and evaluated the consequences of what he called "Adverse Size Effect" and wrote an early paper entitled "Small is Dutiful". Further detailed studies confirmed this theme (that the smaller collieries performed more effectively than the larger ones). Eventually the Coal Board's Economic Adviser (E. F. Schumacher) came around to Revans' way of thinking and published a book, "Small is Beautiful" in 1973.

Revans wrote that:

My experiences ... brought me to question whether the senior brethren of the industry could teach their successors much worth knowing, since so many seemed largely incapable of learning anything themselves.

...

To put it simply, the elegant self-assurance of the plans prepared by the high-level experts were no match for the robust vulgarity of the colliery yard...It was impossible to open up any discussion of size-effects as communication, morale, and autonomous learning...To most servants of the Coal Board in 1950, as to those of the National Health Service today, the key to successful reorganization...is still a matter of the "right" central plans fed into the "right" administrative structure.[10]

Manchester University

Upon leaving the Coal Board, which was increasingly run by bureau-crats and administrators far removed from both the pit faces and dawn choruses alike, Revans became Professor of Industrial Administration at the University of Manchester, starting in 1955 and ending in 1965.

Michael Bowman, at Revans' ninetieth birthday celebration, told the story of his interview for the post. As he sat before the panel, a senior member recollected Revans' career as an athlete and Olympic jumper – also his penchant for leaping over bars (as in "pub") when suitably pro-voked. "Go on Reg, jump over the table", came the challenge – and that is exactly what he did! Not surprisingly, very little else seems to have been remembered about the interview by anyone, including Reg.

Projects undertaken during this period included an experiment in Lancashire factories which showed that it was possible to quantify workers' feelings about management – confirming that the art of listen-ing is highly desirable.[11] He also introduced "The Manchester Schools Project", showing that teaching styles affect the incidence and degree of antisocial behavior. Studies also included an effort to understand more fully how nurses, factory workers and management might learn how to better collaborate together.

It was during this period that Lord Pratt (as he later became) asked Revans to look at the problem of loss of nurses in the Manchester area during their training years. Echoes of 1938 rang in Revans' ears and he approached the problem in typical Revans fashion. Talks took place with nurses and trainees themselves, and much was learned when con-fidence and trust had been gained over a cup of tea at three o'clock in the morning, when wards were quiet and senior staff mostly sound asleep.

Analysis of sickness, accident and absenteeism records (indicators of low morale) showed that there was an extremely strong correlation between the incidence of these factors and the size of the hospital. When nurses were working in the larger hospitals, the records showed staff being off work not only more frequently, but also for longer periods than when they were working in the smaller hospitals: more evidence that "Small is Dutiful".

Revans advocated the idea of Business Schools and, in 1965, funds became available to set up within the University "The Manchester Business School". His notion had been that such an institution would be along the lines of the Coal Board Staff College (based at Nuneaton, manned by colliery staff themselves) and Revans wanted the same approach for the Business School concept: that it would be manned by business people themselves who would "learn with and from each other", creating their own resource, identifying their own problems and formulating their own solutions.

Revans recalled how this idea was greeted with derision by his academic colleagues. Businessmen were to have nothing to do with the diagnosis or choice of solutions. It led to a parting of the ways, since Revans and the rest of the faculty were like oil and water. It was a case of inbred traditions trumping new ways of thinking about management and business.

The Belgian years (1965–1975)

Revans left Manchester and, from 1965 to 1968, he worked out of Brussels as the research fellow of the European Association of Management Training Centers (EAMTC). This was a loose federation of over 40 institutions of university rank from 14 different countries in Western Europe. Revans himself indicates how this research came about:

> I had been President of this Association and was familiar with its endeavors to make more realistic much of its work. My task had been to visit its constituent members and to interest them in trying to develop a research culture specific to European management as such.[12]

Revans highlighted the need for the active participation of managers themselves, and one of the most interesting features of the report is reference to the recommendations made to the Harvard Business School by its Dean, George F. F. Lombard:

> After learning of the efforts being made to bring the universities and business more closely together through management development

now known as action learning, Dean Lombard strongly urged his own colleagues to build upon the European example.[13]

Lombard emphasized Revans' message; namely, that "a central problem of organizations was for managers to understand the effects of their management upon those being managed".[14]

From 1968, Revans started to work officially for the Fondation Industrie-Université in Brussels as well, where his main focus of work at this time was the design and implementation of the Inter-University Advanced Management Program launched in 1968. Belgium had a population of approximately 10 million at the time. It stood at the bottom of the international league of OECD nations in terms of year-on-year improvement in economic performance. Traditional economic measures had been tried but without much impact. It was becoming imperative to improve the country's economic performance and the Inter-University Advanced Management Program was designed to meet these ends.[15] The five universities of Belgium that had an interest in management training collaborated together and involved themselves with Belgium's 23 largest organizations, between them representing 52 percent of the country's capital base.

Action learning was used as a major tool for addressing the complex and daunting problems being experienced by these lead organizations. As designed, senior executives from one industry were asked to examine a major problem in another industry for which they had no expertise or background. It was Revans' technique for breaking them away from ingrained assumptions and arriving at fresh questions. The executives were organized into action learning sets (teams) of five, where they could exchange views on what they were experiencing and learning; learning from and with one another in the process. Additionally, executives were matched and exchanged between industries as a part of the process.

Within a few short years, Belgium moved from the bottom of the OECD league in terms of its year-on-year improvement right to the top, ahead of Germany, Japan and the U.S. The Inter-University Advanced Management Program had undoubtedly contributed to this end. The King of the Belgians made Revans a Chevalier – a Knight of the Order of Leopold – in recognition of his efforts.

The Hospital Internal Communications (HIC) Project

Also started in 1964–1965 (at the end of his time at the University of Manchester) was the Hospital Internal Communications (HIC) Project, involving London hospitals. This project ran concurrently with the project in Belgium. It involved ten London hospitals that came together in a program of action learning. Within these hospitals the general wards were mainly involved, while the gynecological wards chose not to participate. This was a blessing in disguise, for it enabled controlled comparisons to be made. Note was also taken of socioeconomic intake, and other factors, in order to ensure that other effects would not distort the picture. Neither was this a data-starved study, with the resultant statistics arising from a few dozen or a few hundred events. Indeed, the figures were of great statistical significance – involving 33,000 participating general medical and surgical cases compared with 29,000 obstetric and gynecological patients whose wards were not involved in the program.[16]

What was the outcome? Morale indicators all improved (absenteeism, minor accidents, staff turnover). Hospital "hotel" costs improved on a per patient basis (such as linen and kitchen services), and the waiting lists disappeared. Eventually Professor George Wieland of the University of Michigan devoted two years to an in-depth study of the program. He identified the cause of the mysterious disappearing wait lists. He took a look at the average lengths of stay of the patients and noted that, while there had been little change in nonparticipating wards, there had been a 25 percent drop in the average length of stay among patients in those wards participating. Quite simply, patients had been getting better more quickly. Intercommunications had been improved as a result of the program – better communication between nurses with physicians, between patients and physicians, between family members and hospital staff. It elevated staff morale and, when morale is high, performance improves and patients benefit both physically and nonphysically to the extent that they recover more quickly.

From Higher Downs

By 1974–1975 Revans left Belgium and resettled permanently in the U.K., when he was around 70-years-old, but the only retiring he did was to his home at 8 Higher Downs, Bowden, Altrincham, Cheshire. His activity level remained high. He was an advisor to the General Electric Company's executive program at this time. Books, too, continued to appear. In 1980, *Action Learning: New Techniques in Management* was published. His mammoth work *The Origins and Growth of Action Learning* was published in 1982, to be followed quickly by *The ABC of Action Learning* (1983) and *Confirming Cases* (1985).

In 1995, the University of Salford in Manchester created the Revans Centre for Action Learning and Research, and Revans' archive, containing many of his papers together with some unpublished books, were moved there. For many years, Janet Craig, a close friend of Revans, would spend a week or so each month organizing the archives and attempting to retain as much as possible for posterity. In an archive review in the late 1980s, it was found that Revans had upwards of 600 correspondents of which 400 were judged to be current (i.e., active within the last six to nine months).

As a hobby, Revans indulged in woodwork, with the home containing bookcases, cabinets, frames, benches, chairs and tables which he had either made from scratch or adapted.

An event that occurred near the end of his time at Higher Downs was the Action Learning and Mutual Collaboration Congress, held at Heathrow, England in 1995. Over 80 people from 17 countries attended the congress. Emphasis was on inviting practitioners, rather than an abundance of academics or consultants. As a follow-on to the Congress, international collaboration was fostered among the academic centers of Salford (U.K.), Richmond, Virginia, and Atlanta (U.S.), and Ballarat (Australia), each with their collaborative networks as well. Lex Dilworth of Virginia Commonwealth University described it as a "network of networks".

From Tilstock

Shortly after the death of his wife Norah, Revans (now approaching 90-years-old) moved to Tilstock near Whitechurch to live with his eldest daughter Marina. As we have already mentioned, his archive and many books were moved to the University of Salford where they were incorporated into the university library. After an initial absence, visitors began to attend Revans at Tilstock – and his pattern of response remained the same. His mind remained sharp and perceptive.

In 1996, a Summer Program was held at the University of Salford involving 31 graduate students from the United States, Canada and Australia. Lex Dilworth from Virginia Commonwealth University, and David Botham, Director of the Revans Centre (then renamed the Revans Institute for Action Learning and Research) at the University of Salford, partnered in setting up this two-week program. Revans participated throughout. This was an intense action learning experience involving major problems facing two large hospitals in the Manchester area and the National Health Service.

Basics of action learning

Revans made a concerted effort to have us understand action learning, even though we may never fully understand action learning itself. Revans resisted the temptation to define action learning or prescribe restrictive parameters. If we are to understand the man at all, it is through his lifelong deeds. They provide abundant clues.

He tells us that we should be "Learning from and with each other" and he gave us the learning equation as a guide. [Q=Questioning Insight, P=our text book or established knowledge, and L=Learning.] The Learning Equation he described as L=P+Q, but with the Q being the first thing to be addressed.

With System Alpha, Revans shows us a means of strategic analysis posing three Diagnostic and three Therapeutic Questions (i.e., What's happening?, What ought to be happening?, and How do we make it happen?). The five steps of System Beta spell out the process which also reflects our natural approach – Survey, Decision, Action, and Review, leading to Learning. System Gamma addresses the symbiosis of Alpha and Beta, and emerging from within the Learning Equation – reflects the changes which must take place within ourselves for any *real* learning to have taken place.[17]

Revans would say that the fresh questions he is asking us to consider are not new at all, and he refers us to the Karma, Buddha, Confucius, Plato, Aristotle, Christ and Mohammed, to name but a few:

Who am I?
What can I know?
What ought I to do?
What is the Nature of our being?
What is our Place and Purpose in the Universe?

Anecdotes

During the 1980s, two Nobel Prize winners had their prize stripped from them when it was discovered that they had falsified their data results. Revans (who knew the integrity of the Nobel laureates he worked with in the 1930s) was deeply dismayed, but not surprised. We are told that one day, in 1987, the phone rang at Higher Downs and it was a request from a Scandinavian body that wished to nominate Revans for the 1988 Nobel Prize for Economics. Revans apparently told them, "I know nothing about economics" and hung up the phone. He did not seek awards.

He was also a passionate opponent of the use of jargon, and man-agement jargon was high on his list of pretentious twaddle. He noted that academics of almost any hue can resort to mumbo-jumbo to baffle their audience and hype their own image. Said Revans: "It is the lifelong ambition of every professor to give a lecture about which no one in the audience understands a single bloody word".[18]

His view of facilitators (for action learning sets) were very clear indeed, though some refuse to understand his message when he says they are "for-silly-taters" (idiots). He also speaks of facilitation as "apprenticeship for White collar crime" and facilitators as "supernumeries".

Revans was always abstemious about food, but even he could not do without it. When he did eat, his choice was heavily fish or dairy ori-ented. He consumed copious amounts of milk, cheese, cream, and but-ter. Salt was used liberally, as was sugar. His diet was enough to give a cardiologist a heart attack; yet clearly, even in his nineties, it suited him well and he thrived upon it. Large pans of milky coffee would be brewed and then be continually warmed for consumption over the next couple of days.

After his wife Norah died, Reg's eating became a matter of concern. Often, he would work around the clock and forgot all about meals, so absorbed was he by his studies – particularly if they involved mathem-atical analysis, a subject that he found especially interesting. The effects began to show to those who knew him well. Attempts to keep the fridge stocked involved removing last week's fish dinner (half eaten but being saved), overripe cheese and various attempts by his daughter Marina to leave him pies and stews that had only to be heated up to provide an excellent meal.

Honors

His home at Higher Downs was filled with numerous plaques, memen-tos, awards, scrolls, and other acknowledgements from grateful individ-uals and organizations – from Hong Kong to Katmandu, and from the Arctic Circle to Australia. Some gifts were carved from wood, stone and marble.

Clutterbuck and Crainer (1990) wrote *Makers of Management: Men and women who changed the business world*, a book about the 24 people living and dead who have contributed most to modern management. Revans was included, alongside Henry Ford, his friend Schumacher and others. Revans was described by Igor Ansoff in the book as "an amazing and underestimated man".[19] In 1997, Revans was granted the Freedom of the City of London (similar to what some cities grant as the "keys to the city"), allowing him to drive sheep across the Westminster bridge.

A few indicative attributes

There is no attempt here to portray any definitive list, or to say what might have been more important influences than others. It does allow us to catch a glimpse of a man who became so dear to so many.

Humility: His own example of the willingness to learn – to read from and listen to others. When evaluating a management issue, he would characteristically talk to the workers first and learn first hand of their challenges – as he did when he went down into the mines with the miners for several months to experience life at the coalface.

Resolve: He was extremely successful as a solo athlete. For over 60 years he educated people in action learning, and undertook innovative experiments that were well ahead of their time, and in the face of frequent ridicule and rejection by traditional academics.

Integrity: He never claimed to have invented action learning, but simply refers us to evidence of this approach/philosophy/behavioral trait as developed elsewhere in various cultures and civilizations.

Awareness: Social cognizance – he was always the champion of the underdog – a passionate believer in participation, and a man who had real respect for those engaged with soiled hands in the real "here-and-now".

Sensitivity: He was early influenced by the sight of seamen in bare feet coming to his childhood home during the investigation of the *Titanic* disaster by his father. He never forgot this, and always was sensitive to the plight of the common man. He did not behave as an aristocrat.

Compassion: Revans knew the tragedy of two world wars, and had seen the impact first hand in directing emergency services for the East End of London during the World War II Blitz.

Patience: He was patient with those who were slower than others in understanding concepts. He was not pedantic.

Impatience: He had no patience with those who were exploiting their fellow human beings.

Assiduity: He was a master teacher. Few have found anyone else so prepared to listen to their problems and difficulties. He allowed people time to find answers for themselves.

Concern: Revans' deep humanitarian concerns were evidenced not only by deeds in his life, but also by his words. How many would have given up their love of physics because of concern that the science was turning to development of weapons of mass destruction? Revans did this readily and never looked back.

Last days

A few days before Christmas, 2001, Revans was moved to Westlands Care in Wem where he could receive greater support as the frailty of his years began to show. After his 95th birthday on May 14, 2002, some friends from the U.K. and Germany gathered with him for lunch in a local pub. Six professors, with masters and doctoral students too, found Reg his usual attentive self. He was quiet and thoughtful, and still showed all the powers of mental assimilation we had always known. He reflected on the conversations and then made his typically lucid, pertinent and deeply insightful contribution.

Over the summer he eagerly monitored events, especially in Romania, wanting to know of the people, their aspirations and their interest in Action Learning. Professors Barker, Botham, and Morris continued to visit him. He posed problems for further consideration, such as "What is the role of the university?" and "What is knowledge?" Just as "Gamma" had been a major study area with Albert Barker only a few years earlier, so too, in the autumn of 2002, Reg and Albert resolved to use the winter months to think about action learning as a cybernetic process in relation to cybernetics in the widest context – physical, intellectual, emotional and spiritual, to study these alongside genetics and the quantum physics first unfolding in his youth and developing since (remembering that Reg himself was a physicist), and to explore the whole cybernetic process as an inherent element in Creation itself.

In November, we began to detect tiredness, and Reg's physical condition deteriorated towards the end of the year. He slept a lot over Christmas and New Year, finally succumbing to the eternal rest he so deserved during the evening of January 8, 2003.

Notes

1. Recollections in the family vary and the house no longer exists.
2. As recalled by Revans on various occasions, including London, July 16, 1998.
3. As recalled by Revans on various occasions, including London, July 16, 1998; and Revans 1994 video at Virginia Commonwealth University during his time there as Distinguished Visiting Scholar.

4. Ferdinand Terroux went on to become a Professor in Physics at McGill University.
5. Attributed to Einstein in the *New Statesman*, April 16, 1965.
6. Revans, R. W. (1982) *The Origins and Growth of Action Learning* (Bromley: Chartwell-Bratt), pp. 23–9.
7. Revans, recollection of conversation, summer 1995, passing through Dagenham by car en route to Cambridge.
8. Revans, in conversation, but also reflecting the thoughts of Piaget; see Revans (1982) *The Origins and Growth of Action Learning*, pp. 772–86.
9. The numbers are from Kynaston, David (2008) *A World to Build: Austerity Britain, 1945–48* (London: Bloomsbury), p. 185. On the report, see an excerpt in Revans (1982) *The Origins and Growth of Action Learning*, pp. 30–1.
10. Revans, R. W. (1980) *Action Learning: New techniques for management* (London: Blond & Briggs), pp. 103–4, 106, 108.
11. Revans, R. W. (1980) *The Origins and Growth of Action Learning*, p. 210.
12. Ibid., pp. 226–7.
13. Ibid., p. 230.
14. Ibid., p. 231.
15. Revans, R. W. (1980) *Action Learning: New techniques for management*, pp. 39–48.
16. Revans, R. W. (1988) *The Golden Jubilee of Action Learning* (Manchester: Manchester Action Learning Exchange).
17. Revans, R. W. (1980) *The Origins and Growth of Action Learning*, pp. 329–48.
18. These are favorite comments – frequently heard by associates at the Revans Centre and elsewhere.
19. Cited in Clutterbuck, David and Crainer, Stuart (1990) *Makers of Management: Men and women who changed the business world* (London: Guild Publishing), p. 127.

3
Reg Revans: Sources of Inspiration, Practice, and Theory

Yury Boshyk, Albert E. Barker, and Robert L. Dilworth

Reg Revans chronicled his own evolution to what eventually became called "action learning" (Revans, 1980; 1982). To illustrate this journey, we will examine in chronological order earliest developmental experiences, followed by his work experiences with his first employer, the Essex County Council in 1935–1945; then with the coal mining industry (1944–1950); and as a consultant to the industry and as an independent researcher (1950–1955).

In this chapter, we look at some of the sources of his inspiration, theory and practice during his earlier years that have not been previously published or, for that matter, much talked about during his lifetime, except with his closest friends. His experiences of his parents and childhood, his Quakerism, Cambridge and the Cavendish Laboratory, his role in World War II, and his more personal experiences in the coal mining industry before its official nationalization in 1947 – all are moments and situations highlighted in this chapter. By 1947, Revans was 40-years-old and starting a new chapter in his life that would take him personally and professionally in new directions with a second marriage, and as independent consultant, researcher, professor, and pioneer of action learning.

Parents and childhood

In an obituary on the occasion of his father's death, Revans wrote the following – perhaps revealing some of the sources of his own character, behavior and inspiration:[1]

> OBITUARY NOTICE: Thomas William Revans
>   Mr. T. W. Revans died on December, 13, 1936, after a short illness, at the age of fifty-nine. At the time of his death he held the post of

Chief Ship Surveyor in the Mercantile Marine Department of the Board of Trade, and was a member of Council of the Institution ... [sic] He was apprenticed at H.M. Dockyard, Portsmouth, attending the Dockyard school, where his technical education developed on sound lines. In 1932 he was appointed Chief Ship Surveyor, and it was during his short tenure of office that the provisions of the Safety of Life at Sea and Load Line International Conventions were put into operation by the Board of Trade.

The manner on which consequent technical problems have been solved is a testimony to his sound judgement, technical knowledge and experience. He had an encyclopaedic knowledge of the Board of Trade Regulations and Instructions, which was at all times available to his staff and others who sought his assistance. In the interpretation of theory his outlook was predominately practical, and his authority was always exercised in the direction of relating theories to practical considerations. His outstanding characteristics were his ability to take broad views, his constant concern to keep purely technical considerations in their proper relation to wider issues, and his profound belief that regulations – even those for which he had been largely responsible in framing – were made for man, and not man for the regulations. But, if these were the characteristics which earned him the respect of all those with whom he came in contact, the qualities which earned him the abiding affection of his colleagues, and all others who were privileged to know him well, were his kindliness, concealed under what seemed at first acquaintance a somewhat brusque manner, and above all his never-failing sense of humour, which gave a characteristic and a quite unique flavour to every conversation with him.

Mr. Revans took a keen interest in the Institution. The papers read at the meetings and the discussions of them were carefully examined by him in relation to his duties, but he considered that his official position precluded him from entering into the public discussions at the Institution meetings. (The Institution of Naval Architects, 1937)

On other occasions when discussing his sources of inspiration, Revans noted the depth of influence of his father's comments on the major lessons learned from his investigation of the *Titanic* disaster in 1912. It is worth quoting here as it clarifies a major insight from his father. He considered it a fundamental philosophical assumption of action learning.

When I was a little boy, I was four years and eleven months old, a terrible thing happened in the Atlantic Ocean [12 April, 1912] ... A vessel called *Titanic* struck an iceberg and sank and something like fifteen hundred people lost their lives...It so happened that my father was what is called a ship surveyor. Most of the ships in the world had been either built in England or were insured in London. Our Board of Trade, our Ministry of Trade of course had a great responsibility for ensuring that when vessels crossed the sea they were reasonably stable.

My father who was a naval architect (and I myself) was born in Portsmouth, the great naval centre of Britain. My father became very much concerned with the design of vessels, the insurance of them, the way their crews were trained, the authority of their captains or masters, as they were called then, and so forth, and I picked up a lot of this when I was a little boy and then suddenly I heard about the *Titanic* disaster. Some of the survivors came to our house because my father was very much engaged in the inquiry [about the *Titanic* disaster] and of course as a little boy...I didn't learn all that then but some years later...when I must have been between fourteen or fifteen years of age, I asked my father what he had learned from it...[He said:]..."What I learned from the *Titanic* inquiry was to discriminate between cleverness and wisdom"...The inquiry went on for many months and we had all kinds of experts who knew about how to design the ship, we knew the crew members who were warning the lookouts to watch for icebergs and so forth...But it never occurred to anybody that in trying to avoid the iceberg in the way they did, what they were doing was ripping the vessel open from stem to stern...It never occurred to them that...if they had run straight into it [the iceberg] the vessel was designed in such a way that it would not have sunk...."

I had many discussions with him about that but that is the origin of how I was brought up to say "look, if you think you are trying to understand something make very sure that you ask yourself questions about what you mean by understanding it; do you know the limitations of what it is you are on about?"

Why I was wandering on about the *Titanic* is because I think we must grasp the fact that the way people look at the life they live is very powerfully determined by their experiences as little children.[2]

Influences from Revans' childhood are described in this 1997 unpublished typescript. He tries to explain to himself the deeper reasons as to why he left his career in physics in 1935.

My mother...[pointed] out three major influences upon me before the First World War. I had been born in 1907, and, two years later, the family moved from Portsmouth to Birkenhead; my father was a naval architect, brought up on shipbuilding, and soon to be appointed His Majesty's Principal Surveyor of Mercantile Shipping, stationed close to Whitehall. He had a major assignment in reporting the loss of *Titanic*, and my mother insisted that he had very quickly identified this as lack of responsibility, and as he pointed out to me at least twenty years ago, those nominally in charge of large and complicated enterprises may seriously reduce their presidential power by [not] discriminating too fully between cleverness and wisdom. It was a clear objective to defeat the Cunard's trans-Atlantic record by *Mauritania* with keeping *Titanic* at top speed, even if icebergs and fog had been reported in some historical records, but splitting the vessel from stem to stern by refusing to collide head on merely meant overcoming the latest cleverness of *Titanic*'s designers, so ensuring that the dozen or so bulkheads would prove ineffective in introducing new-fangled ideas about limiting the volume of flooding, and so preserving flotation. This was to illustrate the need for those in command of complex systems to ask fresh questions when the unexpected may arise.

My mother had reminded me of how I had acted a couple of years before, when Florence Nightingale had died [13 August 1910], for the nurses at our local hospital, where my mother was an energetic voluntary worker, helping to scrub the floors and to sweep the corridors, had been instructed to turn up in black for a memorial service, and to treat such visitors as myself, brought by my mother to the same formality, with utter and dignified reservation. Since, as a little boy of three, the nurses had picked me up and thrown me one to another, I was apparently so shocked at how they even neglected to look at me, and all disguised behind their black cloaks on this particular occasion, that I burst into a screaming fit, and had to be taken home by my mother. Over the next few months I was constantly picked up and cuddled by the nurses themselves, all trying their very best to explain to me why the Florence Nightingale memorial service implied our need to change behaviour.

This particular incident I cannot remember, but "social behaviour" as a determinant of humanity's future was made most powerfully clear to my local Sunday-school class through the newspaper accounts of Captain Scott's South Pole visit in 1911–12. The sacrificial awareness of Lawrence Oates was illuminated by our teacher as an up-to-date illustration of what Jesus Himself had suffered on behalf of us all in Calvary; *Chamber's Encyclopaedia*, 1955, vol. X may still remind some that *self-awareness* may not have disappeared:

> From Eaton ... Oates was one of the party of five who reached the South Pole on 17 January, 1912. On the return journey, beset by difficulties, the party was weatherbound. Oates, suffering from severe frostbite, and believing that his crippled condition would retard his comrades and imperil their safety, walked into the blizzard and gave his life. (Oates was but 23 years old at the time)

My three infant recollections, of technological shortsightedness, of social unawareness and of personal evaluation, may well have influenced me to give up nuclear physics and to take up education, [in 1935]."[3]

Spirituality, Quakerism, and the practice of the "Clearness Committee"

We know from Revans' close friend Albert E. Barker that Revans was a member of the Christian Protestant group, the Society of Friends, or Quakers. They are known for their "inward spirituality", or respect for the "Inward Teacher" – "the aspiration of private devotion, not of united worship"(Brayshaw, 1969, pp. 252–4).[4] Most are tolerant towards other religions. Quakers put "great emphasis upon the equality of believers", which accounts for "the absence of clergy and also explains why anyone may speak a word in worship based upon the leading of the Spirit". Their active opposition to war and social protest against slavery and inequality are also well known, as is their philanthropy. Quakers played an important role in British society, especially in healthcare, education and commerce. Among the firms started and developed by Quakers were the "chocolate dynasties", Cadbury's, Fry's, and Rowntree's (the so-called chocolate three); Barclays (brewing and banking); Price, Waterhouse & Co. (accountancy); and many others. The Quakers of Portsmouth, the place of Revans' birth, were known since early in the eighteenth century for the ceramic arts (Comfort, 1968, pp. 110–30).

Revans attended meetings of Friends, as Quakers call themselves, during his Cambridge days (1928–1929) when he was a graduate student there. Revans attended these Saturday meetings and among the Friends was Sir Arthur Eddington (1882–1944), the Plumian Professor of Astronomy from 1913 to 1944, and a Cavendish Laboratory member, where Revans was also doing his research (Barker, 2009). Einstein felt that Eddington was only one of the very few who fully understood his theory among the many colleagues who claimed to have done so, and, not surprisingly, because Eddington proved Einstein's theory to be correct through a series of studies of a solar eclipse in 1919. Eddington was very well-known in British society for his work and popular explanations of science – including, of course, relativity theory.

Eddington may have had a considerable impact on Revans. First, perhaps, influencing his choice to study astrophysics and astronomy (that is, variable stars) and no doubt reinforcing the religious foundation of Revans' outlook on life. Eddington was also a very religious person. According to Herbert Dingle (1954, pp. 25–7): "he was especially anxious to harmonize his religion with his scientific convictions". In particular, he wanted to ensure that the religious or spiritual side of humanity was an experience that was viewed as being just as relevant as the scientific approach to the external world. In Eddington's words, "We have to build the spiritual world out of symbols taken from our personality ... as we build the scientific world out of the symbols of the mathematician."

Revans' was a private man and he did not write or speak much about his religious beliefs, even though it is clear from reading much of Revans' work that his writing (from about 1956 onwards) is often interspersed with quotes from religious sources, mostly from the Bible, describing it on one occasion as "expressing the eternal truths of human behaviour" (Revans, 1962, p. ix). In several of his publications, he equated action learning as being, at root, very much part of several religious traditions, be it from the Hindu, Buddhist, Confucian or Islamic civilizations. On one specific occasion, he wrote an article on the relevance of the Bible for executives and the world that they confronted (Revans, 1982, pp. 200–9).

We also often see in Revans' writing clear statements on ethical values and principles such as honesty and social responsibility, advocating, at the same time, that behaviour be grounded in humility, and respect for other people and their points of view. Social harmony among classes, employers and employees, and among nations was of great concern to him and Quakers as well.

As a Quaker, Revans was a pacifist, and one of the reasons he left the field of nuclear physics is because he was distraught to see government's growing interest in the military applications of the research being done at the Cavendish Laboratory. And as a Quaker he refused to be involved in "warlike preparation" (Comfort, 1968, p. 153).

Throughout his life, Revans was concerned with and actively participated in peaceful protest, and enabling harmony among nations, peoples, and classes. His involvement in the Campaign for Nuclear

Disarmament (CND) movement with Bertrand Russell and others (for which Revans was sometimes accused of being a communist), his Liberal political orientation, as well as his wish that action learning be used to bring people together to resolve mutual concerns and problems for the benefit of a more peaceful society were all part of his world view.[5]

He changed his focus to embrace the world of education as a humanist, reformer and pioneer. Like the sciences, education too was going through major changes. In the 1930s, the needs of a more technologically evolving society were not being served by the old system, which was very clearly delineated by class differences and privileges with no technical education of significance, thus further disenfranchising the less fortunate with limited educational opportunities. We can appreciate Revans' antipathy to the class nature of the U.K. when, as a scientist, merit, humility and achievement were values most pronounced and shared by his community. He did sometimes comment on this in his writing (and to his friends), expressing his concern about the great divide between what he called "the artisan" and "the clerk", between those who work to "survive" and those who work to be "fulfilled". His was an approach and philosophy that today we might refer to as being inclusive of diversity and involving participative management.

We believe the Quaker influence on Revans' thinking and work can be seen most clearly in the striking similarity between the Quaker practice of the "Clearness Committee" and the action learning "sets" (teams or groups) advocated by Revans. The latter were to be groups of no more than eight people, whom he at first referred to as "comrades in adversity" and later as "partners in adversity. They came together voluntarily to address their common problems and issues, and collectively were to help each other help themselves, preferably without outside assistance.

The Quaker practice of the "Clearness Committee" seems to have been a fundamental source of inspiration to Revans. We have included a description by the American Quaker Parker J. Palmer on how the "Clearness Committee" is organized and used in the Quaker practice and tradition, because we feel it sheds light on assumptions behind some action learning practice.[6]

> The Clearness Committee: A communal approach to discernment
>   Many of us feel torn when we face a deep personal problem, question, or decision. On the one hand, we know that the problem is ours alone to resolve, and that we have the inner resources to resolve it – but those resources are too often obscured from our own view by layers of inner "stuff". On the other hand, we know that friends and

colleagues and family members might help us find our way – but by exposing our problem to them we run the risk of being "invaded" by their judgment and advice. As a result, too many of us privatize these vital moments of our lives rather than opening ourselves to the power of community. At the very point where we need all the resources we can get, the point where we must make a critical decision, we feel cut off from our own resources and the resources of others.

For people who experience this dilemma, I want to recommend an approach invented by the Quaker community, an approach that protects individual integrity while drawing upon communal wisdom, an approach that I have experienced with great personal benefit. It is called "the clearness committee."

If the name sounds sixty-ish, it is – 1660-ish! From the beginning of their history, Quakers needed a way to draw on inner and corporate resources to deal with personal problems because the Quakers had no clerical leaders to "solve" the problem for them. The clearness committee is testimony to the fact that there are no real experts or authorities on life's deepest issues (be they clergy or therapists or consultants), except for the expertise and authority that lie within each of us waiting to be released.

Behind the clearness committee is a simple but crucial conviction, without which the practice makes little sense (and can even become destructive): Each of us has an inner teacher, a voice of truth, that offers the guidance and power we need but that is often obscured by various forms of inward and outward interference. The function of the clearness committee is not to give advice or "fix" people from the outside in, but to help people remove the interference so that they can discover their own wisdom from the inside out. If we do not believe in inner wisdom, the clearness committee could become an opportunity for manipulation. But if we respect the power of the inner teacher, the clearness committee can be an occasion for helping someone name and claim his or her deepest truth.

The work of the clearness committee is guided by the following simple but crucial rules:

1. The person who seeks clearness (the "focus person") chooses his or her committee – five or six trusted people with as much diversity among them as possible (gender, age, background, etc.). Sometimes it is helpful for the focus person to consult with someone else about who might serve. A minimum of five and a maximum of six, plus the focus person, are the best numbers to work with, based on experience.

2. The focus person writes up his or her issue and circulates it to committee members in advance of the meeting. There are three sections to the write- up: a concise statement of the problem; a recounting of relevant background factors in the person's life that seem to bear on the problem; and an exploration of any hunches the person may have about what lies ahead. Most focus people find that in writing a five or six pages statement of this sort, they are taking their first steps toward inner clearness.

3. The committee should meet for about three hours, with a break in the middle, with the understanding that there may be a need for a second or even third meeting down the road. A clerk (chairperson) and a recording clerk (secretary) should be chosen, though taping the meeting is a good alternative to having a recording clerk. The clerk opens the meeting and closes it, and serves as a monitor in between, making sure that the rules are followed closely. The notes of the recording clerk (or the tape) are invaluable aids to the focus person in retrieving insights well after the meeting is over.

4. The meeting begins with the clerk calling for a period of centering silence, and inviting the focus person to break the silence whenever he or she is ready with a fresh and brief oral summary of the issue at hand. Then the committee members may begin to speak, governed by a simple rule, yet one as difficult and demanding as any they have ever been asked to follow: Members are forbidden to speak to the focus person in any way except to ask honest, caring questions – no more and no less. This rule has astonishing implications, since it prohibits us from dealing with each other's problems in the presumptuous manner to which we are accustomed! The rule means: no offering of advice; no "Why don't you..."; "My uncle had the same problem and he..." no "I know a book/therapist/diet that would help you a lot." Nothing is allowed except authentic, open, challenging, loving *questions* so that the focus person can remove impediments to his or her inner truth without being burdened by the agendas of committee members. Even if I presume to "know" the answer to your problem, my answer is of no value to you. The only answer that counts is one that arises from your own inner mystery. The simple discipline of the clearness committee is designed to give you greater access to that mystery – and to prevent other people from defiling it.

5. Committee members should ask questions that are intended to serve the focus person's needs rather than to satisfy their own curiosity. Committee members should ask questions that are brief and to the point rather than larding them with background issues and qualifications. Not only does this guard against the tendency to turn questions into speeches; it also helps the focus person gain sharpness of insight that is dulled when the questioner wanders. Committee members should trust their intuitions in asking questions; if a question comes to you with force, ask it, even if it seems off the wall. (Once, when I was trying to decide between several job offers, a committee member asked me, "What color do you associate with each of these opportunities, and why?" A bizarre question [that] gave me deeper insight into the choice I needed to make.) Throughout the meeting the clerk (and all committee members) should be ready to overrule questions that are really judgment or advice in thin disguise (e.g., "How could you so be so stupid?" or "Can't you see that it's your mother/father?, or, "Don't you think you should quit this job?").

6. Normally, the focus person responds to the questions as they are asked, in front of the group, and the responses generate more questions. Though the responses need to be full, they should also be relatively brief, so that time remains for more questions and answers, thus deepening the process for everyone. Some questions seem to evoke one's whole life story in response – resist the temptation to tell it! The more often a focus person is willing to answer aloud the more material he or she, and the committee, will have to work with. But this should never be done at the expense of the focus person's need to protect vulnerable feelings or to maintain privacy. It is vital that the focus person have absolute power to set the limits of the process. So the second major rule of the clearness committee is: It is always the focus person's right to choose not to answer a question. The unanswered question is not necessarily lost; indeed, it may be the question that it so important that it keeps working on the focus person long after the clearness committee has ended.

7. The pacing of the questioning and answering is crucial – it should be relaxed, gentle, humane. The Clearness committee is not a cross-examination; a machine-gun fire of questions makes reflectiveness impossible and leaves the focus person feeling invaded rather than evoked. Do not be afraid of silence in the

group. Instead, value it, treasure it. When silence comes it does not mean that the group has reached an impasse, that nothing is happening. It may well mean that the most important thing of all is happening: New insights are emerging inside of people, from their deepest sources of guidance.

8. A three-hour meeting (with a break in the middle) seems to be the right length for a clearness committee. Don't end early for fear that the group is "out of questions"; patient waiting will be rewarded with deeper questions that have yet been asked. About half an hour before the end of the meeting, the clerk should ask the focus person if he or she wants to suspend the "questions only" rule and invite committee members to mirror back what they have seen and heard. "Mirroring" does *not* mean giving advice or attempting to "fix" the person. It means simply reflecting back the focus person's own words and moods to see if he or she recognizes the image – and with each mirroring the focus person should have a chance to respond. (For example, I was once told by a committee member that, in his view, I had already made the vocational decision that I thought I was unclear about; when he presented the evidence of my own words, I had to agree.) In the last ten minutes of the meeting, the clerk should invite members to celebrate and affirm the focus person. This is an important time, since the focus person has just spent three hours making him or herself very vulnerable. And there is always much to celebrate, for in the course of a clearness committee people reveal the gifts and graces which characterize human life at its deepest levels.

The clearness committee works best when everyone approaches it in a reverent (which does not exclude playful!) spirit, inwardly affirming the reality of each person's inner guidance. We must abandon the pretense that we know what is best for another person and learn to ask those honest and caring questions that can help that person find his or her own answers. We must give up the arrogant assumption that we are obliged to "save" each other and learn, through simple listening, to create the conditions that allow a person to hear the voice of wholeness within.

The clearness committee is not a cure-all. It is not for all people or for all problems. But for the right person, with the right issue, it is a powerful way to rally the strength of community around a struggling soul, to draw deeply from wisdom within all of us. The clearness committee has its dangers. It can be exploited by manipulative individuals – as can every form of human interaction. But if the spiritual discipline behind the clearness committee is understood and embraced, the committee becomes a way to renew community in our individualist lives, a way to free people from their isolation without threatening their integrity, a way to overcome the excesses of professionalism in human care, and to open new channels for the spirit to move with power and healing in our midst.

The Cambridge years and the Cavendish Laboratory (1928–1930, 1932–1935)

In 1928, Revans was awarded the Sudbury–Hardiman Research Studentship at Emmanuel College, Cambridge, and started work on his doctorate. He was the last postgraduate student of J.J. Thomson, the 1906 Nobel Prize winning scientist who discovered the electron, former head of the Cavendish Laboratory (to 1919) and Master of Trinity College. Revans worked in the Cavendish Laboratory under the new director, Ernest Rutherford from 1928–1930, and then from 1932–1935, when he obtained his doctorate and left Cambridge.

It is of interest to note that there was a strong relationship between Thomson and Revans. They shared a love of sports, a sense of humour, humility and faith. As a human being, Thomson was highly respected and loved, as can be seen from this funeral oration by Professor G.M. Trevelyan, Thomson's successor as Master of Trinity College, Cambridge:

> I am incompetent to judge the late Master's scientific achievement. But Professor Bragg has written of it: "He, more than any other man, was responsible for the fundamental change in outlook which distinguishes the physics of this century from that of the last."
>
> I will leave it at that. But we are here to-day to remember 'J.J.' as our friend, his unaffected modesty, the most beautiful of all settings for superlative powers of mind; his ever-active love of the College; his interests in its athletic as well as its academic success and failures from day to day; his evident desire to be regarded as an ordinary plain man among ordinary plain men, though his genius had in fact raised him so high above our heads. (Rayleigh, 1942, p. 287)

As an academic supervisor, Thomson created a sense of confidence and self-reliance in his students, and Revans was no exception. When Revans later wrote about Learning = Programmed information and (more importantly) Questioning Insight, and then about how opposed he was to interventionist facilitation, one can see this as being very much Thomson's approach to learning as well. In Thomson's own words:

> In my opinion research has great educational value and can be made a good test of a man's mental power. I have often observed very striking mental development in students after they have spent a year or two on research: they gain independence of thought, maturity of judgement, increased critical power and self-reliance, in fact they are carried from mental adolescence to manhood. It is essential, however, that when using the dissertation as a test of mental power, other things should be taken into account besides the scientific importance of the results it contains... I think when once the research has been started, the student should be encouraged to try to overcome his difficulties by his own efforts, and that the assistance given by the teacher should not be more than necessary to keep him from being disheartened by failure, and to prevent the work getting on lines which cannot lead to success. (Thomson, 1937, pp. 283–4)

Revans often spoke and wrote about the intellectual and social climate of the Cavendish, also captured in this passage from Larsen (1962, pp. 59–60):

> For those fortunate enough to be students or researcher workers at the Cavendish, the twenties and thirties were a most exciting period. The "Cavendish tradition", says Calder, "broke down the isolationism of research... It was a case of taking the informality of the common-room into the laboratory, retaining, and, indeed, encouraging the individuality of the scientist however junior, and making the professor the mentor rather than the master of research. At the same time, it was what we might call today a 'working-party' in which everyone swopped ideas, and, when necessary, lent a hand with the other's chores... It was a nursery in which infant 'genius' was given its fling", says Calder. "It was in the best Montessori tradition; the 'infants' were encouraged to use their hands as well as their heads and to 'make do and mend'".

Of the 15 or so new research students who were admitted yearly, at least half completed their previous studies at Cambridge and the other

half came from all over the world, but all had to go through an obliga-
tory carpentry course to make them self-reliant in the building of their
experimental equipment. Revans' love of carpentry (described by his
daughter Marina in Chapter 4 of this volume) and his gift for it perhaps
spring from this period.

There were, at any given time, about 40 people in total at the
Cavendish, almost all focusing on the director's (Rutherford's) main
research interest, the interior of the atom. Students were expected to
carry out their research in three years and, at the end, gain their Ph.D.
and ideally have been published. In the meantime, they were members
of a special community with clear values and traditions. For example,
the Laboratory itself was closed for *everyone* at 6 pm, a practice started
by Thomson and continued by Rutherford to encourage reflection and
the reading of scientific journals, and to ensure that no one's health
was ruined by overwork. Another feature of this community was the
seminars and clubs for discussion and fun. While the circle around the
Soviet scientist, Kapitza, certainly was full of mirth (and great discussion), every second Wednesday afternoon Rutherford would preside over
a meeting of the researchers, the so-called Cavendish Physical Society.
According to Cathcart (2004, p. 117):

> This was the formal embodiment of the laboratory's research com-
> munity and so the first meeting of every year, in the autumn, was
> like an AGM, with the director providing a *tour d'horizon* of progress
> both "in house" and internationally. At other sessions there would
> be guest speakers or lectures from Cavendish researchers – anyone
> with an important paper coming up in the journals was likely to
> be asked to address this forum. Rutherford's introductions and clos-
> ing remarks were often to be savoured since when he disagreed with
> something as he frequently did, he had the greatest difficulty conceal-
> ing it ... Every other Wednesday afternoon, when the Physical Society
> did not meet, Chadwick and Fowler convened their Colloquium, a
> forum whose job was to close the gap between theoreticians and
> experimenters. This was deliberately held in a room "small enough
> to be full" so that discussion would be freer, and most of the papers
> were delivered by younger researchers on work in which they were
> not personally involved.

Another fortnightly event was the evening meeting of the
Cambridge Philosophical Society, which Rutherford did much to
revive in the 1920s, and besides these official events there were several clubs, of which the most active was the Kapitza Club.

These gatherings reflected the excitement and passion that dominated the new and exciting field of atomic physics and deepened the culture of constructive criticism, pragmatism, and cooperation to be found among colleagues. Of all of these meetings, one in particular stood out for Revans. This was in 1932, on the eve of Chadwick's public announcement about having split the atom (April). It was a comment by Rutherford that became a fundamental intellectual, cultural and behavioral foundation of action learning. Many years later, Revans recalled the general context and the specific moment:

> The Cavendish Laboratory at Cambridge in the 1920s and 1930s was without any doubt whatsoever, the greatest concentration of intellectual ability on human record. I worked in the Cavendish Laboratory as a research fellow, and at that time the great interest was in what has since become known as atomic energy – [that is] where does the atom get its energy from?
>
> The director of the Laboratory was Lord Rutherford who was the first architect of the atom together with the Danish scientist Niels Bohr. I was the last doctoral student of Sir Joseph Thomson and in a sense J.J. Thomson was the founder of modern technology because he was the first to identify the electron which is of course an element in atomic structure...
>
> While I was there, a totally new object was discovered, called the neutron. It was the discovery of the neutron, in the Cavendish, by our research group, that of course laid the foundation for atomic fission, smashing up atoms and generating electricity.
>
> But the important thing was this: whereas my father on asking why the *Titanic* had sunk realized that all the experts who had helped design and run that vessel were insisting upon concentrating on their own narrow field whatever it might be, in the Cavendish the spirit was quite different. Although these different Nobel Prize winners all had different suggestions as to what the cause of atomic fission was – one of them saying it must be high speed beta particles, others saying that it can't be that at all, that it's gamma radiation or alpha particles or something – although they argued among themselves they didn't try to impress each other on how clever they were, and that *their* idea must be the one that was finally suggested. They used to argue with each other and say, "well old chap, if you think *that*, that's very interesting, because what I'm now trying to understand is not so much what it is you're actually thinking but what is it about your past experience which has led you to think in that way?".

In all my years in the Cavendish, although we had eleven Nobel Prize winners, all competing with each other to explain the causes of atomic fission they were not in any way hostile to each other, they were saying – "if my theory is a mistake *here* and doesn't work, what can I learn about why I pursued this long argument by listening to somebody else talking about his difficulties?"

I can remember once Lord Rutherford saying... just a few weeks before Chadwick came out with the final evidence that none of the previous theories would work, that it was a new object altogether, the neutron that caused this, Rutherford was chairman of a seminar and he said at the end of it: "Well boys we've been arguing for the past four hours we'd better get away now and go to hall and get our dinner... What's impressed me for the past four hours is my own bloody ignorance; what does *your's* look like to you yourselves?"

It was this comment by Rutherford which I have kept in my mind... [and] since 1933... I have been interested in how is it that people change their minds and their opinions particularly when they're responsible for running some important system, and... this simple idea that in order to understand better what is it we are trying to do we should be exchanging our ideas with others who say, "well, I see that you have a few doubts about what it is you're after, I have got a few doubts too; can't we do something different?" Most people when they realize that they've got doubts about something, they shut up and they don't discuss it, they pretend to everybody else they haven't got any doubts. This, I think, is responsible for the mess the world is getting into and only if people admit they have doubts, however important they are, however many papers they have published – only if they say "things are happening here which I'm afraid I don't fully understand", only if they meet other people who share their view, do they begin to explore their difficulties do we make any real progress: that is the foundation of action learning... And let me add that... it's high time the world started to ask itself a few fresh questions. (Revans, 1994)

Seen from the outside, some German and American physicists looked down on the Cavendish Laboratory researchers, considering them to be "half physicists" because they were perceived as being either not theoretical enough, or unable or unwilling to link more thoroughly theory and experimentation (Crowther, 1974, p. 233). Later in his career Revans would surely have been reminded of this attitude in his own work in education when he fought back against academic critics who maintained that his ideas about action learning were not grounded in theory. As a partial rejoinder, he would paraphrase Nietzsche that "no good idea was ever adopted before it was ridiculed" (Revans, 1962, p. 11) and "the value of any new proposal can be estimated by the ridicule and resistance with which it is first saluted" (Revans, 1982, p. 498).

Finally, it was also at Cambridge that Revans met some colleagues who became lifelong friends and who also supported him and his work over many decades. Among these was Vivian Bowden (1910–1989), later Lord Bowden, who was also a Ph.D. in physics, and a pioneer in both using computers and in encouraging knowledge about their coming impact. A good example of this was his edited book *Faster than Thought: A Symposium on Digital Computing Machines*, published in 1953. In that same year, he was made Principal of the Manchester College of Science and Technology and was, no doubt, one of the people who was instrumental in recruiting Revans to his professorship there in 1955. As a member of the House of Lords, he on several occasions mentioned Revans' contributions, including his work in Belgium.

World War II

Revans was placed in charge of Emergency Services in the east end of London during the war years and in particular during the "blitz" of London, from 1940–1941. It was under such extreme circumstances that Revans got his seminal experience with what we would call today "crisis management". These, indeed, were seminal years of management experience. Yet, to our knowledge, we have no published article or passage in his work that describes these years in his development. Instead, there is a poem that Revans wrote in August 1945, a few months after the war ended in May, that captures the atmosphere, and his thoughts and feelings at the time (Barker, 2004, pp. 40–4).

Elegy to the Second Great War

1.
Across the skies the flame of battle runs,
the chorus of destruction sinks away,
now mourn the solemn thunder of the guns
the vanquished grandeur of your yesterday.
2.
A wound of unimpassioned hate is torn
in this dark street, where cheerful humour bides

 submerged beneath necessity forlorn,
and none from none adversity divides.
3.
Around this smoking gap the neighbours crowd,
and strive in vain to give their eager aid;
the clarion of vengeance calls aloud
for these whose final tragedy is played.
4.
Herein there lived some family alone,
to whom in death no tinselled glory came,
nor serenades of flattery are blown
to boost the methodologies of fame.
5.
The image of some artisan obscure
who, in the stakes of life, had drawn no prize,
but knew the human values that endure,
whereon defenceless charity relies.
6.
Who saw the plans of life's eternal round
uncamouflaged by fashion or by taste;
who made impartial circumstance the ground
on which his true philosophy was based.
7.
Who lived deprived amid excess, where still
the hopes of true democracy run cold,
and served the mints of lucre with the skill
that turns the brass of others into gold.
8.
Who some relentless engines well obeyed,
and planned his daily life at its behest,
'til cold depression froze the gears of trade
and brought this economic game to rest.
9.
Who knew the pain of idleness enforced,
when stark attrition mocks at self respect
and legal truth, from moral right divorced,
the claims forever of poverty reject.
10.
With many a doctrinaire illusion fraught
the priests of economics chant their creeds,
and many a futile formula is sought
for those whose chief possessions are their needs;

11.
Until the old diplomacies contrive
the dividends of carnage to restore,
the thirst for national glory to revive
and lead their shouting countries into war.
12.
The past factitious quarrels to decide,
for dim, conflicting ends to give their lives,
to set the truths of history aside...
once more the Youth of tortured Europe strives.
13.
And these, here dead, of whom this record tells,
for whom no voice of memory replies,
what happiness within their story dwells,
and comfort for the living soul supplies?
14.
What star above this desolation burns
to show the doubting moralist his path?
Or who the pointing hand of God discerns
Amid the grim and sordid aftermath?
15.
What was the debt to destiny they owed
and fully with their lives alone repaid?
What fault, what sin, what stroke at Honour's code
against them in the Scales of Justice weighed?
16.
Do these enact their artless plays in vain
whose empty scenes the wit of wealth derides?
Are they, then, held by Fortune in disdain
who know not Power nor Envy as their guides?
17.
Though for these dead their fellowship allayed
the social wrongs their chronicles indict,
while ne'er for proud success has pity stayed
the doubts that Fame and Flattery excite.
18.
To fear the cold paralysis of loss,
and live by lurking misreport obsessed;
to hear a modern order rate as dross
the lustre of some proud heraldic crest;

19.
To cry alarm lest liberty derange
the pauperised allegiance of the poor;
to dread the tidal waves of social change
that supplement the hurricanes of war.
20.
To apprehend the sure corroding force
of dark oblivion, swift to overcast
the obelisks of fame, that strew the course
where Man escapes the bondage of the past;
21.
These were the aching doubts, the parasites
of postured Dignity, to them unknown;
the mental hawks that mark Ambition's flights
and scorn to call these nameless ones their own,
22.
In whom from chill Austerity there grows
the fortitude such experts know by name;
and knowledge of Vitality that shows
to them the warmth of Man's undying flame.
23.
Who spreads the fame of Charity abroad
where simple friendship prospers unbeguiled?
To share privation asks for no reward
nor honour fades by usury defiled.
24.
The thoughts of these, the people of the soil,
by pride in race or flag were unadorned,
but they, by sacrifice and patient toil,
redeemed the name their treaty-mongers pawned.
25.
Now victory rewards their silent force,
though politicians claim it as their help,
like sneaking curs that bait the loaded horse
and swell with proud achievement as they yelp;
26.
While chill remorseless Science taps again
the atavistic springs of murderous lust,
and statesmen mouth their duty to maintain
the smouldering fires of rancour and mistrust.

27.
For now the struggle ends, and on its field
be stricken down the hopes of human kind,
are these the newer tyrannies to yield
the plans on which our world is redesigned?
August 1945

Work in the coal mines and the coal industry (1944–1946)

Management and the coal mines (1944–1945) in the U.K.

During the war, Revans became deeply involved in the coal industry, one of the most important industries of his day and one with which he was to be associated from 1944 to 1955. During this period, he even became a Chartered Mining Engineer, a professional qualification from the Institute of Mining Engineers (MIMinE). In his writing, he acknowledges the early and profound influence on him by Sir Hubert Houldsworth (1889–1956) (Revans, 1980, pp. 109–17) who is credited with "doing" action learning in the mines he managed well before Revans. Later, and for a brief period (due to his untimely death), Houldsworth became Chairman of the National Coal Board from 1951 to 1956. In these two excerpts from a speech and from his unpublished writings we see the influence on Revans of the miners, "partners in adversity". For more details on this time in his life, see Chapter 6 in this volume.

My first paper on action learning came out in 1945, and I wrote it the year before, in 1944. During the war... the most important and serious problem we had in Britain at the time was where do we get the energy from to run all the war industries, for the making of guns, aircraft... and of course the fundamental problem was how do we make our coal mining industry more efficient. I was asked to go and study this and so off I went... I actually went to work in the pits, worked with the men and I lived in their houses, if you can call them that, in the mining villages. I began to see very clearly that the complexities of trying to understand what was happening in the coal mine was so great that it was virtually impossible for the people who said "we're in charge" to understand what the real problems were.

I recommended that what we needed was a totally new form of Staff College, that this Staff College should exclude all experts who said that they know how to run coal mines: they never had run one, and most of them had never been down one. I said the only way we were going to solve this is to get the managers themselves together so let's have a Staff College which is no more than a very nice comfortable residential home to which twenty or thirty managers can come and then they can meet there and argue amongst themselves as to what their problems are. It was extraordinary, in those days the coal industry was privately owned, – it was taken over by the government, it was nationalized, after I had written my paper – and the private owners saw so clearly that what I was saying was the simplest of common sense that they said "OK get on with it." (Revans, 1982, pp. 30–1; Revans, 1994)

The Staff College was not formed until 1955, 11 years after his proposal, and five years after he had resigned from the National Coal Board. See Chapter 6 for further details.

Educational activity and action learning with volunteer coal miners from Central and Eastern Europe (1946)

This unpublished note by Revans illustrates his passion, creativity, and commitment to learning, and the obvious pleasure he took from seeing "comrades" or "partners in adversity" achieving the "impossible" through their own collaborative efforts.

> When the industry was nationalized in 1946 [officially January 1947] I was invited to join the staff of the National Coal Board as director of education. My suggestions about a novel Staff College were necessarily postponed, since the Board had plenty of other things to attract its attention, reallocating the duties of a million men who had previously worked for more than eight hundred separate companies.
>
> An interesting educational sideline that seemed, at first approach, to have nothing to do with action learning but plenty to distract attention from novel staff colleges, was to teach English to thousands of volunteers from Eastern Europe coming to work in our pits. Since they spoke over twenty mutually unintelligible tongues and many were illiterate, or did not know the Latin alphabet, we had other educational problems. But, helped by I. A. Richards, pioneer of Basic English, and his Harvard collaborators, we developed a form of action learning to achieve what professional teachers held to be an impossible task. *Operation Babel* was to help anybody between twenty and thirty years old, from Estonia, Poland, Hungary, The Ukraine and many other cultures, to speak and read English enough to join a mining course within ten weeks.

Operation Babel took place in six former British and American air-fields, where our recruits were cared for by women refugees from the same countries; this kept alive the national cultures of costume, dance and song. Efforts by conscientious bureaucrats to suppress foreign activities of this kind, in the belief that Anglicisation would be thereby accelerated were shown to have an opposite effect. Not for many years was this understood; the "foreigners" did not object to officials forbidding them to wear "fancy dress around the local village after dark", since their war years had inured them to the alien jack-in-office. It was the insensitive assault upon the heart of the individual identity that inhibited the capacity to learn – as was later discovered among hospital nurses ... The medium of learning was through mass conversation with a man going through the simplest of movements on a cinematograph screen, posing questions and inviting answers with audiences able to attend for all hours of the day and night. The activities unfolded [as] ... the sound-film grew in complexity, calling for the mastery of increasingly elaborate sentence patterns in English; the students also worked together, with their own languages as the first medium of exchange, to correct each others' mistakes. It was a superb application of the notion of 'comrades in adversity' on which all action learning must ultimately depend.

The whole operation, since it aimed to develop skill sufficient in ten weeks differed in some ways from most action learning; all 'goals' were intensively programmed, because what was to be learned was *necessarily* settled from without. But our plan to encourage questioning insight, defined as the principal objective of the proposed staff college, was spontaneous in the extreme; every participant was given a copy of Breughels' *The Wedding Feast*, so reminiscent of the Danube and the Volga valleys that the painter was thought to be a Slav, and asked to write an essay on what he made out of it. They discussed this task amongst themselves; one participant was so outstanding that he later became a professor of Spoken English at an American University. (Revans, 1985)

Notes

1. Revans typescript "Obituary Notice". From a copy from the Revans Archive, University of Manchester (formerly housed at Salford University, Revans Institute) provided by Donna Vick and Robert L. Dilworth.
2. From a videotape of Reg Revans's speech at Virginia Commonwealth University, February, 1994. Provided by Robert L. Dilworth.

For the records of the inquiry by the Board of Trade see: http://www.paper-lessarchives.com/titanic.html

It is interesting to clarify Revans' point here. In an article in *The Times* (London) in 1971, Revans was quoted as saying that (in another context) the Belgian executives in his program there were "experienced people, and their vision is not obscured by technical knowledge ... They are able to see beneath the technical surface." See Dixon (1971).
3. Revans typescript, "Entry of Girls into the Nursing Profession". From a copy from the Revans Archive, University of Manchester (formerly housed at Salford University, Revans Institute) provided by Donna Vick and Robert L. Dilworth.
4. See also James A. Beverley, *Religions A to Z: A Guide to 100 Influential Religious Movements*. Nashville: Thomas Nelson, 2005, pp. 182–3.
5. Robert L. Dilworth in discussions with Revans and Revans' correspondence with him. Dilworth and Boshyk interview with Albert E. Barker, January, 2009.
6. *Source*: http://www.couragerenewal.org/parker/writings/clearness-committee; another version is also available at: http://www.fgcquaker.org/library/fosteringmeetings/0208.html

References

Barker, A. E. (2009) "Bio-Chronology: RWR Milestones". Unpublished article and background information for Chapter 6 in this volume.

Barker, A. E. (2004) *An Introduction to Genuine Action Learning* (Oradea, Romania: Oradea University Press).

Brayshaw, A. N. (1969) *The Quakers: Their story and message* (London: Friends Home Service Committee).

Cathcart, B. (2004) *The Fly in the Cathedral: How a group of Cambridge scientists won the international race to split the atom* (New York: Farrar, Straus & Giroux).

Comfort, W. W. (1968) *Just Among Friends: The Quaker way of life* (Philadelphia: American Friends Service Committee).

Crowther, J. G. (1974) *The Cavendish Laboratory, 1874–1974* (New York: Science History Publications).

Dingle, H. (1954) *The Sources of Eddington's Philosophy* (Cambridge: Cambridge University Press).

Dixon M. (1971) "David, Goliath and Dr. Revans", *The Times* (London), 8 November, Section D, p. 15.

The Institution of Naval Architects (1937) 2, Adam Street, London, W.C.2.

Larsen [Lehrburger], E. (1962) *The Cavendish Laboratory: Nursery of genius* (New York: Franklin Watts).

Rayleigh, Lord (1942) *The Life of Sir J.J. Thomson* (Cambridge: Cambridge University Press).

Revans, R. W. (1994) From a videotape of Reg Revans' speech at Virginia Commonwealth University, February, 1994. Provided by Robert L. Dilworth.

Revans, R. W. (1985) "Chapter I, Some Opening Evidence of Action Learning at Work around the World: Action Learning in the Coal Industry, Alternative

Approaches". Undated but from 1985, from a typed manuscript provided by Robert L. Dilworth and Donna Vick.

Revans, R. W. (1982) *The Origins and Evolution of Action Learning* (Bromley, U.K.: Chartwell-Bratt).

Revans, R. W. (1980) *Action Learning: New techniques for management* (London: Blond & Briggs).

Revans, R. W. (1962) "Preface", in D. N. Carofas, *Programming Systems for Electronic Computers* (London: Butterworths).

Thomson, J. J. (1937) *Recollections and Reflections* (New York: Macmillan).

4
Revans: The Man and His Legacy

Compiled by David Botham, Robert L. Dilworth,
and Yury Boshyk

Introduction

This chapter is a compendium of recollections and reflections especially written for this chapter by those who knew him well or who have
closely studied his work. There are a number of perspectives included,
and we feel that what emerges is a mosaic of Revans – his personality,
values, core beliefs, and what constitutes his legacy.

When those who knew Reg describe his strengths, interests, and
idiosyncrasies, there are a number of words that come to mind. They
include *venerability, wisdom, perspicacity, tenacity, generosity, humility,
kindness, grace, dynamism, inspirational* qualities, his tendency to be a
*maverick, provocativeness, innovativeness, forthrightness, integrity, dignity,
confrontational* nature at times, and *athleticism*. He could also be viewed
as a *philosopher*.

Each commentary will begin with a few words about the person contributing the thoughts and their relationship to Reg.

Others, of course, have commented on Revans' legacy and about the
person. For those readers who would like to see the sources of these
published accounts and comments, please refer to Chapter 8 ("Action
Learning Today: Resources, Networks, and Communities of Practice").
For other details, please see Chapter 6 ("Milestones in the History and
Worldwide Evolution of Action Learning").

Glimpses of his personality and character
(Robert L. Dilworth)

I have written this comment from my experiences with Reg, including information gleaned from dialogue with David Botham, Albert

Barker, Verna Willis, and others. I had regular contact with Reg beginning in 1991, and we became close colleagues and friends. Revans' last
publication was a foreword he wrote for a book Verna J. Willis and I
wrote on action learning: *Action Learning: Images and pathways*. Revans
died in 2003.

Anonymous benevolence

In April 1995, in initiating the First Action Learning and Mutual
Collaboration Congress at Heathrow, England, with many countries
represented, Reg learned that the East European invitees were having
difficulty funding their travel and accommodations. He quietly drew
on his own meager financial resources to cover their expenses. This was
typical of Revans. He was a man of action and did not make a point of
calling attention to his personal acts of benevolence.

Spartan existence

Reg Revans was Spartan almost beyond measure. He consumed little
food and, when he went to a restaurant, most of the serving went into a
paper bag to be taken home. His refrigerator, especially after his second
wife Nora died, could be described as a grotto of paper restaurant bags
and other leftovers. Family and friends would periodically clean out
the refrigerator to protect his health. Ideas, concepts and taking action
fully occupied his time, and when he was performing research or writing, which it was virtually continuous, he could be as if in another
world. He took almost no interest in money, material things, or creature
comforts.

Significance of graffiti

Seeing graffiti on walls as he rode around London on a bus, Reg remarked
"The graffiti is a result of youth searching for their personal identity
and a means of expression." That was a reflection of his depth of insight
and wisdom. He had many books in his personal library, and a number
of them related to psychology. He was a student of human behavior.

As world traveler

When he traveled the world, he packed light. Clothes worn for travel
were essentially the clothes he wore during the trip. He usually had a
very small bag that he carried on the plane, and it was mostly filled with
books and papers. For overnight trips, he might carry only a "thin" valise, and it would be so stuffed with books and papers that it looked more
like a basketball than a valise.

Dealing with conflict

During a meeting in England in 1994 with 12 members of an international advisory counsel, including representatives from the United States, China, the United Kingdom, South Africa, India, Australia, and Romania, a harsh confrontation occurred between attendees. It became so loud and offensive that two women who were present left the room. Revans sat there passively throughout, not commenting one way or the other, but he was listening closely. After a while the "storm" quieted down, and a decision was made by the group to have each member report on their individual perspectives. Why did the confrontation occur, and how had each member contributed to it? It took two hours to go around the table. Many attendees humbly testified that they recognized that they had contributed to the melee. They also talked openly about what they thought had brought it on and apologized for their part in it.

When the round was finished, Revans was asked for his views. He broke out in a big smile and said, "There has been some bloody good learning taking place this evening. It's getting late. I'm going to bed." He realized that the evening had been, in the end, extremely constructive in bringing the group together, and every individual had obviously learned a great deal from the experience. Revans' basic interest was in having people learn from and with each other. That had happened. He listened rather than intervened, wanting the group to guide its own learning. To him, the evening had been a great success.

Revans as Johnny Appleseed

He was like "Johnny Appleseed". He would visit places around the world, inspire people, and then what he started would frequently blossom into something important. In 1996, he had six graduate students at Virginia Commonwealth University shadow him during a week-long visit to the institution as an action learning team. Initially, they treated Revans with awe, as if he were some form of "guru". They would ask him questions as if he were the worldwide expert. He would immediately disclaim any special expertise or gift. When they asked him what he thought, he would invariably respond, "But what do you think? That is what is really important."

During the week, he would spend some time with them in dialogue off to one side, always primed by questions. He suggested to them that they might want to attend a conference in Bologna, Italy the following month and give a presentation on action learning. The students had never worked together before, had only a rudimentary understanding of action learning, and most were struggling to cover college expenses.

However, the confidence shown in them by this 87-year-old Englishman inspired them. They decided to follow his recommendation, and after much belt tightening they came up with the money. They went to Bologna and gave a presentation that was favorably received. One of the students could only scrape together US$300.00, not enough to cover the trip. She donated the money to the other five to help them meet expenses.

Reg had also recommended to the action learning team of students that they consider setting up an International Center for Action learning in Richmond, Virginia. A week after he returned to England they had done so, even to the extent of having business cards printed up. They then presented to the City Council of Richmond a proposal for forming action learning teams of students and parents to better understand and resolve issues confronting young adults. This was too far out of the ordinary for the City Counsel to grasp or support. The students then formed an alliance with the Department of Corrections and worked with a mixed gender action learning team of six "last chance paroles". These individuals had violated their parole twice and, if they did so a third time there would be no chance of further parole. The action learning format worked well and the Corrections people were surprised at the mature dialogue that developed within this team. One of the team members was able to escape his downward spiral and was later hired by the Department of Corrections to work with other last chance paroles.

The story does not end there. The action learning team of students remained active for two years. One of them, Donna Vick, was selected as the first Distinguished Revans' Scholar and given a fully paid scholarship to obtain a Ph.D. from the Revans Centre for Action Learning and Research at the University of Salford in England when it was created in 1995. She completed her degree work and was able to join their faculty.

All of this sprang from the visit of an 87-year-old man who then proceeded to change the lives of the students involved. If Revans were alive today, he would almost certainly say, "I did not change them. They changed themselves." This is but one of many examples of Reg as Johnny Appleseed.

Children taking the lead

Reg was always intrigued by the harmony he could witness with children at play. They could operate much more harmoniously than adults, were spontaneous in their expressions, and felt secure exploring new ideas. Why was this lost when those children were subjected to highly regimented classrooms that did not allow them full opportunity or space for using their God given intellectual powers?

Reg visited Melbourne, Australia and worked with the local police on problems affecting a large apartment complex in Melbourne that housed immigrants – the Carleton Estates. Thirty-five languages and dialects were spoken there. The various nationalities and ethnicities had congregated on given floors and there was territorialism, friction, and even active conflict between the groups. In the meantime, Reg observed that there was almost no conflict on the playground at the complex. Blacks, Whites, Asians and a representational sampling of all the different nationalities and ethnicities interacted comfortably.

The children ended up taking the lead in defusing the conflict. With money provided by the local police, they started a newsletter that covered events and other information across the ethnic fabric of the tenants. The children came up with the idea of having murals painted on each floor to depict the heritage of the people who lived there. This was accomplished, with the local police once again funding the project. As Reg had observed on seeing the graffiti in London, people need to display their identity, even as they search for it. Revans had been a quiet presence, gently asking questions as the process went forward, working with the local police officials and the children.

The frictions that had been in evidence calmed, with harmonious relations becoming the behavioral norm, founded on respect for one another. Eight years later, Reg returned to Carleton Estates. Had the changes brought lasting harmony? For all intents and purposes they had, and he left satisfied. Some more "apple seeds" had taken root and grown into robust trees. That was the most significant reward that Reg could receive. It far exceeded any titles or monetary award.

No computers allowed

Reg never joined the computer age. He refused to use a personal computer or a word processing program. His typewriter was not even electric. He handled a huge volume of correspondence and other writing the old fashioned way. When he made a mistake, he would dab white-out on it and then type over it. As he became older and his hands began to shake, much of the white out would end up on the typewriter keys rather than the paper. The keys would end up sticking together from all the white out droppings, and would not always print clearly. His friend Albert Barker would periodically clean the keys as well as he could.

I should be running them, laddie

When Reg visited George Washington University in Washington, DC in 1991, he found himself waiting for an elevator with his professor host. It did not come quickly and Reg lost patience. Noticing a stairwell, he said, "Let's walk." He caught the host off guard, and she ended up following his lead for the nine-floor climb. As they proceeded up the flights of stairs, Reg heard some students behind him remark – there was nothing wrong with his hearing – "Look at that poor old man climbing the stairs!" Reg turned around and said, "Right you are. I should be running them laddie" and, even though he was 84 at the time, he then proceeded to do so.

This would have been no great surprise to those who knew him. He had represented Great Britain in the 1928 Olympics. While at Cambridge University, he broke their record for the long jump, a record that was not broken for over 30 years. He was unusually fit and energetic for his years.

A human Rolodex

He had an unusual ability to recall numbers, addresses, and the names of people he had not seen for years. It was phenomenal. Numbers also fascinated him. On one occasion, when he had asked for a phone number to add to his "Rolodex", he started to laugh. When asked why he was laughing, he said the integers came together in an interesting way. And then he said, "Only a mathematician would understand the humor."

This is a good place to underscore his versatility and range of interests. He spoke Swedish (his first wife was Swedish) and German, and had a working familiarity with several other languages. He was a physicist, economist, educator, artist; furniture maker, musician, and more than a few would label him as a philosopher as well.

A daughter's view

What follows has been extracted with permission from remarks that Marina Blanc, Revans' eldest daughter, made on the occasion of the celebration of the 100th anniversary of her father's birth in 2007. The remarks were given at the Manchester School of Business at the University of Manchester.

His memory

When he was 92 years old, I took my father to Birkenhead [where he had lived in very early childhood] to see if he could find the house in which the family had lived, and I was startled to realize what a phenomenal memory he still had. I drove in from the wrong road (for him), and he was somewhat concerned because he remembered the house being on the left, and all the left side houses had been razed to the ground. When we came to a cemetery gate, however, he recognized this as being opposite his front door. The old house was still there.

Love of music

From an early age, he developed a great affection for music and, as he was not able to sing, he would whistle everything. Here, his incredible memory served him well and he was able, from snip-its, to identify most symphonies and concertos, etc. We used to have bets as to what was on the radio when we were out driving. He always got the composer right, but sometimes could not name the composition. I did not stand a chance.

Fascination with nature

He grew to be fascinated by what happened in nature. His knowledge of British birds and trees was phenomenal. If he could not see a bird sitting conveniently on a branch, he could identify by its call, flight, or feathers. He recognized trees by their silhouettes if he was too far away to see the bark or pick a leaf.

Art

Apart from athletic endeavors, he developed an interest in art. He executed many paintings, cartoons, and even illustrated small books for children. He painted portraits, street scenes, and drew such a detailed black and white sketch of Emmanuel College that I had always thought it was a photograph. He had an enviable skill with a pencil, but also found time to play the trumpet. We all knew he could write books and articles on action learning, but how many of you knew that he also wrote poetry and plays? He was a man with many, many gifts, most of which he kept hidden.

Concern for those less well off

Reg would never stand on ceremony and, even when the King of Belgium gave a dinner in 1971 to honor Reg as a Chevalier (he was designated a knight), having eaten the starter, he refused the main course and turned his plate upside down. He protested that there were others who needed the food more than he did.

Focus on how people learn

He was fascinated with how people learn and was convinced that "hands on" learning was more valuable than "book learning" would ever be, both to the individual and to society. This did not keep him from reading, though. He was addicted to books. He read and collected books all his life.

Furniture maker

He made furniture, a large dining table from one plank of elm, on an oak chassis; a sofa frame that took a single bed base and served its time in both capacities; a sideboard – still with me, small tables, armchairs, one made from an acacia tree that fell in the garden.

Patient teacher, but with a ferocious temper at times

He was a patient teacher, but also had a ferocious temper and, when something went wrong, you escaped to your bedroom.

Tastes in foods

Reg's preferred foods gave me concern: he loved cheese, cream, and butter, and used salt liberally; not for him the five fruit and vegetables a day. He had coffee with his sugar, ate chocolate biscuits by the tin-full, and his diet was enough to drive a cardiologist to a heart attack; yet, he reached the age of 95. He did love fish, so perhaps this compensated.

Religious beliefs

I never discussed religion with Reg. That he sent me to a Quaker School may have some bearing on his belief, but as we know from reading his papers, he knew the Bible very well indeed.

Love of walking

His love of walking continued throughout his life and, at Cambridge, he and Vivian Bowden [a fellow graduate student in physics] walked for miles together.

[A note from Albert Barker: During Reg's final illness, shortly before he died, Reg learned that Vivian Bowden was near death at a nursing home just a couple of miles away. When Barker visited Revans one night, Reg told Albert to go cheer up Vivian. "He needs more support than I do." Barker immediately went down the road to comfort Vivian, who was dead by morning.]

Declining health

In 1997, Reg began to feel the strain of a youthful injury. When he was an Olympic athlete, he had injured his left ankle. "It will be all right when it is mended, but when you are 80 it will give you some trouble", young Revans was told. Reg was lucky enough for the ankle to wait until he was 92 before it bothered him. It made walking difficult, and he finally began to slow down.

David Botham, Friend and Protégé of Revans

I knew Reg very well and spent one evening a week with Revans for 20 years, not to mention the interaction I had with him at other times in my role as the head of the Revans Center for Action Learning and Research, established in 1995.

Revans the maverick

Revans was a maverick in many respects; always testing the ground up ahead and willing to take on the established ways of thinking. He was a man ahead of his time and an early proponent of experiential learning, as opposed to didactic approaches to learning, such as a professor imparting knowledge to a passive audience of students. *For Revans, the way to learn was to grapple with real problems, with the participants learning from and with each other.*

The humanitarian

While Revans was a scientist, he was also a humanitarian and came to believe that action learning could be a force for bringing people together in open dialogue to solve the world's problems. He felt that real learning was a social process in which others need to engage.

The importance of fresh questions

It was consistently argued by Revans during the many presentations he gave during his lifetime that action learning centered on the posing of fresh questions. The posing of questions can be attributed to a Socratic idea (469–399 BC) intended for seeking new knowledge. Plato (427–347 BC) developed it into a method of philosophical training by means of questioning games. The games were later used by Aristotle (384–322 BC) as the first systematic epistemology and logical system in the Western tradition on which all hypothetical-deductive thinking was largely based.

Action learning as an autonomous learning process

One of the most challenging consequences of the Revans legacy is the relationship between action learning operating as an autonomous learning process for participants, and those charged with the task of organizing, sponsoring and advising action learning programs. Much debate has occurred over the nature and, sometimes, worth of such arrangements, which in general has led to polarity, with some favoring utter and complete autonomy for action learning sets so that only participants are allowed to learn from and with each other. Others strongly favor the inclusion of sponsors, advisors, consultants and facilitators (Garratt, 1983). Revans consistently, and sometimes angrily, spoke out against inclusion of people external to the set and strongly advocated for autonomy (see, for example, Revans [1984, pp. 209–20]).

He challenged all who offered their professional expertise as set advisors and/or facilitators. He found it particularly galling when people would suggest that they were admirers of his concepts and practicing them, when they were leaning heavily in the direction of having external "experts" constantly intervene in set deliberations and dialogue.

Emphasis on research

Another serious difference between the Revans approach and the majority of current trends in action learning lies in his strong belief and emphasis on research. Consequently, all of Revans' action learning programs were systematically researched, largely by Revans himself as the very basis of his continuing scholarly contributions. It can be argued that Revans adopted a classic action learning stance in the sense that he introduced action learning programs in the major implementation phase in order to observe change and reactions to such a way of understanding organizational behavior (see, for example, Revans, 1971, pp. 148–201 and his descriptions of management education through action learning.)

How he related to action learning sets (teams)

Revans had a clear view of his own relationship with action learning teams. First, he anticipated that conscious learning would take place in the team that would be accessible. Second, he exercised grace and politeness, and waited to be invited to a team meeting rather than thrust himself on the participants, and he demonstrated a sobering level of humility around his own learning needs, thus avoiding the arrogance associated with the sole experience of subject knowledge.

Hesitancy to define action learning

Some suggested that Revans failed to offer, or avoided offering, a definition of action learning. They try to point out that the understanding of the process would have been easier if he had. However, the argument is not entirely valid. While Revans would profess to avoid defining action learning – preferring to explain it in terms of what it was not – Revans did, in fact, provide a definition which has been largely overlooked, if not completely ignored. He stated:

> Action learning is a means of development, intellectual, emotional or physical that requires its subject, through responsible involvement in some complex and stressful problem, to achieve intended change sufficient to improve his observable behavior henceforth in the problem field. (Revans, 1979, p. 4)

Relevance of action learning to the here-and-now generation: The very heart of his legacy

Revans' work, like all legacies, is meaningless unless it has relevancy to the here-and-now generation. Therefore, there is still much more to be done to introduce Revans' approach to aspects and interpretations of action learning. For example, Reg's writings did not receive wide readership in the United States. Therefore, the specifics that had been addressed by Revans did not, for the most part, receive much serious review in America. The potential of action learning came to be appreciated from those portions of Revans' work that were picked up in the journals and the literature. There were also people who had worked with Revans that also helped to spread the word on his philosophy and conceptual thinking. But, over time, these rather narrow penetrations of thought related to action learning came to be further diluted.

You can encounter a rather wide spectrum of applications that are labeled as action learning but, when examined, they seem to have a limited relationship to what Revans had in mind. This is not to say that Revans had a rigid interpretation of what constituted action learning, because he did not. He recognized that it could be realized in different forms, but he became concerned when he saw tight control of the applications and little empowerment of those supposedly engaged in action learning.

For the reasons just highlighted, Revans' legacy does not usually find full expression. However, when his concepts are examined closely and related to the challenges that we face today in organizations and management, it becomes apparent that there are important lessons and approaches that are as applicable today as when Reg first articulated them. He was one of the pioneers in stressing the advantages of small teams that are empowered. He referred to this as "small is dutiful". We see this today in self-directed teams, leaderless teams, and in philosophies that emphasize closeness to customers and allowing workers that are in constant contact with customers to make decisions that can immediately satisfy customer needs. By returning to the roots of action learning, it should be possible to enhance the forms of action learning in use today.

Revans would often talk about little children and how easy it was for them to communicate openly with one another and explore the world about them. They felt safe talking to one another as they played together in small groups. Reg observed this willingness to disclose and be spontaneous, and how it could be driven out of them by what occurred in highly controlled classroom environments and in their workplace, where the authoritarian model might still largely hold sway. A genuine action learning experience – with the team empowered to range freely in its thinking in trying to better understand the problems at hand and how to solve them – could approximate the phenomenon so common with little children. It is a matter of being set free from the restrictions that can often confine thinking, engaging in open dialogue in an atmosphere of trust and mutual support, without someone looking over their shoulder, as can occur when external facilitators are present. This is the very essence of what Reg tried so hard to communicate, but his thinking was frequently rebuffed because it simply did not fit into the traditional mold of education and learning systems. To the extent that such true empowerment is practiced, it represents his legacy. It is the very essence of action learning.

Comments on Revans (Mike Pedler)

Mike Pedler is a leading academic and consultant on management and leadership issues. Widely published, he is the editor of *Action Learning Research and Practice* – the first international journal on action learning. Mike knew Reg and had worked with him.

A perspective on Revans and his legacy

I have said on many occasions over the past 30 years, although it is frustrating: Revans' refusal to define action learning except in the negative, is actually a source of its longevity and its potential for reinvention. To him action learning is *not*:

> Job rotation ... project work ... case studies, business games and other simulations ... group dynamics and other task free exercises ... business

consultancy and other expert mission ... operational research, industrial engineering, work study and related subjects ... simple commonsense. (Revans, 1998, pp. 89–103)

He could no doubt add a longish list of more recent but soon-to-be-dead techniques, but this is what maintains action learning's vitality. It is an idea, a philosophy, a discipline and also a method, but never just a method. We will always be asking the questions "What is action learning?" and "Am I doing it right?"

Another question that this prompts us to ask is "What are other people doing in the name of action learning?", and this question encourages us to share our practices and our accounts of our practices with one another in order to learn more. In a paper with John Burgoyne and Cheryl Brook, we ask, "What has action learning learned to become?" (Pedler et al., 2005), and note a number of recent practice developments that Revans either did not sanction, or actively campaigned against, such as the now widespread use of facilitators.

This is both worrying and reassuring: we have to continue to ask "Are we getting it right?", whilst experimenting with new forms and approaches – an apparent paradox that is part of the discipline and life-long learning.

The influence of Revans' religious or spiritual beliefs is another relevant question. I once drove him from Altrincham to Huddersfield, during which he more or less continuously quoted the Bible. He told me that his mother had read it to him as a child and that he remembered it, often word for word. Yet, he was mainly interested in the spirit behind the words. When he quoted Buddha on how to ease suffering it was because the principles of Buddhism were consistent with action learning.

More Calvinistic principles drove his famous (and sometimes infamous) moral judgments. He could resemble an Old Testament preacher when he scorned the latest gimcrack ideas in the management literature or railed against the *"canaille"* of the consulting profession. He was himself a consultant, but one who did not charge for his services, who did not necessarily seek out the powerful and was willing to spend his time with whoever was interested for the price of his "bus fare". If he were a consultant, this made him a rather unusual one.

My first encounter with him was at a meeting in the then Yorkshire Regional Management Centre in 1976, where he spoke about management and development in terms that few people present could relate to. He used there the famous questions from Belgium, "What is an honest man? and "What must I do to become one?", presenting management development as a moral practice. We were developing people, seeking to influence their conduct and their direction. This did not seem to resonate with most of my colleagues, concerned – then and now – with teaching marketing or finance.

At the close of the day, Revans took books from a battered bag. "The publishers are not making a good job of selling these", he said, "so anyone who wants one can have it for one pound sterling." He sold two copies. My copy of *Developing Effective Managers* (1971), his most ambitious attempt to theorize about action learning, has been with me ever since, not least to mark a day on which I changed my direction.

Comments about the uniqueness of Revans (Alan Mumford)

Alan Mumford has long been associated with action learning. He was a Professor of Management at the International Management Centre (IMC) in the U.K. and has done much work with management development and action learning around the world. He is also the codesigner, with Peter Honey, of the learning style questionnaire (LSQ) based on David Kolb's research on learning styles. The following comments are taken from an interview with him in March, in London.

Uniqueness of Revans

Revans' uniqueness in first identifying, and then campaigning for, action learning is clear, and those managers who have gone through the process can testify to its attractiveness. His ideas are also now at least partially accepted by some of those institutions and academics he previously described as offering "an inexhaustible avalanche of lofty hokus-pocus". Indeed, a leading member of the management education establishment claimed a few years ago that all business schools now use action learning.

A matter of charisma and presence

I went to the annual Conference of the Institute of Management...and there was Reg post-Belgium [Revans had spent an extended period in Belgium from 1965–1975, working on several projects – among them what came to be called the Belgian Experiment], doing his piece. I had read about him but I had never heard him before, and it was a most extraordinary experience. He had presence...and, like a number of people who have it, you cannot describe it. He just held it. He and I performed together on the same occasion, at a conference in Dubai, and actually it was the longest conversation I ever had with Reg. There he was talking to 80 or 90 what we call 'Gulf Arabs" – he did his hour piece on action learning and he was wonderful, and they thought he was wonderful. Reg gave a brilliant delivery.

He absolutely squelched a very senior guy who really wanted to say "this is all a load of rubbish – anecdotal experienced people, people working on projects, what they need surely is what we all know managers need: A strong intellectually-based, knowledge based discipline, not bits of ..." and Reg stamped him into the ground, in the nicest possible way – another Reg experience.

Inveterate hankering of the tutor

All of us have favorite quotations from Revans. Mine is that action learning attacks "the inveterate hankering of the tutor to be the center of attention". This struck me as being an elegant and important statement – just as true, incidentally, for people who describe themselves as facilitators as it is for stand-up lecturers. There is a certain irony involved because, of course, Reg was a superb speaker – but that is a role in which you are inevitably the center of attention.

Oration versus written communication

I was the 'orator' when Reg was awarded a doctorate [honorary] by the International Management Centre. I said there was a significant difference between Reg as a speaker, and Reg as a writer. As a speaker, I described Reg as being very clear in the construction of words and sentences, which was logical and entirely easy to follow. In contrast, his writing, although never difficult to understand, was as I described it "dense". He came up to me after the ceremony. I was not sure what to expect. He was not at all a man given to easy flattery, so I did not expect the usual "Thank you so much Alan. A nice talk." In fact, Reg seized on the point I had just made. He was interested to tell me how nice it was that someone should compliment him on his facility in both spoken and written communications. What he said was that I was the first person who had apparently noticed the significant difference in the two styles. He obviously approved of my comment – which was some relief to me, as I had not been at all sure he would appreciate the second part.

What Reg meant to me (Verna J. Willis)

Beginning in 1994, when Verna J. Willis met Reg Revans, she became deeply engaged in action learning. She ended up with a nationally recognized and award-winning program in human resource development (HRD), which employed action learning in a way that held closely to the principles that Revans articulated. She had a chance to work with Revans, including a sabbatical at the Revans Centre for Action Learning and Research at the University of Salford in England. She ended up being involved with action learning in Australia, the Ivory Coast of Africa, Great Britain, and Romania. Willis was the first to use the term "Chief Learning Officer" (CLO), and one of her doctoral students, Gary May, was the first person to occupy a CLO position.

Like many others, I freely acknowledge that encountering Reg Revans and the way he thought and lived helped not only to reset and enhance the patterns of my professional life, but also to reassert my personal values inside and outside my work life. Six years previously, I had moved from corporate management of a training and development unit into a university faculty post purposely to create new employee development degree programs, and see if I could make a difference in the way organizations imagine and realize learning.

I had become thoroughly jaded by disappointing in-house learning events and the use of fairly standardized 'learning technologies' available in the marketplace. Most of the latter were copycat products that promised far more than they delivered, for few of them induced fruitful mindset alterations or behavioral changes. I kept wondering how to find or create something fresh, something real, something that truly engaged learners and made them responsible for what they learned and how they changed accordingly. They were far too easily gratified – lulled into doing nothing – by the clever stagecraft of legions of "stand-up trainers" who lived in our organization or were contracted from outside.

In 1993, I joined with like-minded faculty colleagues and a few senior corporate trainers in the U.S. to charter the Academy of Human Resource Development (AHRD). We believed that, in a formal alliance, we could strengthen our efforts, gain greater public understanding and acceptance of our emerging discipline, sharpen our teaching, and better support our students who were working out on the threshing floor of our new field.

Thus far, all of the above has been a prelude to what this story is really about: my energetic and deeply rewarding engagement with action learning. My introduction to Reg Revans and his expression of action learning occurred in 1994 in San Antonio, Texas, at the first official gathering of the new Academy. He had been invited there by colleagues (Dilworth, Dixon, and Marsick) who knew him and were confident of the importance of his contributions. It was fortuitous.

What Reg described sounded "right on" to me, affirming my thoughts abut the dysfunctions of consultant-led "learning" that I had observed in microscopic detail in my seven-year corporate stint and my three years' of overseas assignments in higher education. What was more important, of course, was his affirmation of what I deep-down knew, but had never found words to express: that people truly learn when they question what it is they think they know, unleash their curiosity, believe in themselves and their capacities, and internalize new findings and personal responsibility to act on those findings.

I believe nearly everyone senses this "freedom to learn" and act in Revans-style action learning, though it remains a frightening prospect for some. We recognize both of these reactions over and over in post-learning essays and oral debriefings. Action learning seems to be something we have longed for all our lives, perhaps having had glimpses of it earlier. (My glimpses occurred in a 1930s one-room schoolhouse, where learning with and from each other was perfectly ordinary, and definitely exciting.) Perhaps action learning seems most formidable if we have been conditioned to bow to "expert wisdom", to depend heavily on authority figures to put us safely through our learning paces.

In retrospect, I believe that we, the highly professional, highly experienced founders of the new Academy – admitted or not – had few reliable answers, and were instead "partners in adversity" [a Revans term]. We were in the midst of a torrent of "complexifying" elements in our work, though we were dedicated to creating learning organizations. But very few of us became devotees of action learning at the time.

It is a simple truth that great power lies in learning humbly "with and from each other" [a frequent expression by Revans], but how we spread that truth is another matter. I left Reg's keynote session thoroughly curious about what more I might learn from him and from those who valued what he stood for. The odd thing is that I recognized that what Reg gave voice to, I already agreed with, but I felt I had been given no permission to act upon it. I know mine is not an unusual case. Most of us probably do not know how much of this remains untapped.

Reg's words enabled me to reinstate the knowledge that permission is an internal matter, not awarded by authorities of any kind. Shortly after, I became brave enough, with strategic intent and actions but no sponsorship, to launch action learning at a very conservative university. Within a handful of years, action learning at Georgia State became a touted conduit to and from the outside world of commerce, government, and civil society, and our efforts to link up with the "real world" were accorded generous publicity.

I believe that Reg, by nature and upbringing, thought holistically. I am certain that that he was among the first of the great systems thinkers to embrace what Ervin Laszlo is now calling "a cosmology of wholeness" that does not view any part of life, society, earth, or universe as separate from any other part. One might alternatively call it "ecological thinking" on a grand scale, involving DNA, cells, particles, environments as well as "inner" and "outer" space. Reg was far in advance of authors like Margaret Wheatley and Peter Senge in applying general systems principles to institutions and business organizations, emphasizing the democratizing, humanizing aspects of such principles. He inhabited no ivory tower but, instead, engaged as strategist, tactician, and day laborer in pursuit of a more collaborative, more consciously interdependent world.

I think he deliberately avoided the jargon of the many disciplines he knew about, so as to find an oral language understandable to everyone from coconut- and oil-pressers to royalty. There is a touching story in one of his unpublished manuscripts that makes this perfectly clear. He walked out of a Washington, DC conference of the American Psychological Association at which, as I recall, he had himself been a presenter. Dismayed at the tedium, the surfeit of intellectualism and pontification he experienced there, he began to wonder about the city. He came upon an outdoor assemblage of people strangely dressed, "hippie-era people" who were happily engaged in singing, picnicking, and enjoying each others' company. They welcomed him into their gathering, and he stayed on, singing gospel music with them. The contrast between the rule-driven precincts he had just left and the spontaneous welcome he had just received must, indeed, have been stark. It has been several years since I happened on this manuscript in the Revans Archives at Salford University, and I found the account so personal that I could not bring myself to copy it. Now I wish that I had. I have thought since that nothing ever gave me more insight into the man than his record of this incident. This is the same man, of course, that saw such suffering in England during the air attacks by Germany in World War II. In light of such indelible experiences, I suspect he frequently found difficulty aligning himself with people and events that were less real, arresting, or life changing.

Sifting through the dozens of adjectives and characterizations in a vain attempt to "crystallize" the Reg I knew for four short, intensive learning years, I have fallen back on one simple word. Reg was, and is, an authentic *presence*. I would capitalize this word, except Reg would not himself have countenanced the emphasis. Yet, as I have noted above, Reg was, and is, a *vital presence* in my personal and professional life, a sort of culminating influence. Among other dispensations, he validated my own overarching, systems-oriented world view and helped me to realize how I could strike a better balance between trying to change the world and being changed by it.

This is the kind of presence Reg exemplified, no matter how sternly prophetic, informally witty, or reflectively silent he became, or how stubbornly he repeated his favorite themes. He was calmly alive and alert, "the actual person that is present, of a visible or concrete nature", with "stately or distinguished bearing", yet with a quality of poise and effectiveness that enables a performer to achieve a relationship with the "audience". I mean all of these things and more. There was a steadiness about him, and a genuine openness to others that won human trust and confidence across the nations he visited. I also acknowledge that he was wary of pretentiousness, even when being an idiosyncratic presence was clearly a delight to him; it was also an ego burden for such an essentially humble man to carry. He quickly disposed of it by disclaiming his own uniqueness.

I am convinced that, beyond all his words, his presence is what Reg offered and still offers to those who have most closely followed his precepts and patterns of action learning. It is the presence of self that constitutes Reg's legacy, embodying for all time his own life's work, his mental and moral philosophy, his own seeking and sharing of what he found to be the world's wisdom. He never stopped searching while I knew him, and I often wished – for my own edification – that I could make a list and read everything he valued enough to keep in his pared down library.

A notation made by R. L. Dilworth when Revans was briefly a scholar-in-residence at Virginia Commonwealth University reads: "Jan Brandt [one of Dilworth's graduate students] in discussing the dynamics of their action learning experience [expressed an] analogy to Quaker culture and convention at meetings: [that one] 'cannot ask questions they know the answer to.'" This is the only reference I have found to the influence of the Quaker meeting house rules on the importance of the "Q" [Questioning Insight] in Revans' formula for learning. Raised in that faith, it is no wonder that Reg searched always for fresh questions, and never – to my knowledge – suggested that finding answers was anything more than a temporary resolution in a changing world that would drive learners forward to new questions. He found in other faiths a similar emphasis on the importance of the mutuality of learning. Thus, a life of learning must forever be a quest, a process, and a dynamic existence. Such a dynamic forbids "idolization of past experience", and locates action learning naturally in a community of reflective, questioning learners.

I recall one occasion when I felt Reg was excluded from the community, when others present gave no mind to what he wanted: a spirit of inquiry regarding texts to be found particularly provocative. I was on study in residence for two months at the Revans Centre. When Reg brought in a suitcase full of books in which he had marked the texts he would like to explore with us at the next staff meeting; I volunteered to copy, collate, and distribute these. I read them with interest and looked forward to making connections between them, action learning, and the work of the Centre. But somehow, when he came for the staff meeting, we never got around to his materials. I am not sure why, but suspect it was the immediacy of other issues. I was saddened because he felt that we needed new questions and that, in ignoring this, we blinded ourselves to Reg as a vital presence, forgetting his reason for being there.

Proponents and practitioners of action learning can easily fall into this pattern of exclusion of people and questions outside of their immediate concerns. This tendency, I believe, constantly poses the need for us to test the temper of action learning. Failure to acknowledge the "Reg presence" may have far reaching effects, over time, on his life legacy. If we are not vigilant, we may too often settle for being clever and not wise.

But, despite this warning, I see opportunities for expansion of Reg's points of view and his faith in action learning, Contributors to this book testify to the widening use and variety of venues, as well as a renewed allegiance to the importance of every individual member in team (set) activity. Action learning is not – and never has been – "owned" solely by the profit-making sector that is most able to support it financially. It may be that the times are right for ever-broader reliance on action learning, as we face a catastrophic breakdown of human societies everywhere. We appear to be arriving at a greater enlightenment about our local-to-global responsibilities to one another, in our common humanity. I am particularly hopeful, since I have investigated how action learning is being used in nation-building and economic development, even in the poorest communities. Action learning has gone global, even as Reg predicted. His grass-roots realism – we hope – has begun to come of age.

A Summary: Proof of the power of action learning

We have just been through a variety of perspectives on Revans as a man and what constitutes his legacy. The most important proof of action learning can be gleaned from what those who have been through a true action learning experience say about it.

Verna Willis – in her action learning program at Georgia State University, and the same was true of the program created by Lex Dilworth at Virginia Commonwealth University – operated in very close alignment with Reg's precepts, including minimal facilitator interventions in the process, letting the action learners learn by doing, in dealing with major problems being confronted by large organizations and companies, public and private outside the university. Problems addressed met Revans' tests – they were highly complex, urgent to the companies owning the problem, and even falling in the category of being seen as insoluble. Action learners were thrown into the deep end of the pool, confronted with problems in which they had little or no expertise. Their associates were often unfamiliar to them, although they were also graduate students. As already mentioned, the problem was totally unfamiliar to most.

So what happened? Willis conducted a well-engineered analysis of the comments contained in the student essays using a software program to help in sifting through the reflections of the students as they completed the action learning experience – five weeks, in the case of Willis's program. Some categories were entirely expected and even prompted, through critical incident type questions, such as when were you most engaged? and When were you most distanced? But other categories emerged that were not expected, such as "transformation". It could be said various ways, such as "This experience has profoundly changed me."

What follow are some verbatim comments by the students that related to transformation. They represent a "mirror" in terms of what happened when the Revans' precepts were employed in a pure form. How do they match up with what Revans seemed to have in mind? To the extent they do match up, they can perhaps be seen as proof of principle and a reflection of Revans' legacy in practice.

Student 1: Reflecting on the past five weeks, I realize this class has basically built an awareness in me. First, an awareness of the fundamentals of action learning, and secondly, an awareness of myself. The latter awareness opened my eyes to the way I now think of myself and group dynamics. It is actually a relief knowing that I don't have to be the expert, but that I may call on my intuition, common sense, and creative thinking that I feel are my strong points – those traits about myself that I did not put much "worth" into because I felt if I didn't know everything there was to know about a subject, then I should squelch my ideas and keep my mouth shut. Now I know better! I also find it easier to deal with (problematic) others in a group situation. Whereas in the past I was intimidated by the very knowledgeable people, now I see them in a whole new light. If they were being cocky, I would hold back. Now I can assure myself that they aren't so smart after all if they cannot open their minds to learning; sounds silly, but now I do not feel intimidated.

Student 2: What I gained after several weeks in this course is the realization that exploration of others and ourselves is what true learning represents. It is the exploration aspect of learning that I think gets ignored in most situations where a group of people come together. Action learning gave me new insights into just how "problems solving" oriented we have become in this society. The linear pathway straight to the solution bypasses the process of questioning, exploration, and reflection. The end result is we end up forfeiting the growth that could have been found in the interaction process of individuals working together. I have truly gained a new appreciation for the value of being open to questioning and exploration, while at the same time letting go of the requirement of being the expert who has to come up with a solution. Now I realize if a solution is needed in certain situations, one of the best ways to achieve it is through questioning and exploration.

Student 3: I would like to state that action learning has affected me in many ways. It definitely has not been just another learning theory added to my knowledge. In many ways, I have begun to view it more as a life philosophy that I could use in all areas of my life. It has helped me realize that it is OK to just question and reflect without having to come up with an answer right at the moment. I found that learning does come from openness and relinquishing the expert role. I also realized that when you question and explore, you are also able to drop many of the value judgments that you may normally place on individuals. That even though you might not agree with someone's ideas, when you use action learning, you can still reflect on those ideas and ask fresh questions that could help expand you own awareness.

Revans' legacy is very much alive, to the extent that practitioners heed what he had to say and practice it – not slavishly, for that is far removed from Reg's intent – but by keeping it visible and adapting it to different contexts, venues and cultures.

References

Dilworth, R. L. and Willis, V. J. (2003) *Action Learning: Images and pathways* (Malabar, FL: Krieger Publishing).

Garratt, B. (1983) "The Role of the Learning Group Adviser: A process of phased redundancy? *Management Education and Development*, 14(3), pp. 201–7.

Mumford, A. (March 8, 2008) Interview in London by Yury Boshyk.

Pedler, M., Burgoyne, J., and Brook, C. (2005) "What Has Action Learning Learned to Become?" *Action Research: Research and Practice* 2 (1), spring, pp. 49–68.

Revans, R. W. (1998) *ABC of Action Learning* (London: Lemos & Crane).

Revans, R. W. (1984) "On the Learning Equation". *Management Education and Development* 15 (part 3), pp. 209–20.

Revans, R. W. (1982) *The Origins and Growth of Action Learning* (Bromley: Chartwell-Bratt).

Revans, R. W. (1979) "The Nature of Action Learning". *Management and Educational Development*, 10 (part 1), pp. 3–23.

Revans, R. W. (1971) *Developing Effective Managers* (New York: Praeger).

5

National Level Experiments with Action Learning: Belgium and Beyond

Robert L. Dilworth, David Bellon, and Yury Boshyk

Introduction

There have been two notable examples of action learning being employed at the national level, both of them by Revans – the Belgian and Egyptian (or referenced as the Nile) projects (1968–71). Revans also was involved with public service initiatives in both India and Australia, but on a much less ambitious level than in Belgium and Egypt.

National-level action learning initiatives are difficult to engineer from several standpoints. There are political factors to contend with, and it can be difficult to line up influential supporters because of their diverging interests. In Belgium and in Egypt, it was a case of both the public and private sectors being involved, which can further complicate coordination and planning.

In the case of the Belgian Experiment, the constellations were right, with highly influential people willing to support the initiative in key positions. Further, the industrial productivity of the nation was a source of grave concern at the time. Therefore, there was a receptivity to new ideas and approaches that might help reverse the negative economic trends. Action learning was one of several programs decided on to move the country forward. It was also fortuitous that Revans was a known commodity in European management circles, and in a position to step in and assist with the action learning component. The timing was good all the way around.

The Nile project was, in effect, the offspring of the Belgian project, even umbilically tied to it in some respects. There is much that can be learned from both projects. South Africa has been considering undertaking a national-level action learning program that draws on what was learned during the Belgian venture. We will examine outcomes of the two projects in our chapter summary and their implications in launching new efforts.

The Belgian Experiment

Reginald W. Revans, the principal pioneer of action learning, would single out several of his major initiatives for emphasis. They were the National Coal Board, the Hospital Internal Communications (HIC) Project, and the Belgian Experiment, and he would occasionally refer to the Nile project. His first action learning program was developed with the National Association of Colliery Managers in 1952.

> Under the aegis of the National Coal Board, 22 bold members of that body formed a consortium to examine the four main problems of their daily operations... in their own pits and those of their colleagues. (Revans, 1983, p. 56)

Over the three years that the National Coal Board program existed, there was an exchange of experiences between those involved. This was in line with Revans' core belief that we need to learn from and with each other. While Revans labels this action learning, it came before Revans' conceptual framework for action learning had fully matured.

The HIC Project, involving London's ten largest hospitals, ran from 1965 to 1969 (Revans, 1985, pp. 17–19)) and overlapped with Revans' effort in Belgium. The HIC project, while having many of the basic trappings of action learning, did not use action learning teams *per se*. It did call for the staff of one hospital to examine the practices of another hospital, thus falling in line with Revans' belief that more can be learned by having people deal with unfamiliar settings and problems (see Chapter 1). Groupings of people sent from one hospital to another involved three or four individuals. These were informal groups. The various groups were brought together periodically to discuss what they had learned and surface ideas for improving hospital operations. This led to at least a score of initiatives being launched. The results were quite striking and are reported elsewhere in this book.

Belgium was obviously the "crown jewel" to Revans. He would almost always turn to the Belgian Experiment when outlining what constitutes action learning in its most fully developed form. This initiative seems to include some of his best thinking on the subject of action learning.

As will be explained, he would attribute major advances in the Belgian economy to the Belgian Experiment.

In 2007 and 2008, David Bellon of Belgium, with the encouragement and support of Yury Boshyk, performed some important investigative work on the Belgian Experiment. He was able to locate some of the individuals who had assisted with the research in the 1960s, or had been a part of the actual action learning teams and experience. Many have passed from the scene by now, but those who Bellon was able to contact had rather vivid memories of their experience. In various ways, it seems to have been a pivotal point in their lives. Their perspectives add a fresh stream of research information to that already available.

It is important to understand some of the antecedents to the initiative in Belgium, and the dynamics that drove it. First, it was a confluence of interests, both national and individual, that came together in a powerful way. When the two Treaties of Rome were signed in 1957, establishing the first foundations of the European Union (EU) and the European Atomic Energy Community (ECSC); six countries were signatories (Belgium, France, Italy, Luxembourg, the Netherlands, and what was then West Germany). Brussels was selected as the capital of the European Economic Community (EEC), as it was called then and remains so today. There were expectations set for economic performance, and Belgium was the laggard among the EU countries. There was a sense of urgency in Belgium at the national level to reverse this trend.

Individuals in a position to exert influence on events now came into play. The first was Gaston Deurinck, who had founded the Belgian Productivity Centre. He was later to help establish the Fondation Industrie-Université in 1956, becoming its Managing Director, and the European Association of Management Training Centres (1959). The latter was merged into what is, today, the European Foundation for Management Development (EFMD) in 1971. Deurinck was well-connected to the academic institutions in Belgium and well-versed about things American as he had studied in the U.S. on a scholarship. The latter was important, as both the Fondation and the EFMD were supported by the Ford Foundation. Deurinck was, in turn, the brother-in-law of Max Nokin, President of the Société Générale (the largest holding company of its day in Belgium). He had 15 companies over which he had direct influence, and this no doubt helped involve many large and well-known Belgian companies in the experiment (DeSchoolmeester, 2007).

At the time (1965), Revans was working in Brussels for three years as a research fellow of the European Association of Management Training Centers, and had served for a time as its President. He had just left his position by mutual agreement, as a professor of Industrial Administration at the Manchester Business School at the University of Manchester – a position he had earned in large part because of his outstanding record with the National Coal Board. In any case, from conversations with Revans (with Robert L. Dilworth) the situation became untenable for Revans at the University of Manchester, and he resigned his professorship in 1965.

We will now focus in on some of the most significant aspects of the Belgian Experiment. Here are the ingredients of what constituted a high potency advocacy for the Belgian Experiment.

1. A country that felt itself on the cusp of greatness, but needed to prove itself;
2. A businessperson with considerable clout and influence (Gaston Deurinck), including academe, who wanted to move the Belgian economy along, and get some credit for it in the process;
3. A business magnate who was the brother-in-law of Deurinck (Max Nokin) who also wanted to move the economy forward, and his business interests along with it;
4. A professor and prognosticator of management and action learning (Revans), emerging from a bad professional experience (University of Manchester), who was highly motivated to make his mark, perhaps vindicate himself, and build his theories in practice;
5. Academics in Belgium (e.g., Andre Vlerick, for whom the Vlerick Business School is now named), who were "tuned" into the moment and ready to try new things).

It would be hard to imagine a more powerful tonic for launching a major new program. This was a marriage of mutual interests. While the Belgian Experiment germinated with Deurinck, he needed an agent and intellectual "engine" and innovator to give it life. He knew Revans through the European Association of Management Training Centres. He also knew that Revans could be depended on to do something highly innovative and make a difference. Revans became the key ingredient in the mix, the seasoning that brought the flavors together.

This led to the creation, by the Fondation Industrie-Université, of the Inter-University Program for Advanced Management – a consortium of the five universities in Belgium and its 21 largest firms. (Revans, 1971, p. 3). Revans outlines the essence of the program this way:

In the spring of 1968 the five universities of Belgium and a score of her larger firms set up a consortium in which each enterprise exchanged a senior manager with another for a year, to work on a strategic problem of the receiving partner. The universities provided support in the form of research method, experimental design, and other techniques. There were thus three parties to the program:

- Senior managers learning how to tackle unstructured situations
- Business enterprises learning about their dynamics and inertias
- Teachers of Management learning to examine the action problem at first hand (Revans, 1982).

The conceptual design

The Belgian Experiment was inherently different from any action learning program before or since (except perhaps for its virtual Siamese twin, the Nile project, to be addressed later). Here is the core essence of program design, as a backdrop for the program specifics we will be covering.

Business and Academic institutions formed a consortium and worked together closely.

Senior managers considered to have high potential were designated by their firms as possible participants. They then went through a panel selection process to determine if they had sufficient motivation and the attributes to be successful:

- Each individual selected, or "fellow" as they were called, was assigned a tutor to help prepare him for the program
- Each fellow was matched with a fellow from another industry, and they were, in effect, exchanged
- Fellows were formed into action learning teams, usually five members to a team
- Each member of this team (the Diagnostic team) had their own individual assigned problem to pursue and, by design, they were from an industry far removed from their own (Revans' belief in removing people from their familiar settings and problems in order to generate fresh questions and innovative thought)
- As each fellow grappled with the problem he or she had been given, they shared their concerns and learning with others in their action learning team who were pursuing different problems.

Each firm with a problem being addressed had a client organization designated within the firm that would be responsible for implementing the recommended solution team and action plan, once determined. Along the path to arriving at a solution, they were to be kept informed of progress being made. Therefore, they were primed and motivated to spring into gear when the nature of the problem had been identified; namely, launch of an action learning set to deal with the implementation. The fellow in the diagnostic set would then finish the last four months of the year-long assignment helping to move the implementation along. This is one of the most intriguing design features of the Belgian Experiment, and truly unique.

Revans was very clear about the importance of the secondary, implementation oriented-action learning team in the receiving company. There had to be a "Framework of Welcome", with "buy in" for the recommended solution and action plan, when it was received in the client organization. Further, the action learning team to handle the implementation phase had to have three types of people in it (those who Care, those who Know and those who Can (Revans' overview of the Belgian Experiment).

The program ended up going through four cycles, each a year in length in a biannual pattern. Before each program year began, participating executives were selected. They were drawn from a pool nominated by the major firms of senior executives who were deemed to have high potential. The candidates appeared before a selection panel of five to six people who assessed their qualifications and motivation level.

Daniel Deveusser, one of those selected, recalled the selection interview during an interview with David Bellon on December 5, 2007. He was asked two questions:

- What do you feel about such a challenge?

(Deveusser states "All I had to show was my motivation")

- Were you expecting some more university studies here?

(Deveusser already had three Master's Degrees, and told them "No", which is what they apparently wanted to hear.)

Each selectee was designated a "fellow". This term was selected by Revans for a purpose. Two of the definitions for the term are "equal" and "comrade". Revans believed deeply in egalitarianism in action learning, everyone to leave their mantle of authority at the door when they entered an action learning team. Participants were organized into action learning teams of five members.

Over the four one-year cycles of the program in Belgium, we know that no more than 40 executives were exchanged between enterprises over the four cycles. Revans launched a replica of the Belgian Experiment in Egypt in 1970, with 13 nationalized enterprises exchanging senior managers. Called "The Nile Project", it used the staff at Al Azhar University as academic advisors. Revans states that:

> in Egypt and Belgium fifty managers have actually been exchanged between fifty enterprises. (Revans, 1982, p. 399)
>
> The one-year program cycle can be broken down this way:
> * a preparatory tutorial phase,
> * a two-month orientation course,
> * a three-month diagnostic phase,
> * a visit to America of about a month,
> * an action phase of four months.
>
> (Revans, 1982, p. 330)

Let us examine the program components more closely. The preparatory tutorial phase involved interaction with each designated fellow to review the program and the expectations. The tutor was apparently assigned six months before the start of the program.

> This tutor first advised each participant how to go about it, either by reading or written exercises, to maintain the academic standard necessary for entering the formal scheme. (Revans, 1971, p. 6)

Two-month orientation phase

This phase, according to Revans, dealt with "action ideas, such as interviewing and sampling, the nature of motivation, risk and learning" (Revans, 1982, p. 330). It is interesting to note that this front end orientation phase, except for about a week, ended up being a series of lectures or, in Revans' parlance, Programed Knowledge, or P – exactly what Revans suggests should not occur in starting an action learning related effort. He emphasizes beginning with Questioning Insight, or Q. The strong inclusion of P in this instance may have been a compromise on his part with those in the academic community in Brussels in the interest of program harmony and gaining their support. In any event, it happened. After events in Manchester, he may have been disinclined to stir up another hornets nest. Dirk Deschoolmeester, when interviewed by David Bellon, explains the use of lectures during the orientation phase this way:

> I guess Professor Revans expected each of the participating schools to bring one of their courses into the program ... for example Philippe

Dewoot might have given two to three days on strategy...Professor Vanlommel was asked to give a little module in cost control...because the participants expected to receive some kind of course in this program rather than just talk philosophy about systems.

Some participants in the Belgian Experiment, based on interviews by David Bellon in 2007 and 2008, believed that this front end loading of lectures was less than inspiring. From what participants had been told, this would not occur, and when it did, they could find it counterproductive. In part, they were receiving instruction on things that they already knew. Here is what Daniel Deveusser, one of David Bellon's interviewees, had to say:

> It was really a fiasco...We were already grown up within our organizations, we were managers...at such training you do not tell things everyone should know...It was really not good...even Gaston Deurinck [the head of the foundation] gave a lecture. It was not what we expected.

The first week of the orientation phase was viewed more positively. It was seen as providing useful tools, including interview techniques and some work with learning styles and psychological tests. There was also sensitivity training (also referred to as T Groups). Some, including Deschoolmeester, apparently found this aspect a problem point in the orientation in that it triggered conflict and, in their view, was of questionable value. It is worth noting that this kind of training can trigger a wide range of responses, but it may well have helped open up communications and thought processes. You would have needed to be there to judge the dynamics.

Three-month diagnostic phase

The diagnostic phase centered on delivery of an action plan, together with a practical roadmap for what needed to happen, by whom, and by when. It involved asking many "Why?"-type questions in getting to the bottom of what was occurring and how to go about resolving it.

Revans' favorite story related to a banker who had been given a thorny problem plaguing Belgian's largest steel company to diagnose. The problem had persisted for some time, despite concerted efforts to solve it by both internal and external consultant teams of experts in the steel industry. The problem related to alloy steel. The company had some of the most modern technology in the world for production of alloy steel. However, they could not seem to get it out of the door. Sales sagged, and the Japanese were gaining market share, forcing the company to sell off some of its assets to remain solvent. It was clearly an urgent situation.

The banker, who knew next to nothing about the steel industry, began interviewing people throughout the company, including a number of hours spent with the chief executive officer (CEO). A picture gradually started to emerge of what was going on – and it was entirely different than expected. It took a nonexpert in steel to figure out the nature of their problem and, when they learned what it was, the senior executives were amazed that they had missed it in all of their studies. They had simply been looking in all the wrong places, using the lens that came from their long-held underlying assumptions and expertise. They had been entrapped by their own assumptions and knowledge.

The problem related to compensation. The entire remuneration system for the company, from entry level to corporate boardroom, was predicated on the "tonnage of steel shipped". That translated to pig iron and other heavy steel products, *not* lightweight alloy steel. They had to reconfigure their compensation system and probably negotiate with the Labor Council in the process (Revans' 1994a).

Problems rooted in metrics are not all that uncommon in business. Steve Kerr, when CLO for General Electric, told the story of how performance in producing chandeliers was measured in the old Soviet Union. Like the Belgian steel company, it was also related to weight. The heavier the chandelier, the better. Finally, matters came to a head when chandeliers began breaking loose from ceilings and killing people. The ceilings could not withstand the weight (Steve Kerr in discussion of metrics with Dilworth).

Visit to America (one month)

Revans indicates that the purpose of the American visit was to submit action plans to the criticism of informed opinion, both in the leading business schools and at the headquarters of major firms (Revans, 1982, p. 330).

Daniel Deveusser in his interview by David Bellon states:

> The visit to the United States lasted only one week...we went to the States just to make a presentation of our project. I gave mine at IBM. Others went to General Electric...some presentations were not ripe yet. Some were just theory. Some were good. It was really not the best moment.

The action phase

As already highlighted, this phase involved the fellows, who had performed the diagnosis and created the action plan, working with the client organization in the receiving enterprise in helping to guide the implementation. This also entailed helping to "seed" the implementation team in getting it up and running.

Revans had formulated a very advanced approach in this design, because it has been found time and time again in business operations that the strategic implementation often falls short in matching up well with the strategic formulation. Here, we see a mechanism for establishing a nexus and alignment between strategy as conceived and what actually transpires.

Impact of the Belgian Experiment

As pointed out in discussing the dynamics that gave impetus to the Belgian Experiment, there were important reasons for wanting it to be successful. There was a thirst for positive results. Revans preformed many statistical analyses of the Belgian economy during the experiment and for at least the next 30 years. He hinged his analyses on what he termed "National Spontaneity", and tied them to his learning equation – L (for Learning) equals P (Programed Information) plus Q (Questioning Insight).

The performance of the Belgian economy did show a remarkable upward spike about the time the Belgian Experiment was put in place and in the ensuing decade. Revans seemed to believe that the "National Spontaneity" (his expression) resulting from the Belgian Experiment had played a significant role in lifting the economy. A lengthy report that he prepared for the First Action Learning and Mutual Collaboration Congress in 1994 is entitled "Action Learning or Partnership in Adversity: The Economic Effects of National Spontaneity". It establishes the linkage with the learning equation and underscores the importance of asking "Why?"-type questions in order to grasp what is really taking place, and, in effect, "get out of the box". He expresses his philosophy this way in one section of the report (p. 9):

> Only *the awareness of one's own inability to grasp what is happening* can be the valid starting point of one's race against a quickly changing world, so that it is not merely the event around one that may need deeper examination. It is one's own personal responsibility to recognize one's inner helplessness that is now so imperative. It is not what we are drilled by others to do in this rapidly-changing world of

today that is the essence of salvation, but what we ourselves, as different individuals, may learn from the practical interpretation of our immediate and threatening embarrassments.

He goes on to say (p. 9) that:

Our first declaration is that we need to learn as rapidly as the world around us is changing; our second is that learning consists of both what we pick up from others and what, from here-and-now experience, we find out for and about ourselves.

What we see in his basic treatise on National Spontaneity are the threads of two philosophical constructs that did not emerge until much later. The first was "Emotional Intelligence", and the second, related specifically to his National Spontaneity argument, are behavioral economics and behavioral finance. Behavior, mindset and emotions do influence economic activity (e.g., the Consumer Confidence Index). This seems to be Revans' underlying theme. In sum, he is saying we need to exercise both sides of our brain, the emotional and intuitive side as well as the fact-driven, hard analysis side.

There is substance in the way Revans philosophically frames things. However, when it comes to ascribing Belgian's economic progress to the Belgian Experiment he seems to go too far. That he does see such linkage is clear. In a compendium of documents prepared for distribution at an International Action Learning Seminar in 1996 (Revans, 1995) he uses some statistics and rationales he has used repeatedly over the years with regard to the economic performance of Belgium. He states (p. 4):

Since the majority of Belgium's largest enterprises agreed in 1968 to try a new form of managerial development, now known as action learning, and derived from managers working together as comrades in adversity upon real and threatening troubles that all are ready to admit they do not understand, it is interesting to see from Table Three [a table encompassing economic performance from 1953 to 1987] that Belgium is alone among the twelve economies monitored by the U.S. Bureau of Labor Statistics to show any improvement in output per hour after that year.

He goes on to say:

The difference of over three percent in Belgium's performance relative to the other eleven manufacturing economies is very highly significant; some assignable cause must have been introduced during 1968, but it has been impossible to suggest what this might have been...were it other than the action learning program designed to achieve operational improvement in manufacturing and overseas markets. (p. 4)

In all fairness to Revans, few would argue that the Belgian Experiment did not have a favorable impact. It may have even to some degree changed management thinking in those areas that were impacted by it. It was certainly a new way of dealing with executive development. However, cause and effect relationships are hard to prove, and there are reasons to damp down just how much influence the Belgian Experiment with action learning may have had on the economy:

1. It was not the only initiative in being by the Foundation and by others;
2. There were a number of exogenous factors at work in the world economy;
3. This period saw the beginning of a strong upsurge in the world economy;
4. There were only 40, or fewer, executives involved in the Belgian Experiment, and while some of the problem solving (like the example in the steel company) was obviously very significant, others produced less meaningful results.

What did those interviewed by David Bellon have to say about the impact of the experiment on the Belgian economy?

Leopold Vansina:

> It would not be scientifically correct to say that the Belgian economy jumped as a result of the experiment...the number of participants was far too limited to achieve such impact...also the era was one of the most glorious economic periods of the century. Everyone was booming.

Daniel Deveusser:

> How to measure the impact of the experiment is a good question. The number of people who passed through the program was limited. We are talking about 40 people. It is impossible to say that this made a difference.

Professor Dirk Deschoolmeester:

> Revans always said that Belgium became the most productive coun-
> try, and he had statistics around that, and he said this is thanks to
> our efforts. In my opinion he exaggerated on that, but it could be
> true. But I do not see a tangible relationship between the experi-
> ment and economic performance. The country is too big for that.
> The experiment was very small. But it is interesting that Max Nokin
> was using this to show things were moving, to shareholders.

Dirk Symoens:

> Trying to make a relation between the increased productivity figures
> of Belgium and relate them to bi-yearly programs was very emotional
> but, in fact, rather weird.

From his experience with all the interviews, David Bellon makes this
observation:

> A lot of the people interviewed perceived the experiment as "inter-
> esting". However, not one of them linked the experiment to a better
> performance of the economy. Research also revealed that this experi-
> ment was one of many (see also Activity Reports of the Fondation
> Industrie-Université in which the experiment took only 2–3 pages per
> report). From a political viewpoint, it seems the Belgian government
> launched a large wave of initiatives which ultimately lead to an uplift
> in the economy. The experiment was not of major importance for the
> Belgian political establishment. It was one initiative among many.

The Nile Project

As we outlined in discussing the Belgian project, some very important people were in a position to promote the effort. Similar good luck
and networking helped bring the Nile project into being. Professor
Saad Ashmawy of the Department of Business Administration at
the University of Cairo had been a doctoral student of Revans at the
University of Manchester.

Revans was invited to speak in November 1969 at a seminar on problems of productivity in the Middle East in Cairo, Egypt. In his remarks,
Revans struck one of his favorite themes. He said:

> [O]nly Africans can understand and develop Africa, that Africans can
> be effectively taught only by their own responsible study of African

problems, and that if the intervention of Western professors is not to be actually harmful (in addition to being unconscionably expensive), a great deal of thought needs to be given to their role. (Revans, 1982, p. 373)

Revans gave examples of his work with London hospitals and Belgian enterprises. Presiding over the session was Abdel El Abd, Director of Training of the Central Training Organ (CTO) of the United Arab Republic. He saw the wisdom of Revans' philosophy and appears to have been primed to receive the message. He had a close relationship with the Inter-University Program in Belgium and was well aware of the Belgian Experiment with action learning.

From this catalyst, an active collaboration quickly developed, including a decision to inaugurate a smaller version of the Belgian Experiment. Managers from Belgium started coming to Egypt to assist in setting up the program, and managers from Egypt went to Brussels. However, the first task in Egypt was to interest the presidents of some of the major companies to participate and free up some of their high potential executive talent to serve as fellows and go through an exchange of executives with other companies. Thirteen companies were ultimately enlisted to participate:

1. The National Bank of Egypt
2. The Automotive Repair Company
3. The Eastern Tobacco Company
4. The Coke Company
5. The Metal Construction Company
6. The Cooperative Petroleum Company
7. The Sugar and Distillation Company
8. The Organization for Metal Industries
9. The Alexandria Soap and Oil Company
10. The Plastics and Electric Manufacturing Company
11. The Tanta Oil and Soap Company
12. The Copper Factories Company
13. The Soyof Spinning and Weaving Company (Revans, 1982, 379–380).

While this diversified list of companies signed up to participate, there were some caveats. They agreed with having the executives work on projects with which they were unfamiliar. However, they also decided that there should only be a limited number of project themes. Three themes were initially decided on: the relevance of training, the sources of motivation, and the flow of productive operations.

Rather than run through an in-depth examination, the program pieces in the Nile Project – since they largely followed the pattern used in Belgium – we will cover a few highlights and areas that seem in need of particular attention.

The induction of fellows phase in Eqypt "opened up with a part-time Induction Course concerned with the skills of interviewing, and with such ideas as self-awareness, the nature of learning and the origins of reinforcements of resistances to change (Revans, 1980, p. 55).

The highlighting of potential resistance during the induction phase was in some ways a harbinger of what was to come. Hurdles and resistance were encountered, but especially at the end when it came time for the fellows to outline their findings and recommendations to top management.

> At these meetings, each set of fellows, backed by a few counterparts, gave an account of his findings and recommendations, outlining his methods, his evidence, and so forth. The frankness with which some of the visitors described what they had seen, supported by the conviction with which they urged their recommendations for action, had never been anticipated and aroused more than a little defensiveness and recrimination. (pp. 56–7)

One top manager described the dynamics that unfolded this way:

> At first I refused to accept the fellow's report about my company. Then I tried to find reasons for persuading myself not to accept it. I thought – and how sour were my thoughts! – and the criticisms were against us, against my staff, and against me. But as I hear it this room tonight, the same criticism is being made by all the fellows, against their own companies as much as against the others, since they all worked in pairs; it is a common feature of the whole programme. We are all of us in the same boat. This makes the findings of all the fellows very important and very relevant. (p. 57)

Revans was dissatisfied with one aspect of the Nile Project – the implementation phase. He states his displeasure this way:

> We did not, during the development of the Nile Project, appreciate the importance of the client group for implementation, or therapeutic, phase of the projects; the Egyptian fellows were not advised to make a team out of those, who would be called to answer the questions 'Who knows? Who cares? Who can?' (p. 58)

Revans goes on to say:

> Our ignorance of the implementation process was brought home
> very clearly when, at the end of the first Nile Project, most of the
> Egyptian managers came to Belgium to compare progress with the
> fellows of the Inter-University Programme [Belgium]. (p. 59)

What were some of the positives of the Nile Project? Six of the 13 fellows were rewarded at the end with major promotions (Revans, 1982,
p. 423). This clearly suggests that their worth was reinforced to top
management, and that recriminations were perhaps minimal. Overall,
the fellows reported that they had learned a great deal, including better
self-knowledge.

After organizing a second program in action learning from his own
university in Cairo, Professor Ashwamy helped create a similar program
in Libya.

Lessons learned

What broad lessons learned can be drawn from the Belgian Experiment
and the more limited project in Egypt?

1. It suggests that national initiatives are worthy of further consideration. In fact, there is a case – Revans certainly visualized it – for
   using action learning on an international scale to deal with disputes,
   as well as the development of programs that require several international players;
2. The Belgian Project in particular showed great promise in opening
   up communications and bringing some solution opportunities to
   bear on persistent and urgent problems, by getting people to think
   differently and operate outside their comfort zones;
3. You can argue over some of the apparent contradictions and flaws in
   the two programs, but the pluses seem to exceed the minuses by a
   significant margin;
4. The benefits derived from the program in Belgium, in terms of greatly
   improved economic performance, seem a bit overstated.

Applying knowledge gained in the Belgian
Experiment to other national efforts

When asked for their thoughts on implementing the Belgian model elsewhere, two of the individuals David Bellon interviewed, each a veteran

of the Belgian Experiment, said this:

Dirk DeSchoolmeester

> The only thing I can say is just do it. Revans was more the feminine way, the soft skills, reflect, propose again. You have to accept that the approach is more feminine, I do not mean women doing it. The masculine way is more that we shoot from our hip and we will solve it. You know that there are political systems all around so you reflect, you propose, you try again. That's what I like about Business Process Management [DeSchoolmeester teaches the subject in an interdisciplinary way]. We know it will take time. Some managers do not like that. They are more 'give me what is'. That's more like solving puzzles. That's not Revans. Living in modified environments, that's what I have learned. Revans' approach was more a slow methodology than an analytical one.

Daniel Deveusser

> They should be prepared to be strategic and engage in long term thinking. For high level executives, a year is too long. Three or four months should be sufficient if it is intense and with a group, not individuals. Young graduates need a longer time... You need an organization that supervises the whole program. It needs to be structured.

Those contemplating other national level programs should bear in mind:

1. The Belgian model used in the 1960s cannot be used without significant adjustments. The world has changed;
2. Both Belgian and Nile experiments seemed a bit heavy on formal instruction prior to launch. The fellows, by definition, were high performers and highly experienced. As those who were interviewed in 2007 and 2008 by David Bellon (who had participated in the Belgian Experiment) suggest, they were being taught things they already knew and that seemed out of place in this kind of program;
3. Whatever the model, as Revans continuously emphasized, it must be fitted to the culture and context. It must be tailor-made for the nation and setting in which it will be used;
4. The core essence of what was done in Belgium – which aligns rather directly with the basic precepts of action learning – can still serve as the central design.

References

Barker, A. E. (2008) Telephone conversation with Robert L. Dilworth in July.

Blain, J. (2008) Executive Development Center, Manchester Business School. Email to Robert L. Dilworth, July 28, with announcement of new Academy for Action Learning and Research. The official dedication ceremony took place on November 26, 2008.

Botham, D. (2008) Former Director of the Revans Centre for Action Learning and Research at the University of Salford in England. Telephone conversation with Robert L. Dilworth in July.

DeSchoolmeester, D. (2007) Interviewed by David Bellon in Belgium in October.

Drieghe, L. (2008) Interviewed by David Bellon in Belgium.

Deveusser, D. (2007) Interviewed by David Bellon in Belgium on December 5.

Kerr, S. (1992) Chief Learning Officer (CLO) for GE. A conversation with Robert L. Dilworth in Miami, Florida on the use of metrics.

Revans, R. W. (1995) "Past, Present and Future of Action Learning – First Example: The Economic Miracle of 1990". Unpublished paper distributed in 1996 at the International Action Learning Seminar at the Revans Centre for Action Learning and Research (later redesignated as an Institute).

Revans, R. W. (1994a) "Detailed Overview of the Belgian Experiment", in an Address to staff and faculty of the Defense Systems Management College at Fort Belvoir, Virginia, in February 1994. Contained in an unreleased DVD by Robert L. Dilworth.

Revans, R. W. (1994b) "Action Learning or Partnership in Adversity: The Economic Effects of National Spontaneity". Unpublished report distributed by Revans in 1994 at the First Annual Action Learning and Mutual Collaboration Congress at Heathrow in England.

Revans, R. W. (1985) *Confirming Cases* (Manchester: RALI [Revans Action Learning International] Ltd).

Revans, R. W. (1983) *The ABC of Action Learning* (Bromley, U.K.: Chartwell-Bratt)

Revans, R. W. (1982) *The Origins and Growth of Action Learning* (Bromley, U.K.: Chartwell-Bratt).

Revans, R. (1971) *Developing Effective Managers* (New York: Praeger).

Symoens, D. (2007) Interviewed by David Bellon in Belgium.

Talpaert, R. (2007) Interviewed by David Bellon.

Vansina L. (2007) Interviewed by David Bellon.

Part 2

The Evolution of Action Learning

6
Milestones in the History and Worldwide Evolution of Action Learning

Yury Boshyk, Albert E. Barker, and Robert L. Dilworth

Introduction

This chapter was written to assist those who wish to gain a comprehensive understanding of action learning's origins and evolution. There is much diversity of thought and interpretation about action learning's major principles and development. With this in mind, we have tried to clarify the chronological and intellectual evolution of action learning as well as how it was, and is, practiced. We have emphasized the life, thinking, and experience of action learning's principal pioneer, Reg Revans, as he and his work are less well-known today when compared with other approaches to action learning, especially in North America.

Other perspectives and practices of action learning that are not directly linked or related to Revans' influence or thinking have also been included. We make no judgment on what is or is not "true" action learning – only that there are many action learning tributaries and, although many call themselves "action learning", there are fundamental differences between and among them. It is crucial, however, that we understand the different philosophical, theoretical, and intellectual foundations because, as Kurt Lewin once stated, "there is nothing as practical as a good theory". Moreover, the various applications of action learning all flow from certain theoretical assumptions.

In some circles, there is still harsh and bitter criticism about what is "true" action learning, and attempts abound in defining action learning "typologies" – something that action learning's principle pioneer lamented in the later years of his life. In his correspondence in the 1990s, Revans encouraged people to come together to debate each others' perceptions in a manner reminiscent of his Cavendish Laboratory days. This is the spirit in which we offer this survey.

Reg W. Revans consciously discouraged biographies about himself. However, he did share some of his more personal details and his professional history with his close friends, Albert Barker, David Botham, and Robert L. Dilworth. We have, therefore, relied on their recollections and have supplemented these with our own research and documentation. We have sometimes provided a "context" for the event mentioned to help the reader appreciate the background to a publication or activity, and we encourage readers to consult the endnotes for these and more detailed comments on the subject in question.

Concepts and terms such as systems theory, systems thinking, organizational learning, organizational systems, action research, action science all spring from the well of a new and more "people centered" way of looking at the world and, in particular, in management practice. Revans was aware of these tributaries, and even espoused his commitment to some of their principles as, for example, "action research", "action science", "systems thinking", and what he termed the "learning system" of an organization and of an individual adult learner. For this reason, we have included mention of some of these parallel developments during Revans' lifetime and in the context of action learning's evolution and linkages. Also included are books and other events referenced by Revans in his writing and correspondence.

The section on Resources and Networks in this volume (Chapter 8) provides further details on publications by Revans and by others mentioned in this overview.

We have tried to place Revans' life in chronological order with other events following so, for example, an entry for the year "1973" will first mention events in Revans' life and then these will be followed by other developments. Revans was sometimes referred to as "RWR" (Reginald W. Revans) and, on occasion, we use the short form here as well.

1907–1925: Early years

1907: (14 May) Birth of Reginald William Revans in Portsmouth, U.K. Father: Thomas William Revans, Principal Ship Surveyor, Board of Trade. Mother: Ethel Amelia Revans.[1]

1910: RWR accompanies mother on her voluntary hospital work. Attends Florence Nightingale's memorial service.[2] A family connection to health care and service is evident. Revans' mother is a volunteer in the city's hospital while younger brother John (1911–1988), a medical doctor, had a distinguished career in health care and was knighted for his efforts.[3]

1911: Publication of Frederick Taylor's *The Principles of Scientific Management* and Frank Gilbreth's *Motion Study* establishing what Kleiner refers to as "scientific management", whereby "the numbers as the dominant method for drawing efficiency from people" prevailed. It started to be challenged seriously in the 1920s.[4]

1912: Family moves to Foxbourne Road, Ballam, London; the year of the *Titanic* disaster, an event that was to have a profound impression on Revans (see Chapters 2 and 3). RWR was educated at Battersea Grammar School, London.[5]

1914–1918: Revans sees the social impact of World War I. Every street and every family knew their dead.[6]

1920: "Social psychology begins to study organizational behavior";[7] publication of Kurt Lewin's, "Die Sozialisierung des Taylorsystems" (Humanization of the Taylor System).[8]

1921: Publication in the U.K. of *The Human Factor in Business* by B. Seebohm Rowntree, a Quaker and member of the chocolate-making family. He was active in the Acton Society Trust, which was also supported by the Joseph Rowntree Social Service.[9] Revans' research on the conditions in the mines and retail outlets was published by the Acton Society Trust in 1953 as *Size and Morale: A Preliminary Study of Attendance at Work in Large and Small Units*. See 1953.

1925–1935: University years

1925: RWR enters University College, London.

1926: Pioneering efforts in educational theory; for example, publication of Eduard C. Lindeman's *The Meaning of Adult Education* and, in 1924, Eugen Rosenstock's *Andragogik* (Adult Education) was published in Germany; in 1927: Eduard Lindeman and Martha Anderson publish *Education Through Experience*, a summary of the adult education movement in Germany.[10]

1928: RWR awarded a B.Sc. from University College, London with First Class Honors in Physics.[11]

1928: RWR awarded the Sudbury–Hardiman Research Studentship at Emmanuel College, Cambridge, and started work on his research as the last doctoral student of J.J. Thomson. He was the 1906 Nobel Prize winning scientist who discovered the electron, and was later Master of Trinity College. Revans worked in the Cavendish Laboratory, then under Ernest Rutherford.[12] (see Chapter 3).

1928: RWR attends Quaker House of Friends gatherings on the corner of Emmanual Road on Saturdays. Eddington, Cambridge Professor of Astronomy who proved Einstein right in 1919, was also at the Cavendish and attended the Quaker meetings.[13]

1928: RWR is a member of the British Olympic team for the long-jump at the Amsterdam Olympics (17 May–12 August); he is also the holder of Cambridge undergraduate long-jump record, 1929–1962.[14]

1930–1932: RWR attends the University of Michigan, in the U.S., as a Commonwealth Fund Fellow[15] and goes to study physics (astrophysics and astronomy).[16] And in 1930 RWR took part (16–23 August) in the inaugural British Empire Games in Hamilton, Ontario, Canada.[17] Naturally enough, athletics was a lifetime passion.

1932: RWR married Ann-Ida Margareta Åqvist, a librarian from Göthenburg, Sweden, whom he met in Ann Arbor, Michigan. During this time, he also met Raoul Wallenberg, who was studying architecture at Michigan.[18]

1932–1935: Back to Cambridge

1932: RWR returned to the U.K. to take up a Research Fellowship at Emmanuel College, Cambridge University, where he was later awarded a Ph.D. (1935). He is part of the Cavendish Laboratory[19] (see Chapter 3 for more on his Cambridge years).

1932: (4 May) Einstein visits Cambridge for a lecture and visits the Cavendish Laboratory with Revans in attendance.[20]

1932: Eric Trist (1909–1993), one of the founders of the Tavistock Institute for Human Relations, and later acquaintance and somewhat colleague of Revans during the days when Revans was at the National Coal Board (NCB) (1947–1950), then a graduate student of literature in Cambridge shows Kurt Lewin around Cambridge. Lewin had just fled Germany to escape persecution from the Nazi regime. He was on his way to the U.S. where he is considered to have been one of the pioneers of many developments, including T-(training) groups, sensitivity training, the National Training Laboratory, "action research", and Organization Development. There is no evidence that Revans and Lewin ever met[21] (see 1949).

1933: (November 15) Revans' scientific publication on his research on ionic sound waves: "The Transmission of Waves Through an Ionized Gas". In 1961, researchers commented on the accuracy of the research. Revans' comment on this was: "Total acknowledgement of Revans' pioneering work, in spirit quite unlike that of social science, management education, etc."[22] For a more detailed explanation of his area of research, see the endnotes to this entry.[23]

1933: The publication of Elton Mayo's *The Human Problems of an Industrial Civilization*. Considered to be one of the founders of "humanistic psychology".

1933: The publication of *The Nature of Learning in its Relation to the Living System* by George Humphrey. Inspired by Einstein and applying early systems theory to psychology.[24]

1935: RWR receives his doctoral degree Ph.D. from Cambridge as a result of five years' scientific research at Cambridge and in the U.S.[25]

In an article, Revans' comments on his scientific training and research:

> I had been raised in the austere school of experimental physics which taught me one could never know what the atom *was*; all we could hope for was to observe how it *apparently behaved*. Action learning descends from this ethic: something exists not for what it *is*, but by what it can *do*. It is idle, indeed, fraudulent, to take students through the contents of books, except as the overture to application that can test the rigour of the argument.[26]

1935: RWR leaves Cambridge.[27] Several years later, he was to explain his reasons for doing so:

> From 1925 to 1935 my field of interest had been atomic physics, and I had worked for my doctorate under Sir J.J. Thomson in the Cavendish Laboratory with its many Nobel Prize winners. Two non-academic interests were then diverting my attention from the vital significance of my research field, the first being the likelihood that nuclear energy might amplify our impending disagreements with Adolf Hitler and Benito Mussolini, and the second that my tiny daughters had deflected my attention from nuclear physics towards human survival. The inherent variability of that epoch may well be recalled in *The Thirties*, Malcom Muggeridge's account of how we must all be

more fully aware that the more the world is changing, the less we must rely upon expert forecasts of what tomorrow will reveal.[28]

The writings of Sir John Sargent (1888–1972) in 1933 also encouraged Revans to enter the education field.[29] It could be considered that Revans was following the Quaker tradition with many of its adherents active in the field of education (and health care) (see Chapter 3).

1935: Kurt Lewin appointed professor of child psychology at the University of Iowa in the U.S.

1935–1945: Pioneering work in education and health care – World War II

1935–1945: RWR takes up the position of Deputy Chief Education Officer to the Director of Education, John Sargent, Essex County Council, in Chelmsford "and held this appointment for ten years". "I got the job of developing the forms of education alternative to the traditional grammar schools"[30] Helps launch one (perhaps two) Technical Colleges in Essex, but never saw them built during his tenure.[31]

Revans' comments about the cultural and political setting at the time, as well as his views on education and its role in society are of interest:

> We can find, in modern times…examples of the divergence between the practical outlook of technology and trade, on the one hand, and the enduring classical and literary outlook of the educationist on the other. The *Spens Report*, published in 1938, advised us to set up technical high schools as equal alternatives to the traditional grammar schools. It was not only industrialists who came to be alarmed by the success of the grammar schools in draining the nation's talent into literary occupations, and leaving the less able pupils to enter industry; our system of public education had tended to make the clerk and the typist more important in the eyes of the nation than the artisan and the nurse. In the words of the Spens report itself:
>
>> A careful study of the present position has led us to the belief that the existing arrangements for the whole-time education of boys and girls above the age of eleven in England and Wales have ceased to correspond with the actual structure of modern society and with the economic facts of the situation.
>
> The spirit of this is now written into the Education Act, 1944, although as long ago as 1936 the Essex Education Committee [when Revans was Deputy Education Officer for Essex County

Council, 1935–1945] had persuaded the Board of Education, as it then was, to allow them to open the first technical high school in the country.[32]

It is interesting to note in this article the opening words, which are so characteristic of Revans' (perhaps Quaker inspired) belief in harmony:

> My task is to discuss education in industry, and to stress, if I can, the importance of education in establishing and maintaining that harmony between all those engaged in producing and distributing the world's wealth that is known as good industrial relations. [Disharmony or] cleavage exists today between ... the university and the technical college ... between the grammar school and the technical secondary school ... but the true antithesis is that between fulfillment and survival; between the enrichment of human life and experience, on the one hand, and our physical survival on the other.[33]

During this time, RWR had his first experience with the business world, Ford of Dagenham's, regarding including workers in management decisions (see Chapters 2 and 4).[34]

1936: RWR's father, T. W. Revans, dies on December 13, 1936, after a short illness, at the age of 59. See Chapter 3, for Revans' comments about his father.

1936: Publication of what is considered to be a classic study of systems thinking from Plato onwards, Arthur Lovejoy's *The Great Chain of Being*.

1937: Untimely death of Ernest Rutherford of the Cavendish Laboratory.

1938: During his time with the Essex County Council, Revans was asked by a colleague with responsibility for health care to investigate why there was a shortage of nurses and a high rate of attrition during their training period. This experience started his long-term engagement with work in hospitals.[35] At this time, Revans submits his "Memorandum to the Essex Education Committee", one of the important foundations for his thinking about action learning, according to Revans.[36]

1938: Publication in the U.S. of John Dewey's *Experience and Education,* often cited by Revans.

1939: (3 September) Britain declares war on Germany. With the war, Revans is in charge of emergency services for the East End of London, the area worst hit by Germany's bombing of London. This constant problem-solving and practical work under great pressure had an influence on him, reinforcing his public spirit and engagement as well as his management skills.[37]

1939: Publication of Peter Drucker's first book, *The End of Economic Man*; and Fritz Roethlisberger and W. J. Dickson's *Management and the Worker*.

1940: (30 August) Death of J. J. Thomson, RWR's supervisor at Cambridge University.

1940: Saul Alinsky (1909–1972), the founder of modern community organizing in the U.S., creates the Industrial Areas Foundation to help prepare hundreds of professional community and labor organizers, and thousands of community and labor leaders (see 1971).

1940–1941: September 1940 to 11 May 1941, German "blitz" against Britain.[38] Revans was in charge of emergency services in the East End of London, as noted above (1939).

1944–1950: Coal mines and miners – years at the Mining Association of Great Britain and the National Coal Board

1944: While apparently officially still with the Essex County Council, Revans asked to study how the coal mining industry could be made more efficient to better assist the war effort; namely, by generating more power for greater manufacturing capability. He starts this assignment by living with the miners and going into the coal pit to better understand the situation.[39]

In Revans (1945, pp. iii–iv) the Introduction by Robert Foot, Chairman of the Mining Association of Great Britain, provides a valuable context to the situation:

> Early in the war there occurred a real slump in recruitment in the Coal Industry, which fell quite suddenly to less than half the normal rate and this situation was undoubtedly accentuated by the high wages (swollen by overtime earnings) that were obtainable in munitions and other war industries. [In 1938, the number of miners was 787,046; and the "corresponding numbers of boys under 16" were 27,469.]
>
> The need for stimulating recruitment and particularly recruitment from mining families, had been fully recognized by the Industry, which has adopted plans for education and training designed to ensure that whatever colliery a new entrant might join, big or small,

in any part of the country, he would find from the very first day that a path was open to him, if he had character, determination and ability, to the highest placed in the Industry.

But it was also realized that merely to attempt to attract recruits by giving them these opportunities was not enough; and that to the workers in the Industry there must be assured a wage, a stability of employment and general conditions that would give them a good standard of living throughout their working life; that as a principle the earnings of the underground workers should be maintained at a level in each district which would give them there the pride of place amongst the industrial workers; and that the best modern principles of labour administration and management must be applied throughout the Industry and maintained at every colliery in the country.

1944: Kurt Lewin cofounds the Research Center for Group Dynamics at MIT, Cambridge, Massachusetts.

1945: Publication of Elton Mayo's *The Social Problems of Industrial Civilization*.

1945: (May) With the end of the war, Revans becomes Director of Recruitment, Education and Training with the Mining Association of Great Britain (the association of the mine owners, as the industry was still privately held).[40]

1945: (October) Publication of *Plans for Recruitment, Education and Training in the Coal Mining Industry*, "Prepared by Dr. R.W. Revans, B.Sc., Ph.D., in conjunction with The Recruitment, Education and Training Committee of the Mining Association of Great Britain with an Introduction by Robert Foot, Chairman of the Association." The Committee was organized in the spring of 1944 and it seems Revans may have worked on the study from that time on, even though officially still in his previous job in Exeter. Revans was not appointed Head of Recruitment until May of 1945 (p. vi of Plans).

This Report contains themes and states assumptions that Revans, at this time 38, was to use later in the development and extrapolation of action learning, management and executive development and education. For example, it is worth quoting the following on leadership development and management education:

The essential qualities which the manager of a large undertaking should possess, and in future it would appear that all undertakings will be large, can be listed under two headings. He must, on the one hand, have a broad understanding of the technicalities of coalmining, and, on the other, the ability to handle successfully a wide and miscellaneous assortment of spirited workmen. There may be some variety of opinion about the relative amounts of time that a manager is called upon to devote to exercising these two rather distinct sets of abilities; some have said that they spend three-quarters of their life dealing with labour and personnel questions, and only one-quarter on the purely technological business of coal-production; others have estimated the division to be even more lop-sided. With these comparisons in mind we can hardly be satisfied that the present systems for the education and training of managers are entirely adequate, since the time and energy devoted to the acquisition of technical knowledge during the courses of instruction far outweigh the consideration given to the study of the management of men. Nor do we believe that the right balance is necessarily restored during the first five years in which the future manager starts to collect his practical experience in the pits; there is no evidence that the handling of men *ipso facto* teaches the principles of how to handle men smoothly and successfully, any more than practical experience of coalgetting *ipso facto* reveals the most successful methods of production.

And this applies not only to coalmining alone; all industry must be alive to the need for the systematic training of executive and supervisory staff on questions of labour management and direction. While it will always be true that some men are endowed better than others with gifts of leadership, it will be equally true that those gifts can be developed under proper tutelage, or by example. It may be many years before the study of industrial psychology deserves the respect now given to mathematics or chemistry, but that there are laws of mass human behaviour is now well established; it remains for those laws to be simply codified and then put into a form that those interested in industrial training can use. For the present, we must be content with suggesting a period of directed practical training in mine administration, with visits to a proposed Staff College, but the industry must never lose sight of any progress made elsewhere in the subject of labour management and must be quick to employ its results. (p. 53)

The study covered the following subjects:

1. An Educational Program for Juvenile Entrants into the Mining Industry, with a special note on recruitment;

2. The Supply of Instructors in Mining Subjects;
3. The Recruitment, Education, and Training of Under-Officials;
4. The Education and Training of Managers and Higher Officials;
5. The Recruitment and Training of Craftsmen for the Mining Industry;
6. The Education and Training of Higher Technical Officers;
7. A Staff College for the Mining Industry.

The head of the Association, Robert Foot, also commented that:

> Each subject is surveyed dispassionately and with a truly liberal approach; and the consequent recommendations are inspired by vision – without being visionary – and are at the same time eminently practical. (viii)

The meaning of this "liberal approach" was clarified by Revans in a section of the report dealing with "the education and training of higher technical officers" in which the "importance of a liberal outlook" is discussed (pp. 89–91): Its main features were, among other things, humility, and a respect for facts and scientific analysis, and respect for people.

Among other things, Revans recommended the creation of a Staff College which would emphasize learning from fellow managers rather "than from academic courses of most kinds".[41] To Revans this was the "first statement of the [action learning] theme", more specifically, that "managers should be encouraged to learn with and from each other in the course of doing their everyday jobs rather than by listening to specialist tutors".[42]

The Staff College was not built during RWR's time at the Mining Association and then the NCB but, it seems, only in 1955.[43] In that year, the NCB Annual Report was discussed in Parliament, where the Paymaster-General stated:

> Recently, there has been established by the Coal Board a staff college, which, I think, is of very great importance, because it is very much needed in the industry. It will be giving courses for men between the ages of 30 and 45, refresher courses for senior colliery managers, and will be arranging the sort of industrial symposia among leading members of the industry which have proved so valuable in other industries. In addition to the staff college, there are courses for managers and refresher studies in techniques and modern methods.[44]

1946: RWR involved in teaching English using action learning to Displaced Persons from Central and Eastern Europe. They were volunteer miners (see Chapter 3).[45]

1946: (Spring) The "Miners' Charter" drawn up by miners in the U.K. demanding "modernization of existing pits", five-day work week, "proper training for young miners" and improved social and welfare provisions.[46]

1946: The founding of the Tavistock Institute of Human Relations in London with a grant from the Rockefeller Foundation.[47]

1946: The first use of the term "action research"; earlier, in 1945 by John Collier (1945), commissioner of Indian Affairs in the U.S. federal government from 1933–1945; and then by Kurt Lewin (1946) who stated that "there can be no action without research, and no research without action".[48]

1946: Publication of Saul Alinsky's *Reveille for Radicals*, later republished in 1969 (see 1940 and 1971).

1947: (1 January) Nationalization of the coal industry in the U.K. preceded by the formation of the NCB (1946); RWR, therefore, works in the private sector from 1944–1946. At the time of nationalization, there were 970 pits, 692,000 miners; and coal made up more than 90 percent of Britain's energy requirements.[49]

Great strife in the industry during this time; absenteeism rates "were still high (running about 15 per cent)". Great shortages of coal and everyone was cold, with plant closings due to lack of energy, blackouts; more strikes after nationalization than before and unhappiness with centralization of decision-making in the NCB. But some progress noted as well: "working conditions improved markedly... training was introduced for newcomers before ever they went down to the coalface. A ban was introduced on young boys going underground before they were sixteen. We had a national safety scheme, with proper standards at every colliery. And for the first time, pithead baths became a standard facility... There were also improved wages, and, despite ministerial and NCB misgivings, the introduction of the five-day work week."[50]

An interesting comment about Revans' work during these years was also provided by Charles Margerison:

> [T]he problems that he and his colleagues faced at the NCB were enormous. There were so few people available to manage and work the mines, due to the losses during the war years. It was not appropriate for those who returned to be off the job attending courses.

Therefore, Revans adopted a system he had seen in the research laboratories where colleagues shared and compared their problems, their ideas and findings at the workplace.

He invited coalmine managers to do likewise, by visiting each other's mines, usually in small groups, which he called 'a Set' of managers. One of the managers could be managing safety arrangements very well. If so, he was asked to share his methods. Another might be doing well on productivity and teamwork. Another manager might be controlling costs well. By their visits and discussions to each other's mines, they learned best practice. In addition, they also had mutual support and confidence from each other to introduce the new methods to their own mines.[51]

1947: Revans' divorce from his first wife (see 1932).

1947: (12 February) In the U.S., the untimely death of Kurt Lewin (born 9 September, 1890). Lewin is considered to be the founder of social and applied psychology (behavioralism) and one of the first to study group dynamics and organization development, and also the founder of action research, sensitivity training and the National Training Laboratory in the U.S. It is of interest to note the role of the U.S. government and military in helping to develop this field further, and the number and rapid spread in the 1950s of "change agents" or Organization Development (OD) practitioners throughout the corporate world in the U.S., a situation that was not comparable nor available to Revans and his supporters in the U.K. and other parts of the world.[52] Revans' view of what he called "group dynamics", and how it differed from his understanding of action learning, was summarized as follows (Revans, 1980, 309–10):

> Since an essential process in any action learning programme is the set [group or team] discussion, itself inextricably associated with the projects deep in managerial reality, it is not seldom asserted that group dynamics and its many derivatives have long supplied us with all that action learning may have to offer. Because the set helps its manager-participants to correct their obliquities of vision and to master their infirmities of resolve, and employs for these useful purposes the managers themselves, would not the set be greatly helped if the participants openly and courageously embraced all that the behavioural sciences have to offer? I cannot dispute this claim, as I do not know what all the contending schools of inter-personal psychology are on about. I can only stress that action learning is about real people tackling real problems in real time, observing the

impartial discipline of the business setting, and looking after a lot of people without much interest in group psychotherapy of any kind. Such exercises as sensitivity training, transactional analysis and so forth are not, it seems, *by their very nature*, riveted firmly to the here-and-now demands of industrial or commercial achievement. My criterion is simple: "Does the programme require that, after the therapeutic episode, the subject tries himself out afresh in the real world and produces the evidence of improvement that will convince *external and disinterested observers*?"

1948: First Conference held at Oxford in 1948 on the "Education of the Young Worker" in which Revans played a prominent role, and in which he is mentioned. See *The Education of the Young Worker* (*1949*).[53]

1948: Publication of Norbert Wiener's, *Cybernetics, or the Control and Communication in the Animal and the Machine*. One of the early founders of systems thinking. Revans contributed an article to a book honoring Wiener (1894–1964), entitled "The Structure of Disorder", edited by J. Rose (1969), *Survey of Cybernetics: A Tribute to Dr. Norbert Wiener.*

1948: RWR's action learning work with Displaced Persons from Central and Eastern Europe, voluntary miners who came to the U.K. and needed to learn English quickly (see Chapter 3).[54]

1948: Publication of Kurt Lewin's *Resolving Social Conflicts: Selected Papers on Group Dynamics.*[55]

1949: Eric Trist, Tavistock Institute of Human Relations, together with Ken Bamforth, studies coal mines in Haighmoor, U.K., and their ground-breaking research is later published in 1951.[56] It is interesting to note Revans' comment on this research and the Tavistock Institute:

> [T]he Tavistock Institute carried out a famous experiment (to which I contributed nothing but from which I learned a lot). The Institute persuaded the management of a Durham coalmine to allow the 41 miners who had previously worked on three separate shifts now to work together, in smaller groups, on the same shifts... It is true that the Tavistock researches into the power of groups owed nothing to action learning (as that term is now employed); those researches were self-standing, and, as far as I am aware, did not recognize the virtues of smallness, at least in the sense that smallness by itself has the advantage of encouraging spontaneous learning... We must be grateful to the Tavistock – perhaps for some time yet.[57]

Eric Trist (1909–1993), psychologist and later a leading figure in the field of Organization Development. He was one of the founders of the Tavistock Institute of Human Relations in London. Trist was influenced by Kurt Lewin, whom he knew. The Tavistock Institute for Human Relations worked closely with the National Training Laboratory in the U.S. Later in his career, Trist used the term "action learning" when describing his university-based work at York University in Toronto, which may have been a source of some confusion for some since his orientation and approach had no connection with Revans' philosophy or approach.[58]

1949: (July) Revans is Chairman of the Second Oxford Conference on "The Education of the Young Worker", focused on vocational training. In the published report on the conference (1950) we can see his profound dissatisfaction with the increasing bureaucratization of society and the coal industry. We see an example in the following account which also shows Revans being true to his belief that those close to the matter should be involved:

> Sir Geoffrey Vickers, then Revans' boss at the Coal Board, tells the story of a post-war meeting at which a group of his managers was selecting slogans for recruitment posters. Just as the men had the slogans all formally arranged in their selected order of preference, Revans came in and objected: "Most of us are closer to 50 than 15", he complained. He insisted that the list should be submitted to the young men at the Coal Board's nearby apprentice training school. This was duly done, with two classrooms asked to rank the slogans in their own order of preference. The results from the two classes were almost identical: more than 90% of the boys had selected the slogan their directors have ranked last – because the older men dismissed it as "too idealistic".[59]

1950–1955: Years as an independent research consultant

1950: Publication of *The Education of the Young Worker*, a report of the Second Conference. (See 1949 and endote).

1950: Revans resigns from the NCB and becomes an independent researcher and consultant on the management of coalmines from 1950–1955.[60] Revans disliked the Chairman of the NCB at this time, Sir Geoffrey Vickers (a lawyer by background). RWR "spent several years working closely with the National Association of Colliery Managers, to examine, in the mines themselves, the operational problems in which these managers saw themselves, or thought they saw themselves, confronted". During this time Revans learned a great deal from Sir Hubert Houldsworth (1889–1956) and credits him with the notion of "small is dutiful" and of practicing action learning in the coal industry even before Revans. In 1951, Sir Hubert was made Chairman of the NCB and this may have been a contributing reason why, despite his resignation from the NCB, he still decided to work with the organization from 1950–1955 as a research consultant.[61]

1951: Publication of RWR's article, "Education in Industry", in *Education in a Changing World: A Symposium*, edited by C. H. Dobinson.

Revans' main points here were that "the art of management is the art of getting people to do things", that is, management is about people and consultation, especially with workers (miners). The problem is not a lack of theories or teachers in education and industry but that there is an exclusion in education of those who work and know. Business realities can be analyzed, and analysis can help enterprises and managers get things done better.[62]

1951: Publication of Kurt Lewin's *Field Theory in Social Science: Selected Theoretical Papers*; and Trist and Bamforth's study of a Durham mine in the U.K. (see 1949).

1951: In Japan, the Deming Prize for quality improvement is introduced.

1952: RWR officially appointed Research Consultant in the NCB's Headquarter's Department.[63]

1952: Publication of W. Ross Ashby's *Design for a Brain*, a systems theorist from the U.K., who, along with Wiener, "initiates a 'machine' view of systems. Ashby along with Wiener develop the notion of feedback and of single-and-double loop learning (the latter including learning about learning). They are considered to be the two of the early founders of modern systems thinking".[64]

1953: Revans' research on the conditions in the mines, a large company, and retail outlets was published by the Quaker-founded Acton Society Trust as *Size and Morale: A Preliminary Study of Attendance at Work in Large and Small Units*. See this endnote for more details on the content and context of this publication.[65]

1954: Revans as a consultant to the NCB, also works with E. F. Schumacher, the author of *Small is Beautiful: Economics as if People Mattered* (see 1973). Schumacher joined the NCB in 1950 as Economic Advisor. They worked on a report studying the colliery management structure, which also had the support of the National Association of Colliery Managers.[66]

1954–1956: RWR launches what he referred to as "the first-ever action learning programme" for managers of coal mines in the U.K.: it ran from February 1954 to November 1956 and Revans called it "A Consortium of Pitmen."[67]

1954: Publication of Abraham Maslow's *Motivation and Personality*.

1955: RWR marries Norah Mary Merritt, of Chelsmford, formerly in the British diplomatic service, based in the Washington embassy.[68]

1955–1965: The Manchester years

1955–1965: RWR joins Manchester College of Science and Technology as Professor of Industrial Administration. From 1953, the College was led by his good friend from Cambridge, B. V. Bowden (later Lord Bowden) and, at the time when Revans joined the College, it had just achieved independent university status (1955–1956). In 1955, the College already had a long history of research and work in the area of management studies. In 1966, its name was changed to the University of Manchester Institute of Science and Technology.[69] RWR focuses on publications.

1956: RWR's article "Industrial Morale and Size of Unit" published. Republished in 1960 in *Labor and Trade Unionism: An Interdisciplinary Reader*, edited by Walter Galenson and Seymour Martin Lipset, pp. 295–300. The editors comment that:

> The paper by R.W. Revans shows the empirical connection between the size of a plant and its strike propensity, and suggests that in large plants strikes are due to the "distance" of the worker from his supervisor, producing a feeling of arbitrariness and of lack of confidence, since managerial representatives are not close enough to know the real work situation, or able to render assistance to the production process. Revans assumes that the worker *is* [sic] interested in production, and where this goal is interfered with by poor organization, and inadequate supervision, morale drops and absenteeism goes up.[70]

1956: From this time on we begin to see references and quotes from the Bible in many of RWR's publications; his religious views are explicit but not prescriptive.[71]

1956: Creation of the Fondation Industrie-Université in Brussels. The formal name of the foundation was: *Fondation Industrie-Université pour le perfectionnement des dirigeants d'enterprise* (FIU). According to one scholar, it was a mixture of Belgian companies and universities and its goal was to promote "university-based management education through intensive networks". The Foundation's "central policy" was to "speed up the legitimization process of management studies into the university systems". Max Nokin was the President of the FIU. He was also chairman of the Sociéte Générale, a holding company comprising large companies especially in the banking and energy sectors. Gaston Deurnick (1922–2000) was the director of the FIU and he was also the brother-in-law of Max Nokin.[72] Revans was to become a Fellow of the Fondation in 1965 and he was associated with it for ten years. He later described Deurnick as a "most remarkable man".[73]

1957: Treaty of Rome lays the integrationist and cooperative foundations for the creation of the European Economic Community and for what is today the European Union. A similar pattern repeated itself in all walks of life throughout Europe, including management education. Revans played a role in this trend when he became President of the European Association of Management Training Centres (EATC) in 1961.

1957: The publication of Chris Aryris' *Personality and Organization: The Conflict Between the System and the Individual.*

1958: RWR's unsuccessful attempt at trying to persuade "a group of Manchester industrialists that the College of Science and Technology should stage a full-time three month experimental course for practicing managers".[74]

1958: The formation of the Campaign for Nuclear Disarmament (CND) formed in the U.K. and still in existence today. Revans was politically a Liberal, a member of the Liberal Club, and was active along with Bertrand Russell and many other prominent citizens in the CND. His comment on this experience is of interest: "I joined the CND and spoke at public meetings. This, no doubt, led me to be seen as a communist; it may have had a long-delaying effect upon the spread of…genuine action learning."[75]

1959: Formation of the Brussels-based European Association of Management Training Centres (EAMTC), a grouping of some universities but mostly highly selective private-sector management development and training centers, among them CEI [later IMI and then merged with IMEDE to form IMD in 1990] in Geneva, IMEDE in Lausanne, and IPSOA in Turin, with Gaston Deurnick as its head (as he was with the 1957-founded Fondation Inter-Université (FIU), see above). Revans would later become President of the EAMTC while still a professor at Manchester, and then, as a Fellow of the EAMTC, after he left the university and moved to Brussels in 1965. From its origins, and then under Revans, the "EAMTC deliberately practiced elitism: it was a select grouping of institutions. Membership criteria was clearly laid down...EAMTC developed a...[broad] spectrum of activities ranging from inter-centre twinnings, through staff training to working groups on management and examining the real operations of management training centres..." In 1971, the EAMTC, along with another organization, the International University Contact for Management Education (IUC), became the European Foundation for Management Development (EFMD), still an active organization based in Brussels. All these organizations, the FIU, the EAMTC, and the EFMD were founded with the help of grants from the Ford Foundation.[76]

1959: Publication of Matthew Miles' book *Learning to Work in Groups* in the U.S. synthesized more than ten years of experimentation, study and learning about group work.[77]

1959–1960: RWR begins research on life in hospitals, and especially the problem of the high turnover of nurses in the Manchester area (reminiscent of his research in Essex in the 1930s) together with a group from the Manchester College of Science and Technology, Department of Industrial Administration. This research was initiated by Professor Robert Platt who was responsible for the 1961 report, "Medical Staffing Structure in the Hospital Service: Report of the Joint Working Party".[78]

1960: RWR's important study, "The Hospital as an Organism: A Study in Communication and Morale" published.[79]

1960: Publication of Chris Argyris' *Understanding Organizational Behaviour*.

1960: Publication in the U.S. of Douglas McGregor's, *The Human Side of Enterprise*. Edgar H. Schein wrote that this book

gave to the academic and industrial community [in the U.S.] a set of values about people in organizations which were widely held but had not been clearly stated or examined. Ironically, Doug did not intend to state values. Instead, he intended to point out that the assumptions upon which traditional principles of management rested were out of step with what psychology has learned about human behavior. He meant his book to be a plea for self-examination on the part of managers, in the hope that they would examine their own assumptions and bring them into line with what is known and what they wish to accomplish.[80]

1961: Revans becomes President, European Association of Management Training Centres (a Brussels-based organization) for three terms. He was President from 1961/2, then 1962/3, and 1963/4.[81]

1961: Publication of *New Patterns of Management* by Rensis Likert, University of Michigan, a pioneer in what later was to be called Organization Development (OD).[82] In this work, he mentioned research done by Revans:

> Revans (1957) has demonstrated marked relationships between the size of an enterprise and such variables as absence, accidents, and strikes. He found that both the total size of the enterprise and the size of the work groups within the organization are related to the above variables. He has found that for coal mining, quarries, hospitals, and telephone exchanges, the larger the unit, the less favorable are the results so far as absence, sickness, accidents, and strikes are concerned. Two reports dealing with the adverse effects of increased size have been published by the Acton Society Trust (1953; 1957). Other material dealing with the relation of size to the functioning of the organization appears in *Large-Scale Organization.* (Milward, 1950)[83]

And in another part of the book:

> The larger the work group, the greater the difficulty in building it into a highly effective group. Seashore (1954) found that group cohesiveness, i.e., attraction of the members to the group, decreased steadily as work groups increased in size. This finding is supported also by other data. (Indik, 1961; Revans, 1957)[84]

1962: RWR's article "Hospital Attitudes and Communications" is published in *Sociological Review Monograph* (July).[85]

1962: RWR's article "The Hospital as a Human System" published in *Physics in Medicine and Biology.* This article was later republished in 1990 in *Behavioral Science* and the comments on the article at that time are of interest, as they emphasize RWR's belief in and use of systems thinking:

> As early as 1938 Professor Revans was concerned with a systems approach to health care. Perhaps his clearest presentation of his

ideas on this topic appears in the following article. For more than 50 years, he has made recommendations for improving health care in numerous countries, and although health delivery systems have become more complex in that half-century, his concepts seem to be as relevant today as they were when the article was first published. Particularly remarkable are his... relating of the concepts of physics to communication and information flow in a human system, including such ideas as noise and feedback loops. In addition, he recognizes the promise of digital computers, linear programming, and simulation for improving effectiveness of human organizations such as hospitals.[86]

1962: The demand for management educators is on the rise in Europe. The European Productivity Agency issues the "Fischer Report" suggesting that 500 "management teachers" be educated and trained by 1970.[87]

1962: The publication of D. N. Chorofas's book *Programming Systems for Electronic Computers*, dedicated to "Professor Revans" and with an insightful "Preface" by him on the future of computers and software and their significance. Revans' professorial responsibilities included teaching about computers and their use.[88]

1962–1968: RWR's articles popularizing some of his concepts and ideas are published in the left-of-center *New Society* magazine in the U.K. It is easy to see why Revans felt aligned with the objectives of the publication. From the editorial of the first issue, 4 October, 1962:

> It is in the belief that the human sciences must come into their own that *New Society* is now launched... we shall not ignore ideas or theories... but we aim, above all to link the study of society with practice: to tell the manager what the psychologist has to say, to make the town planner aware of what the social anthropologist is revealing... and – in each case, equally important – vice versa. The experience of the practitioner and the research of the academic are complementary, and our contributors will be drawn from both groups".[89]

The social sciences were clearly becoming more appreciated and respected at this time.

1963: Publication in the U.S. of B. Frank Brown's book, *The Non-Graded High School*. RWR states that Brown in the U.S. discussed "our learning equation [L(earning) = P(rogramed information) + Q(uestioning Inquiry)] almost at the very same time as I was into it."[90]

1964: Revans involved in a Ford Foundation-sponsored project in Nigeria: Revans' own account is a very good example of how he worked as a consultant-adviser.[91]

1964: Publication of RWR's book *Standards for Morale: Cause and Effect in Hospitals*.[92] From the 1964 Foreword: These studies of life in hospital occupied nearly twenty persons from time to time over the course of five years." (p. vii). And from the "Introduction: The Adjustment to Change" section:

> This essay describes the work and conclusions of a small group at the Manchester College of Science and Technology (none of whom was medically qualified); we spent about four years in a number of hospitals, mainly in the North of England, observing, discussing and analyzing a variety of human problems, beginning with the adjustment of the student nurse to her professional task. Our group was drawn from the Department of Industrial Administration; its members could claim to previous research in the field of administration and some had responsible experience in industrial management. (p. xi)

From the Acknowledgments section:

> [T]he thesis [of the research and the book is that] ... the stability of all institutions – not hospitals alone – that are based on authority, and that must work through situations of command and obedience, depends upon their capacity to learn. Control systems to keep informed those who are in charge are not enough; the stoker in the engine room no less than the captain on the bridge needs to understand what is going on. We must give more thought than we have in the past to the problems thrown up by change and emergency at all levels and this demands that many of those in authority shall have a new perception of their relations, both formal and informal, to their social need. (pp. ix–x)

The study and the book:

> showed that low morale, particularly among nursing staff, tended to be associated with communication problems ... [and] led Revans to suggest that the effectiveness of a hospital communication system was likely to exert a major influence on both staff stability and length of patient stay.[93]

1964–1965: Initiation of the Hospital Internal Communications Project (HIC Project)

As a result of RWR's previous work in hospitals (see *Standards for Morale*) and his "views on management and management education":

> Janet Craig [assistant director] of the King's Fund Hospital Centre [King Edward's Hospital Fund for London, and the Hospital Centre maintained by the Fund in the West End of London] ... [initiates] ... a series of collaborative discussions between Revans and a number of hospitals on how these ideas could be put into practice ... These meetings took place during late 1964 and early 1965, and from them a plan to carry out the H.I.C. Project was evolved. Ten [London] hospitals, comprising seven general hospitals, one teaching hospital, one paediatric hospital, and one mental hospital, agreed to participate.[94]

It is of interest to note that one researcher at the time described Revans as carrying out "action research" and Organization Development (OD), which was somewhat misleading and contributed to the confusion between action research and action learning, and identified Revans as another practitioner of OD and action research:

> This chapter provides a brief account of a four-year action-research [sic] project that can be described as an attempt at organizational development (or change) in hospitals. The Project was initiated by Professor R.W. Revans with the primary aim of trying to help small teams of senior administrators, doctors, and nurses from ten 'self-selected' hospitals in the London area to make better use of their own resources in identifying and tackling their working problems. After an initial period of training, the teams selected and carried out nearly forty projects in their own hospitals, assisted, when requested, by a small central team.[95]

The "Educational Assumptions" of the project, as described by Revans, are worth noting:

> The assumptions of the Project can be stated simply:
> 1. that most people are normally willing to work at whatever they are doing;
> 2. that, in this work, they welcome, and may even seek, opportunities for self-expression;

3. that one important aspect of self-expression is self-development, which demands learning;
4. that, since the learning process requires one to follow the effects of one's own performance, true self-expression must depend upon, among other things, a two-way communication process with others in the work situation.[96]

The HIC Project was supported by the Department of Health and Social Security and aided by the Department of Community Medicine at Guy's Hospital Medical School, where Revans also became a Research Fellow in 1965, perhaps after resigning from the University of Manchester in 1965.[97] The HIC Project was completed in December 1968 when Revans was based primarily in Brussels. He travelled to the U.K. very often and remained involved in the project.

1964: Publication of *The Managerial Grid* by Blake and Mouton.

1965: Publication of RWR's book *Science and the Manager*.[98]

Of the eight chapters in this book, five were reprinted from previous journal articles. The three new chapters were "The Sampling of Shop Floor Attitudes", ""Decisions, Communications and Morale", and "The Nature of Operational Research". Other articles were: "Science and the Manager", "A Study of Technical Knowledge", "The Pathology of Automation", "The Scope of Management Control", and "Industrial Relations and Industrial Training". We see many themes here that later emerged in greater depth in Revans' writing, among these the rate and extent of change outlined here in the chapter "Decisions, Communications and Morale". In the Preface, Revans outlined his plans for his next publications, indicating the direction of his work and thinking: "Of the matters dealt with in these papers, I hope in the near future to treat at greater length in forthcoming books on *sampling shop floor attitudes* and *decision making* [his emphasis]. The present volume is to be followed by a second volume of collected papers around the theme of management education". (See 1966.)[99]

1965–1974(5): Self-exile

First phase of the Belgian years (1965–1968)

In 1965, RWR resigns from the University of Manchester as he is not in agreement with the orientation of the new business school.[100] Apparently, Revans wanted to base the Manchester Business School on the principles and values of the Staff College that he proposed to the owners of the coal mines in 1945, in which those with experience in business and management would be most involved in the new institution and would engage with the business community in a more respectful way, unlike the traditional university models. When his concept was not accepted, he resigned, forfeiting his pension as well. The dynamic growth of business education during Revans' most active professional life began around this time. In 1970, about one eighth of all undergraduate students in the U.S. studied business but, by 1990, one quarter of all U.S. students and about one quarter of all postgraduates studied business. In the U.K., 1965 marked the formation of two business schools, the London Business School and Manchester Business School, the latter as part of a university. The number of MBA programs in the U.K. increased from 26 in 1985 to about 100 in 1994.[101]

1965: Revans becomes a Senior Research Fellow for three years at the European Association of Management Training Centres (EAMTC), based in Brussels. See 1959. According to Revans, "this was a loose federation of over forty institutions of university rank, in fourteen different countries of Western Europe. I had been President of this association and was familiar with its endeavours to make more realistic much of its work. My task [from 1965] was to visit its constituent members and to interest them in trying to develop a research culture specific to European management as such." It was a condition of membership that a center offered a management course to senior executives or engaged in research in the field of general management.[102] At the same time, he continues his association with health care in the U.K. by also becoming a Research Fellow at Guy's Hospital Medical School in London, where he will continue his research and change initiatives in this sector (see 1964).

1965–1975: RWR begins his association, as a Fellow, with the Fondation Industrie-Université, Brussels, Belgium (see 1956). Revans' main focus was the design and implementation of the Inter-University Programme for Advanced Management (started in 1968) and later "the Inter-University College for Doctoral Studies in Management" (1969).[103] Gaston Deurinck was the founder and director of both the EAMTC and the Fondation. It took Revans almost three years to implement the Inter-University Programme.[104]

1966: Publication of RWR's *The Theory of Practice in Management*.[105]

A follow-up companion volume to *Science and the Manager* (1965), it focuses almost exclusively on management education and the world of the manager. It includes the following eight articles: "Management Education and the University Tradition"; "The Design of Management

Courses"; "The Theory of Practice"; "The Nature of Managerial Judgement"; "The Elements of Organisation"; "The Manager's Job"; "Our Educational System and the Development of Qualified Personnel"; and "The Development of Research into Management and its Problems".[106] The topics and themes are self-explanatory with much on the nature and pace of change.

1967: As part of his work with the Brussels-based European Association of Management Training Centres, Revans' *Studies in Institutional Learning,* is published by the EAMTC.

1967: (June), Revans participates in a conference held in Barcelona at the IESE Business School to discuss the creation of a doctoral program at this School. Among those present was the Senior Associate Dean of the Harvard Business School, George F.F. Lombard, and pioneer in the field of organizational behavior. He was impressed by Revans' discussion of a proposed program for Belgian senior executives (started in 1968) and this initiated a report by Lombard to his colleagues that led to a lively discussion about the case study method and the relevance of Harvard's approach.[107]

1967: (November), RWR stimulates the organization of what he referred to as the "Milwaukee Consortium", involving six Wisconsin companies and the University of Wisconsin at the Milwaukee Speech Communication Center. One of the interesting approaches developed was what may be called today the "outside-in" interviews with non-participating companies and the development of action plans or programs to address their problems and dilemmas. Of interest as well is Revans' "hands off" approach, for he did not return to Milwaukee after the initial meeting and let the Milwaukee team implement their own approach.[108]

1967: Publication of Edward de Bono's *The Use of Lateral Thinking.*

1967–1968: Revans takes part in seminars run by Professor Réne Clemens, Institute of Sociology, University of Liège, Belgium, clarifying and developing new "action learning" concepts.[109]

1968: (December) RWR clarifies some of his theoretical concepts for what later would be component parts of "action learning", as developed in the first year of the Belgian Inter-University Advanced Management Program for which he was responsible in his role at the Fondation. He does so in a paper presented at a meeting in London where he first introduced the concepts of "Systems Alpha, Beta and Gamma". For more on these concepts, see Chapter 1 by Dilworth in this volume and the endnote for this entry.[110] Of significance is that a clarification of values, ethics and sense of purpose were seen as the very core of managerial behavior and effectiveness, the starting point for action and learning. We should also note Revans' comment that "the theory of the approach [action learning] was far from fully developed by 1970".[111]

1968: (December) end of the Revans-led Hospital Internal Communications (HIC) Project in London, started in 1964–1965 (see 1964–1965).

1968–1974: Second phase of the Belgian years and preparation for the return to the U.K.

1968: (March) The official launch of the Revans-designed and developed "First Inter-University Programme for Advanced Management" (prepared for over three years and completed in July 1969), involving five universities in Belgium and 21 of its largest firms.[112] For further details, see Chapter 5 in this volume and sources cited in the endnote.

1969: Formation of the Inter-University College for Doctoral Studies in Management (CIM) in Brussels with the help of the Fondation (see 1959) and the Government of Belgium. Revans is associated with this institution as well.[113]

1969: (June) Start of a project for "the mentally handicapped" entitled "Coordination of Services for the Mentally Handicapped" with Revans' participation, which also resulted in publications by Revans and colleagues on this project during and after its completion (21 September 1972).

This project was described by Nancy Foy in 1972 as follows:

His [Revans'] special favourite is the study he helped organize on social services for mentally handicapped children. In one set of conclusions it is shown, after intensive interviews carried out by doctors, nurses and social workers themselves, that while each one thinks he or she has a direct function relating to handicapped people, no one thinks he or she has a coordinating function – that was always "someone else's job". Yet the truth of the matter is, as Revans points out fervently, that every one of the people dealing with handicapped children can deeply affect the child's welfare by whether or how he coordinates with other services, agencies, and experts. This was another typical grass-roots Revans study, done on a slender budget by people in the field under the auspices of the Hospital Centre. The study noted such unfilled needs as genetic counseling – expert calculations to help parents of retarded children to decide whether to have more offspring, as well as their need for emotional support and the inability of the general practitioner to provide it. [114]

1969: Publication of Eric Trist's article "On Socio-Technical systems", in W. G. Bennis et al. *The Planning of Change*, emphasizing Tavistock Institute's close relationship with U.S. Organization Development thought leaders and practitioners.

1970: Second Belgian Inter-University Program for Advanced Management launched.

1970: Publication of RWR's article "The Managerial Alphabet", in *Approaches to the Study of Organizational Behaviour: Operational Research and the Behavioural Sciences*, edited by Gordon Heald.

About the Belgian experience and Revans' conceptual and theoretical underpinning of learning and managerial behaviors: Systems Alpha, Beta, and Gamma.[115]

1970: Publication of Paulo Freire's *Pedagogy for the Oppressed* in English.[116]

1970–1971: Egypt, Revans-associated project jointly sponsored by "The Development Centre of The Organisation for Economic Cooperation and Development (OECD), Paris, and The Central Training Organ of the United Arab Republic, Cairo and by Professor Saad Ashmawy, Al Azhar University, Cairo. Dr. R. W. Revans of the Foundation for Industry and the Universities, Brussels, acted as a technical adviser". This was an attempt to use some of the organizing details and conceptual frameworks developed during the Belgian project for Egypt. For further details, see Chapter 5.[117]

1971: Publication of Revans' *Developing Effective Managers: A New Approach to Business Education*.

This volume is a detailed description of the Belgian Inter-University Program for Advanced Management and includes Revans' theoretical assumptions as well.[118]

Dedicated to Hans Hellwig, the German economist and journalist, pioneer in German management education, and leading member of the European Association of Management Training Centres and the European Foundation for Management Development.[119] See Chapter 5 in this volume, for further details.

1971: Publication of *The Nile Project* report with Professor Saad Ashmawy, Al Azhar University, Cairo [and Dr. R. W. Revans] [November] "A Monograph upon which the Fondation Industrie-Université contribution to the 1972 ATM [Association of Teachers of Management] Conference was based."

The following excerpt from an article by Nancy Foy describes the nature of the project, which was an attempt to introduce to Egypt the learning concepts and practical approaches developed from the Belgian experience:

> In Cairo, the two-year-old Nile Project first involved 13 national companies, under government sponsorship, with some assistance from [the] OECD to bring Revans in. This year [1972], the project continues under Professor Saad Ashmawy, who studied urban transport systems with Revans in Manchester in the early 1960s.

She adds later in the article:

> [I]n 1971 [1969–1970] came the invitation to Egypt. "Rather than impose Western miracle cures, I simply tried to work out an Egyptian programme for the Egyptians", says Revans. Remembering that three of his former doctoral students from Manchester were in the country, he insisted that they become the nucleus of the Egyptian programme, which was scaled-down to half-time participation [compared to Belgium] (since none of the companies felt it could part with a key manager full-time for an entire year) and concentration on two major problems: incentives, and management training itself. Several of the Belgian 'graduates' also flew to Cairo to speak to the top managers of the Egyptian companies and to describe their own experiences as fellows. The Nile Project is now going into its second year, and discussions are being held, with OECD encouragement, between Egypt, Iraq and Syria regarding a further cooperative venture.[120]

1971: (3 June) Revans receives the "Chevalier, Order of Leopold, Belgium", in appreciation of Revans' contribution to Belgium in his role as Director of the Inter-University Program for Advanced Management.[121]

1971: (October) The "corporate" organization, European Association of Management Training Centres (EAMTC), joins the "educational" organization, the International University Contact for Management Education (ICU), to form the European Foundation for Management Development (EFMD) in Brussels.[122]

1971: Publication of *Changing Hospitals: A Report on the Hospital Internal Communications Project*, edited by George F. Wieland and Hilary Leigh. Introduction by R.W. Revans. In this introduction, Revans also discusses "organizational learning" and hospitals as "learning organizations": "If they are to be learning organizations, those who command them must learn too; they must be open to the questions and criticisms of their juniors and they must be willing to perceive that even the most humble members of their staff may have constructive ideas". He also extrapolated on what he termed "social learning" and "change agents" as a new social role.[123] The editors do not make a completely positive assessment of the HIC Project; a more positive assessment came a few years later by the same researcher in Wieland (1981), *Improving Health Care Management: Organization Development and Organization Change.*

1971: Revans was planning to have his ideas and experience disseminated in the U.K. in a consulting form. At the May 1971 conference of European Management Education held in London, a reporter commented on this conference and Revans' remarks there.

> He [Revans] added that although his type of [Belgian] programme had not been run in the U.K. as yet, one would be organised before long by a commercial company of management consultants. He would not name the company. I will. Business Intelligence Services plans to start introducing the programme to top managements in May, to close the application lists in November, and start the work in March 1972.

What is also of interest is Revans' comments on the Belgian experience and the questions asked of him, especially about the power of exchanging executives to look at other company problems:

> [Revans] used the story [of David and Goliath] to illustrate a central point of his prescription. This is educating by sending an experienced, highly intelligent manager from one type of business – who is linked into the knowledge resources of one or more management schools – to act as a consultant in an entirely different type of company. The first Belgian programme, which involved five universities and a score of companies working together, used this method with 20 consultant-students. A logistics expert from Esso, for example, went to identify, consider and actually tackle a basic strategic problem of the Bank of Belgium. The method worked, Reg Revans assured us. Not only did the 20 "students" learn a lot, each also had an educating effect on between five and 15 other people in the organisation where they went to work. "Ah," came an objection from the floor, "but what about the dangers of having your problems tackled

by someone who, however intelligent, is ignorant of the indigenous technicalities of your business?" It was then that David and Goliath was evoked. "These consultants [said Revans] are experienced people, and their vision is not obscured by technical knowledge...They are able to see beneath the technical surface. What is more, employees speak to them freely because they are not involved in the promotion race."[124]

1971: Geert Hofstede joins IMEDE (now IMD, the International Institute for Management Development) in Lausanne, Switzerland and starts his work on international employee values and cultures.[125]

1971: Publication of Saul Alinsky's final work, *Rules for Radicals: A Pragmatic Primer for Realistic Radicals*. (See 1940.) Alinsky had an influence on an entire generation of U.S. social activists in the 1960s, including Hillary Clinton and, later, Barack Obama. Many Organizational Development (OD) academics and practitioners were also influenced by Alinsky's philosophy and methods. Approaches to executive development and OD such as "leaders teaching leaders" and the telling of "stories" can be traced directly to Alinsky's writing, training, and activities as a community activist.[126] As far as we could ascertain, Alinsky did not know of Revans and vice versa.

1972: Publication of Gregory Bateson's *Steps to an Ecology of Mind*, "early precursor to learning systems theory. Formulates a theory of deutero-learning or 'learning how to learn,' which is very close to Ashby's earlier double-loop learning theory" from 1952. "While the individual learns, the organization learns *how* to learn."[127]

1972: Revans as Distinguished Visiting Scholar, Southern Methodist University, U.S. and launching the first action learning university-level course with C. Jackson Grayson, the Dean of the business school.[128] (See also 1979).

1972: Publication of RWR's edited book (but chief author), *Hospitals: Communication, Choice and Change: The Hospital Internal Communications Project Seen from Within*.[129]

1972: (Autumn) Revans' article "Action Learning – A Management Development Program" published in *Personnel Review*. This is the first time it seems that Revans uses the term "action learning" in published form.[130]

1972: (November) Nancy Foy's article is published, entitled "The Maverick Mind of Reg Revans". This is the first time in print that the term "action learning" is used by someone other than Revans, who did so a few months earlier in his article in *Personnel Review* (1972). The brief introductory description of the article by the editor(s) is as follows:

> The most iconoclastic of the new management teachers is unquestionably Reg Revans, a Briton who is based in Brussels. Revans' approach to education, called Action Learning, founds the training of managers firmly on reality and experience. Revans was a prophet too little honoured in his own country. Now Britain is taking up the practical philosophy described by Nancy Foy.

And, in Foy's words, she describes Revans and action learning as follows:

> Dr. Reginald Revans is an iconoclast. The icons which he most often casts out of the temple are sacred middle-men of education and management – the teachers and training centre managers. Revans calls his approach to education Action Learning. It could as easily be called direct learning, or experience-based learning, except that the latter has come to have connotations of sensitivity training. Revans' version is simply learning-by-doing. He believes that the student at any age or phase of his working life is more likely to learn from doing something himself than by reading or hearing someone else talk about it.[131]

Nancy Foy played a very important role in publicizing Revans' ideas in her publications, in both her articles and books (see Chapter 8 in this volume). Born in California and educated at Smith College, she was a freelance journalist and management consultant, contributing to such periodicals as *Management Today, New Scientist, The Economist, The Financial Times* and the *Harvard Business Review*. She later became Manager of Environment and Communication for Standard Telephones and Cables Limited, a British subsidiary of ITT, and a Fellow at the Oxford Center for Management Studies, in Oxford, U.K.

1973: Revans and a few colleagues form *Action Learning Projects International*, at some point in 1973. According to one of its first members, Ali Baquer:

> Until the early 1970s, RWR had been working out, testing and developing his theories of Action Learning from a number of platforms – the universities in Belgium, or the King's Fund or the Nuffield Foundations or projects in Sweden, India, Australia, Nigeria, Egypt

and many other countries. It was then felt by some that Action Learning should have a home, a professional base, a formal platform. Action Learning Projects (ALP) International was formed and the names of Reginald W. Revans (UK), David Sutton (UK), Ali Baquer (India), R. S. Ware (Australia), F. Musschoot (Belgium) and G. Morello (Italy) were printed on ALP's letterhead.

Apparently a few months later, most probably in late 1973 or early 1974, new members were added to ALP International and a new agreement was drawn up. Baquer's account continues:

Later on ALP had a metamorphosis and a group of ten professionals, on the basis of their collective experience of being involved in different operational exercises of Action Learning in diverse organizations, had set up the Action Learning Projects International with its headquarters in Southport, Lancashire (England) to give an institutional base to RWR's approach. ALP International's Directors included Janet Craig, Ali Baquer, David Williams, Anita Loring, Diana Cortazzi, David Sutton, Alan Lawlor, David Casey, Jean Lawrence and of course Reginald W. Revans. This assortment of talent displayed a wide spectrum of experience from the polite bedside manners of a nurse to hard-nosed management consultant. Each ALP director was committed to the Action Learning approach and each had a full range of expectations from this collective effort, depending on the action learning programmes that he or she had been through.

ALP International began in all earnestness by offering a positive and constructive service for organizational development and human resource growth through a range of techniques, extensible to any situation. ALP declared that those running any kind of organisation, shall be provided with opportunities to engage in "learning by doing" with those who provide and receive its services. In the initial phase, ALP had modest success. Sir Arnold Weinstock of GEC was impressed with an interview of RWR on BBC TV [November 1973] and invited him to use his approach to improve the effectiveness of managers in his company. ALP also got a project in North Derbyshire Hospitals for the Mentally Handicapped [1975]. But the discussions at the meetings of ALP Directors were almost always bogged down with financial problems, consultancy fee structure, expenses and the like. ALP succeeded in coming out with several publications [from 1973 on] to disseminate its philosophy and approach in the hope of getting work, so that expenses of running an office, an income for the Directors, who were unable to earn on the days they worked for ALP was available. By the time I returned to India in 1976, I do not recall if a satisfactory system for financial resources had been worked out, despite the support of RWR.[132]

1973: (November) Revans is interviewed on a BBC TV program along with a Belgian executive about the Inter-University Advanced Management Programme of Belgium. It was seen by Sir Arnold Weinstock, managing director of the U.K. enterprise, General Electric Company (no relation to General Electric, in the U.S.) and led to a major action learning intervention at this company (see 1974).[133]

1973: Revans' report (along with Ali Baquer) published as "But Surely That is Their Job"?: A study in practical cooperation through action learning. One of the first publications by ALP International.

> This describes how about 150 persons involved in the services for the mentally handicapped – general practitioners, mental welfare officers, members of voluntary organizations, health visitors, neighbours, teachers in special schools, among others – drawn from several different areas of England, from Tyneside to the South Coast, came together to identify their unseen problems; to design, test and apply their own survey instruments in order to identify more closely what these problems were and how to tackle them; to try out proposed solutions and to evaluate their results; and generally to make the services better by helping each other understand them better. The new self-perceptions achieved by such action-oriented and mutual support are eloquently described by the social workers themselves in their own report.[134]

1973: Publication of *Small Is Beautiful: Economics As If People Mattered* by E. F. Schumacher, Revans' colleague who worked with Revans on a task force when RWR was a consultant to the NCB, where Schumacher was Economic Advisor from 1950–1970. Revans also emphasized the commonality of his conceptual thinking and practice with that of Schumacher. Revans often mentioned his approach as being based on the notion of "small is dutiful".[135] Schumacher's book was very influential and coincided with the energy crisis of 1973 and emerging environmentalism.[136]

1973: Publication of Malcolm S. Knowles', *The Adult Learner*, considered one of the pioneering studies in this area.

1973: Publication of *Toward a Sociology Ecology* by Fred Emery and Eric Trist. "Since the 1950s these two British experts, building on Bertalanffy's work on open systems, had been propounding a practical dynamic systems view of organizational development. [They] stressed the socio-technical side of organizational design as opposed to scientific Taylorism."[137]

1973: The U.S. Army became one of the first institutions to support and foster Organizational Development but, since it did not like the term, it was called Organizational Effectiveness instead. In the early 1970s, the U.S. Army established an Organizational Effectiveness (OE) School at Ft. Ord in California, and the training of Organizational Effectiveness Staff Officers (OESOs) became an official Army activity in 1973. The Army ultimately had about 2,200 OESOs and they had an impact on the culture of the Army. The program, however, was disbanded in 1984 by General John Wickham who claimed that OE was "just good leadership" and now that "we have trained good leaders, we don't need specialists". The U.S. Navy, however, copied the program but most of the OESOs in the Army left for the private sector, an important development for the spread of OD in the U.S. Some businesses, like General Electric, claim to have modeled their development of "change agents" in their companies on the Army's experience.[138]

1974–2003: Revans – Back to the U.K: The explication, adoption, and evolution of action learning worldwide: Theory and practice

1974: RWR returns from Belgium to settle permanently again in the U.K. at the age of 67.[139] But he still keeps some affiliations with Belgium. For example, he is a Fellow with the Inter-University College for Doctoral Studies in Management Sciences.[140] He also takes on consulting assignments with "the International Labour Office, the Government of India, the Foundation for Industry and the Universities, Brussels, and the Organization of Economic Cooperation and Development [OECD]."[141] In the 1970s, Revans was also associated with several universities, among them the University of Leeds, as an 'External Professor" (Professor of Praxiology).[142]

1974: (October) Opening residential course of General Electric Company's (U.K.) first action learning program and the engagement of RWR as Adviser to the program, as a member of Action Learning Projects International (ALP) (a limited company for contractual reasons for the GEC program).[143]

It is interesting to note the following comment by Revans on how important the GEC work was to clarify details for him and on the practicalities of designing and implementing action learning:

> Until the GEC action learning programme was run in 1974, no particular attention had been given to detailed logistics; earlier experiments (collieries, 1952; hospitals, 1964; Inter-University Programme [for Advanced Management], 1968) had assumed homogeneous project design, with all participants working on comparable problems in comparable settings and on comparable terms. The variety of attacks suggested within GEC made it desirable to identify more clearly the relations between all parties involved, and to discriminate between familiar and unfamiliar problems in familiar and unfamiliar settings.[144]

1974: Publication of Chris Argyris' and Donald A. Schön's *Theory in Practice: Increasing Professional Effectiveness*. Explication of 'double-loop' learning' and distinction between espoused theory and theory-in-action and their application to organizations. Like Revans, Argyris was influenced by the theories of systems thinkers Wiener (1946) and Ashby (1952). Argyris was a student of Kurt Lewin, one of the pioneers of organizational development (OD). Several decades later, Peter Senge, author of the *Fifth Discipline* and a student of Argyris, also uses a systems approach to his writing on learning organizations.[145]

1974: Publication of *25 Action-Learning Schools* by the Association of Secondary School Principals (NASSP), USA. No direct link with Revans or his understanding of "action learning" is made. The term is used to denote schools that tie work to learning, in what would be described as "work-study" cooperative programs between schools, industry and government, and further, school curriculum that involves voluntary participation and engagement in community work. In the early 1970s, the NASSP held several conferences on "action-learning" and published the results.

1975: RWR's article "Helping Each Other to Help the Helpless" published, on the work with service providers for the mentally handicapped. "A Study of Coordination in the Services for the Mentally Handicapped, conducted largely by those who provide those Services" (p. 205). See also 1969, regarding the study (when it was started). Foy (1972) mentions that this project is the one she was most proud.

1975: Publication of *Illuminative Incident Analysis* by Diana Cortazzi and Susan Roote, with a very interesting Preface by Revans. The book's dedication is to Revans and reads:

> "For Professor Reg Revans
> thank-you is a small word
> so we decided on action instead.
> 'Why,' said the Dodo,
> 'the best way to explain it
> is to do it.'" (Lewis Carroll: *Alice in Wonderland*)

Mike Pedler comments that this book is "an imaginative approach to visualizing problems and action learning situations by drawing them – another product of the HIC Project."[146]

1975: RWR's note about the learning organization, or what he called the "learning system", made in response to a report issued by the Science Research Council and the Department of Industry, entitled *The Teaching Company*.[147]

1976: (January) Several action learning and "self-help" initiatives were under way in the U.K. From a letter to *The Times* (London) from Bob Garratt, a colleague of Revans', we learn:

> there are people actually taking action through various forms of self-help. More remarkable is that there are a growing number of groups springing up spontaneously to help such risk-takers. The mutual aid programmes developed are not just for industrial managers to develop their organizations and themselves by facing and tackling, live, their crucial organizational problems. They include a major trade union tackling an internal dilemma, and many civil servants learning how to solve their own organizational problems. Such action learning activities include GEC's Developing Senior Managers Programme, Manchester Business School's Joint Development Activities, the newly sponsored Institute of Works Management's Managerial Clinics, and Action Learning Projects' Consortium to name only a few.

Garratt worked with Revans on the GEC program.[148]

1976: Publication of Revans' book *Action Learning in Hospitals: Diagnosis and Therapy*.[149] He was the editor and "main author" from among several contributors, among them Janet Craig and Nelson Coghill. The Foreword is by Lord Platt of Grindleford. This is the first time *in book form* that Revans uses the term "action learning" (see 1972), though those working with him were still referring to the approach used as "action studies" and also "action learning", as, for example, Nelson F. Coghill (Chapter 15 in this book). In Chapter 14, Revans discusses "eight major action learning projects", or "experiments" as he calls them, that provide a chronological evolution of his practice "before and since the HIC Project". These were: "The Nigerian Project, The Wisconsin Project, The Belgian Consortia, The Nile Project, Coordinating services for the mentally handicapped, the General Electric Company [U.K.] programme, The India Project [The Bureau of Public Enterprise, Ministry of Finance], and the Panchayat Project [Government of Bihar in India]."

In the Preface to the book Revans makes it clear how action learning can be used to change the work environment and the life of workers:

> By providing the conditions in which persons can cooperate in the antecedent design and subsequent review of their own tasks, a few managements are opening to their organizations a new quest for efficiency and for morale: ... Most of our present confusion about worker consultation, worker participation and worker control can be traced to one simple failure: we do not sufficiently appreciate that what concerns the workman most, what absorbs the greatest share of his life, and what he knows more about than all others in the world, is the job at which he gains his living. Nothing is more a part of him than is the very job he does. This book is very much an illustration of how such self-involvement in one's own job may be secured ... Action learning offers one opportunity.

1976: (November), David Clutterbuck's perceptive article, "Whatever Happened to Action Learning? While the traditional massive projects continue, the future of the technique seems to lie in less ambitious undertakings". It describes Action Learning Projects' programs and approach and predicts that there will inevitably be an evolution in action learning's philosophy and practices, including shorter programs than in other countries in order to meet the needs of U.K. businesses.[150]

1976: Publication of David A. Kolb's *Learning Style Inventory: Technical Manual*. An expert in organizational psychology, he developed a strong research interest in learning methods and approaches in the 1970s, including the development of "Learning Styles", that was most clearly articulated in his 1984 book, *Experiential Learning: Experience as the Source of Learning and Development*.

1977: Publication of *More than Management Development: Action Learning at GEC*, edited by David Casey and David Pearce. A detailed description of the senior executive program involving GEC personnel, Revans and the Action Learning Projects International team. The program was launched in 1974. RWR has an article in this book entitled: "Action Learning: The Business of Learning about Business".[151]

1977: (April) "Action Learning Comes to Industry", article in the *Harvard Business Review* by Nancy Foy.

This appears to be the first time something is written about action learning primarily for a U.S. readership. This article is thoughtful, rich in detail and even suggests ways to initiate and implement "do-it-yourself" action learning programs in companies. Most of the examples of previous action learning experiences are from the GEC program but other examples of work done by Revans with other companies are also mentioned; and there is a brief biographical outline on Revans in the text. She also deals directly with some points of view that are critical of action learning; that is, that it is just another form of professional consulting, case studies, a task force, job rotation, and that action learning is just another way of describing group dynamics or T[raining]-groups. Her discussion of these issues is thoughtful and worth considering, as they continue to be brought up in one form or another. One also sees how the editors of the *Harvard Business Review* simplify the philosophical concepts behind action learning and reduce it to a method: " 'Action learning' is precisely what it sounds like – learning by experience, through solving a real company problem where there is a need for a solution ... [and creates in the process] an effective way to provide a pool of seasoned managers".[152]

1977: (January) Creation by Revans and some colleagues of an Action Learning Trust (ALT).

> *The Action Learning Trust* is a non-profit making, educational charity set up to promote the ideas of action learning; it has a substantial record of unpublished work upon the topic that can be made available to members. The offices of the Trust are at the headquarters of the Institution of Industrial Managers, 45 Cardiff Road, Luton, Bedfordshire, UK. The Trust hopes to work on its mission in cooperation with the International Consortium of Improving Productivity (a foundation of Houston, Texas); with Kepner-Tregoe Inc [a consultancy] (of Princeton, New Jersey); and with Utbildningshuset, the present publisher [the Swede, Bertil Bratt, who also owned Chartwell-Bratt], of Lund, Sweden. All have much to do but nothing is as powerful as an idea coming into its time.

The first chairman of the Trust was Mike Bett, personnel director of the General Electric Company.[153] The ALT published newsletters and pamphlets (sometimes from previously published materials) and also organized seminars for companies, as this announcement indicates:

> [The ALT advertised that it would be holding two one-day seminars] "for Industry" on "How to Start Your Own Action Learning Programme", organized by ALP [Action Learning Projects] International, London, 8 March, and 15 March, Birmingham. "Each seminar will be given by a team of four speakers involved in current programmes, from this list: David Casey, Bob Garratt, Alan Lawlor, Jean Lawrence, David Pearce, Reg Revans, David Sutton".[154]

It seems that the ALT was in existence up until 1982, the date of its last newsletter.[155]

1977: Possible formation of *The International Foundation for Action Learning* (*IFAL*) "an educational charity [and membership organization] [formed] by supporters of the work of Reg Revans". Whereas the Trust was to raise funds by undertaking action learning programs for companies, IFAL, it seems, was to be focused on undertaking action learning with charities or not-for-profit organizations, but this activity did not materialize according to a former IFAL head, Jean Lawrence. IFAL is still active today. It publishes a newsletter and organizes meetings not only in the U.K., but also in affiliated branches in the Netherlands, Sweden and the U.S.[156]

1977: (December) Formation of the Management in Lund (MiL) Institute (also sometimes referred to as the Management Institute in Lund) in Lund, Sweden, in order to "bring in more of the Scandinavian cultural roots into management and leadership". Towards the end of the 1980s, MiL, and its sister organization in the U.S., LIM, developed what they later called "Action Reflection Learning" independently of Revans, also trade marking this term for their consulting work. Revans nevertheless occasionally participated in MiL annual conferences as an invited guest, and due to his first wife's Swedish roots, he had a very good network there and familiarity with the language.[157] For more details on the organizational and intellectual origins of MiL and "Action Reflection Learning", as well as Revans' connection with Swedish supporters of his work and ideas, see the endnote to this paragraph prepared by one of the founders of MiL, and its president for 32 years, Lennart Rohlin.[158]

1978: (July) The publication of Revans' *The ABC of Action Learning: A Review of 25 Years of Experience*. A brief and succinct 38-page self-published exposition of action learning. This was the first edition of what seems to have been six editions. It appears that, in the same year, another edition was published by the Action Learning Trust.[159] The book is "dedicated to Janet Craig whose support made Action Learning possible in the country of its origin". It was with the HIC project (1964–1965) that Revans established his lifelong relationships with Nelson Coghill (MD and CEO), Dr. Margaret Ullyat, Professor John Butterfield (later Lord Butterfield and Vice-Chancellor of Cambridge University) and Janet Craig. She was a Nursing Sister, later Deputy Matron at St. Thomas's and Matron at Great Ormond Street, Director of Nurse Training and Development at the King Edward VII Fund, a "professional nurse", and for those who knew her, "a tower of strength to us all". She also catalogued Revans' archive.[160]

1978: Revans' action learning work in Australia.[161]

1978: Founding of Action Learning Associates by Alan Lawlor, George Percy, George Boulden and Reg Revans.[162]

1978: Report issued by the European Economic Community, *Management Education in the European Community* "provided sober testimony to Revans's contribution" as head of the European Association of Management Training Centres and for his work in Belgium.[163]

1978: Publication of *Organizational Learning: A Theory of Action Perspective* by Chris Argyris and Donald A. Schön. There is no reference to Revans, only to Eric Trist from Tavistock, and, it appears, no mention of Revans in all of Argyris' and Schön's books.[164]

1978: Action Learning Group, formed in the Faculty of Environmental Studies, York University, Toronto, Canada. There is no connection to Revans, his theories or practice. Eric Trist, one of the founders of the Tavistock Institute of Human Relations and a strong advocate and practitioner of "action research" in the U.K. was, as a new faculty member at York, one of the members of the Group. The use of the term "Action Learning" may have caused some confusion in some circles and was the start, it seems, of several such developments. (See 1985, on General Electric and Noel Tichy, and 1987 on Marvin Weisbord).[165]

1979: (April) "First international conference on action learning" held by the American Productivity Center, Houston, Texas with Revans in attendance.[166] He was a colleague and friend of C. Jackson Grayson, head of the Center, and former Dean of the Southern Methodist University's business school (see also 1972). Its creation in 1977 and Grayson's appointment were carried out by President Nixon. It was later renamed the American Productivity and Quality Center in 1988.

1980: Publication of Revans' *Action Learning: New Techniques for Management*

The book's dedication reads: "To Norah and Andrew for making endurable ten years of exile in quest of educational reforms": to his second wife Norah and their son.[167] The "infinite variety" of Revans' action learning programs and approaches are outlined in many sectors (health care, mining, business, public service, and education) and in many countries (Belgium, India, Australia, Egypt and the Middle East, the U.K. among others). The second part includes articles about his research and studies; the third section "social and educational issues" discusses his work among miners and teachers, and an article on "worker participation in action learning"; and finally, the last section, entitled "Logistics and Methods" deals with the practicalities of designing and implementing action learning, particularly in the business world. The subtitle was chosen by the publisher and not by Revans.[168]

1980: RWR makes mention of a "World Institute for Action Learning":

> At the time of writing [1979–1980], Professor Ashmawy is working with the Saudis on setting up in Cairo a Pan-Arab Programme for Managerial Self-Development, and proposals have also been put forward for a World Institute for Action Learning primarily to help the underdeveloped countries both marshal their own strengths more effectively, and reduce their dependence upon the not-seldom-bogus expertise of the foreign consultant.[169]

1980: Publication of an article often referred to by Revans entitled "Managing Our Way to Economic Decline" by Robert Hayes and William Abernathy in the *Harvard Business Review* in which American management education and practices are criticized. The editor's note states from its republication recently:

> This 1980 article, with its scathing and richly documented criticism of U.S. managers' focus on short-term financial gain at the expense of long-term competitiveness, sent shock waves through American business when it was first published. The inroads that European and Japanese companies have made into traditional U.S. industrial strongholds since then prove its prescience.

1981: Publication of *Management and Industrial Structure in Japan* by Professor Naoto Sasaki, Sophia University, in which he thanks Revans, and provides a glimpse into Revans' encouraging approach to other authentic researchers. Sasaki was a visiting fellow at the recently formed European Institute for Advanced Studies in Management (EIASM) in

Brussels and describes his first meeting with Revans:

> One morning, at the breakfast table in a humble hotel on Rue de
> la Concorde, an old gentleman talked to me, who turned out to be
> Dr. Reginald W. Revans of Fondation Industrie-Université. Dr. Revans
> soon discovered my poverty and kindly introduced me to Dr. Michael
> Z. Brooke in order to get his help to extend my "tour" to the U.K.
> Dr. Brooke was at the University of Manchester and was editing a
> series of international business publications. After a few months he
> asked me to write a book on Japanese management for his series and
> so this book was conceived.
>
> In the writing of it I have never forgotten what Dr. Revans told me
> when I was hesitating whether to return to Japan or not. He said,
> "Professor Sasaki, Japanese organizations have got so many good
> things which the Western organizations have not got. If you write
> a book on Japanese management, go back to your own country, see
> your organizations with your own eyes and touch them with your
> own hands.[170]

1981: Revans' *The ABC of Action Learning* (1978) appears in Swedish,
published by Bertil Bratt.[171] There will be three other editions, in 1983,
1986, and 1989.

1981: Publication of George F. Wieland's edited book, *Improving Health
Care Management: Organization Development and Organization Change.*
This contains a more positive assessment of the Hospital Internal
Communications Project than Wieland's previous assessment (in
Wieland and Leigh, 1971) and is worth citing here because of its descrip-
tion of Revans' practice, and the author's attempt to place Revans'
approach in an Organization Development (OD) framework:

> The HIC Project was most unusual in its provision of free choice
> in this form. [Free choice meaning offering both action and under-
> standing kinds of intervention and allowing the client, or client
> subsystems, to choose either]. Revans emphasized that only hospital
> staff knew their own problems and could solve them, and having said
> this he withdrew from active management of the project. Although
> he continued to play an inspirational role and motivational role, he
> refrained from pushing his theories, models, or ideas onto the hos-
> pital staff. Thus it was up to the hospitals and to individual hospital
> team members to decide what their problems were (psychological dif-
> ficulties or structural ones requiring managerial action), and it was

up to them to invite central team help. Some hospitals teams waited for months before inviting central team members (to the great dismay and intense frustration of the central team members). One team proceeded to work without any direct team help at all. (p. 458)

One might well ask if the HIC was organization development. As mentioned above (see also Wieland 1979), the HIC Project was, in general and on average, more shallow than the usual OD [Organization Development] effort. Many of the hospital team members did not want a deep intervention, and the physicians in particular were in a position of sufficient power to prevent such interventions whenever they were undesired.

But there is a more positive reason for choosing such a relatively shallow approach to OD: there is likely to be more "carry over" as Straus (1976) terms it. More individual change is carried over into organizational change. To understand this, one may array OD efforts along a continuum of individual to organizational focus, with T[raining]-groups ... at the individual end of the continuum. Process facilitation and team building, i.e. work on the interpersonal problems of organizationally related individuals, are in the middle of the continuum. HIC is further toward the organizational end of the continuum, since it deals with relations among the top staff members of the organization as well as with their more distant organizational responsibilities (interpersonal relations of near and distant subordinates, as well as structural and technological problems in distant corners of the organization.

By directly involving organizational concerns (following Revans' prescriptions for learning by doing or action learning) the HIC Project would seem to have dealt with the problem of carry over

...

But we have been speaking of the HIC Project *in general* as being relatively shallow. As we have seen, some interventions were quite deep. Team members were confronted with survey data, or with perceptions of training group members, that questioned their attitudes, styles of management and the like. With support from superiors, as well as peers and central team members, they made efforts to assimilate these data, and psychological change apparently ensued.

...

The HIC Project was in part an effort in organization development, but because it made provision for client choice (by avoiding high consultant power and also by providing a variety of change program alternatives), it was also an effort in traditional management consultancy aimed at managerial action. Normally the OD consultant is highly committed to his or her humanistic values and world view (an understanding view in which psychological and interpersonal problems are important) and is quite antipathetic toward an action-oriented approach. Because the HIC Project allowed both approaches to organizational improvement (and thereby caused conflict and confusion) it provided the potential for learning about the situations in which one or the other approach was more appropriate.[172]

1981: Revans' article on Jean Piaget's (1886–1980) theories about learning in childhood. Revans maintained that Piaget's work showed that "all learning is the product of action, seemed to answer in one sentence the objections of the management professors that action learning is without adequate 'theory' ".[173]

1981: Publication of R. Meredith Belbin's *Management Teams: Why They Succeed or Fail.*

1982: (15 February) Revans writes the "Clive Memorandum" with several colleagues from Foster Wheeler and the Action Learning Trust to explore the creation of a company "to market action learning...to top managers". It represents yet another initiative by Revans to create an organizational and consulting framework for his work on action learning around this time. We have already mentioned the first international conference on action learning in 1979, and proposals in 1980 for a "Pan-Arab Programme for Managerial Self-Development", as well as a "World Institute for Action Learning primarily to help the underdeveloped countries". We mention later the Institute for Action Learning formed in Sweden in 1982. Also in this year, it seems that some initiatives evolved or came to an end as, for example, the Action Learning Trust (formed in 1977). In 1983, Revans becomes President of the International Management Centre from Buckingham (IMCB), in the U.K. and he announces the formation of Revans Action Learning International Limited (RALI) and the Foundation for Action Learning (see 1983).[174] The "Clive Memorandum", after a meeting at the Clive Hotel in Manchester, was prepared on 12 February, 1982.[175]

1982: Publication of Revans' *The Origins and Growth of Action Learning.* This 800-page volume is a collection of Revans' writings, most of which were published before but in less accessible form. As the title indicates, this a retrospective look at action learning's origins and evolution and, as such, helps the reader understand the chronological development of his thinking and practice.[176]

1982: Creation of the Action Learning Society – "Föreningen Action Learning" – based in Lund, Sweden, formed by Lars O. Andersson and Lennart Rohlin of MiL, Revans' publisher Bertil Bratt, and Lennart Strandler, from the Swedish Employer's Federation.[177] The Society issued the following announcement about its foundation:

> The Action Learning Society was founded in Lund in 1982. According to the statutes the purpose of the association is [as follows]:
> The ALS [FAL] supports knowledge development about and application of Action Learning, meaning learning directly related to action. The main ideas behind Action Learning have been formulated in the works of Reginald W. Revans.
> The main purpose of the Society is to be a forum for the exchange of experiences between people working with Action Learning within different sectors of the society. The main activity is a conference organized on a yearly basis focusing on this purpose as well as activities connected to this conference.
> Apart from this, the association shall not engage in educational or consulting activities.[178]

The Society it seems, later became known as the Scandinavian Action Learning Society.[179]

1982: Publication of *The Manual of Learning Styles*, by Peter Honey and Alan Mumford. A reworking of Kolb's learning style into a language and context more in keeping with managerial language, behaviors and practices.[180]

1982: The creation of the International Management Centre from Buckingham (IMCB), in the U.K. Since it was to be based on action learning principles, Revans agreed to lend his name as President from 1983 to 1985, and then Emeritus President. In either role, he played no operational role in IMCB and his relationship with the private institution was apparently strained.[181]

1982: Publication of *In Search of Excellence: Lessons from America's best-run companies* by Thomas J. Peters and Robert H. Waterman, Jr.

1982–1983: Revans, along with his publisher, Bertil Bratt (Chartwell-Bratt), and "his long-term industrial supporters Foster Wheeler Power Products" form the Revans Action Learning International Limited – RALI". In the announcement of RALI's formation we read:

> The term 'action learning' has been used to cover a number of very different approaches to management development and problem

solving, many of which bear little resemblance to the original principles conceived by Revans, so the full benefits have not always been realised. To re-establish action learning in its most potent form, Reg Revans, his publishers, Chartwell-Bratt, and his long-term industrial supporters Foster Wheeler Power Products have made the decision to form a new company – Revans Action Learning International Limited – RALI.

The principle activity of RALI will be the planning, implementation and management of action learning programmes, but in addition to these commercial objectives, RALI is deeply concerned to establish the validity of action learning, not only as an approach to economic reinvigoration in a failing culture, but as a medium of social regeneration to help with the problems of the inner cities, of unemployment and of disengaged youth; it has application not only to the creation of industrial wealth, but also to the problems of our schools, our hospitals, and other social services. Thus RALI is willing to work with business schools, trade unions, local authorities, management consultants, professional associations, training boards, government departments, teachers' organizations, and so forth.

The last paragraph on this page is a note to explain the above text and it is of interest to note that "Foster Wheeler's Power Products were part of the first industrial consortium-type action learning programme in the U.K. and Foster Wheelers group chairman, Don Newbold, made possible by his generosity the publication of the first volume of Reg Revans' collected papers, for which he wrote the foreword.[182] The Consortium program involved "Foster-Wheeler Power Products, Cable and Wireless, Imperial Group, Ciba-Geigy and others, [and they] have kept together in the exchange of senior managers to work full time upon the problems of their counterparts."[183]

1983: Publication of another edition of Revans' *The ABC of Action Learning*. "Published for Revans Action Learning International Ltd., by Chartwell-Bratt (Publishing and Training) Ltd. Cover and artwork by the author."[184]

1983: Publication of *Action Learning in Practice*, edited by Mike Pedler. One of the best collections of practitioner experiences. Includes articles by those who worked with Revans.

1983: Announcement by Revans of the creation of "The Foundation for Action Learning", but it does not seem to have been active unless it was the progenitor of the International Foundation for Action Learning, still in existence to this day.[185]

1983: Publication of Donald A. Schön's, *The Reflective Practitioner: How Professionals Think in Action*. Discussion about "reflection-in-action", "reflection-on-action". No mention of Revans, although Eric Trist (Tavistock) mentioned briefly.

1984: RWR's *The Sequence of Managerial Achievement*, a compendium of previously published articles. Revans mentions that action learning programs had been organized in the following countries: Australia, Bahrain, Belgium, Britain, Egypt, Finland, India, Libya, Norway, Saudi, and Sweden.[186]

1984: Publication of David Kolb's *Experiential Learning: Experiences as The Source of Learning and Development*.

1985: Publication of RWR's *Confirming Cases*. Examples and descriptions of action learning programs and interventions especially in the business community.[187]

1985: Publication of *Leaders: The Strategies for Taking Charge* by Warren G. Bennis and Burt Nanus. Revans considered Bennis a supporter of his form of action learning and they corresponded.

1985: (September) Noel Tichy joins General Electric's Management Development Institute in Crotonville, New York for a two-year period (from the University of Michigan, where he was a professor in the Business School) as part of the staff involved in executive education. Tichy states that he introduced "action learning" to GE during this period. It should be noted that while his use of the term "action learning" was a dynamic expression that appealed to management, it was used out of the context that Revans had defined. Tichy later outlined his understanding of action learning as: "The process of developing employees on hard (e.g. marketing, financing) and soft (e.g., vision, leadership, values) skills by having them work with others on real organizational challenges and reflecting on their decision-making and experiences throughout." It is, however, significant to appreciate that his role at such an influential company and his use of the term "action learning" led to considerable confusion about what the term "action learning" actually meant. He also used phrases such as "compressed action learning" in his writing that further clouded the issue. His followers, such as Dotlich and Noel (1998) (the latter being a former GE colleague) have continued this approach with acknowledgement to Tichy's consulting work. In their context, therefore, action learning is another dimension of Organization Development.[188]

One U.S. academic, Nancy Dixon, has called this approach to action learning, the "modified or perhaps Americanized version of action learning". While a considerable "improvement over more traditional lecture-based programmes", she maintains that this form of action learning is really a more sophisticated version of a task force and lacks the depth that one sees in Revans' action learning approach. In particular, the "Americanized version" does not usually involve the *implementation* of team recommendations and, at the same time, does not maximize individual development and behavioral change – both important to Revans, she states. Other differences are that, in Revans' approach, participation is voluntary and not required, and action learning tends to be extended over a period of nine to twelve months, and not three weeks to three months in length as in the U.S. experiences. Dixon also asserts that "it is important to acknowledge that even in its Americanized form, team members *do* learn and teams *do* assist organizations in addressing difficult problems – it is just that they fall short of their potential. It is as if many US companies have grasped the outward form of Action Learning, that is, teams working on problems, without, however, attending to its essence."[189]

1985: The English-language publication of Norberto Odebrecht's *Survival, Growth, and Perpetuity.* One of Brazil's executive leaders, owner of its largest engineering and construction company, outlines his learning philosophy as "learning through work", societal engagement and sustainability. First Portuguese edition published in 1983.

1986: Revans made Professorial Fellow in Action Learning, University of Manchester.[190]

1986: (Approximately) Formation of the consulting group Leadership in International Management (LIM) in the USA with Lars Cederholm, Lennart Rohlin, Tony Pearson, Ernie Turner and Victoria Marsick and, somewhat later, "associates" included Judy O'Neil, Bob Kolodny, and Sue Lotz. Tony Pearson and Ernie Turner remained in LIM. Victoria Marsick, Judy O'Neil, and Karen Watkins went on to form Partners for the Learning Organization. All became, in one way or another, associated with Action Reflection Learning (ARL).[191] (See 1977.)

1987: Special issue of *Journal of Management Development,* in honor of Reg Revans on the occasion of his 80th birthday, edited by Alan Mumford.

1987: Retirement of Gaston Deurinck (head of the Fondation, Brussels); considered by Revans to be a "remarkable man".[192]

1987: Publication of *Making Managers* by Charles Handy, Colin Gordon, Ian Gow, and Collin Randlesome, adapted from their study in 1986 and then subsequent report, "The Making of Managers" in April 1987 commissioned by the National Economic Development Council, The

Manpower Service Commission and the British Institute of Management. There are several references to Revans' contributions in the book:

> Professor Reginald Revans, the architect of Action Learning has been the unseen, and too often unacknowledged, inspiration behind much of the best practice discovered in the study in Britain and elsewhere.

And ...

> There is more than one way to learn. All countries use traditional learning practices involving teaching and practice, formal study and formal examinations (Japan is perhaps more traditional than most). But each country recognizes that there are other forms of learning which are important, if not more so. America has exported its case studies, its business games and management exercises. Japan has elevated the mentor role into a formal requirement of every manager. In Japan, too, they recognize that watching and listening to others can open one's eyes to new possibilities; they therefore encourage subordinates to sit in on discussions among their superiors, they avidly study their competitors, both on paper and on site, they routinely expose their own ideas to everyone concerned before coming to any decision. Britain has contributed the concept of action-learning, originally formulated in Belgium by Professor Revans but since then widely imitated and adapted. It is based on the idea that managers learn best by finding real solutions to real problems in the company of friendly peers who use each other as a 'set' of consultants. Germany has cultivated the model of apprenticeship and France the science of rational analysis.[193]

1987: Marvin R. Weisbord in *Productive Workplaces: Organizing and Managing For Dignity, Meaning and Community*, a very influential book, states incorrectly that:

> Lewin intended his enhanced problem-solving model to preserve democratic values, build commitment to act, and motivate learning – all at once. Indeed, some people have renamed the process "action learning" to more accurately indicate its nature. (Revans, 1982)

This perhaps further confused the differences between the two very different approaches, between action research and action learning, and certainly misinterpreted Revans' orientation.[194]

1987: Publication of Donald A. Schön's, *Educating the Reflective Practitioner: Toward a New Design for Teaching and Learning in the Professions.* No mention of Revans, but there is reference to Trist and Tavistock.

1988: (February) Sir Douglas Hague, Chairman of the Economic and Social Research Council (ESRC) of the U.K. wrote: "'We are in a new industrial revolution which requires management trainers to develop 'action learning' from real experience with business and industry, rather than getting tied up with theory and academia'". Sir Douglas was at this time, and earlier, from 1967 to 1979, a member of the Price Commission, which controlled prices in the U.K., and also advisor to the Prime Minister's Policy Unit. In 1963, he was one of the founding professors of Manchester Business School so he was no doubt very familiar with Revans and his philosophy. Among other things, he was, in 1991, the author of *Beyond Universities*.[195]

1988: (July) First "global action learning" Business Management Course (BMC) at General Electric. GE's approach was widely adopted and adapted by other leading companies, as for example, Johnson & Johnson, and some Korean companies. The approach was very much in the mold of a "modified or Americanized version of Action Learning".[196] (See 1985, September.)

1988: Publication of Revans' *The Golden Jubilee of Action Learning: A collection of papers written during 1988* and published by the Manchester Action Learning Exchange (MALEx), University of Manchester, Manchester Business School, and prepared by Barry Caidan on the British Institute of Management (BIM) and Albert E. Barker from MALEx. On the occasion of the 50th anniversary of Revans' 1938 memorandum celebrated by the University of Manchester Business School and the British Institute of Management. Revans delivered the keynote address.[197]

1989: Lord Butterfield's speech in the House of Lords outlining the need for "genuine" action learning in the National Health Service.[198]

1989: *Sri Lanka Journal of Development Administration*, Special issue on Action Learning, edited by Eric J. de Silva.

1989: General Electric in the U.S. launches "Workout", considered by some to be a form of action learning.[199]

1990: Revans included in *Makers of Management: Men and Women Who Changed the Business World* by David Clutterbuck and Stuart Crainer. In the section on "The Behavioural Scientists", they describe him as "a prophet long unrecognized in his own country and now perhaps the bitterest of gurus". Elsewhere in the entry, Revans is described as "'an amazing and underestimated man'" by Igor Ansoff, one of the most influential "fathers" of modern strategic management.[200]

1990: Publication of Chris Argyris' *Overcoming Organizational Defenses: Facilitating Organizational Learning.*

1990: Publication of Peter Senge's *The Fifth Discipline: The Art and Practice of the Learning Organization.* No mention of Revans, or action learning, but some discussion about "action science" and Chris Argyris' influence on Senge. (See 1974).

1991: RWR publishes his article "Action Learning in the Third World", and is listed as Visiting Professorial Fellow, Institute for Development Policy and Management (IDPM), University of Manchester.

1991: The Action Learning Action Research and Process Management Association founded in 1991 following an inaugural Research Symposium in Brisbane in 1989 and a first World Congress, also in Brisbane, in 1990. The organization established itself as the world's earliest action research professional association. It was the first to mount World Congresses for this field, bringing together theorists and practitioners with novices, innovators and managers. Renamed ALARA in 2007, the association has held seven World Congresses in Australian and International settings, numerous Australian national conferences, and local workshops and seminars for members and their networks. Twenty-six volumes of the Association's Journal have been produced, and it has established a part-time professional administration, and an online presence at http://www.alara.net.au/

1991: Publication of Geert Hofstede's *Cultures and Organizations: Software of the Mind.*

1992: (25–27 November), Revans makes one of the keynote addresses at the Second International Congress of Educating Cities, in Gothenburg, Sweden, along with Farrington, Freire, and Sapp. Revans maintains that civil society in cities and other communities can best be addressed through action learning and the personal responsibility of citizens, not through policies designed by civil servants and experts.[201]

1992: Publication of Chris Argyris' *On Organizational Learning.*

1992: Publication of the article "Action Reflection Learning" which outlines a specific approach to action learning, written by Victoria Marsick, Lars Cederholm, Ernie Turner and Tony Pearson, and more rooted in the interventionist use of applied psychology and education theory, with little that is from Revans.[202] (See 1977, December.)

1993: Publication of Chris Argyris' *Knowledge for Action: A Guide to Overcoming Barriers to Organizational Change.*

1993: Publication of *Organizational Learning II: Theory, Method, and Practice* by Chris Argyris and Donald A. Schön.

1993: (7 May) Formation of the Academy of Human Resource Development (AHRD) at Georgia State University in the U.S. Revans was the keynote speaker and received an award for his services to the field at the first ever AHRD conference, 3–6 March, 1994 in San Antonio, Texas. The AHRD was a grouping of academics who wanted to deepen and propagate the professionalization of Human Resource Development (HRD) practice. At the time, there was considerable discontent in this field as it was felt that the HRD role in corporations and government were populated by too many untrained "Training Coordinators". The academics were at first organized in what was called the Professors' Network within the American Society for Training and Development (ASTD), but they became disenchanted with this organization and so many left it to form the AHRD. Robert L. Dilworth was the first editor of its newsletter, called the *AHRD Forum*, the first issue of which appeared on 1 November, 1993.[203]

1994: (7–11 February) Revans as Distinguished Scholar in Residence at Virginia Commonwealth University.

1994: (Autumn) RWRs' spiral-bound work: "Action Learning or Partnership in Adversity: The Economic Effects of National Spontaneity". This was prepared by Albert Barker for the First International Action Learning Mutual Collaboration Congress in 1995. Mostly about the Belgian experience (1965 onwards).[204]

1994: Formation of the Dutch Action Learning Society by Otmar Donnenberg and colleagues.[205] Although acquainted with Revans and in correspondence with him, this Society was also influenced by Organizational Development theory and practices.

1995: Revans' "Disclosing Doubts", an extended essay on "spontaneity economics" prepared for the Heathrow conference (see April, 1995).

1995: (17–25 April) The First International Action Learning Congress for Mutual Collaboration Congress at Heathrow with 80 participants from 18 nations. Revans actively participated.[206]

1995: (22 June) The Revans Centre (later renamed the Revans Institute, December 2000) for Action Learning and Research was dedicated at the University of Salford. Professor David Botham is appointed Director.

Revans already, by then, Professorial Fellow of the university. Official transfer of Revans' archive and books to the University Library. Apparently, as of June 2009, the Institute is in discussion to perhaps relocate itself and the collection to the University of Manchester.

1996: (Summer) International Action Learning Seminar at the Revans Centre for Action Learning and Research at the University of Salford involving action learning team members from Canada, Australia, the U.S, and the U.K. (total of 31 people in five teams). Organized by David Botham, Director of the Revans Centre and Robert "Lex" Dilworth from Virginia Commonwealth University, with Revans deeply involved over a two-week period on action learning involving some hospitals in the area. Among the other participants were Alan Mumford, Mike Pedler, Krystyna Weinstein, and Verna J. Willis.[207]

1996: Publication of the Brussels-based European Foundation for Management Development's, *Training the Fire Brigade: Preparing for the Unimaginable*. A short history of the EFMD published with a few references to Revans, especially the strict standards he adhered to and demanded from the European Association of Management Training Centres (EAMTC) members when he was President; the stimulating character of their meetings; and his influence on the Stockholm School of Economics. A collection of short articles on the past and the challenges ahead by prominent contributors. Among the most thoughtful is that by Per-Jonas Eliaeson, Professor at the Stockholm School of Economics about the need for cooperation not competition among and between business schools, as well as between faculty and participants. He writes:

> Too rarely do our faculty see themselves as learners and the participants as the experts; too rarely do they see their task as coaxing and coaching managers in learning to learn; too rarely does the learning process start months before the "programme" by going into the sending organisation, understanding the participants' (preferably more than one) unit's culture and problems, and end after the learning-doing-reflecting period spread over 18 months. We have developed quite successful approaches, stimulated by Reg Revans' ideas of getting chief executives to explain their unresolved issues which can then become foci of their own managers' learning in programmes.[208]

1996: (20–21 June) The first annual Global Forum on Executive Development and Business Driven Action Learning is held at the Theseus

Institute, Sophia Antipolis, France. The Global Forum is an annual "by-invitation-only" community of practice that brings together practitioners from multinational companies, public and civil sector organizations, academics and consultants – and all who use action learning in a variety of ways and in different industries and fields.[209]

1997: Publication of *Action Learning at Work*, edited by Alan Mumford.

Mumford was a Professor of Management Development at the International Management Centre from Buckingham (IMCB), in the U.K. from 1983–1992, and Visiting Professor after that.[210]

1997: First issue of *Link-up with Action Learning*, the newsletter of the Revans Centre for Action Learning and Research.

1998: Republication (in edited form) of RWR's *The ABC of Action Learning*.[211]

1998: Two special issues on action learning, *Performance Improvement Quarterly*, a journal of the International Society for Performance Improvement, edited by Robert L. Dilworth.

1998: Publication of *Action Learning: How the World's Top Companies Are Re-Creating Their Leaders and Themselves* by David Dotlich and Jim Noel.

The authors make no claim or connection to Reg Revans' work or theory, or previous contributions to action learning, except through the consulting work of Noel Tichy for Honeywell from the University of Michigan. Jim Noel was formerly at General Electric's Crotonville, and the description is mainly from this and a few other experiences in the U.S.[212]

1999: Publication of *Action Learning*, edited by Wojciech W. Gasparski and David Botham, which arose from the Heathrow conference (see 1995).

1999: Publication of what is perhaps the first book in German on action learning, edited by Otmar Donnerberg, *Action Learning: Ein Handbuch*, and publication of Michael J. Marquardt's *Action Learning in Action* in the U.S.

1999: (4 February) Lord Butterfield in the House of Lords comments on the contribution made to the National Health Service (NHS) by Revans:

> 90 [92] year-old Professor Reginald Revans of Manchester did the NHS a great service when he studied action learning in London hospitals. He really showed that if managers share their difficulties and

help each other in their diversities, hospital performance statistics improve.[213]

2000: Death of Gaston Deurinck (10 May, 1922 to 24 February, 2000).[214]

2000: Publication of *Business Driven Action Learning: Global Best Practices*, edited by Yury Boshyk. The term and approach of "business driven action learning" is introduced to emphasize a different focus and emphasis for action learning for the business community. This volume is written by practitioners from companies and organizations around the world that designed and implemented executive and management programs and who have a holistic, performance based, and "ecumenical" view of action learning. Most of the examples are more within the context of the "modified or Americanized version of action learning".

2002: Publication of *Action Learning Worldwide: Experiences of Leadership and Organizational Development*, edited by Yury Boshyk; one of the first volumes to include a variety of approaches to action learning in the public, private, and not-for-profit sectors covering North and South America, South Africa, Europe, China, Hong Kong, South Korea, and Japan.

2003: Publication of *Action Learning: Images and Pathways* by Robert L. Dilworth and Verna J. Willis with a preface by Revans authorizing this book as an authentic reflection of his views and approach to action learning. This was also Revans' last published contribution in his lifetime.

2003: (8 January) Death of Reginald Revans at the age of 95.[215]

2003: (23 October) African Regional Forum (Mbizo) on Business Driven Action Learning organized by Mike Stonier from the Gordon Institute of Business Science, University of Pretoria (based in the Johannesburg suburb of Sandton), in affiliation with the annual Global Forum on Executive Development and Business Driven Action Learning, an international community of practice. Two (2004, 2006) such regional gatherings have taken place in South Africa since then.

2004: (April) The launch of the journal *Action Learning: Research and Practice*, edited by Mike Pedler.

2005: Formation of the Korean Action Association (KALA) with Kyung Roh Yoon, DuPont Korea, as its first president. On 25 November, KALA held its first Action Learning Symposium in Seoul. (See www.kala.or.kr)

2007: The popularization of research done in the neurosciences and in neurobiology on "brain plasticity" showing that the adult brain generates new neurons. "Biologists had long believed that this talent for neurogenesis was reserved for young, developing minds and was lost with age". Learning "enhances the survival of new neurons in the adult brain", with major implications for adult learning and action learning.[216]

2008: (17–19 March) First International Action Learning Conference held at Henley Management College, U.K., organized by a group associated with the journal, *Action Learning: Research and Practice*. The theme of the conference was "Action Learning: Practices, Problems, and Prospects". This is to be a bi-annual event.

2008: (26 November) Dedication of the Revans Academy for Action Learning and Research at the University of Manchester.

2009: (6 March) First Nordic Regional Forum on Business Driven Action Learning held in Stockholm. This Regional Forum, like its Korean and Southern African counterparts, is associated with the annual Global Forum on Executive Development and Business Driven Action Learning, a community of practice.

2009: (6 June) Untimely passing of Robert L. (Lex) Dilworth (1936–2009), one of action learning's leading authorities and practitioners.

Notes

1. See Chapter 3 in this volume quoting Revans' obituary about his father; "Revans, Reginald W." in [Anonymous] 1987 (*Who's Who*, 1987), p. 1468; The most unusual interpretation on Revans' background is as a German Jew who migrated to the U.K., in O. Zuber-Skerritt, 2001, p. 14.
2. Albert E. Barker, 2009.
3. "Revans, John", [Anonymous] *Who's Who*, 1987, p. 1468. Among his publications was the book, *The Future of Healthcare Education*.
4. Kleiner, 1996, inside introductory but not numbered pages in something called "Timeline".
5. Barker, 2004, p. 17.
6. Albert E. Barker, 2009.
7. Kleiner, 1996, inside introductory but not numbered pages in something called "Timeline".
8. "Praktischer Sozialismus", 1920(4), 5–36, as cited in Weisbord, 1987, p. 387.
9. Comfort, 1968, p. 127.
10. Miles, 2003, p. 56.
11. Revans, 1972, p. 36; and *Who's Who*, 1987.
12. Barker, A. E., 2004, p. 20; Revans (1994a, video).
13. Barker, 2009; and Yury Boshyk and Robert L. Dilworth interview with Albert E. Barker, January or February, 2009.
14. *Who's Who*, 1987.

174   *Yury Boshyk, Albert E. Barker, and Robert L. Dilworth*

15. Revans, 1972, p. 36, mentions 1928, but he seems to be mistaken. See Commonwealth Fund, 1990, p. 313, and *Who's Who*, 1987.
16. Commonwealth Fund, 1990, p. 313; *Who's Who*, 1987; Revans, 1945, p. vii. During this time he kept a notebook, passed on to and now in the possession of Albert E. Barker: "R.W. Revans: His Book. Meditations upon nothing in particular in Canada and U.S.A. during the years 1930–1931–1932 in which he does not guarantee the truth nor the accuracy of any single statement". On the top of the page Revans has also written "University College, London; Emmanuel College, Cambridge; The University of Michigan".
17. *TimesOnline*, 2003, obituary on Revans.
18. Barker, 2009; *Who's Who*, 1987, gives her name as Annida Aquist which is a modernized version. Revans uses the more traditional spelling in his dedication in Revans, 1982, on the inside cover. Ann-Ida Margareta and Revans divorced in 1947 and had three daughters: Marina, Vendela, and Barbara.
19. Commonwealth Fund, 1990, p. 313; *Who's Who*, 1987.
20. Cathcart, 2004, p. 252.
21. Weisbord, 1987, pp. 70–105.
22. From the Revans Archive: "confirmation of earlier researches of Reg Revans, carried out in Cavendish from 1928 onwards and published in *Physical Review*, no: 44, 1933." Total acknowledgement of Revans pioneering work, in spirit quite unlike that of social science, management education, etc. [Revans' comment]. Revans Archive, RWR3/1/5 Ionic Sound Waves.

    The full title of the 1961 article is as follows: I. Alexeff and R.V. Neidigh, Oak Ridge National Laboratory, Oak Ridge, Tennessee, USA. "Observation of Ionic Sound Waves in Gaseous Discharge" in "Proceedings of the Int. Conf. on Ionization Phenomena in Gases", 1961, 5th, 2, PP 1141–1786, 6844.68, N.L.L.

    The Laboratory was operated by Union Carbide Corporation for the U.S. Atomic Energy Commission. The last paragraph reads:

    > In general, these observations agree well with those of Revans whenever the two sets of observations overlap. Many oscillations which have been found in plasmas may be due to standing ionic sound waves. Their analysis could be useful in determining the temperature of the electrons (p. 1529). (Revans' 1933 publication is cited.)

23. From the concluding paragraph of Revans' 1933 article:

    > It seems to be established that an ionized gas is capable of generating and transmitting oscillations of its constituent ions. In the highly ionized gases of the stars and their atmospheres, these oscillations may be of profound importance, especially in disturbed areas such as sunspots, granulations, and faculae.
    >
    > In conclusion, the author wishes to thank most heartily, Sir J.J. Thomson for his continued advice and help, and the Governing Body of Emmanuel College, Cambridge for a studentship which made the work possible. The experiments were completed at the University of Michigan while the author was a Fellow at the Commonwealth Fund. (p. 802)

    Professor Donald R. Sadoway, John F. Elliott Professor of Materials Chemistry, Department of Materials Science and Engineering, Massachusetts Institute of Technology, asked to comment on this article states:

    > What Revans was studying was gas discharge in mercury vapor under condition where the mercury atoms break up into electrons and ions.

This state of matter is known as a plasma, a term coined by the American scientist Irving Langmuir because to him the glow inside the tube reminded him of blood plasma. Revans found that both in a spherical bulb and in a long cylindrical tube the discharge became oscillatory at a certain combination of voltage and current. In other words, the plasma behaved like a violin string, i.e., standing waves of a fixed frequency plus overtones or harmonics of this fundamental frequency (whole number multiples of it). Revans measured the temperature of the plasma and found that when the system became oscillatory the temperature spiked. ... I wonder whether it is the case that J. J. Thomson had worked out the math and Revans was a skillful experimentalist who made the measurements that squared with the previously derived predictions. (Email to Yury Boshyk, 15 February, 2009)

24. Miles, 2003, p, 44.
25. Revans (1945), p. vii; *Who's Who*, 1987.
26. Revans, 1980, p. 70.
27. He is displeased with the way science was turning to the development of weapons of mass destruction. Barker, 2004, p. 22 comments on "interest displayed by government departments, particularly those concerned with military matters". The moral concern about "the use that may be made of their particle research became a disturbing factor at the Cavendish". A fellow student at the time, Ferdinand Terroux, who later became a professor of physics at McGill University in Montreal, also shared these misgivings. For more on the role of government and private sector funding of research, see Crowther, 1974.
28. From an unpublished typescript by Revans, entitled "SALFORD – or Sincere Action Learning Fellowships Orchestrate Rigorous Darwinism", Revans Archive. Copy provided by Donna Vick and Robert L. Dilworth.
29. Revans, 1982, p. vii and extracts, chapter 3, pp. 18–22.
30. Revans. 1972, p. 36; and *Who's Who*, 1987.
31. Barker, 2004, p. 22.
32. Revans, 1951, pp. 20–1.
33. Revans, 1951, pp. 18–19.
34. For more on the Ford corporation at this time, see Saul Gellerman, 1966, pp. 69–70, with an interesting excerpt from Richard Austin Smith, *Corporations in Crisis*, New York: Doubleday, 1964, p. 16.
35. Barker, 2004, p. 22.
36. Revans, 1982, chapter 4, "The Entry of Girls into the Nursing Profession", pp. 23–9.
37. Barker, 2009, and interview with A. E. Barker, February, 2009.
38. For more background, see Gilbert, 2008, p. 21.
39. "Before taking up the post of director of education and training at the Mining Association, Revans spent several weeks living as a miner in Durham and learning the importance of team working. Colliery managers could learn more from each other, he realized, than from management trainers who had never been down a mine" (from *The Times* obituary.) Also, Revans, 1994 (video) Virginia Commonwealth University discussion. For some context to the situation at this time, see Tiratsoo, 1998, p. 141.
40. Revans, 1945, p. vii; and Revans, 1972, Autumn, p. 36.

41. Revans, 1945, p. 111; and Revans, 1982, chapter 5, pp. 30–1; see also, Revans, 1982b, p. 64.
42. Revans: "first statement of the theme [action learning] in October [1945]" Revans, 1983, inside page, p. 2; and Revans, 1982, pp. 30–1.
43. Revans, 1988, p. 140. In another, more detailed reference, Revans, 1982b, p. 64, Revans wrote: "The Mining Association did not go ahead with this proposal, since the coal industry was soon thereafter nationalised, [January 1947] and it was some years before the National Coal Board did set up its own staff college and partly implemented the first recommendations."
44. NCB (Annual Report), House of Commons Debate, 28 February, 1957, 565 cc 1407–523 1407. Available at http://hansard.millbanksystems.com/commons/1957/feb/28/national-coal-board-annual-report
45. Revans, from a typed manuscript provided by Robert L. Dilworth and Donna Vick entitled: "Chapter I, Some Opening Evidence of Action Learning at Work around the World", undated but seems to be from 1985.
46. Kynaston, 2007, p. 189.
47. Trist and Murray, 1993, p. xi.
48. Cited in Burke, 1987, p. 54.
49. Kynaston, 2007, pp. 185–205, 185, 188.
50. Kynaston, 2007, pp. 203–4, citing an original source.
51. Margerison, 2003, pp. 2–3.
52. For more on the history of the National Training Laboratory see its Web site. Available at http://www.ntl.org/inner.aps?id=178&category=2
53. Published as *The Education of the Young Worker: Report of a Conference held at Oxford under the auspices of the University Department of Education*. Oxford University Press for King George's Jubilee Trust, 1949; see also Revans, 1982, p. 819.
54. Kensit, 1948. This was the NCB's training magazine. From the Revans Archive: RWR3/11/2. Revans' comment: "One of earliest references to action learning."
55. Revans never seems to have made a published comment on Lewin, his philosophy or practice.
56. Trist and Bamforth, 1951.
57. Revans, 1984, the article "Kindling the Touch Paper", pp. 73–4.
58. See Trist and Murray, 1993. For more on Trist, see his autobiography, available at http://www.moderntimesworkplace.com/archives/ericbio/ericbio.html

    And also good on Trist and "work life" improvements in various regions of the world, see the article by E. Mumford, 1999. This article by the following is also of interest when compared with Revans' approach:

    It is important to recognize that, unlike much of today's reorganization, the rationale behind the Tavistock approach was not to increase production but to reduce stress and provide a better work environment for the miners. The fact that production did go up once the new system was introduced was an unexpected benefit and surprise to the Tavistock Group. (p. 32)
59. The quote is from Foy, 1972, p. 163. On the increasing bureaucratization of society, Revans (1950, p. 10):

    The danger is that, as more and yet more organizations appear, all pledged to help the [worker] lead a fuller and happier life, he will be taken still more closely in hand by an increasing number of zealous officials, each surveying him with an ever-narrowing particularity. In describing him each will use his own particular departmental measure; each will see him a living expression of a particular departmental policy; each will deliver to him their own particular message of salvation, and hold before his eyes their own model of perfection. (p. 10)

Revans was also irritated with the lack of fact-based discussion:

perhaps the lesson that those who attended the Conference will longest remember is our extreme difficulty of seeing clearly what is in fact going on; we could not make up our minds on many issues simply because we did not accurately know the facts. In planning future conferences of this kind we shall endeavour to acquaint ourselves better beforehand with the statistics, though nearly all of us are uneasy about the implication that to get them might mean a good deal of further clerical work. (Revans, 1950, p. 12)

Perhaps this drove Revans to the next phase of deeper research into the circumstances of the coal industry, coal miners and managers and management that he undertook after resigning from the NCB in 1950. Albert E. Barker also tells us about the fact that Revans did not get along with the head of the NCB, Sir Geoffrey Vickers. (Interview with Yury Boshyk and Robert L. Dilworth, 14 February, 2009).

   Revans' 1945 recommendation for the creation of a Staff College was not acted upon while he was with the NCB and this must have been frustrating (Revans, 1988, pp. 140–1).

60. In *Who's Who*, 1987, the entry for Revans reads: "Research on management of coalmines, 1950–55".

61. Revans, 1966, pp. 1–2; for a description of Houldsworth and his practice, see Revans, 1980, pp. 109–18. Another version about Revans' 1950–1952 years is provided by Nancy Foy (1972, pp. 166, 168):

   The beginnings of Action Learning were demonstrated in Revans' own life. In 1950 he resigned from his head office job at the Coal Board, installed his family in a country cottage, and went to live and work in the pit with miners. "I became convinced we really knew nothing about mining accidents", he says – he made the change after three terrible disasters. After two years underground, doing grueling physical tasks, he was invited to come back and take charge of an NCB inquiry into mining accidents.

62. R. W. Revans mentioned as with an M.A., D.Ph., and Education Officer, the NCB. The symposium that looked at questions about the implementation of the 1944 Education Act in the U.K. and the modernizing changes that came to the educational systems of many countries after the war.

63. Revans, 1972, p. 36.

64. "Living systems" as opposed to "machine systems" are the two major models of systems thinking. The former can be traced in the ideas of Lovejoy, Ludwig von Bertalanffy, according to Miles, 2003, p. 45.

65. Although there is no name on the 44-page pamphlet, it is by Revans. See Revans, 1982, p. 819. There were two parts of this study, but the second (1957) is not by Revans. On the inside cover of the first pamphlet we read the following:

   The Acton Society Trust is a non-profit-making Trust set up for the purpose of promoting economic, political and social research, and for the publication of material in keeping with its aims. It has no connection with any political party and was founded by the Joseph Rowntree Social Service Trust.

Likert (1961, p. 38) states that two reports were published "dealing with the adverse effects of increased size"; this one, and one in 1957. The latter's details are as follows: "Size and Morale, Part II: A Further Study of Attendance at Work in Large and Small Units", London: The Acton Society Trust, 1957, 37 pages. In both cases, the author is listed as The Acton Society Trust and the title is "Size and Morale". However, in this latter report, on the inside cover is a note stating that: "The research on which this paper is based was principally carried out by B. W. Gussman, B.A., a former member of the Society's research staff". It is interesting to quote the exact words from this later work for they are both complimentary and critical of Revans' study (Part 1) in 1953:

In 1953 the Acton Society Trust published [Revans' study], under the title *Size and Morale*, the results of an enquiry into the statistically observable relationship between the size of a number of otherwise similar undertakings – in a coalfield, in a large industrial organisation, in a commercial group – and certain indices of morale among the workers employed in these undertakings. 'Size' was defined not, as an economist might define it, according to capital invested or to output, but according to the numbers of workers on the books. 'Morale,' a much more bibulous indice and quantitatively elusive notion, was measured by various indices of which the most important was the negative one of absenteeism

...

The results of the enquiry were...extremely suggestive. In the coalfield studied, not only was lost time found to increase with size, but it also established statistically that in similar geological conditions output per man-shift tended to be no higher – and was often in fact appreciably lower – in large pits than in small. There was an interesting tendency, too, for any general improvement in output to be more marked in the smaller pits... [Another Acton Society Trust report published in the same year, "The Worker's Point of View", "showed that a greater interest in matters associated with their place of work than those in larger pits. Wages did not appear to have any effect on morale...This last finding was not indeed new, but it was interesting to find it statistically confirmed".]

All this evidence, striking as it was, was entirely quantitative: and thus not very useful as a guide to policy...The fact that the size of the unit in which people work is related to their behaviour is not an explanation of the relationship. These earlier studies stopped short at statistical demonstration; they made no attempt to explain what they demonstrated in sociological terms... Here evidently, was a matter calling for closer study by different techniques; techniques which should aim to establish the underlying causes producing the inverse size-morale correlation. That this enquiry is urgently needed hardly required stressing, whether its assumed purpose is the material one of improving productivity and so raising the standard of living, or the social and ethical one, more particularly bound up with the Acton Society's aims, of achieving harmonious human relationships for their own sake. It is necessary because the big organisation is necessary [and now a reality for good reasons...]. (pp. 2–3)

That, however, is no reason for paying an unnecessarily high price, in terms of social disharmony and unhappiness, for the advantages of size; let alone for actually losing a large part of those advantages through the frictions, wastes and explosions generated by that social disharmony. *Size and Morale* showed, in unmistakable terms, that a price is paid; in so doing it gave, for the first time, firm and quantitative substance to an already widespread commonsense impression. But towards the next stage of enquiry – the enquiry in to the 'how' and 'why' of the size effect – it did no more than point the way. The next stage called for a different approach, the approach of the social scientist working less on statistical aggregates than on individual situations; for the supplementing, so to speak of the bird's eye survey by the worm's-eye view ... (p. 3)

This quote provides us with an understanding of Quaker values regarding the emphasis on harmonious societal relationships, the increasing influence of the social sciences, and perhaps explains Revans' later deeper study of sociology in Brussels, with Professor Clemens in the 1960s. Joseph Rowntree was a Quaker, philanthropist and choclatier. He contributed to many other causes, among them substantial funding for the Liberal Democratic Party. Also of interest, is that the Director of the Trust, T.E. Chester, became the first Professor of Social Administration at Manchester University in 1953, two years before Revans was recruited to his professorial position in Manchester in 1955. For further details and context about business education in Manchester at this time, see Wilson, 1992, p. 19.

66. "The Report upon a Study of Colliery Management Structure":
In February 1954, the Board commissioned Prof. R.W. Revans to undertake a survey of the management structure of a group of collieries. He was assisted by a team consisting of ... Mr. E. F. Schumacher (economic advisor)" and other names are mentioned. The project also had the support of the National Association of Colliery Managers. (Revans, 1982, pp. 48–9)
Schumacher (1911–1977) joined the Coal Board in 1950 as Economic Adviser.

67. "Revans' earlier notions about Action Learning now began maturing – starting around 1952. Between February 1954 and November 1956 Revans instigated at the Coal Board [sic] what he describes as the first-ever Action Learning Programme! He called it a 'Consortium of Pitmen!'" (Barker, 2004, p. 25); see also Revans, 1982, pp. 38–55, chapter 7, "A Consortium of Pitmen", where he also writes about "the involvement of managers, 1953–1956" (p. vii) – that is, the National Association of Colliery Managers; see also Botham, 1998, pp. 40–2, who describes this program in greater detail.

68. *Who's Who*, 1987; she passed away in 1994 (*TimesOnline*, 2003; Barker interview, 14 February, 2009).

69. It is interesting to note that the motto of the college was "Scientia et Labore" (Knowledge and Work). For more on the background to developments in Manchester, see: Wilson, 1992; Keeble, 1984, 1992; Wilson, 1996, p. 138–9. The formation of business schools and schools of management was a

worldwide trend at this time. See Engwall and Zamagni, 1998. On Revans'
work during this period, see Barker 2004, p. 26.

70. Summarizing the content by the editors (Galenson and Lipset, 1960), we
read: "The concept of morale, absenteeism, accidents, some figures for
British coal mines, strikes, depersonalization in large work units" (p. xviii).
In commenting on the readings in the section where RWR's article appears
"Factors Shaping Occupational Behaviour", the editors make the following
comment:

> A variety of factors, which are unrelated to the internal political structure
> of unions or the nature of their leadership, decisively shape the typical
> behavior of persons in diverse occupations; and these different behavior
> patterns have in turn decisive effects on patterns of trade union action,
> our main concern here. Mining unions, for example, tend to have a
> high strike record and to be extremely militant in almost every coun-
> try in the democratic world, regardless of whether they have demo-
> cratic or dictatorial government, or are led by Communist, Socialist, or
> Republican...leadership. Variations in the size of plant, "climates" cre-
> ated by different types of management, the ecological location of diverse
> industries, the degree of opportunity for labor mobility, the opportuni-
> ties for individual advancement, the status differences between manual
> and non-manual jobs, are some of the elements that are linked to vary-
> ing responses by workers to their occupations. The papers which follow
> discuss some of these points, and indicate their consequences for the
> formation of unions, their propensity to strike, and the morale of work-
> ers. (p. 293)

71. See, for example, Revans, 1956; 1982, pp. 62, 84, 139–140, 181: "God the
creator" and "all human beings are imperfect images of God, their Creator".
See also Lessem, 1982, pp. 9–11.

72. According to Bertrams, it was a "mixture of industrial business schools
and University training centers". Its goal and that of its Director, Gaston
Deurinck (1922–2000), was to promote "university-based management
education through intensive networks", and the Foundation's "central
policy" was to "speed up the legitimization process of management
studies into the university systems". Max Nokin was the President of
the FIU. He was also chairman of the Societé Générale, a holding company, leading a group of large companies especially in the banking and
energy sector. Nokin was also the brother-in-law of Gaston Deurinck.
This would prove to be of importance for Revans when he worked on
the Belgian Experiment in 1965. Deurinck also was also a tutor to the
King of Belgium. More detailed background information can be found in
Bertrams, 2001, and 2006.

73. Revans described Deurinck as a "most remarkable man" (Revans,
1980, 41).

74. Revans, 1966, pp. 1–2. For more information on Revans' activities at this
time at the College, see Revans, 1980, pp. 129–39.

75. Reg Revans to Robert L. Dilworth, 18 June, 1995; and interview with Albert
E. Barker, 14 February, 2009.

76. Founded by "the heads of several European institutions similar to the
five Belgian centers, it was agreed to launch the EAMTC, which was a

select group of institutions (IPSOA in Turin, IMEDE in Lausanne, CEI in Geneva,...[sic] with Deurinck at its lead". See Bertrams, 2001. In the words of one observer:

> Unlike the IUC (International University Contact for Management Education), the EAMTC deliberately practiced elitism: it was a select group-ing of institutions. Membership criteria was clearly laid down...EAMTC developed a broader spectrum of activities [than the IUC] ranging from inter-center twinnings, through staff training to working groups on management and examining the real operations of management training centres...It was a mixture of industrial business schools and University training centers. Merger talks [with the IUC] started around 1963 [when Revans was President of the EAMTC] and idled through the sixties...the marriage was consummated in October 1971 in Amsterdam and the IUC and EAMTC merged to become the European Foundation for Management Development (EFMD), also sponsored by a $150,000 dona-tion by the Ford Foundation. (European Foundation for Management Development, 1952, pp. 27–8)

77. Still an excellent source to this day.
78. Revans, 1964, pp. vii–ix. Research continued until 1964, according to Revans, 1982, p. 613. Sir Robert Platt was responsible for the 1961 report, "Medical Staffing Structure in the Hospital Service: Report of the Joint Working Party" (HMSO 1961). Sir Robert was the Chairman. On Platt, see: http://www.rcplondon.ac.uk/heritage/munksroll/munk_details.asp?ID=3584
79. In "The Proceedings of the 6th International Meeting of the Institute of Management Sciences", (7–11 September, 1959, Paris), vol. 2, pp. 17–24. This was part of Session 8 (Measurements in Management), with Revans as President of the session (Président de séance, and presenter, Prof. R.W. Revans, The Manchester College of Science and Technology) London: Pergamon Press, 1960. In volume 1 of the Proceedings, Revans is cited as arguing for the introduction of the scientific method in management research and thinking (p. 427).
80. Schein, 1967, p. xi.
81. Rowbottom and Greenwald, 1962, RWR is listed as "Professor of Industrial Administration, University of Manchester, [and] President, European Association of Management Training Centres". In 1963/64, RWR cited as President, European Association of Management Training Centres (Revans, 1964).
82. Rensis Likert (a professor at the University of Michigan) was very much influenced by Kurt Lewin. He was a strong advocate both in his research and published work on participative management; that is, management that involves all stakeholders, workers and managers. He believed that the task of management was to assure participation in all respects. Considered to be one of the founders of Organization Development. See Burke, 1987, pp. 28–31 and Weisbord, 1987, pp. 192–4.
83. Likert cites Revans (1957, 1959) in his text, relating to the size of an enter-prise or organization and a team p. 38 and p. 176 respectively.
84. S. E. Seashore, Group Cohesiveness in the Industrial Work Group. Ann Arbor: Institute for Social Research, 1954 (Institute directed by Likert); B. P. Indik's work was a doctoral dissertation, University of Michigan.

85. Cited in Revans, 1964, p. 133.
86. See the introduction in Revans, 1990.
87. European Foundation for Management Development, 1997, p. 35.
88. For example, in the Revans Archive there is a reference to his presentation on 2 July, 1965 at Fresno State College. RWR is described as an "Expert on Data Systems". See Revans Archive, RWR3/6/16/44.
89. Barker, 1972, pp. 11–21.
90. Revans letter to Robert L. Dilworth, 11 January, 1992.
91. Revans, 1974, pp. 133–5.
92. Revans has the titles on the front page as follows: "MIMinE [Chartered Mining Engineer, Institute of Mining Engineers]; Professor of Industrial Administration, University of Manchester; President, European Association of Management Training Centres". This work was republished Revans, 1976.
93. Leigh, in Wieland and Leigh, 1971, p. 25. There is a very positive summary of the research in Gellerman, 1966, pp. 69–73.
94. Leigh, in Wieland and Leigh, 1971, pp. 25–6; and Revans, 1971b, in that volume, pp. 14–15.
95. Leigh, in Wieland and Leigh, 1971, p. 31.
96. Revans, 1971b, p. 7.
97. Revans, 1980, p. 30, and *Who's Who*, 1987.
98. Listed in the book as Professor of Industrial Administration, The Manchester College of Science and Technology. Lessem, 1982, p. 9, writes that this was his first book, but this is not correct.
99. Revans, 1965, p. xi. For a review of the book, see Anderson, 1965.
100. Revans, 1982, pp. 226–7.
101. Jean Lawrence, a colleague of Revans', stated that Revans resigned because he was not made the Dean of the new business school (Yury Boshyk interview with Jean Lawrence, February, 2009). For Revans' views on events and issues leading up to the formation of the Manchester Business School, see Revans, 1966, pp. 1–7. For the larger context of trends in management and management education, see Stiefel and Papalofzos, 1974, p. 162. On the growth of business education, see Amdam, 1996, p. 2.
102. Revans, 1982, pp. 226–7. Described as Senior Research Fellow, first with the EAMTC and then later with the Belgian Fondation-Industrie-Université, in Revans, 1972, p. 36.
103. Revans, 1982, pp. 360, 496. See also Bertrams, 2001, for this period.
104. Reg Revans spent three years helping to prepare the top management of Belgium for this critical experiment in action learning. He was the principal of the staff called upon to organize it, that is, to contrive the conditions in which very senior managers would learn with and from each other while tackling real problems alike in real settings in real time. (Revans, 1983, p. 2)
105. Listed in the book as Professor of Industrial Administration, Research Fellow European Association of Management Training Centres and billed as a "companion volume" to Revans, 1965.
106. Some of the articles were republished from journals (two, from 1962 and 1964) and others were addresses he made at conferences or meetings (four, from the period between 1962 and 1965.

107. Revans, 1982, pp. 230–4; and Revans, 1984, p. 19. Accessed 11 November, 2009, on Lombard, see http://www.hbs.edu/news/releases/062504_lombard.html
    See also the Lombard Papers finding aid at Harvard Business School that houses his correspondence with Revans and his publications, accessed 11 November, 2009, available at http://oasis.lib.harvard.edu/oasis/deliver/deepLink?_collection=oasis&uniqueId=bak00036

108. Revans, 1982, pp. 233–324; Revans, 1974; see Levy (2000) on the details regarding the role of the "outside-in" role of country coordinators or outside-in interview/dialogue experiences.

109. Revans, 1982, p. 566.

110. This paper by Revans was later published as "The Management Alphabet" in Heald, 1970 and republished in Revans, 1982, chapter 30, pp. 329–48, with an explanatory note. Several years later, in 1990, he mentioned that " 'The feeble and ill-informed concepts that I had struggled to distil from what went on in the mines and hospitals were replaced by the clear and decisive enunciation of Belgian scientists, engineers and bankers". See Clutterbuck and Crainer, 1990, p. 126.

    In Revans' words: System Alpha:

    > the design of a management decision, or of that set of potential decisions generally called a strategy, demands information about three critical elements: the **value system of the managers; the external system that they exploit; and the internal system by which they exploit it**. The structured interplay of these three sets of information is the design process of a management decision; it is here called System Alpha.

    There are several questions associated with this phase (see Revans, 1982, pp. 332–3);

    System Beta: or the "cycle of negotiation", has five management tasks associated with it:

    1. A **survey stage** in which data upon all three design elements of System Alpha are identified;
    2. A **trial decision stage**, in which a first design, using System Alpha, is selected from among a number of alternative designs;
    3. An **action stage**, in which the trial design is implemented, either in whole or in part, either in reality or in some simulated form;
    4. An **inspection or audit stage**, in which the observed outcome of the action stage is compared with the outcome expected when the when the first design was selected; and
    5. A **control stage**, in which appropriate action is taken on the conclusions drawn from the inspection (such conclusions will be to confirm, modify or reject the first design, or to repeat the cycle of negotiation in the light of experience gained from its first application) (Revans, 1982, p. 334);

    The following paragraphs suggest that the definitions of Systems Alpha and Beta are secured through the posing of questions.

    > The ability to pose questions seems to be determined by the use made of the answers to them, and those that have not acquired the capacity to listen to what is said to them cannot learn to pose questions. (Revans, 1982, pp. 338–45)

    good questions follow;

System Gamma: (Revans 1982, pp. 345–8) but a more succinct explanation is in Revans, 1971, p. 146: "The symbiosis of a person changing a
situation (action) and of a person being changed by this action (learning)
embraces both system alpha and system beta, and is here called system
gamma."
111. Revans, 1982, p. 349.
112. Revans, 1971, p. 27; and Revans, 1982, p. 496.
113. Bertrams, 2001.
114. Revans and Baquer, 1972; the project was completed on 21 September,
1972, with a press conference about the report and the research method
and results. It is worth noting that the approach was referred to as "participative research" and "action research" by the journalist. The words "action
learning" were not mentioned at all in this report by Revans (Foy, 1972,
p. 166). See also Revans, 1975: "Acknowledgements. The field researches
on which this essay is based were conducted between 1969 and 1972 in
collaboration with Ali Baquer, Janet Craig and Diana Cortazzi, to name
only a few of those, who, with the support of the King Edward's Hospital
Fund for London, managed to interest a large number of social workers in
taking a new look at themselves" (Part II, p. 211). See also Revans, 1976,
pp. 150–1.
115. This seems to be the first time Revans' Systems Alpha, Beta and Gamma are
mentioned (not as mentioned in Lessem, 1982 in Revans, 1971).
116. Revans was a fellow guest speaker along with Freire in Gothenburg Sweden
in 1992. See Gothenburg City (1992).
117. Ashmawy 1972; Ashmawy and Revans 1972; also Revans' comments on
Ashmawy and Egypt project: Revans, 1980, and, 1982.
118. Revans commented on the background to this publication and subsequent
developments in a letter to Robert L. Dilworth, 4 September, 1995:

In 1971 a New York publisher, Praeger, brought out a book of mine,
Developing Effective Managers, which I wrote under pressure from
both Harvard and MIT Business Schools. In 1965 the Belgian banks
and industries started action learning, and Belgium was so effective an
international trading economy that many US Corporations asked the
participating managers themselves to visit their own headquarters and
tell their own managers just what it was they were doing. When some of
the US Business Schools heard about [this]...they too sent out the same
kind of invitation, but sometimes to ridicule the very suggestion that it is
from other managers that genuinely responsible organizers may understand more fully their own personal duties. Massachusetts Institute
of Technology was 100% supportively convinced Belgium was right;
Harvard had one or two doubters, although George Lombard, its Dean
was (and still is fully) convinced; Philadelphia [Wharton Business School]
was actively hostile, for its Dean had just before been given some international award for commercially supporting traditional rigmarole. But
MIT and George Lombard convinced the Belgians that they should make
their mission known, so that I was nominated as their scribe.
   Developing Effective Managers came out in February, 1971...shortly
after [the book had appeared] I had a phone call from Jack Grayson, then
Dean of Southern Methodist Business School in Dallas, Texas; he said he
had read as far as page 40 and was so impressed, that he could be in

Brussels next morning if I agreed to introduce him to the real Belgian managers at once; Ross Perot imposed the urgency because he was convinced traditional management education was dangerous and, as the richest man in the United States, had challenged all directors of business schools – to send him fresh suggestions, that he would subsidize, for running better programmes. So, Jack Grayson immediately came, was deeply impressed with the outlook of the Belgian top managements, and asked me to return to Texas as soon as possible.

119. Hellwig and Bertsch, 1997, p. 176. Hans Hellwig, Dr. rer. pol. (Ph.D. in Law), born 10 February, 1913; 1932–1937: Studies LLM; 1937– 1943: Editor of the *Frankfurter Zeitung* (newspaper); 1937– 1949: Soldier and POW; 1950–1964: Editor *Deutsche Zeitung and Wirtschaftszeitung* (economics); in 1959 promotion to Chief editor; 1965–1982: Managing Director, Society for Management Development and Manager Baden Badener Business Dialogs; 1974–1982: Member of Board, Wuppertaler Kreis (Leadership Society) and from 1976–1981: Society of Business History; 1967–1983: Professor at the Technical University in Aachen. It seems that Hellwig was also a board member of the EAMTC and EFMD and would have known Revans in that capacity (Liliana Petrella email to Yury Boshyk, 14 May, 2009). The business dialogues still continue to this day and constitute a very influential network in Germany.

According to Otmar Donnenburg, Hans Hellwig was connected with the Deutsches Institut zur Förderung des industriellen Nachwuches and participated in the work of the Wuppertaler Kreis (an association of institutes for the development of industrial leaders in Germany) and in the Baden-Badener Unternemergespräche zur Förderung des industriellen Führungsnachwuchses (an association for the promotion of industrial leaders). The Wuppertaler Kreis brought about a substantial change in the methods of management training (participative learning instead of pure classroom teaching), in the post-war period. For more on Hellwig, see the web site of the Wuppertaler Kreis: http://www.wkr-ev.de/ (accessed May, 2009. Email to Yury Boshyk, May 15, 2009.

120. Foy, 1972, pp. 79, 81; Clutterbuck, 1974.

121. *Who's Who*, 1987; see also, accessed 11 November, 2009, http://en.wikipedia.org/wiki/Order_of_Leopold_%28Belgium%29

122. For a detailed description about the formation of the European Foundation for Management Development (EFMD), see Bertram, 2001, who states it was in 1971, whereas the EFMS's Web site gives the date as 1972.

123. Revans listed as Research Fellow, European Association of Management Training Centres, Brussels; and Guy's Hospital Medical School, London. *New Society*, 30 March, 1972, also reported on the seeming lack of success of the HIC Project. See Revans, 1988, p. 143.

124. Dixon 1971, p. D15. During this time Revans was a keen traveler, laying the foundations for action learning programs throughout the world:

In 1971 Action Learning circumvented the globe; in the summer of that year I visited New York (to discuss the publication of Developing Effective Managers, where it had appeared), Dallas (where Southern Methodist University was initiating a programme), Sydney (to lay the foundations of future programmes), Singapore (where discussions about starting a programme continue), Delhi (now the headquarters of a programme run by the Government of India) and Cairo (to follow up the Nile Project). (Revans, 1997, p. 3)

125. Clutterbuck and Crainer, 1990, p. 246.
126. Use the quote from Control Your Destiny and methods like Leaders teaching leaders…Tichy and Sherman. Alinsky, 1972 pp. 63–97; and accessed 11 November, 2009, http://en.wikipedia.org/wiki/Saul_Alinsky.
127. Miles, 2003, p. 46.
128. *Who's Who*, 1987; see Foy (1972), for excellent description excerpt on Revans' experience.
129. Foreword by W.J.H. Butterfield, Guy's Hospital Medical School (October 1970). Pioneer of research and treatment of diabetes. After 1975, Lord Butterfield of Stechford became Master of Downing College and Vice-Chancellor of Cambridge University. Revans' book was in press when Wieland and Leigh's volume was published.
130. Botham 1998, p. 61, in References also cites the following unpublished source by Revans from 1970, which mentions the term "action learning": "Action Learning Itself as a Theme for Doctoral Dissertations"; see also Coghill (1983) bibliography, but note that it was "published" by Action Learning Trust and Revans used Action Learning as a term retroactively, especially in the cataloguing of his publications and documents. We should therefore proceed with caution on these pre-1972 references to "action learning". We should also bear in mind Revans' comment that "the theory of the approach [action learning] was far from fully developed by 1970" (Revans, 1982, p. 349).
131. Foy, 1972, p. 79; also excerpts in Revans, 1988, pp. 143–4.
132. Ali Baquer's memoir of Revans in *Link-up 2* [2]. 2002–2003. Manchester, Revans Institute for Action Learning and Research, Salford University. Much of this issue is about Revans as he passed away in January of 2003. See also, from the Revans archive, *Memorandum and articles of association of Action Learning Projects International Ltd*. Manchester: Hutton, Hartley & Co. Ltd, [c.1974] (Revans Archive RWR4. 07/11/02).
133. On GEC, see accessed 11 November, 2009, http://en.wikipedia.org/wiki/General_Electric_Company_plc
   The General Electric Company or GEC was a major UK company involved in consumer and defence electronics, communications and engineering. … It was renamed Marconi Corporation plc in 1999 after its defence arm was sold to British Aerospace. In 2005 Ericsson purchased the bulk of Marconi and the remaining businesses were renamed telent [sic].
   On Weinstock, see Brummer and Cowe, 1998.
134. Baquer and Revans, 1973; also Revans, 1976, p. 175.
135. Revans, 1980, pp. 103–26.
136. Revans, 1982, pp. 48–9.
137. Miles, 2003, p. 46.
138. Correspondence between U.S. Brigadier General John Johns who was in charge of Ft. Ord and the training until 1978, and Robert L. Dilworth, 27 April, 2009, forwarded to Yury Boshyk, 27 April, 2009. In Tichy and DeRose, 2003, p. 158, the details on the Army are not correct.
139. Revans, 1981, p. 518.
140. In December, 1974, Revans submitted his article, Revans, 1975. He is described as part of the "Interuniversity College for Doctoral Studies in Management Sciences, Eendrachtstraat 51, 1050 Brussels (Belgium)".

141. Description on the dust cover of Revans, 1976.
142. *Who's Who*, 1987; Revans as a Visiting Professor of Praxiology, University of Leeds, according to Casey and Pierce, 1977, p. 3.
143. Casey and Pearce, 1977, p. 145. "Action Learning Projects International, Ltd., A non-profit organization spreading action learning ideas in the UK and overseas. 97 Roe Lane, Southport, Merseyside PR9 7PD, England". Among those involved outside GEC were: "Directors of ALP: Professor Reg Revans: Adviser to the whole programme; David Casey: Coordinator and ALP project adviser; Jean Lawrence: ALP project adviser. ALP Resources: Professor Tony Eccles: ALP project adviser; Bob Garratt: ALP project adviser". Another group of non-GEC people involved were from the Dunchurch Industrial Staff College (DISC): "Ray Godsall: Director; John Teire: Coordinator". DISC was "a commercially run management training centre owned by GEC" (Casey and Pearce, 1977, p. 16). On ALP see Jean Lawrence's article in Casey and Pearce, 1977.

    The "key dates were as follows: November 1973: First meeting between Professor Revans and Sir Arnold Weinstock; May 1974: Participants and projects named; October 1974: Opening residential course at DISC; November 1974 to January 1975: Diagnosis of projects. Sets met regularly; February 1975: Mid-programme residential course at DISC; March 1975 to May 1975: Implementation of projects. Regular set meetings resumed" (Casey and Pearce, 1977, pp. 9–11).
144. Revans, 1982, p. 613, chapter 44. Also note the use of "set advisers" from both GEC and ALP, and described in Casey and Pearce, 1977. According to Pearce (interview with Yury Boshyk, 2009), Revans himself was an active set adviser. In the Revans archive there about eight publications by the ALP ranging in size from 3 pages to 40, and from 1973 to 1980 (RWR3, in the archive).
145. Argyris, it is claimed, also comes from this 'machine systems' thinking tradition developed at MIT with the work of Jay Forrester (*Industrial Dynamics* published in 1961) which are "closed systems". The "organic view of organizations", tracing its roots to Aristotle and Goethe, was represented later by Capra (1996) and Wheatley (1992) according to Miles, 2003, p. 46.
146. Revans, 1998, p. 142. Today, this approach is referred to as "graphic capture" and is used widely in management education and executive development programs. See, for example, the Dow Chemical experience, Guillon, Kasprzyk, and Sorge (2000), pp. 14–28.
147. Revans, 1982, pp. 606–12.
148. Letter to *The Times*, 9 January, 1976 from R. Garratt.
149. On the cover Revans is described as: "Professor R.W. Revans was formerly research fellow, Emmanuel College, Cambridge, Guy's Hospital Medical School, London, and the European Association of Management Training Centres, Brussels. He has been Professor of Industrial Administration, University of Manchester, and Visiting Professor, Southern Methodist University, USA. He is now a consultant with organizations which include the International Labour Office, the Government of India, the Foundation for Industry and the Universities, Brussels, and the Organization of Economic Cooperation and Development [OECD]."
150. Clutterbuck, 1976. pp. 47–9.
151. Casey and Pearce, 1977, pp. 3–6.
152. Revans, 1982 – in the bibliography, the date of this article is mistakenly given as 1972.

153. Revans, 1982, p. 819. *Who's Who*, 1987, lists him as "Founder, Action Learning Trust, 1977"; Revans, 1977; About the role of Bett, see his foreword in Pedler, 1983, p. viii. Kepner-Tregoe, a consultancy still in existence, authors of *The Rational Manager* (1965). Benjamin B. Tregoe was very much concerned with developing the questioning skills of managers and executives, similar to Revans with the "Q", and perhaps this is one reason why they wanted to cooperate. See Tregoe, 1983.
154. Revans, 1977.
155. See the Revans archive: RWR3/1/3 Action Learning Trust 1979–1982. Newsletters and Annual reports.
156. Interview with Jean Lawrence, 27 February, 2009. One of the founders was Nelson F. Coghill, formed around the same time as Action Learning Trust according to Lawrence. The Trust was for work with business and others while IFAl was formed to do charitable work, but the latter (charity work) never materialized she said. In 1983, Nelson Coghill was the chairman of the Action Learning Trust and the director was Charles Simeons.

Today (2009) "IFAL's administration base is located at the University of Lancaster, but IFAL remains an independent organization". For recent information about IFAL and its activities see www.ifal.org.uk

Note: The IFAL Web site states that IFAL traces its formation to 1977, as "formerly the Action Learning Trust", but this it seems is inaccurate. The Action Learning Trust was in existence 1977–1982. The IFAL and their archives and books may be relocated to Manchester to the Revans Centre (Jan Hall conversation with Yury Boshyk, 22 May, 2009).
157. Marsick, 1990, p. 25; Rohlin et al., 2002, pp. 8 and 17–22 ("The Story of Mil").
158. Email from Lennart Rohlin to Yury Boshyk, 19 February, 2009:

The MiL Institute was formed as a not-for-profit foundation in December 1, 1977, with Per Lindblad (VP at Handelsbanken and a prominent figure at the Chamber of Commerce) as Chairman and Lennart Rohlin as Dean and President. Per Lindblad stayed on as chairman for 17 years and Lennart Rohlin stepped down as CEO in January 2009 after 32 years.

This formal step was preceded by a two year long development process involving about 100 actors from 30 of the largest corporations in southern Sweden (including some CEOs), from the academic world and a few consultancy firms. During this process of co-production several new concepts were developed in cooperation across all borders ("The MiL Model" including "The Actor Model", "The Management Model" and the "Action Strategy for Change and Development"); the longest and most advanced management development program in Sweden was designed ("The MiL Program", 50 days over one year); and the necessary formalities were created together with the stakeholders. Beyond the founding corporations and individual actors, one of the stakeholders was The Economic Research Center at Lund University. EFL, as the Swedish name goes, was founded ten years earlier with Lennart Rohlin as one of the enrepreneurs and its COO since its beginning. Curt Kihlstedt, Sven Åke Nilsson, Lars O Andersson and Gösta Wijk, all professors at Lund University, and Einar Mörck, Executive Vice President of Trelleborg AB, should be mentioned as five of the most important individuals in the founding of MiL. Einar Mörck was chairman of EFL at the time and Curt

Kihlstedt its CEO. Sven Åke Nilsson left his tenured position at the university to become one of the first full time employees in MiL and its first Executive Vice President. Lars O Andersson and Gösta Wijk made the founding politically possible in the academic environment.

The co-producing process preceding MiL was designed as an open ended inter-organizational Organizational Development (OD) process in which each individual actor has as much say as anybody else, it was a true cooperative initiative where practitioners and academicians worked side by side on equal terms. Eventually MiL came to exist of two main networks, the member corporations and the MiL Faculty with a small full time staff coordinating the whole thing.

When the co-producing phase in 1976 and 1977 resulted in the new concepts (eventually named "The MiL Model") and the new program design, several of the actors almost simultaneously mentioned that what have been created was similar to Action Learning. Consequently we invited Reg Revans to one of our meetings in 1977. Although there were important differences to his concept of AL, he embraced and felt stimulated by our work and he made a marvelous work in legitimating the approach of ours in the minds of some individuals who still were doubtful about the approach we have created. Later, after having run the first successful MiL program in 1978–79, we invited Reg Revans again.

During the 80s Reg Revans visited us a couple of times and it was always very stimulating having him around with his combined supportive and critical mind. He was impressed by the involvement and active support we have managed to elicit among our soon over 100 members, mainly large international corporations. He appreciated our basic values of diversity, democracy and inclusion, creativity and innovation. He was especially fond of the fact that we were (and still are) a network of independent actors more than a formal organization and that we were (and still are) not-for-profit. The profits we did (and do) make were mainly put into a research foundation, resulting in up until now in nearly 200 scholarships. In the 90s the contact with Jean Lawrence ... [head of IFAl at the time] ... became more frequent. As an example, her choice of venue for IFALs first international conference ... became the MiL Campus ...

The first intellectual influences behind MiL are as diverse as the original group of nearly 100 developers. When it comes to learning philosophy and our humanistic values, it would be obvious to mention names such as Piaget, Freire and Kirkegaard, but there are of course also influences from Kolb and other learning theorists as well as Fritz Perls and others from the Gestalt field. Interestingly enough there were not a single individual among the developers with a specialist academic background in pedagogics! And, as mentioned above, few were aware of Action Learning. There were, on the other hand, quite a few with backgrounds similar to mine: strategy, organization and business administration in general. Some influences might have been on a very personal level and not very well known. An example of my own is James Bugental, a Californian psychotherapist whose book Tony Athos put in my hands at Harvard.

The popularity of Action Learning boomed in Scandinavia during the early 80s and even though there were some important differences between AL and the MiL Model, we went with the boom and started to talk more about AL, which we have avoided during the first years of MiL. The downside of popularity, however, often is that each and everybody jumps on the bandwagon and eventually everything with some components of Action became labelled AL, including initiatives that we would not like to become associated with. So we were just in the process of turning back to our original trade mark on our combined concepts for change, development and learning, i.e. the MiL Model, when we in the mid 80s met with Ernie Turner, Lars Cederholm and some of their colleagues in the US. They became interested in setting up a subsidiary in the US based on the MiL Model. We became interested in supporting the formation of an independent organization with which we could have mutually refreshing conversations and perhaps some common business assignments. LIM was eventually formed and in the process we invented Action Reflection Learning, ARL as a proper label of the shared learning philosophy and methodology originated as the MiL Model. There was of course also a more factual reason for adding the R. From the beginning we stressed the importance of Reflection (on Action) as a precondition for Learning. Ernie and Lars both became members of MiL Faculty, and Lars, who moved back to Sweden in the late 90s still is.

The ARL concept was then further developed on both sides of the Atlantic Ocean, and sometimes by cooperative efforts. As an example, Victoria Marsick, professor at Columbia University and then member of LIM, was invited on a MiL Scholarship to Sweden to do research on the experiences and effects of MiL Programs in the late 80s. Together with US colleagues, she went on developing categories of different forms of Action Learning and a lot more. This kind of work made the field develop into maturity far beyond its wild character of the early 80s. LIM people were frequent and appreciated guests at the yearly MiL Days and eventually, Isabel Rimanoczy and Ernie Turner, who met at MiL Campus in 1994, published a standard textbook on ARL in 2008.

159. In 1978, Action Learning Trust, 45 Cardiff Road, Luton; "Published by the author", Revans, 1982, p. 717, endnote, 6; see also Revans, 1983, p. 9, where Revans states that this work first appeared in July, 1978.

There seem to have been six editions of this work in English: the first edition in 1978, published by Revans and titled "The ABC of Action Learning", copyrighted by Revans and republished in Swedish in 1983, stating that this was based on 25 years of experience; then 1983 pre-Chartwell-Bratt publication; in 1983, published for RALI by Chartwell-Bratt (joint copyright, cover design and artwork by the author); then Revans 1998 edition, edited by Pedler; then in 2004, 1983 version published by Barker, 2004. In one bibliography (www.emeraldinsight.com), the publication details for the first edition are as follows: "Birmingham: F.H. Wakelin Ltd. Mention is made that the first edition was published with the 'help of the Forward Engineering Group Training Scheme in Birmingham, England'" (Pedler 1998, p. xii) while Revans is not so direct, just mentioning that this Group was interested in knowing more about action learning (Revans, 1983, p. 9) and implied that he may have mentioned that he had organized programs for this Group: "Management Action Groups of the Institution of Industrial Managers (formerly of Works Managers)... supported by the Training Services Agency of the Manpower Services Commission" (Revans, 1983, p. 58).

160. Albert E. Barker email to Yury Boshyk, 9 January, 2009.
161. Revans, 1985; Revans, 1984, 83–5.
162. Lawlor biographical note in Pedler, 1997, p. xxiv. On Action Learning Associates and their research, see Lawlor, 1985, pp. 275–6, and 223.
163. Clutterbuck and Crainer, 1990, p. 126.
164. *Note*: There is one letter from Argyris to Revans on 7 August, 1980 in the Revans Archive: RWR5/1/3.
165. In 1978 Eric Trist joined the Faculty of Environmental Studies with which his relations had been growing for several years. The purpose was further to develop the socio-ecological perspective, especially in Third World projects, and to foster socio-technical projects throughout Canada. Search conferences have been introduced and teaching begun in futures studies. The center functions as a Canadian Tavistock [Institute]." (Trist and Murray, 1993, pp. 23–4)
166. Revans, 1980 p. 93; and Revans, 1988 on Grayson who headed it up, and Ross Perot; Cole, 1989, pp. 145–7 on the Centre and Grayson.
167. Revans' comment on withdrawal and return in Foy, 1975, p. 83. She describes the terms "penalty box" for those in IBM who were punished and then sometimes redeemed for their mistakes or errors, or until another position was found for "abrasive" colleagues. Foy asked Revans to comment on this practice, which no doubt he could identify with on a more personal level:

    Dr. Reginald Revans, an iconoclastic expert in corporate behaviour, suggests that IBM's Penalty Box has historical utility, reflecting Toynbee's anthropological myth of withdrawal and return. Jesus spent 40 days and 40 nights in the wilderness. Moses went up to the mountain. John Buynan wrote *Pilgrim's Progress* in Bedford Prison. (Hitler wrote *Mein Kampf* in prison for that matter.) Nixon, de Gaulle, Gladstone, Churchill, Lenin, Marx – all had their times in the wilderness and came back from exile or rejection to new power.

168. On the subtitle, see Pedler, 1983, p. 3, in the introduction. For an excellent review of this book, see Pedler 1980, revealing a great deal about Revans' personality and behavior.
169. Revans, 1980, p. 60. Contrary to its own publicity, the Washington-based consultancy with the same name and directed by Michael J. Marquardt has no direct connection to this comment by Revans nor to the work of Revans. He wrote a foreword to one of Marquardt's books (1999), not fully understanding how different Marquardt's approach to action learning was to his, and never having read the manuscript or worked with Marquardt before. According to those who advised Revans to write this introduction, this was done to "publicize" Revans to the Americans and others, since they felt Revans was not given the respect or mention he deserved in the U.S. as the pioneer of action learning (Interview with Albert R. Barker by Yury Boshyk and Robert L. Dilworth, 14 February, 2009).
170. Sasaki, 1981, pp. vii–viii; Revans, 1982, p. 685, chapter 48.
171. Published by the Swedish publisher Bertil Bratt, who also owned Chartwell-Bratt in the U.K., and established the Bratt Institute in Germany. This is the second translation and the first one was in Romanian in 1970, according to the finding aid to Revans' archive, RWR4/1: Books by R.W. Revans.

There was an extensive correspondence between Bratt and Revans from January 1981 to September 1988, Revans Archive, RWR5/1/14. The following account about Bratt was provided by Lennart Rohlin (email to Yury Boshyk, 19 February, 2009):

> Bertil Bratt and Lennart Rohlin knew each other quite well since the late 60s, when they were the two main competitors on the Swedish market for books and learning packages in Business Administration on the College level – Bertil through his book publishing company Studentlitteratur and Lennart as an independent editor engaged as a project leader by CWK Gleerup book publishing company. When the MiL Institute was under construction 10 years later, Bertil took active part in the development process and enrolled his company among the founding corporations. He met with Reg Revans in that process, who got Bertil interested in publishing his big opus "Origins and Growth" (1982). The big British or American publishing companies would not be interested, I remember Reg telling Bertil.
>
> When the first MiL Executive Program (12 days over a year and exclusively for CEOs) was launched in 1981, Bertil was one of the first participants and – according to the MiL Model – also co-designer. Another co-production was the founding of the Scandinavian Action Learning Society in 1982. This was done at a conference in Lund organized by MiL Institute, building on the MiL experiences so far and featuring Reg Revans launching his "big book". Lennart Strandler was also among the three sponsors, besides Bertil Bratt and Lennart Rohlin. Lennart Strandler, a longtime friend of Reg was a big fan of A[ction] L[earning] and he worked hard to get support for these ideas within his organization, the Swedish Employers' Federation.
>
> Bertil Bratt participated in several of our MiL Executive Missions to South East Asia in the mid 80s and our Executive Vice President Sven Åke Nilsson was on his board for many years. In the mid 1980s, Revans "ABC-book" was published by Bertil Bratt with a foreword by another MiL Faculty Member, Lars O. Andersson, who had a very strong position at the Lund University from which he supported the founding of MiL Institute in 1977.

172. Wieland and Leigh, 1971, pp. 460–1. One of Revans' comments about OD was as follows: "the enterprise as a learning system (now marketed as OD)" (Revans, 1982, p. 2).
173. Revans, 1983, pp. 772–86, chapter 51.
174. Revans, 1980, p. 60; Revans, 1983; and in Barker 2004, p. 259.
175. *Source*: Donna Vick and Robert L. Dilworth

> This note [The Clive Memorandum] has been prepared by Reg Revans following a meeting at the Clive Hotel, Primrose Hill on Feb 12th 1982. Present at the meeting were C.E. Hopper, L. Lowe (both of Foster Wheeler Products) [one of Revans' very supportive clients], Chas Simeons of the Action Learning Trust, Walter Riley and Reg Revans. The purpose of the meeting was to settle how a limited company might be established to market action learning of a kind that would appeal to top managers in volume enough to ensure continuous and viable operation into the foreseeable future. The meeting ... concluded that the setting-up of

a company should be seriously considered, and workable proposals were outlined for attracting potential customers. It was, nevertheless, agreed that a clear statement of our marketable product should be prepared. Others present are invited to make any alterations to it they feel necessary or desirable. The financial implications of what might be achieved in the first year of working are put forward solely as a base line from which to start more realistic debate.

176. "Foster Wheeler's Power Products were part of the first industrial consortium-type action learning programme in the U.K. and Foster Wheeler's group chairman, Don Newbold, made possible by his generosity the publication the publication of the first volume of Reg Revans' collected papers, for which he wrote the foreword " (Revans, 1982; and, Revans, 1983, p. 2).

177. Managementprogrammet i Lund, in Revans, 1983b, p. 6 Andersson wrote the foreword; email from Lennart Rohlin, 19 February, 2009:

Scandinavian Action Learning Society [was formed] in 1982. This was done at a conference in Lund organized by the MiL Institute, building on the MiL experiences so far and featuring Reg Revans launching his "big book". Lennart Strandler was also among the three sponsors, besides Bertil Bratt and Lennart Rohlin. Lennart Strandler, a longtime friend of Reg was a big fan of A[ction] L[earning] and he worked hard to get support for these ideas within his organization, the Swedish Employers Federation.

178. Addition to the second printing Revans, 1983b, p. 6.

179. Revans archive, RWR3/19/1 Scandinavian Action Learning Society, "Notice about the 1988 annual conference, held at the new University of Flensburg, on the Danish frontier with West Germany".

180. Interview with Alan Mumford, September 2008.

181. One of the founders of the IMCB describes the early years as follows:

[In 1982], a group of colleagues with whom I worked since 1965 both at Bradford University Management Centre and MCB University Press, resolved to address the challenge of creating...a structure for an Action Learning business school. The school would be committed totally to the process. It would offer the resources and advice appropriate to Action Learning for mid-career managers, both on an open basis and at master's and doctoral levels (MBA and DBA). We called it the International Management Centre from Buckingham (IMCB) and Reg Revans was eventually persuaded to become our President from 1983 to 1985 (and remains associated with us as Emeritus President). (Wills, 1999, pp. 31–2)

Revans referred to the IMC as "a handful of bold and enterprising academics" (Revans, 1984, p. 89).

According to Albert Barker and Robert L. Dilworth, Revans was highly critical of this private institution, but he seems to have kept these doubts to himself and to a close circle of friends and colleagues. Revans is listed in *Who's Who*, 1987, as still President, International Management Centre from Buckingham.

182. Revans, 1983; Revans, 1983, p. 2; The address given for those wanting more information was: "RALI, 1 Fairfield Avenue, High Street, Staines, Middlesex, TW 184AB".

183. Barker interview 14 February, 2009; and Revans, 1983, p. 58: "Foster-Wheeler Power Products, Cable and Wireless, Imperial Group, Ciba-Geigy and others, have kept together in the exchange of senior managers to work full time upon the problems of their counterparts."

184. Note that in Revans, 1982, p. 682, endnote 9, Revans mentions the following: "The ABC of Action Learning. Action Learning Trust, 45 Cardiff Road, Luton, 1978". On the title page, "There can be no learning without action and no action without learning". On the dedication page (p. 5): "A Review of Thirty Years' Experience, dedicated to Janet Craig whose support made Action Learning possible in the country of its origin". Thomas Joh, a South Korean doctoral student at the University of Brussels, but not associated with the Inter-University Program, wrote this dissertation on the attitudes to top management to action learning. Summarized by Revans, 1983, pp. 43–8 in chapter 4, but no mention of the name, and Revans, 1998, pp. 59–70; In the Revans, the name of the student and title of the dissertation are as follows: "RWR3/10/4 L'enterprise face au changement et a l'innovation: Doctoral dissertation of Thomas Joh Tae-Houne, from South Korea, enrolled at Free University of Brussels. Two volumes, 738 pp, 1977". Apparently missing from the archives.

185. Revans, 1983, p. 77; 1983, pp. 3–4; and in Barker, 2004, p. 259.

186. Revans, 1984, p. 38.

187. Telford: Revans Action Learning International (RALI Ltd); republished in Barker and Revans 2004.

188. Tichy, 1993, pp. 130–4. The approach used by Tichy had many elements of Organization Development and was influenced by his study of "change agents" like Saul Alinsky, his supervisor Morton Deutsch at Columbia who was a colleague of Kurt Lewin, the pioneer of "action research", his own experience as an undergraduate student at New York Banker's Trust Company, which convinced him that there was much that behavioral science could do for business, and the five years he spent working with the Martin Luther King Center in the South Bronx assisting in developing its neighborhood health centre, and "with substantial borrowings from others". Among these, was the experience of the U.S. military's development of "Organizational Effectiveness Officers", a model he apparently used for his work at GE (see 1973). On compressed action learning, see Tichy, 2001; Tichy and DeRose, 2003. (Yury Boshyk interview with Tichy, 27 April, 2009).

189. Dixon, 1997, pp. 329–330, 335–7.

190. *Who's Who*, 1987.

191. Marsick, 2002, pp. 298, 310–11. There is no direct link with Revans either with MiL or LIM, see for example, Marsick et al., 1992, p. 64: " British physicist Reg Revans is credited with creating A[ction] R[eflection] L[earning], but the basis of ARL is implicit in the work of many people who have observed that people can learn from their own experiences. Some of the assumptions that have emerged from that work include the following: ... Facilitators can accelerate learning by helping people think critically ... among other key points that echo Revans" (p. 64).

    As we have seen, this was not Revans' approach. Action Reflection Learning as a "philosophy" of both organizations came later around the late 1980s. See Marsick, 2002, Rohlin, 2002, and Rimanoczy and Turner, 2008. On its self-described differences with other forms of action learning see Marsick, 2002, pp. 304–8.

192. Revans archive: RWR3/4/6. University and Enterprise: Facing a New Era. Address by Gaston Deurinck on his retirement in 1987. *IMD Journal*, vol. 3, 1987, pp. 1–3.

193. Handy, Gordon, Gow, and Randlesome, 1988, pp. viii, and p.14.

194. Facing problems that cannot be isolated to a single cause, his [Kurt Lewin's] descendants have been experimenting ever since with his generic road map for getting from here to there. Lewin intended his enhanced problem-solving model to preserve democratic values, build commitment to act, and motivate learning – all at once. Indeed, some people have renamed the process [action research] "action learning" to more accurately indicate its nature (Revans 1982). (Weisbord, 1987, p. 187)

195. Clutterbuck and Crainer, 1990, p. 127.

196. Stephen Mercer to Yury Boshyk, 20 December, 2008:

I don't recall the date of the first action learning Business Management Course, but I believe that it was around 1986. I know that the first Global BMC was July 1988, since I was a participant. The thinking behind the first action learning BMC was that BMC was part of a three program series, in which each program was four weeks in duration, and classroom based. We wanted to get some variety into the series, and for the BMC level, we wanted to focus more on experiential learning. The first step in the migrating process was to kick off the program with three days of Outward Bound type activities. This morphed into doing business related projects. Jim Noel was leading the program at the time, and he came up with the idea of taking it global in 1988 when GE started to think about global business opportunities. At that time we did two domestic sessions and one global session. I attended the 1988 global session, co-program managed the 1989 global session, and took over the program in 1990. That was when you and I first met, and began the process of going full global with all three annual BMC sessions.

See also Mercer, 2000, 2000b; Lee, 2002; Noel, J.L., and Charan, R. 1992.

197. Foreword by Albert Barker and Barry Caidan, 1988; Barker, 2009, p. 7. Also, Revans, 1994b, p. 83, states that:

It was a recount of my Cavendish experiences some years ago that led some local managers to set up MALex, [sic] the Manchester Action Learning Exchange; this hopes to encourage, not only Mancunians to learn with and from each other by bartering their own failure and inadequacy, but similar consortia in all parts of the world that will, sooner or later, exchange internationally accounts of their own achievements and frustrations. Genuine action learning exchanges should be reluctant to purchase the services of experts, even "experts in action learning".

See also Revans, 1988, postscript:

The Spirit of Action Learning, crying from the pages of these papers, calls for more than the willingness to simply read and digest the message.

In Manchester, a group of people have come together to translate these words into Action...and MALex...is the result with the Community Trust for Greater Manchester being our local experience. The publication of the Golden Jubilee Papers is a first attempt to broaden debate and encourage active initiatives.

The Manchester Business School...are providing their support to this project. We are most anxious to hear from others who are willing to join the debate and help actively in working together, across the world, in an effort to bring about a better society for the benefit of all. Please write c/o...Miss Janet B. Craig, Archivist, MALex, Manchester Business School.

In 1992, Janet Craig states that:

> Reg Revans *is* MALEX [sic]. All correspondence and information is chan-neled through him and his contacts. MALEX has no other store of informa-tion and anyone responsible for ensuring the very necessary exchange of information. Reg and Janet are very grateful to Janine Mackey for her help and quick grasp of the situation and what needs to be done to keep Reg's "office" ticking over. For how long can the situation remain unchanged and what in the way of new organisation is needed to take its place?

"Description of the Revans Collection when housed in 8 Higher Downs", October 1992. Revans Archive, University of Salford, U.K.

198. Revans archive: RWR3/2/64 (p. 16) "Lord Butterfield in Hansard.
       16 December 1989, 2 pp. Reference to speech in the Lords – the need to get genuine action learning introduced into the NHS".
199. Ulrich, Kerr, Ashkenas, 2002, p. 11; and chapter 11 for a good summary of the underlying principles and approach.
200. Clutterbuck and Crainer, 1990, pp. 124, 127.
201. Gothenburg City Education Committee, 1992.
202. Marsick Cederholm, Turner and Pearson, 1992. See also Yorks, O'Neil and Marsick, 2002. pp. 19–29.
203. Verna J. Willis to Yury Boshyk, 13 June, 2009:
       The actual chartering of the Academy was initiated at the ProfNet Conference which I chaired in Atlanta, May 8–9, 1993. At that time, senior HRD practitioners and HRD professors were still folded into the American Society for Training and Development (ASTD), budgeted and treated as a special interest group. Most of us were dissatisfied with being a set-aside group with less than complete control of our own agenda. We met in a post-conference session to begin breaking away. It was spear-headed by Wayne Pace of Brigham Young University and Fred Otte of George State (an ASTD board member). Encouraged in previous ProfNet years by the rest of us, these men had already done a good deal of ground work.
       See also Revans archive: RWR3/4/28, "The A.H.R.D. Forum, Editor Prof. R.L. Dilworth. First issue of a newsletter, vol. 1, no: 1, November 1st 1993".
204. Barker who wrote the foreword dated Autumn, 1994. Mostly on Belgium, providing the context for Revans' work there.
205. There is some correspondence between Donnnberg and Revans in the Revans archive. The Society is still in existence. See its Web site.
206. Robert L. Dilworth email to Yury Boshyk, 2 August, 2007.
207. Robert L. Dilworth email to Yury Boshyk, 2 August, 2007.
208. European Foundation for Management Development, 1996, p. 52.
209. At that time it was called the "International Workshop on Strategic Executive Development and Action Learning" and held at the Theseus

Institute, Sophia Antipolis, France. On its origins, see Boshyk 2000, introduction and www.GlobalForumActionLearning.com
210. Mumford, 1997, p. xviii.
211. Part of the Mike Pedler Library. Additions to the original publication
include: with an Editorial Preface by Mike Pedler, a Foreword by David
Botham, a chapter on "The Enterprise as a Learning System", reprinted
from Revans, 1982, pp. 280–6.
212. Dotlich and Noel, 1998, pp. 1 and 3. Entirely focused on large U.S. corporations. Noel was for a time at GE's Crotonville. A recent article "updates"
their previous book, Noel and Dotlich, 2008.
213. www.publications.parliament.uk/pa/ld199798/ldhansrd/vo980204/
text/80204–11.htm
214. David Bellon, email 28 December, 2008 from Dirk Symoens; and in
Bertrams, 2006, p. 432, with photo.
215. Barker, 2009 and *TimesOnline*, 2003.
216. For example, see Shors 2009; Doidge 2007; Begley, 2007; Kegan and
Laskow, 2009.

References

Action Society Trust (1957) *Size and Morale, Part II: A further study of attendance at work in large and small units* (London: Acton Society Trust).
Alinsky, S. (1972) *Rules for Radicals: Pragmatic Primer for Realitic Radicals* (New York: Vintage Books).
Amdam, R. P. (ed.) (1996) *Management Education and Competitiveness: Europe, Japan and the United States* (London: Routledge).
Anderson, J. R. L. (1965) "Man at Work", *The Guardian*, 24 September.
[Anonymous] (1987) Revans, Prof. Reginald William, in *Who's Who, 1987: An Annual Biographical Dictionary*, 1468 (London: A. & C. Black).
Argyris, C. (1990) *Overcoming Organizational Defenses: Facilitating organizational learning* (Boston: Allyn & Bacon).
Argyris, C. (1992) *On Organizational Learning* (Oxford: Blackwell).
Argyris, C. (1993) *Knowledge for Action: A guide to overcoming barriers to organiza-tional change* (San Francisco: Jossey-Bass).
Argyris, C. and Schön, D. A. (1993) *Organizational Learning II: Theory, method, and practice* (Reading, MA: Addison-Wesley).
Ashmawy, S. (1972) "Consortium Revans". *Journal of European Training*, 1, pp. 54–6.
Ashmawy, S. and Revans, R. W. (1972) "The Nile Project: An experiment in educational authotherapy". A monograph upon which the Fondation Industrie-Université contribution to the 1972 ATM Conference was based. Paris: The Development Centre, Organisation for Economic Cooperation and Development (OECD).
Baquer, A. Q. and Revans, R. W. (1973) *"But Surely that is Their Job": A study in practical cooperation through action learning* (Southport: A.L.P. International Publications).
Barker, A.E. and Revans, R. W. (2004) *An Introduction to Genuine Action Learning* (Oradea, Romania: Oradea University Press).

Barker, A. E. (2004) "Professor R.W. Revans: The founding father of action learning – a short bio-summary", in A. E. Barker and R. W. Revans (eds.), *An Introduction to Genuine Action Learning* (Oradea, Romania: Oradea University Press), pp. 17–44.

Barker, A. E. (2009) "Bio-Chronology: RWR milestones", 15 January. Typescript.

Barker, P. (1972) *One for Sorrow, Two for Joy: Ten years of "new society"* (London: Allen & Unwin).

Begley, S. (2007) *Train Your Mind, Change Your Brain: How a new science reveals our extraordinary potential to transform ourselves* (New York: Ballantine).

Bertrams, K. (2001) *The Diffusion of US Management Models and the Role of the University: The case of Belgium (1945–1970)*. Accessed 10 October, 2009, available at [web.bi.no/forskning/ebha2001.nsf/23e5e39594c064ee852564ae004fa010/.../$FILE/C2%20-%20Bertrams.PDF] Bertrams, K. (2006) Universités et enterprises: Milieux académiques et industriels en Belgique (1880–1970) (Brussels: Le Cri).

Boshyk, Y. (ed.) (2000) *Business Driven Action Learning: Global best practices* (London/New York: Macmillan/St Martin's Press).

Boshyk, Y. (ed.) (2002) *Action Learning Worldwide: Experiences of leadership and organizational development* (Basingstoke, U.K./New York: Palgrave Macmillan).

Botham, D. (1998) "The Context of Action Learning: A short review of Revans' work", in W. Gasparski and D. Botham (eds.), *Action Learning* (New Brunswick, US: Transaction Books), pp. 33–61.

Brummer, A. and Cowe, R. (1998) *Weinstock: The life and times of Britain's premier industrialist* (London: HarperCollins).

Burke, W. W. (1987) *Organization Development: A normative view* (Reading, MA: Addison-Wesley).

Casey, D., and Pearce, D. (eds.) (1977) *More than Management Development: Action learning at GEC* (New York: AMACOM).

Cathcart, B. (2004) *The Fly in the Cathedral: How a small group of Cambridge scientists won the race to split the atom* (London: Viking).

Clutterbuck, D. (1974) "An Egyptian project for swapping managers". *International Management*, 29(11), November, pp. 28–34.

Clutterbuck, D. (1976) "Whatever happened to action learning? While the traditional massive projects continue, the future of the technique seems to lie in less ambitious undertakings". *International Management*, 31(11), November, pp. 47–9.

Clutterbuck, D. and Crainer, S. (1990) *Makers of Management: Men and women who changed the business world,* (London: Guild Publishing).

Coghill, N. F. (1983) "A Bibliography of Action Learning", in M. Pedler (ed.), *Action Learning in Practice* (Aldershot: Gower), pp. 277–83.

Cole, R. E. (1989) *Strategies for Learning: Small-group activities in American, Japanese and Swedish industry* (Berkeley: University of California Press).

Comfort, W. W. (1968) *Just Among Friends: The Quaker way of life*, 5th and revd edn (Philadelphia: American Friends Service Committee).

Commonwealth Fund (1990) *Directory of Commonwealth Fund Fellows and Harkness Fellows, 1925–1990* (New York: Commonwealth Fund).

Crowther, J. G. (1974) *The Cavendish Laboratory, 1874–1974* (New York: Science History Publications).

Dilworth, R. L. and Willis, V. J. (2003) *Action Learning: Images and pathways* (Malabar, FL: Krieger).

Dixon, M. (1971) "David, Goliath and Dr. Revans: [European] Management Education Conference", *Financial Times*, 8 January, D15.

Dixon, N. M. (1997) "More Than Just A Task Force", in M. Pedler (ed.) *Action Learning in Practice*, 329–37, 3rd edn (Aldershot: Gower).

Dobinson, C.H. (ed.) (1951) *Education in a Changing World: A symposium* (Oxford: Clarendon Press).

Doidge, N. (2007) *The Brain that Changes Itself* (New York: Viking).

Donnenberg, O. (ed.) (1999) *Action Learning: Ein Handbuch* (Stuttgart: Klett-Cotta).

Dotlich, D. L. and Noel, J. (1998) *Action Learning: How the world's top companies are re-creating their leaders and themselves* (San Francisco: Jossey-Bass).

"The Education of the Young Worker: Report of the second conference held at Oxford in July 1949 under the auspices of the University Department of Education" (1950) Oxford: Published for King George's Jubilee Trust by Oxford University Press.

Engwall, L. and Zamagni, V. (eds.) (1998) *Management Education in Historical Perspective* (Manchester: Manchester University Press).

European Foundation for Management Development (1996) *Training the Fire Brigade: Preparing for the unimaginable* (Brussels: European Foundation for Management Development).

Foy, N. (1972) "The maverick mind of Reg Revans", *Management Today*, November, pp. 79, 81,163,168.

Foy, N. (1975) *The Sun Never Sets on IBM: The culture and folklore of IBM world trade* (New York: Morrow).

Galenson, W. and Lipset, S. M. (eds.) (1960) *Labor and Trade Unionism: An interdisciplinary* (New York: Wiley).

Gasparski, W. W. and Botham, D. (eds.) (1998) *Action Learning. Praxiology: The International Annual of Practical Philosophy and Methodology* (New Brunswick, NJ: Transaction Publishers).

Gellerman, S. W. (1966) *The Management of Human Relations* (Hinsdale, IL: Dryden Press).

Gilbert, M. (2008) *The Routledge Atlas of the Second World War* (London: Routledge).

Gothenburg City Education Committee (1992) "Farrington, Freire, Revans, Sapp: Four of the main speakers at the 2nd International Conference of Educating Cities", November, 1992 in Gothenburg, Sweden (Gothenburg: Gothenburg City Education Committee), pp. 25–7.

Guillon, P., Kasprzyk, R. and Sorge, J. (2000) "Dow: Sustaining change and accelerating growth through business focused learning", in Y. Boshyk (ed.), *Business Driven Action Learning: Global best practices* (London/New York: Macmillan Business/St Martin's Press), pp. 14–28.

Handy, C., Gordon, C., Gow, I., and Randlesome, C. (1988) *Making Managers: A report on management education, training and development in the USA, West Germany, France, Japan and the UK* (London: Pitman).

Hellwig, H., and Bertsch, J. (1997) "Usprung und Werden einer Erfolgsgeschichte", in J. Bertsch and P. Zürn (eds.), *Führen und Gestalten: 100 Unternehmergespräche in Baden-Baden* (Berlin: Springer), pp. 13–24.

Keeble, S. P. (1984) "University education and business management from the 1890s to the 1950s: A reluctant relationship". Unpublished Ph.D., London School of Economics, University of London.

Keeble, S. P. (1992) *The Ability to Manage: A study of British management, 1890–1990* (Manchester: Manchester University Press).

Kegan, R. and Laskow Lahey, S. (2009) *Immunity to Change: How to overcome it and unlock the potential in yourself and your organization* (Boston: Harvard Business School).

Kensit, D. B. J. (1948) "European Voluntary Workers and their English", *Outlook*, July.

Kleiner, A. (1996) *The Age of Heretics: Heroes, outlaws, and the forerunners of corporate change* (New York: Currency).

Kynaston, D. (2007) *A World to Build: Austerity Britain, 1945–48* (London: Bloomsbury).

Lawlor, A. (1985) *Productivity Improvement Manual* (Westport, CT: Quorum Books).

Lee, T. (2002) "Action Learning in Korea", in Y. Boshyk (ed.) *Action Learning Worldwide: Experiences of leadership and organizational development* (Basingstoke, U.K./New York: Palgrave Macmillan), pp. 249–59.

Lessem, R. (1982) "A Biography of Action Learning", in R.W. Revans (ed.), *The Origins and Growth of Action Learning* (Bromley: Chartwell-Bratt), pp. 4–17.

Levy, P. (2000) "Organising the External Business Perspective: The role of the country coordinator in action learning programmes", in Yury Boshyk (ed.), *Business Driven Action Learning: Global best practices* (London/New York: Macmillan Business/St Martin's Press), pp. 206–26.

Likert, R. (1961) *New Patterns of Management* (New York: McGraw Hill).

Mailick, S. (ed.) (1974) *The Making of the Manager: A world view* (Garden City, NY: United Nations Institute for Training and Research (UNITAR) and Anchor Press/Doubleday).

Margerison, C. (2003) "Memories of Reg Revans, 1907–2003", *Organisations and People*, 10 (3), August, pp. 2–7.

Marquardt, M. J. (1999) *Action Learning in Action: Transforming problems and people for world-class organizational learning* (Palo Alto: Davies-Black).

Marsick, V. J. (1990) "Action Learning and Reflection in the Workplace", in J. Mezirow et al. (eds.), *Fostering Critical Reflection in Adulthood: A guide to transformative and emancipatory learning* (San Francisco: Jossey-Bass), pp. 23–46.

Marsick, V. J., Cederholm, L., Turner, E. and Pearson, T. (1992) "Action-Reflection Learning", *Training and Development*, August, pp. 63–6.

Marsick, V. J. (2002) "Exploring the Many Meanings of Action Learning and ARL", in L. Rohlin, K. Billing, A. Lindberg and M. Wickelgren (eds.), *Earning While Learning in Global Leadership* (Lund, Sweden: Studentlitteratur), pp. 297–314.

Mercer, S. (2000) "General Electric's Executive Action Learning Programmes", in Y. Boshyk (ed.), *Business Driven Action Learning: Global best practices* (London/New York: Macmillan Business/St Martin's Press), pp. 42–54.

Mercer, S. (2000b) "General Electric Executive Learning Programmes: Checklist and tools for action learning teams", in Y. Boshyk (ed.), *Business Driven Action Learning: Global best practices* (London/New York: Macmillan Business/St Martin's Press), pp. 179–90.

Miles, D. H. (2003) *The 30-Second Encyclopedia of Learning and Performance: A trainer's guide to theory, technology and practice* (New York: American Management Association).

Mumford, A. (ed.) (1997) *Action Learning at Work* (Aldershot: Gower).

Mumford, E. (1999) "Routinisation, Re-engineering, and Socio-technical Design. Changing ideas on the organisation of work", in W. L. Currie and B. Galliers (eds.), *Rethinking Management Information Systems* (Oxford: Oxford University Press), pp. 28–44.

National Association of Secondary School Principals. 1974. *25 Action-Learning Schools.* Reston, Virginia: The National Association of Secondary School Principals.

Noel, J. L. and Charan, R. (1992) "GE brings global thinking to light", *Training and Development*, 46 (7), pp. 28–33.

Noel. J. L. and Dotlich, D. L. (2008) "Action Learning: Creating leaders through work", in J. L. Noel and D. L. Dotlich (eds.), *The 2008 Pfeiffer Annual: Leadership development* (San Francisco: Wiley), pp. 239–47.

Pedler. M. (1980) "Book review of *Action Learning: New techniques for action learning* by R.W. Revans", *Management Education and Development*, 11, pp. 219–23.

Pedler, M. (ed.) (1983) *Action Learning Practice*, 1st edn (Aldershot: Gower).

Pedler, M. (ed.) (1997) *Action Learning in Practice*. 3rd edn (Aldershot: Gower).

"The Proceedings of the 6th International Meeting of the Institute of Management Sciences, (7–11 September, 1959, Paris) (1960) Volume 2", pp. 17–24. Session 8 ("Measurements in Management"), with Revans as President of the session (Président de séance, and presenter, Prof. R. W. Revans, The Manchester College of Science and Technology) (London: Pergamon Press).

Revans, J. and McLachlan, G. (1967) *Postgraduate Medical Education: Retrospect and prospect* (London: Nuffield Provincial Hospitals Trust).

Revans, R. W. (193). "The transmission of waves through an ionized gas", *Physical Review*, 44, pp. 798–802.

Revans, R. W. (1945) "Plans for recruitment, education and training in the coal mining industry", Prepared by R. W. Revans in conjunction with The Recruitment, Education and Training Committee of the Mining Association of Great Britain, S.l.

Revans, R. W. (1951) "Education in Industry", in C.H. Dobinson (ed.), *Education in a Changing World* (Oxford: Clarendon Press), pp. 18–33.

Revans, R. W. (1953) *Size and Morale: A preliminary study of attendance at work in large and small units* (London: Acton Society Trust).

Revans, R. W. (1956) "Industrial morale and size of unit", *Political Quarterly*, 27 (3), pp. 303–10.

Revans, R.W. (1957) *The Analysis of Industrial Behaviour. Automatic production – change and control* (London: Institution of Production Engineering).

Revans, R.W. (1959) "Operational Research and Personnel Management, Part 2". Institute of Personnel Management, Occasional Papers, number 14, Part 2. London: Institute of Personnel Management.

Revans, R. W. (1960) "Industrial Morale and Size of Unit", in W. Galenson and S. M. Lipset (eds.), *Labor and Trade Unionism: An interdisciplinary reader* (New York: Wiley), 295–300.

Revans, R.W. (1962) "Preface", in R. W. Rowbottom and H. A. Greenwald, *Understanding Management* (Manchester: Whitworth Press), 9–11.

Revans, R.W. (1962) "Preface", in D.N. Chorafas (ed.), *Programming Systems for Electronic Computers* (London: Butterworths), 9–11.

Revans, R.W. (1964) *Standards for Morale: Causes and effect in hospitals* (London: Oxford University Press for the Nuffield Provincial Hospitals Trust).

Revans, R. W. (1965) *Science and the Manager.* (London: Macdonald).

Revans, R.W. (1966) *The Theory of Practice in Management.* (London: Macdonald).

Revans, R.W. (1969) "The Structure of Disorder", in J. Rose (ed.), *A Survey of Cybernetics: A tribute to Norbert Wiener* (London: Illife), 331–45.

Revans, R. W. (1970) "The Managerial Alphabet", in G. Heald (ed.), *Approaches to the Study of Organizational Behaviour: Operational research and the behavioural sciences* (London: Tavistock Publications), 141–61.

Revans, R. W. (1971) *Developing Effective Managers: A new approach to business education* (New York: Praeger).

Revans, R.W. (1971b) "Introduction" [Background to the HIC Project], in G. Wieland and H. Leigh (eds.), *Changing Hospitals: A report on the Hospital Internal Communications Project* (London: Tavistock Publications), 3–24.

Revans, R.W. (1972) "Action learning – A management development program", *Personnel Review*, 1(4), pp. 36–44.

Revans, R.W. and Baquer, A. (1972) " 'I thought they were supposed to be doing that': A comparative study of coordination of services for the mentally handicapped in seven local authorities', June 1969 to September 1972 (London: Hospital Centre).

Revans, R. W. (1974) "The Project Method: Learning by doing", in S. Mailick (ed.), *The Making of the Manager: A world view* (Garden City, NY: United Nations Institute for Training and Research (UNITAR) and Anchor Press/Doubleday), pp. 132–61.

Revans, R. W. (1975) "Helping Each Other To Help the Helpless: An essay in self-organization, (Part I)", *Kybernetes*, 4, pp. 149–55. [Note: Republished in Revans (1982), *The Origins*, pp. 467–92.]

Revans, R. W. (1975) "Helping Each Other To Help the Helpless: An essay in self-organization, (Part II)", *Kybernetes*, 4, 205–11. [Note: Republished in Revans (1982), *The Origins*, pp. 467–492.]

Revans, R. W. (ed.) (1976) *Action Learning in Hospitals: Diagnosis and therapy* (London: McGraw-Hill).

Revans, R. W. (1977) "An action learning trust", *Journal of European Industrial Training*, 1(1), pp. 2–5.

Revans, R. W. (1980) *Action Learning: New techniques for management* (London: Blond & Briggs).

Revans, R. W. (1982) *The Origins and Growth of Action Learning* (Bromley: Chartwell-Bratt).

Revans, R. W. (1982b) "What is action learning?", *Journal of Management Development*, 1(3), pp. 64–75.

Revans, R. W. (1983) *The ABC of Action Learning* (Bromley: Chartwell-Bratt).

Revans, R.W. (1983b) *ABC of Action Learning* (Lund: Utbildningshuset).

Revans, R. W. (1984) *The Sequence of Managerial Achievement* (Bradford, U.K.: MCB University Press).

Revans, R.W. (1985) *Confirming Cases* (Telford: Revans Action Learning International).

Revans, R. W. (1988) "The Golden Jubilee of Action Learning: A collection of papers written during 1988". Manchester Business School and Manchester Action Learning Exchange (MALEx).

Revans, R.W. (1990) "The hospital as a human system", *Behavioural Science*, 35 (2), pp. 108–14.

Revans, R.W. (1991) "Action learning in the Third World", *International Journal of Human Resource Management*, 2, May, pp. 73–91.

Revans, R. W. (1994a) Life History Interview [and] Action Learning and The Belgian Action Learning Program, Including an Address to the Faculty of the Defense Systems Management College at Fort Belvoir, Virginia. Interviews by Robert L. Dilworth et al., during Revans' visit to Virginia Commonwealth University as a Distinguished Scholar (video).

Revans, R. W. (1994b) "Action Learning or Partnership in Adversity. The economic effects of national spontaneity", prepared by Albert E. Barker. S.l. [Typescript and spiral bound. Prepared for the First International Action Learning Mutual Collaboration Congress, pp. 17–25 April, 1995.]

Revans, R. W. (1995) "Disclosing doubts". March. S.l. [Typescript and spiral bound. Prepared for the First International Action Learning Mutual Collaboration Congress, 17–25 April, 1995, as an "Extended Paper".]

Revans, R. W. (1997) "Action Learning: Its origins and nature", in M. Pedler (ed.) *Action Learning in Practice*, 3–14. 3rd edn (Aldershot: Gower), pp. 3–14.

Revans, R. W. (1998) *The ABC of Action Learning*, M. Pedler (ed.) (London: Lemos & Crane. Mike Pedler Library).

Rimanoczy, I. and Turner, E. (2008) *Action Reflection Learning: Solving real business problems by connecting learning with earning* (Mountain View, CA: Davies-Black).

Rohlin, L., Billing, K., Lindberg, A. and Wickelgren, M. (eds.) (2002) *Earning While Learning in Global Leadership: The Volvo MiL partnership* (Lund: MiL Publishers).

Rowbottom, R. W. and Greenwald, H. A. (1962) *Understanding Management* (Manchester: Whitworth Press).

Sasaki, N. (1981) *Management and Industrial Structure in Japan* (Oxford: Pergamon).

Seashore, S. E. (1954) *Group Cohesiveness in the Industrial Work Group* (Ann Arbor: Institute for Social Research).

Schein, E. H. (1967) "Introduction", in D. McGregor, *The Professional Manager*, C. McGregor and W. G. Bennis (eds.) (New York: McGraw-Hill), pp. xi–xiii.

Senge, P. (2009) *The Fifth Discipline: The art and practice of the learning organization* (New York: Currency Doubleday).

Shors, T. J. (2009) "Saving new brain cells", *Scientific American*, 300(3), pp. 46–54.

Stiefel, R. Th. and Papalofzos, A. (1974) "Use of Newer Participation Teaching Methods in Western Europe", in S. Mailik (ed.), *The Making of the Manager: A world view* (Garden City, NY: United Nations Institute for Training and Research (UNITAR) and Anchor Press/Doubleday), 162–200.

Taylor, B. and Lippitt, G. (eds.) (1983) *Management Development and Training Handbook* (Maidenhead, U.K.: McGraw-Hill).

Tichy, N. M. and Sherman, S. (1993) *Control Your Destiny or Someone Else Will: How Jack Welch is making General Electric the world's most competitive company* (New York: Currency-Doubleday).

Tichy, N. M. (2001) "No ordinary boot camp", *Harvard Business Review*, 79(4), pp. 63–9.

Tichy, N. M. and DeRose, C. (2003) "The Death and Rebirth of Organizational Development", in S. Chowdhury (ed.), *Organization 21C: Someday all organizations will lead this way* (Upper Saddle River, N.J: *Financial Times*/Prentice Hall), pp. 155–73. See Mercer email on factual mistakes in this article.

TimesOnline (2003) "Reginald Revans: Management guru who taught executives to value experience over theory and put their people first", *The Times*, 21 February. Accessed 11 November, 2009, available at http://www.timesonline.co.uk/tol/comment/obituaries/article884986.ece

Tiratsoo, Nick (1998) "Management Education in Postwar Britain", in L. Engwall and V. Zamagni (eds.), *Management Education in Historical Perspective* (Manchester: Manchester University Press), pp. 111–26.

Trist, E. and Bamforth, K. (1951) Some social and psychological consequences of the longwall method of coal getting", *Human Relations*, 4, pp. 3–38.

Trist. E. (1969) "On Socio-Technical systems", in W.G. Bennis, K.D. Benne and R. Chin (eds.), *The Planning of Change* (New York: Holt, Rinehart & Winston), pp. 269–82.

Trist, E. and Murray H. (1993) *The Social Engagement of Social Science: A Tavistock Anthology. Volume II: The Socio-Technical Perspective* (Philadelphia: University of Pennsylvannia).

Tregoe, B. T. (1983) "Questioning: The key to effective problem solving and decision making", in Taylor and Lippitt (1983).

Ulrich, D., Kerr, S. and Ashkenas, R. (2002) *The GE Workout: How to implement GE's revolutionary method for busting bureaucracy and attacking organizational problems – fast!* (New York: McGraw-Hill).

Weisbord, Marvin W. (1987) *Productive Workplaces: Organizing and managing for dignity, meaning, and community* (San Francisco: Jossey-Bass).

Wieland, G. F. and Leigh, H. (eds.) (1971) *Changing Hospitals: A report on the Hospital Internal Communications Project* (London: Tavistock Publications).

Wieland, G. F. (ed.) (1981) *Improving Health Care Management: Organization development and organization change* (Ann Arbor: Health Administration Press).

Wills, G. (1999) "The Origins and Philosophy of International Management Centres", in A. Mumford (ed.), *Action Learning at Work* (Aldershot: Gower), pp. 30–41.

Wilson, J. F. (1992) *The Manchester Experiment: A history of Manchester Business School, 1965–1990* (London: Paul Chapman Publishing).

Wilson, J.F. (1996) "Management Education in Britain: A compromise between culture and necessity", in R. P. Amdam (ed.), *Management, Education and Competitiveness: Europe, Japan and the United States* (London: Routledge), pp. 133–49.

Yorks, L., O'Neil, J. and Marsick, V. (2002) "Action Reflection Learning and Critical Reflection Approaches", in Y. Boshyk (ed.), *Action Learning Worldwide: Experiences of leadership and organizational development* (Basingstoke, U.K./New York: Palgrave Macmillan), pp. 19–29.

von Berttalanffy, L. (1950) "The theory of open systems in physics and biology", *Science*, 111, pp. 23–9.

Zuber-Skerritt, O. (2001) "Action Learning and Action Research: Paradigm, praxis and programs", in S. Sankaran et al. (eds.), *Effective Change Management Using Action Learning and Action Research: Concepts, frameworks, processes, applications* (Lismore, Australia: Southern Cross University Press), pp. 1–20.

7
Action Learning in Different National and Organizational Contexts and Cultures

Robert L. Dilworth and Yury Boshyk

Introduction

In June 2008, the authors began a discussion of how well action learning "travels" across national and organizational cultures. Given the rapid growth of action learning internationally, this seemed a good question to be asking. One point of view suggests that action learning is cross-culturally compatible and can be used easily in a variety of contexts. The authors believe that action learning can, in fact, be used in a variety of venues, and action learning's history provides convincing evidence of this. But the issue of cross-cultural compatibility is another matter. For example, setting up action learning teams in Asia with team members of unequal status is usually not going to work. Mixing men and women in a team does not work in most Arab countries, and it also can encounter keen resistance in Asia. And, in organizational cultures that are rather authoritarian or top-down, action learning tends to be more like "project-based" work rather than being more integrative of individual and societal contexts. There is clearly a need to adapt the way action learning is applied based on the national and organizational culture involved.

Our goal in this chapter is to provide practitioners with practical information that can help them avoid cross-cultural problems and enable them to have a successful experience. We are not simply thinking of practitioners or others in the West, as they bring their action learning approaches to other parts of the world. We envision it much more broadly than that. It includes practitioners of any nationality introducing their approach elsewhere. Action learning is dynamic and adaptive, and we can learn from each other across international and organizational frontiers. Those who have been involved with action learning for a long time can marvel at the innovativeness and power of approaches to action learning being used in societies other than our own – whether in India, China, South Africa, Germany or elsewhere – and in a multitude of organizational cultures.

During his lifetime, Revans "the founding father" of action learning, traveled to many countries to discuss action learning and help people come to understand it. Unlike most of his contemporaries, he did not simply try to impose an approach originally conceived in England on others. In this area, as in many others, he was well ahead of his time. He recognized that there are cultural differences, and that we need to be sensitive to the needs of the country or locale where action learning is to be practiced. In his milestone work, *The Origins and Growth of Action Learning*, Revans addresses the fact that lessons from "managers learning from each other, doing real time experiences, can be taken across international boundaries" (1982, p. 373). But he also states, in addressing developing countries, that they "must solve their own problems" in their own way. This is indicative of the way Revans viewed action learning. He believed that those involved with action learning should be empowered and enabled. In a cross-cultural sense, this translates to flexibility in shaping the experience to the environment and the learners. He wrote that "There is nothing more likely to test one's belief in an idea than to try carrying it across a cultural barrier, and to succeed in this the idea must be stripped of all that is not central to it" (1980, p. 53). He also recognized that no one has a monopoly on good ideas. As an example, Naoto Sasaki (1981, p. viii) writes:

> I have never forgotten what Dr. Revans told me when I was hesitating whether to return to Japan or not. He said, "Professor Sasaki, Japanese organizations have got so many things which the Western organizations have not got. If you write a book on Japanese management, go to your own country, see your organizations with your own eyes and touch them with your own hands."

This way of thinking may be one reason why he was received so warmly in his dealings with diverse groups in many countries. He was not dictating a modality to them but, rather, trying to help them understand their problems and deal with them through a form of action learning that aligned with their circumstances and their cultural mores.

Revans' point of view is especially evident when he discusses the contrast between action learning applications in Africa and Europe. He states:

> [The] education of the African must be secured through attack on his present poverty. He must learn, not so much from the scholarship of the European, as from solving the problems that lie before him in Africa. And the educational task of the West is not to instruct him in the achievements of its own past, however successful these may appear to be; still less it is to lay upon him the veneer of an alien culture. (Revans, 1982, p. 373)

In this spirit, and with our intention of providing readers with useful information that they can immediately put to good use, we will cover the following areas:

- *The nature and importance of national cultural differences*
  Why does it matter? It can be useful to have some general grounding in why consideration of cultural differences is important, including an examination of the research that underlies it.
- *A survey of some selected national cultural dichotomies and how they can be related to action learning*
- *Differences between domains, contexts, occupational groups and corporate cultures in adapting action learning approaches*
- *Some rules of thumb that can be helpful*
- *An analysis of the hypothetical introduction of an action learning program in Japan*
  This is designed to create an awareness of what you need to consider in introducing action learning in any country. In this illustration, we use the introduction of action learning from the U.S. culture into Japan. This can be helpful as a general template in the planning and preparation phase involved in undertaking an action learning intervention in any country.

The nature and importance of national cultural differences

Why is consideration of national cultural differences important? The short answer is that not to consider such differences can undermine your effort and even cause it to fail.

Pachter and Brody (1995, p. 277) include an international perspective on etiquette and say this:

> Every culture has a different set of glasses, which affects its vision of reality. What are Americans like? To Mexicans, Americans are emotional and serious, likely to work as a team but rather time-conscious. The Taiwanese see Americans as emotional and fun loving, easy-going although inclined to be independent. To the French, Americans are friendly but aggressive, competitive and entrepreneurial. They're all correct in their assessments, because they are measuring Americans against their own society. Comparatively speaking, Americans are all of these things.

There are at least two fundamental points contained in this statement.

- *We need to understand our own national culture before trying to understand other cultures.* The reality is that we can wear "cultural clothes" and not really know how we are clothed. Culture becomes instinctive to us. We are programmed to operate out of a cultural perspective by our life experiences and education. We need to step back and reflect on who we are, the values that govern us, and how we function in dealing with both personal and work-related issues in our lives. We project our own culture, knowingly or unknowingly, when we deal with people with vastly different backgrounds. We therefore need to have a relatively clear idea of what our cultural trappings are, as well as how they match up with the person or organization with whom we are dealing.
- *Even when we strive to understand other national cultures, we can default to our own.* To the extent we recognize this, we can draw back before committing a gaffe in the way we relate to someone in another culture.

Use of actual examples can be a good way of understanding the importance of taking national cultural differences into account, and there are many examples of issues that caused, or might have caused, serious cross-cultural disconnects. Nancy Adler (1997) tells the story of a dinner hosted by the Chinese in beginning a relationship with a U.S. firm. The Chinese toasted the Americans at the welcoming dinner. The Americans failed to return the toast. The Chinese were deeply offended by this lack of courtesy and attention to protocol.

The Chinese summarily dropped any further discussions with the U.S. firm.

Another example provided by Adler also shows how you can run the risk of a cultural miscue.

A businessman from Scotland was spending two weeks in Japan and had a Japanese businessman traveling with him and serving as an Escort and intermediary with the company. They took their meals together and stayed at the same hotel each night. One night they were having a drink together in the Scotsman's room before retiring for the night. The Japanese businessman suddenly said, "Why don't we sleep together tonight?" Rather than receive the invitation negatively and assume there was a sexual innuendo, the Scotsman instinctively accepted the invitation. He trusted the intentions of his Japanese colleague. A maid brought another sleeping pad into the room. Without knowing it at the time, the Scotsman had paid his Japanese associate a very high compliment. It turned out to be a cultural tradition dating back to the Samurai Warrior era, several hundreds of years earlier. The Japanese businessman was saying in effect that he absolutely trusted his Scottish associate not to harm him while he slept. Without realizing it, the Scotsman had returned the compliment.

Language can get you in trouble in ways you would not have expected. When Bill Clinton was President of the United States, he was to address a large group of students at the National University in Hanoi, Vietnam. A U.S. Department of State Translator prepared the script to be used during the simultaneous translation of his remarks into the Vietnamese language. The Vietnamese students had great difficulty understanding what Clinton was saying. It turned out that the translator at the U.S. State Department had come from the Saigon (Ho Chi Minh City) area in southern Vietnam. The Northern dialect spoken in the Hanoi area is quite different. Dilworth identifies with this example because he almost fell into the same trap. A U.S. Department of Defense translator had translated a speech he was to give in Budapest, Hungary. Based on a hunch, Dilworth had a friend and colleague, who was a native Hungarian speaker, and from the Budapest area, retranslate the script. He discovered that the original translation was badly flawed and would have been an embarrassment if it had been used, especially since Dilworth was representing his country and the United States Army as part of the first senior officer exchange to Hungary in 1989.

There are many ways to define culture. Among a number of definitions of culture presented by Geert Hofstede (2001, p. 10), one of them in particular seems to communicate most clearly:

> Culture determines the uniqueness of the human group in the same
> way personality determines the uniqueness of the individual.

Hofstede goes on to say that:

> Culture is usually reserved for societies (operationalized as nations or
> as ethnic or regional groups within or across nations) ... the word can
> be applied to any human collectivity or category, an organization, a
> profession, an age group, an entire gender, or a family). (p. 10)

(It is instructive to note that in China, the term "family" can be used to
apply to the entire nation.)

Both Hofstede and Trompenaars have undertaken extensive research
in the area of national culture. In the case of Hofstede, he administered over 100,000 survey instruments across 50 countries in his original research study. All persons surveyed were employees of IBM. It
was a very revealing study, and led him to four empirically derived
dimensions of culture, to which he later added a fifth dimension (i.e.,
long term–short term orientation) during a later research study. His five
dimensions are:

1. Individualism–collectivism;
2. Power distance (number of layers between the top and bottom of
   organizations);
3. Uncertainty avoidance (dealing with anxiety and risk);
4. Masculinity–femininity (which now can be described as "achievement versus quality of life orientation");
5. Long-term as opposed to short-term orientation.

It is important to understand these dimensions, because they can
unlock an understanding of why there can be disconnects between
cultures. We will explain them more fully during our examination of
cultural dichotomies, but here is the gist of what these major cultural
dimensions convey, and why not understanding at least their broad
implications can place you at risk in cross-cultural communication. In
terms of Individualism, the U.S., for example, is highly individualistic.
Most other countries outside North America and Western Europe are
highly Collectivistic – just the opposite. Power distance in terms of
hierarchy can be very large in countries like Malaysia, but very small in

countries like the United States. Uncertainty Avoidance, how a culture deals with anxiety and accepts risks, can be very different. The United States tends to be low in Uncertainty Avoidance, whereas many other countries are not. In terms of masculinity–femininity (Achievement versus Quality of Life), the Japanese were the most Achievement driven, with the Swedes at the opposite end. The time dimension is especially telling, with China and Japan having by far the longest time line for their planning. The United States is much lower, and Russia is lower still.

You can readily see how these cultural dimensions, even in a general form, can influence your ability to do business and build a successful relationship with those from another culture. It can have a large bearing on the success or failure of an action learning program. You obviously cannot take cultural differences lightly. You dismiss them at your own risk. Despite this, cultural differences can still be either ignored or given little attention.

Even with growing awareness, "cultural blindness" can still be very much in evidence. It can be seen at times in the readiness of U.S. business executives and university professors to use theories of management that originated in the West, without adaptation, on the assumption that they are somehow universally applicable and will mesh with the host culture. *You obviously need to be wary of the same pitfall in introducing action learning in other cultures.* Geert Hofstede provides some excellent examples of this. One of his examples relates to use of Theory X and Theory Y, a theoretical construct of Douglas McGregor. Theory X relates to leadership styles that are authoritarian in nature; namely, the perceived need to supervise subordinates closely and prod them in order to obtain results. Theory Y operates on the premise that people will strive to do their best without the need for constant oversight and supervision to achieve results. Hofstede points out (2001, p. 387) that Theory X/Theory Y have never been relevant to South east Asia. He states that a distinction more in line with South east Asian culture would:

oppose mutually exclusive alternatives that discount the norm of harmony. The ideal model would be for opposites to complement each other to fit harmoniously together.

Hofstede also calls attention to the fact that a number of U.S. theories of leadership advocate "participative management"; that is, participation in the superior's decision by subordinates *"at the initiative of the superior".* He points out that:

> [I]n countries ... such as Sweden, Norway, Germany and Israel, models of management were developed that assumed the initiative was to be taken by subordinates. (2001, p. 389)

In other words, it was not necessary to introduce a U.S. model for these countries related to participatory management, where the principles involved had long ago been internalized in terms of the way that organizations should be managed.

A survey of some selected cultural dichotomies and how they can be related to action learning

Michael Marquardt of George Washington University, who has written about both cross-cultural differences and action learning, is an important resource. Marquardt (1999) devotes an entire chapter to action learning around the world, and states the following:

> Action learning is a prime management-development and problem solving tool for numerous corporations and public agencies in Western countries and the former British colonies (e.g., Singapore, Nigeria, Malaysia, Hong Kong). Despite its amazing accomplishments in Western countries and Western-headquartered corporations, action learning appears to have been rarely implemented in the remaining 90 percent of the world. (p. 149)

He suggests several reasons for action learning's perceived failure to penetrate more broadly (p. 150).

- Lack of familiarity with action learning
- The non-Western world is simply unaware of the inherent power of action learning to change organizations and people
- Action learning is built on primarily Western cultural values and practices.

Since Marquardt wrote these words, the landscape has been rapidly changing. Action learning is spreading quickly in many areas. Action learning has become almost ubiquitous in many of the largest global companies. It has now, for example, established deep roots in South Korea, and receives strong sponsorship from the Korean Action Learning

Association. While not spreading as rapidly in China as yet, it seems on the cusp of a rapid expansion. In 2008, Robert Weintraub (of IBM) was instrumental in launching an action learning program with one of China's largest telecommunications firm. It apparently proved to be highly successful.

Judging by the cross-section of global companies represented at the Thirteenth Annual Global Forum on Executive Development and Business Driven Action Learning (a community of action learning practitioners) in Seoul, South Korea in June 2008, use of action learning is becoming well-established. Of the 100 invitees, including senior individuals from many global companies, 15 countries were represented. They were Germany, Canada, Israel, Sweden, South Africa, South Korea, Singapore, China, Denmark, France, United Kingdom, Australia, Japan and the United States. Exactly 50 percent of the invitees were from Asian countries. While a skewing effect in the direction of Asia could be expected for a Global Forum being held in Asia, other Global Forums held over the years have reflected broad diversity as well. In 2008, 7 percent of the attendees were from China. South African representatives were contemplating a national level program in action learning.

In exploring the issue of action learning built on Western cultures and values as an impediment to its use in non-Western countries, Marquardt cites research by Hampden-Turner and Trompenaars (1997) that found that "East Asian cultures may, in fact, have several characteristics that make them better suited to action learning". This is an interesting proposition. Their study found that:

> Westerners prefer playing what these researchers call a *finite game*, in which individuals win or lose by specific criteria in universal contests; Easterners play an *infinite game*, in which all players learn cooperatively. (Marquardt, 1999, p. 167)

The Eastern perspective of an infinite game lines up rather well with what Revans would frequently cite as, "Learning from and with each other." Revans seems to have found his way to a similar belief concerning the compatibility of action learning in Asia. He writes (1982, p. 544) that,

> [T]here is a remarkable correspondence between the Buddhist Philosophy and the general theory of action learning...Among its postulates are the following:
>> That persons learn only when they want to learn; they change their behavior of their own volition and not at the will of others;

That the need to solve problems or to seize opportunities engenders the most powerful desire to learn.

Mike Pedler (1991, p. 29) alludes to a meeting he had with Reg Revans, where Revans told him that "Action Learning and Buddhism were one and the same".

Marquardt (1999, p. 167) says this with respect to China:

> Several years ago, Zhou Jianhua, after meeting with Reg Revans in England, returned to Wuxi, in a remote area of China, to introduce the concept of action learning. She was surprised that managers gave there felt so familiar with the process. The managers gave three reasons for their inherent enthusiasm for action learning. It fit with Maoist philosophy ... 'Not only reading is learning, but also doing is learning ...'; Sharing experiences and perspectives is the traditional and popular method of learning in China; The managers had found that the principles of Western management did not provide solutions to their problems.

The compatibility of action learning with management practices and traditions in Africa is also evident in relation to their tradition of *Ubuntu* – "I am because you are and you are because I am" (Christie et al., 1994, p. 123; and Mbigi and Maree, 1995).

Ubuntu is a concept that brings to the fore images of supportiveness, cooperation, and solidarity; that is, communalism (p. 122).

What these views of compatibility of action learning with non-Western cultures provocatively suggest is that action learning may even fit better with some non-Western cultures than it does with cultures in the Western world. Revans encountered resistance to action learning throughout his lifetime, some of them centered in his own country, England. Therefore, it may not be a case of fitting a concept spawned in the West to non-Western contexts but, rather, realizing that action learning *as conceived by Revans* can be a comfortable fit with non-Western cultures and values.

We will now turn to several selected cultural dichotomies that can help explain the differences that need to be taken into account in applying action learning cross-culturally. These are general categories and provide a broad gauged index to cultural differences. They include five empirically derived dimensions of culture developed by Hofstede and already identified. The list could have been considerably longer, but we decided to select just a few dichotomies that we feel will expose some of the most significant areas that need to be understood and taken into account.

Individualism versus collectivism

The difference between individualistic and collectivistic cultures can be a basis for conflict. The United States and Australia have strongly individualistic cultures, as does Great Britain, Canada and the Netherlands. In Hofstede's research, Guatamala was the most collectivistic, followed closely by Panama, Venezuela, Columbia, Pakistan, and Indonesia. Countries falling near the center were Iran, Japan, India, Turkey, Portugal, and Jamaica. What needs to be remembered when dealing with a country like India is that overall ratings do not necessarily tell the story, given the variegated nature of Indian society, with its caste system, religious differences, and the number of languages and dialects spoken.

When you are dealing with extremes on Hofstede's scale, such as individuals from the U.S. culture versus individuals from a country like Korea, Pakistan or Indonesia, the possibilities for misunderstanding or miscues can go up. This can be evident when an American wants to move swiftly to accomplish some end, while the Pakistani counterpart does not have as much independence when it comes to decision-making and needs to obtain a group consensus. A good example of this was when the action learning program director, based in the U.S., encountered resistance to his request that the South Korean country manager nominate a candidate to take part in an action learning program. The manager felt that nominating only one individual from his whole team would undermine the spirit and effectiveness of the entire group, and would also cause problems for the nominated individual.

Power Distance

Power Distance, as defined by Hofstede, relates to the distance between the top and bottom of the organizational pyramid. Based on his research, the power distance in the United States is relatively small, with few organizational layers, and the structure tends to be flat. GE prided itself at one point in having no more than five layers between the line worker and the chief executive officer (CEO). However, there are other countries with even smaller power distances than the U.S., including Austria, Israel, Denmark, New Zealand, Norway, Sweden, Switzerland, Ireland and Finland.

The statistics developed by Hofstede as result of his research with IBM, place Malaysia at the head of the 50-country list in terms of large power distances, followed by Arab countries, Indonesia, Guatemala, Ecuador, and Mexico.

These statistical differences tend to play out in reality, especially when they stand in sharp contrast. An American dealing with a Saudi company (part of Hofstede's Arab Countries category) will almost

certainly encounter some frustration in the form of an entrepreneurial
orientation clashing with a much more hierarchical way of doing business. Some conflict between Malaysian and U.S. approaches to management is also likely to develop.

Masculinity

Hofstede originally addressed this as Masculinity versus Femininity,
but that could be a source of confusion. Therefore, for purposes of clar-
ity, it is now being referred to as Achievement versus Quality of Life
Orientation. Hofstede found Japan to be the most achievement oriented
of the 50 countries he studied. Sweden stood at the opposite end in
terms of its quality of life orientation. The quality of life orientation has
not held back what Sweden has been able to achieve. It is a very successful economy, and the same is, of course, true of Japan at the opposite
pole on this dimension.

Other countries with a high achievement orientation include
Switzerland, Italy, Ireland, Mexico, Germany and Great Britain. The
U.S. tends to the high side as well, but not to the degree of the countries
already mentioned, and Canada is almost squarely in the center of the
two orientations.

Countries with almost the same magnitude of quality of life orientation as Sweden are Norway, the Netherlands, Finland, Denmark and
Chile. The Netherlands demonstrates a strong belief in quality of life.
Time for family and activities outside the work place are considered
very important. The watchword here, if you are dealing with an action
learning program in any of these northern countries and Chile, is not
to intrude on their private space by scheduling events on days that
they consider to be their personal time, including weekends with their
families.

Uncertainty avoidance

This takes into account the degree to which individuals prefer unstructured, ambiguous and unpredictable situations as opposed to expecting
rules, regulations and controls. The country with the lowest uncertainty
avoidance and propensity for risk-taking was Singapore. Other countries with relatively low uncertainty avoidance were the United States,
Ireland, Canada, India, Great Britain, Hong Kong (China was not in
Hofstede's study at the time), Jamaica, Malaysia, and the Philippines.

Countries more inclined to avoid uncertainty and less inclined to
take risks were Belgium, Japan, Salvador, Spain, Panama, Uruguay,
South Korea, and Argentina. While Hofstede's study was extremely

valuable, it is important to remember that it was run within one company; namely, IBM. Therefore, when you look at the results for India they would have come from a highly industrialized area of India, such as Bangalore, rather than from the poorer areas of the country.

Uncertainty avoidance can be a useful gauge in introducing an action learning intervention in another country other than your own. High uncertainty avoidance coupled with large power distance can suggest that your client organization will be inclined to have a highly structured and regulated environment for action learning, one with less empowerment and less free-ranging interaction. France is one country that fits this description based on the results of Hofstede's study. But, once again, it needs to be kept in mind that such study results are not sacrosanct. Hofstede's results are good at showing central tendency but, as Hofstede emphasizes, you can find a wide spectrum of results in the same society. We will address this when we explain the significance of different contexts and occupational groups within societies.

Long- versus short-term orientation

This was the last of the cultural dimensions to be developed by Hofstede. It was brought together in 1985 and involved a sampling in 23 countries. Called the Chinese Values Survey (CVS), it differed from the earlier IBM survey design and purposely leaned in the direction of Eastern values versus those in the West. The fifth dimension, which came to be added as a result of this survey, was long- versus short-term orientation. (Hofstede, 2001, pp. 351–72).

This dichotomy receives attention in both the research of Hofstede and Trompenaars. It is a very important reference point to keep in mind when launching an action learning initiative. Persons who have lived in the United States all their lives will tend to operate with a short-term time line. If you live in Russia, it is even shorter. On the other hand, as already indicated, the Chinese and Japanese have a very long-term orientation, the longest by far of the 23 countries included in the survey. China surpasses all of the countries by a significant margin. These differences can be telling and lead to significant cultural disconnects, and even clashes, unless understood and kept in view. Hofstede indicates that:

> Businesses in long-term oriented cultures are accustomed to working toward building up strong positions in their markets; they do not expect immediate results...In short-term oriented cultures the 'bottom line' (the results of the past month, quarter, or year) is a

major concern; control systems are focused on it and managers are constantly judged by it. (Hofstede, 2001, p. 361)

In long-term cultures, they will not normally take a favorable view of an action learning design – or any other management or educational initiative, for that matter – unless it takes long-term implications into account.

Field dependent versus field independent

This concept came from studies described in Witkin and Goodenough (1981). Witkin had performed groundbreaking research in the 1940s. He discovered that some people are "field independent" and others "field dependent". When a person is field independent, the context is less important than the specific focus point being addressed. This is characteristic of the U.S. culture and other Western cultures. Most of the rest of the world is field dependent, and they tend to orient on the context. That is a significant perceptual difference.

There was some research done in comparing Japanese and U.S. participants in a research study. It demonstrates rather clearly how perspectives can be out of synch, and the differences in perceptions not consciously recognized. Goode (2000) calls attention to some research by Richard E. Nisbett and his colleagues. In one experiment involving students from Japan and the United States, participants were shown an animated underwater scene. One large fish swam among other fishes and aquatic life.

> Asked to describe what they saw, the Japanese subjects were much more likely to begin by setting the scene, saying for example, "The water was green" or "The bottom was rocky"... Americans, in contrast tended to begin their descriptions with the largest fish, making statements like "There was what looked like a trout swimming to the right."

Inductive versus deductive reasoning

In the view of the authors, no dichotomy is more interesting and significant from the standpoint of action learning than this one. Action learning, as conceptually constructed by Revans, begins deductively by asking questions that are holistic and general in nature (e.g., "What is happening?") and then gradually focuses in on specifics and solution sets that flow from this deductive approach.

The United States, Germany, Great Britain, and most Western countries use an inductive form of reasoning, starting with the specifics rather

Table 7.1 A summary picture of national cultural dichotomies

Primarily West	Primarily East
• Individualistic	• Collectivistic
• Low power distance	• Large power distance
• Low uncertainty avoidance	• High uncertainty avoidance
• Achievement orientation	• Quality of life orientation
• Short-term orientation	• Long-term orientation
• Field independent	• Field dependent
• Low context	• High context
• Inductive	• Deductive
• Monochronic (linear; step-by-step)	• Polychronic (multiple venues simultaneously; more intuitive)
• Nuclear family	• Extended family
• Language promotes informality	• Language promotes formality
• Interaction in classroom commonplace	• Expect didactic, one-way communication

than the big picture. Asians, Africans and other non-Western countries tend to orient on deductive reasoning. As has been already pointed out, action learning can potentially fit better with cultures in Asia and Africa than it fits in Western societies. This is another example of that.

A summary picture of national cultural dichotomies

As has been shown by the few select cultural examples just outlined, there are significant differences in the way people perceive their world and operate in different national cultural contexts. This extends to other areas that were not addressed, like language. Table 7.1 was compiled by the authors to show a summary view of dichotomies, including those just covered as well as others. For convenience, we show a contrast between East and West.

Differences between domains, contexts, occupational groups, and corporate cultures in adapting action learning approaches

National culture is only one reference point in adapting an action learning model for another cultural environment.

Domains and sectors

Table 7.2 presents five principal domains and 16 contexts where action learning can occur as identified by Dilworth and Willis (2003, pp. 126–151).

Table 7.2   Principal domains and contexts where action learning can occur

Domain	Context
Academic settings	• Higher education (general) • Adult education and human resource development (HRD) professional programs • Community colleges • Adult education outside academe (e.g., adult basic education)
Private sector businesses and services	• Major private companies • Corporate universities • New economy businesses • Small businesses and non-profit making organizations
Governments	• Federal • State • County and municipal
World	• International organizations (e.g., UN, World Bank, World Health Organization) • Non-governmental organizations (NGOs) (e.g., Doctor's Without Borders, International Red Cross)
System changers	• Organization development (OD) • Chief learning officer (CLO) • Other HRD practitioners

Dilworth and Willis analyzed each sector closely in terms of the driving forces and the retraining forces that might be expected to exert themselves in setting out to employ action learning programs in each of them. The concept of "driving forces" and "retraining forces" is taken from Kurt Lewin's work with force field analysis (Weisbord, 2004, p. 83). You examine the forces in being that can either help or hinder you. Dilworth and Willis based their analysis on long experience with action learning in a number of settings, including internationally. They also drew on the experience of colleagues.

We will not outline here the full scope of this analysis but, rather, provide three examples of how such an analysis can be helpful in Table 7.3.

Occupational groups

Within the same national culture, there can be variations across occupational groups and they can be quite significant. Hofstede calls attention to this in describing a study of commercial airline pilots by

Table 7.3   Three examples of sector analysis

Context	Driving forces	Restraining forces
Major private companies	• Major companies may welcome action learning approaches because they can help to build competitive advantage • The use of action learning in business is growing • Action learning fits well with the development of self-directed teams	• There are hierarchical power structures • Some companies have a fixation with formal methodologies • Traditional HRD practitioners can be one of the major inhibitors because of classroom focus
Small businesses and non-profit making organizations	• Action learning can provide a low-cost, effective route to competitiveness • People are already accustomed to working in small teams to solve problems	• There can be a limited financial base • Expertise and knowledge of action learning within the organization is limited or non-existent
Organization development (OD)	• Action learning aligns closely with organizational development, and can even be considered a preferred intervention in remolding corporate culture • Practitioners have the skill sets necessary to introduce and sustain action learning programs	• Organizational development, like action learning, can elicit major resistances because of its perceived threat to existing power relationships • Cultures not ready to receive major change • Expert focus of OD practitioners can run counter to action learning

Helmreich and Merritt in 1998. The study covered more than 15,000 commercial airline pilots from 23 countries, surveyed between 1993 and 1997. Hofstede compared these results with his major study across 50 countries with IBM. He found that:

> The overall level of individualism for the pilots was much higher than for IBM employees (a mean of 142 instead of 57 for the same countries in IBM)...Pilots seem to be individualists, and pilots from collectivistic countries are more different from their home-country cultures in this respect than are pilots from individualistic countries. (2001, p. 230)

We could provide a variety of other examples from Hofstede's work in connection with differences between occupations. However, most experienced consultants intuitively appreciate that differences exist between occupations. Engineers, for example, tend to engage in linear thought processes by virtue of their education and the kind of requirements they deal with in their work. Our intent is merely to inform action learning practitioners of the need to take occupational differences into account in planning an action learning program.

Fons Trompenaars (1993, p. 64) provides a number of meaningful displays from his research, some of which address the work environment. One of them deals with feeling upset at work, and the percentage of respondents that would not express it openly. Eighty-three percent of Japanese respondents to his survey would not speak up, whereas only 29 percent of the Italian respondents would express it openly. In the United States, 40 percent would make their displeasure known. Here, you see the Asian desire for harmony and avoidance of anything that might work against that.

Another of Trompenaars' displays relates to what makes a good manager, and the percentage opting to be left alone to get the job done. Ninty-seven percent of the Australians prefer to be left alone. The United States also ranks high, with 83 percent wishing to work independently. In Egypt, only 32 percent chose to be left alone to get the job done. Sixty-nine percent of Japanese respondents preferred being left alone (Trompenaars, 1993, p. 143).

Corporate culture

When Geert Hofstede made his initial contact with IBM about running a cultural survey, the initial reaction was that there was really no need for it because at IBM there was only one culture, the IBM culture. IBM does have a strong culture, call it a corporate personality. The large-scale research study that Hofstede ended up undertaking with IBM proved that there are many other cultural aspects to consider. From what we have already outlined, they clearly matter.

It was said of IBM for many years that it lived in the shadow of Tom Watson, its founder, and that his influence could be felt long after he had passed from the scene. The same can be said of Hewlett Packard, and the powerful influence its founders, Bill Hewlett and David Packard, had on the company long after they retired. It came to be known as "The HP Way". If you asked an employee to talk about it, they would refer to it with pride, but were usually not be able to provide much in the way of a definition of what it meant, except for saying that the company took good care of its people. Heavy restructurings, including major downsizing, have tended to wash away some of this image in recent years.

Edgar H. Schein (1992, p. 12) defines organizational culture this way:

> A pattern of shared basic assumptions that was learned by a group as it solved its problems of external adaptation and internal integration, that has worked well enough to be considered valid and, therefore, to be taught to new members as the correct way to perceive, think, and feel in relation to those problems.

There can be a distinction drawn between climate and culture, with climate being more transitory and reflecting the forces at a particular period in time. It can be a charismatic leader that people choose to follow. However, the underlying "river" of culture can flow on and then reassert its influence when that leader departs. A good case example is GE. Jack Welch assumed his duties at GE on April 1, 1981. It was no "April Fools Day" for the company. He swept in like a firestorm, taking a company that was highly successful, turning it on its head, and making it even more successful. Noel Tichy (Tichy and Sherman, 1993, p. 8) says this:

> If Welch's vision shocked GE's workers, his behavior terrified them. While he was talking about "liberating or empowering" GE's employees, they were worrying, with reason, about their jobs. He challenged the time-tested compact that governed GE's relationship with its employees: something approaching lifetime job security in return for loyalty, obedience, and performance. In its place he offered a new principle that struck employees as cruelly Darwinian: "Companies can't give you job security," he said. "Only customers can." In other words, *succeed in the marketplace or you're out of a job.*

He ended up shaking the company from top and bottom, and continued as the Chief Executive Officer for 20 years. It leaves the question: "Did the culture of GE change?" The answer is probably yes, a climate change akin to a hurricane emerged as basic cultural transformation in the company. However, inherent in the corporate culture of GE is an engrained belief in revitalization and renewal, something it has done throughout its long and successful corporate history. That allows us to make the point that corporate culture is not a static thing. It evolves, if the company plans to survive and move with the times.

Some years ago researchers at the University of Chicago studied the corporate culture of an English company named Rugby Cement. Its

President and CEO was Sir Halford Reddish. He was beloved by his people and an inspiring leader. In the winter time, he would ensure that bags of coal were dropped off at the homes of his employees. During the Great Depression, when businesses around the world were contracting, Reddish greatly expanded his production capacity, and when the Depression began to draw to a close and business began to pick up again, he was positioned to grab market share and capitalize on this increased capacity. A few years after Reddish died, the University of Chicago researchers decided to go back to England and rerun their study, to see if the organizational culture still reflected his value set. They concluded that Reddish was still very much alive in terms of the corporate culture.

One of the most brilliant insights on the subject of corporate culture comes from Edgar Schein (1997) at MIT. Dilworth and Willis (2003) allude to the importance of his point of view. Schein has identified what he calls the operator culture, the internal culture of the organization. But Schein finds two other cultures that are important to understand as well, and both come from outside the organization. The first external influence he calls executive culture – what is coming from the wide community of business leaders (such as holders of an MBA). The second external influence he calls the engineering culture – which draws from the worldwide occupational community (e.g., academics, scientists, social workers). These influences can obviously come into conflict. A good example of this potential conflict can be found in universities, where the operating culture can call for teamwork, but the engineering culture stresses "publish or perish", causing professors to prefer individual effort, where their individual accomplishments can be included in their curriculum vitae.

Culture is a complex subject, as should be evident from the ground that has now been covered. Our best advice to you, when it comes to scoping an organization and locale, is to remember that culture is not transparent. It takes time to learn the true values in the culture. As Argyris et al. (1985) point out, there are both espoused theories and theories in use. They explain it this way:

> There are two kinds of theories of action. Espoused theories are those that an individual claims to follow. Theories in practice are those that can be inferred from action. (pp. 81–2)

They go on to say (p. 82) that, "Espoused theory and theory in use may be consistent or inconsistent, and the agent may or may not be aware of any inconsistency."

If you go into an organization and automatically believe that what you are told about the espoused values is true, you are likely to be surprised as you come to learn the inner workings of the organization. There is almost always a gap between the two. It is no different than what occurs with people, who may say one thing while doing another. It can take the form of what is called in psychology "cognitive dissonance", comfortably holding two entirely different points of view that are in conflict, such as espousing the need to live a healthy life while continuing to smoke two packs of cigarettes a day.

Some rules of thumb and resources that can be helpful

We will be outlining a few simple rules of thumb in Table 7.4 that can serve you well and help you prepare for an action learning initiative in a culture other than your own. We use the word "culture" in this instance to include all the bases we have covered in this chapter, including corporate culture. We will then turn to some resources in the literature and online that you can use to inform yourself about another culture.

In sum, the basic rule is to do your homework before entering the other culture and organization.

An analysis of the hypothetical introduction of an action learning program in Japan

We will begin with some brief background notes on Japan to set the stage, and then discuss a hypothetical model to be brought to Japan by a U.S. practitioner. In doing so, we will analyze each major planned ingredient of that model in relation to the Japanese culture and suggest how it needs to be adapted. What we are suggesting is that the same approach can be used to sort out the best way to use any action learning model cross-culturally.

Some background notes

Japan has one of the most homogenous populations in the world. Aside from a small Korean minority, it is ethnically pristine pure and has highly restrictive immigration policies. As Chin-Ning Chu (1991, p. 12) indicates:

> The Japanese have always been the greatest disciples of Chinese wisdom. When it comes to the perfect execution of this principle, the pupil has surpassed the master.

Table 7.4 Some rules of thumb

1	Read about the country and the locale where you will be working. Your hosts will be deeply appreciative of the fact that you have made the effort. This includes reading about the history of the country and region you will be visiting. The standard guidebooks, such as Fodor, can be very useful. The Michelin guidebooks will tend to go deeper than others in dealing with historical detail.
2	Try to identify someone in the organization you will be working with, or even outside it, who can be a collaborator in translating the cultural nuance for you. The ideal person will come from the organization (i.e., living in the corporate culture). Even more perfect is an individual who understands both your culture and the culture in which they live. They can readily crosswalk between the two, telling you what you need to do or avoid doing to help establish your credibility with the host organization. Make sure you select the right collaborator to work with. Get opinions from their parties where possible.
3	Try and determine how action learning is being practiced in the country, locale and organization you will be involved with. In some cases, there may be little or no previous experience with action learning.
4	Avoid use of humor cross-culturally. What may be funny in your culture may be totally misunderstood or taken as a supreme insult in another culture.
5	Discover the espoused values of the organization you will be working with as contained in policies and publications produced by the organization.
6	Get as much background information as you can about the people you will be working with in the organization, including those to whom you must answer. Find out as much as you can about those who are being considered as participants in the action learning experience.
7	Set about studying the business with which you will be involved. Try and "wear their shoes". What are their principal concerns? What are the strategic goals of the enterprise? How successful have they been? Who are their competitors?
8	If very critical remarks are to be translated from your language into another, consider using "back translation" to check its accuracy. You do this by having a second translator take the translation of the first, as translated into the other language, and translate it back into your language. You can then compare your remarks as written initially with the back translation. It will give you a good gauge as to the quality of the first translation.

Perhaps more than any other society, you have to understand Japan's past and traditions to understand Japan today, because Japan did not leave its traditions behind. It still lives by them. An example of this is Mushashi (1982). The author was a Samurai warrior born in 1584. He practiced "Kendo", the way of the sword, a school of thought dating back to 1390. The Samurai ethos itself can be traced back to 792 AD. This book does not go out of style. It stays in print, and the philosophy it contains is passed on to the each successive generation.

> Where a Westerner might say "The pen is mightier than the sword", the Japanese would say 'Bunbu Itchi', or 'pen and sword in accord'. Today, prominent businessmen and political figures in Japan still practice the traditions of the old Kendo schools, preserving the forms of several hundred years ago. (p. 3)

To Japan, economic competition is war by another name: "The highest victory is to win a war without battles" (Chin-Ning Chu, 1991, p. 12).

> The Chinese expression, "Shang Chang ru zhan chan," translates literally as: "The market place is the battlefield." That is how the Asian people view the importance of success in the business world. The success of a nation's economy influences the survival and well-being of a nation as surely as does the course of a battle.

The Chinese practice of *Bing-fa*, which translates into English as "military strategy" (p. 13) dates back to the twelfth century BC. As Chu (1991) points out, the strategies are still operative today. In fact, they are an inherent part of the cultural weave. There are 36 primary strategies, and they are frequently learned by school children. They were captured by Sun Tzu in the fourth century in what is considered "the most complete book of military strategy that has survived to the present". The titles of a few of these strategies will give you an idea about their overall contents – "Display Your Forces in the East and Attack in the West (p. 50), "Kill the Rooster to Frighten the Monkey" (p. 64), Be Wise but Play the Fool" (p. 69), "Attack When Near, Befriend When Distant"(p. 66), "Trade a Brick for a Piece of Jade" (p. 59), and "Knife Hidden Under the Smiling Face" (p. 34).

> Being immersed in Asian culture, one absorbs strategic thinking unconsciously and learns to love the mental thrust-and-parry as a natural part of the human interaction. (p. 16)

Japanese culture is not transparent, and what you experience in interaction may not be a good representation of intentions. This is really the theme of Chu's book, with the suggestion that Westerners can go into discussions and negotiations with the Japanese like babes in arms, assuming that the Japanese somehow possess similar values, a case of defaulting to your own culture when you do not comprehend the other culture. The example of an iceberg can sometimes be used in making the point that only a limited amount of the cultural artifacts are visible. If you compare the U.S. culture with that of Japan, there is more of the U.S. culture visible above the surface. In the case of the Japanese culture, there is much less made visible; Japanese are also less emotive in explaining their intentions. Part of it is a matter of holding their cards close to their chest, but it is also a case of being in a very homogeneous culture, where a bow can take a hundred different forms, with another person from the Japanese culture able to decode the nuance instantly.

Robert C. Christopher (1983, p. 21) issues a warning that Americans need to heed:

> Americans have no idea how the Japanese think and feel. Because we cannot conceive that they could be radically different from our own, we cannot duplicate the logical processes of the Japanese or grasp the value system that underlies Japanese behavior.

Table 7.5 offers a thumbnail sketch of things you need to know about the complex Japanese culture.

A side-by-side comparison of Japan with the United States, in relation to Hofstede's five dimensions and the results of his milestone studies, proves revealing (see Table 7.6).

What this comparison shows is that there is a potential for cultural clash in two areas. The first is in dealing with anxiety and risk (i.e., Uncertainty Avoidance), and the second is in the short-term orientation of the United States, versus the extremely long-term orientation of Japan. In the worst case scenario, this can be "like ships passing in the night".

Analysis of a hypothetical introduction of action learning – U.S. culture to Japanese culture

Table 7.7 presents an analysis of a hypothetical introduction of action learning situation between and U.S. and Japanese cultures. Each U.S. hypothetical design characteristic, *before* applying any cultural "filters", is numbered and immediately followed with an analysis and suggested adaptations for the Japanese culture.

Table 7.5 The complex Japanese culture

1	Decisions are always by consensus. Westerners can misinterpret what this means. It doesn't mean absolute agreement, but it does mean that every voice is heard and listened to before a decision is made.
2	Rank and titles are very important. They will look closely at how you are represented on a business card.
3	Proper etiquette is very important.
4	They are extremely humble about their own individual achievements and can be highly embarrassed to be singled out for praise. The group is what gets recognized.
5	It is a male-dominated society, but when an American woman, for example, is doing business in Japan, they will treat her with respect, as someone who has earned the right to be there.
6	Collective harmony is more important than individual latitude and personal freedom.
7	The Japanese will say "yes" more than "no" in negotiations, but that does not mean that they agree. It is a case of maintaining harmony. That can be disconcerting to Americans, who can find out later that they did not really come to agreement.
8	Relationships are the key to communication.
9	Japanese would rather lose money than lose face.
10	Silence can be seen as expressing something profoundly important.
11	Peace and harmony are valued.
12	Mutual trust is important, and it is not created instantly.
13	They are long-term thinkers and seek a holistic view.
14	Formal attire is usually the order of the day.
15	The bow is the traditional greeting and, as already indicated, the bow can take many forms, each with a distinct meaning. Handshakes can be acceptable, but hugs are not.
16	The family is the foundation of Japanese society.
17	There is a set way for doing almost everything. They like orderliness.
18	Things are done with artistry––such as flower arranging and their tea ceremonies.
19	Most Japanese are associated with two religions, a combination of Buddhism and Shinto. However, there is no particular religious conviction. A Culturegram from Brigham Young University (BYU) says that "work is the religion of most".

Table 7.6   Cultural comparison of Japan with the United States

Cultural dimension	United States	Japan
Power distance	Relatively low	More mid-range
Individualism–collectivism	Extremely individualistic	More collectivistic
Uncertainty avoidance	Low	High
Masculinity (achievement versus quality of life)	Relatively high on the achievement scale	Extremely high
Long-term versus short-term	Short-term	Extremely long-term

Table 7.7   Analysis of a hypothetical introduction of action learning – U.S. culture to Japanese culture

	U.S. culture	Japanese culture
1	Each member of the action learning team to have their own problem/project to pursue that is of major significance to the company.	This approach is in direct conflict with the Japanese culture. They work in teams and groups, not as individuals. You should move the design in the direction of having all members of the team deal with a common problem they are to solve.
2	Team members to be picked by management and required to participate, as specified by the client organization.	Since the client organization wants it this way, you go with it. This design characteristic also fits with the Japanese cultural characteristic of obedience to higher authority. However, if you are working with multiple action learning teams that are to begin work at roughly the same time, you might encourage the client organization to examine the pool of planned participants, possibly with your assistance, in making team assignments that balance skills and backgrounds. You need to tread carefully here so as not to offend cultural sensitivities. At any sign of resistance, you should back off.
3	The team advisor/facilitator (U.S. practitioner) will be non-invasive, allowing the set to function, once it moves into the process, with limited interruptions and interference.	Don't assume automatically that you are to be the facilitator. The Japanese culture, while interactive (e.g., quality circles on assembly lines), is also a didactic one, and somewhat passive when it comes to instruction. They will expect the facilitator to provide structure and act with authority. Therefore, there will need to be more interventions and guidance provided.

Continued

able 7.7   Continued

U.S. culture	Japanese culture
The department head will serve as the sponsor, as specified by the client organization.	You obviously accept this situation, with the hope that the sponsor is at level that will allow the necessary decision-making on team recommendations. You can be fairly well assured that the Japanese management team will have this issue well covered.
The action learning team will be empowered to pursue solutions to the problem, and with the expectation of implementation if the team answers the need.	This is a very bad assumption in relation to the Japanese culture. The team can expect to have their recommendations heard and considered, but their recommendations then need to be run through the consensus process and the management hierarchy. It is likely that they will be modified, or perhaps even discarded. Therefore, the action learning team cannot be made to believe that their recommendations, if sound, will be implemented as presented. They would not believe it if you told them that anyway, because they are a product of their culture and readily appreciate that it is the not the way things are done.
Each team member must be an expert in the problem area involved, as specified by the client organization.	You do what the client wants, even if contrary to what you might view as an ideal state. If what you recommend runs counter to Japanese culture, it is going to be rejected. What they are asking for can be made to work and produce valuable learning.

Summary analysis

You are an outsider to the Japanese culture. You need to present your credentials. An important part of that is to demonstrate that you have a basic understanding of their culture and are humbly striving to demonstrate sensitivity to their values. Using that as an opening wedge, building a relationship with them of mutual trust, and demonstrating your competence, should gradually open up opportunities to influence what happens and have your voice heard. If you come in and give the impression that you have all the answers and anticipate that things will happen rapidly, you can be expect to be summarily rejected.

In the case of Japan, understanding the culture is not a "nice-to-have" preparatory step to practicing action learning there. It is essential that you make a real effort to learn their culture. It is a strong culture, as well as a complex one, and you cannot proceed to do things the way you do things in the United States. If you are clearly well-intended and obviously trying to meet them halfway, they will be warm and gracious hosts.

Conclusion

There is no fixed and absolute way to sort through cross-cultural differences. But you must start with the belief that cross-cultural differences really do matter, as our examples serve to highlight. There are tools and resources to help you along the way. A number of them are explained in this chapter and others in the section of this book on action learning resources and networks.

Culture covers a multitude of areas. You cannot simply read up on a country like Japan and consider the job done. You need to know much more than that, including as much as you can find out about the organization you will be entering and the corporate culture involved. *As a basic rule, get as close to the culture as you can, including interviews of the people that are a part of it.*

References

Adler, N. (1997) *International Dimensions of Organizational Behavior* (Cincinnati: South-Western College Publishing).

Argyris, C., Putnam, R., and McLain Smith, D. (1985) *Action Science: Concepts, methods, and skills for research and intervention* (San Francisco: Jossey-Bass).

Axwell, E. (ed.) (1993) *Do's and Taboos Around the World* (New York: Wiley).

Boshyk, Y. (ed.) (2002) *Action Learning Worldwide: Experiences of leadership and organizational development* (Basingstoke, U.K./New York: Palgrave Macmillan).

Boshyk, Y. (ed.) (2000) *Business Driven Action Learning: Global best practices* (Basingstoke, U.K./New York: Palgrave Macmillan).

Christie, P., Lessem, R., and Lovemore, B. (eds) (1994) *African Management: Philosophies, concepts, and applications* (Pretoria, South Africa: Knowledge Resources).

Christopher, R. C. (1983). *The Japanese Mind: Goliath explained* (New York: Linden Press/Simon & Schuster).

Chu, C. (1991). *The Asian Mind Game: Unlocking the hidden agenda of the business culture – A Westerner's survival manual* (New York: Rawson Associates).

Dilworth, R. and Willis, V. (2003) *Action Learning: Images and pathways* (Malabar, FL: Krieger).

Goode, E. *How Culture Molds Habits of Thought. New York Times*, August 6, 2000 in electronic form, accessed 11 November, 2009, http://www.nytimes.com/2000/08/08/science/how-culture-molds-habits-of-thought.html?scp=1&sq=how%20culture%20molds%20habits%20of%20thoguht&st=cse

Hampden-Turner, C. and Trompenaars, F. (1997) *Mastering the Infinite Game: How Asian values are transforming business* (London: Capstone).

Helmreich, R. L. and Merritt, A. C. (1998) *Culture at Work in Aviation and Medicine: National and professional influences* (Aldershot, England: Ashgate).

Hofstede, G. (2001) *Cultures Consequences: Comparing values, behaviors, institutions and organizations across nations* (Thousand Oaks, CA: Sage Publications).

Inglehardt, R., Basanez, M., and Moreno, A. (1998). *Human Values and Beliefs: A cross-cultural sourcebook* (Ann Arbor, MI: University of Michigan Press).

Marquardt, M. (1999). *Action Learning in Action* (Palo Alto, CA: Davies-Black Publishing).

Mbigi, L. and Maree, J. (1995) *Ubuntu: The spirit of African transformational management* (Pretoria, South Africa: Knowledge Resources).

Morrison, T. and Conaway, W.A. (2006) *Kiss, Bow or Shake Hands: The best-selling guide to how to do business in sixty countries* (Avon, MA: Adams Media Corporation).

Musashi, M. (1982) *A Book of Five Rings: The classic guide to strategy* (Woodstock, NY: Overlook Press).

Pachter, B. and Brody, M. (1995) *Complete Business Etiquette Handbook* (Englewood Cliffs, NJ: Prentice-Hall).

Pedler, M. (ed.) (1991). *Action Learning in Practice*, 2nd edn (Aldershot: Gower).

Revans, R. (1982) *The Origins and Growth of Action Learning* (Bromley: Chartwell-Bratt).

Revans, R. (1980) *Action Learning: New techniques for management* (London: Blond & Briggs).

Sasaki, N. (1981) *Management and Industrial Structure in Japan* (London: Pergamon).

Schein, E. (1997) *Three Cultures of Management: The key to organizational learning in the 21st century* (Cambridge, MA: MIT Sloan School of Management).

Schein, E. (1992). *Organizational Culture and Leadership*, 2nd edn (San Francisco: Jossey-Bass).

Tichy, N. and Sherman, S. (1993) *Control Your Own Destiny or Someone Else Will* (New York: Currency).

Trompenaars, F. (1993) *Riding the Waves of Culture: Understanding cultural diversity in business* (London: Economist).

Weisbord, R. M. (2004). *Productive Workplaces Revisited* (San Francisco: Jossey-Bass).

Witkin, H. and Goodenough, D. R. (1981) *Cognitive Styles: Essence and origins – field dependence and field independence*, *Psychological Issues* Monograph 51 (New York: International Universities Press).

8
Action Learning Today: Resources, Networks, and Communities of Practice

Compiled by Yury Boshyk and Robert L. Dilworth

Publications by Reg Revans

We have tried to make this the most comprehensive bibliography of Revans' publications to date. Its foundation is the work of Lucinda Gibson-Myers and Verna J. Willis, who electronically catalogued the publications from the Revans collection and went to considerable effort to ensure its accuracy. We have also tried to integrate other sources such as the Revans Archive and the International Foundation for Action Learning listing.

The International Foundation for Action Learning (IFAL) also has an extensive listing on Revans' publications but the list is not precise or sufficiently detailed for researchers. See also the Revans' bibliography in 1983, *ABC of Action Learning*, 79–83; and the Revans archive listing, especially RWR 3 [3].

This bibliography is organized chronologically and can be used in coordination with Chapter 6 in this volume, where the reader will find further details about certain publications.

Revans, R. W. (1933) "The Transmission of Waves through an Ionized Gas", *Physical Review*, 44: pp. 798–802.
[*Note*: Based on his research work at the University of Michigan 1930–32. See the commentary on this research in Chapter 6 of this volume, by Professor Donald Sadoway, M.I.T.]
Revans, R. W. (1938) "The Entry of Girls into the Nursing Profession: A memorandum to the Essex Education Committee, 1938". Reprinted in R. W. Revans (1982), *The Origins and Growth of Action Learning* (Bromley, U.K.: Chartwell-Bratt), pp. 23–9.

Revans, R. W. (1945) "Elegy to the Second World War" (Poem), in A. E. Barker and R. W. Revans (eds.) (2004), *An Introduction to Genuine Action Learning* (Oradea, Romania: Oradea University Press), pp. 40–3.
[*Note*: See also Chapter 3.]

Revans, R. W. (1945) "Plans for Recruitment, Education and Training in the Coal Mining Industry". Prepared by R. W. Revans in conjunction with The Recruitment, Education and Training Committee of the Mining Association of Great Britain. s.l.
[*Note*: See also Chapter 6.]

Revans, R. W. (1947) "The Training of Under Officials", Abstract of a paper read before the Manchester Geological and Mining Society in Manchester on 20 February, 1947. Printed in *The Colliery Guardian*, 174(4497): pp.330–4.
[*Note*: The topic is also covered in Revans, 1945.]

Revans, R. W. (1949) "The First 'W. M. Thornton Lecture': The status of the professional association, past and present". Speech given at the Association of Mining Electrical and Mechanical Engineers Annual Convention, London, 29 June, 1949, *The Mining Electrical and Mechanical Engineer: Journal of the Association of Mining Electrical and Mechanical Engineers*, 30 (347), pp. 41–53.

Revans, R. W. (1950) "Why We Held Our Conference", in *The Education Of The Young Worker*. Report of the Second Conference held at Oxford in July 1949 under the auspices of the University Department of Education, 9–13 (Oxford: Oxford University).

Revans, R. W. (1951) "Education in Industry", in C. H. Dobinson (ed.), *Education in a Changing World* (Oxford: Clarendon Press), pp. 18–33.

Revans, R. W. (1953) *Size and Morale: A preliminary study of attendance at work in large and small units* (London: Acton Society Trust).

Revans, R. W. (1956) "Industrial Morale and Size of Unit", *Political Quarterly*, 27(3), pp. 303–10.
[*Note*: Subsequently republished in *Labor and Trade Unionism: An interdisciplinary reader*(1960) W. Galenson and S. M. Lipset (eds.) (New York: John Wiley & Sons), pp. 295–300.]

Revans, R. W. (1957) "Staff Turnover – Its causes and remedies?", in "Programme and papers for the conference on hospital authorities and staff management", Royal Empire Society, 20–22 May, 1957.

Revans, R. W. (1957) "How Much Can – Or Should – A Man Sell?", *Agenda*, 5(3), pp. 33–40.
[*Note*: *Republished in Revans, 1982,* The Origins*: 82–94.*]

Revans, R. W. (1957) "The Contribution of the University to Management Education", *British Management Review*, 15(1), January, pp. 31–7.
[*Note*: Republished in Revans, 1982, *The Origins*, pp. 56–63.]

Revans, R. W. (1958) "The Sister and The Hospital System: Proposed study of her work and opinions", *Nursing Mirror*, 25 April, pp. 261–2.
[*Note*: *This is a weekly periodical.*]

Revans, R. W. (1958) "Theory and Practice: A study of technical knowledge", *Researches and Studies*, University of Leeds Institute of Education, 18, July.

Revans, R. W. (1958) "Is Work Worthwhile?, *Personnel Management*, 40(343), March, pp. 12–21.
[*Note*: Republished in Revans, 1982, *The Origins*, pp. 111–22.]

Revans, R. W. (1958) "Hospital Work Study Course at Manchester College of Science and Technology", *The Hospital*, 54(9), September, pp. 659–63.

Revans, R. W. (1958) "Human Relations, Management and Size", in E. M. Hugh-Jones (ed.), *Human Relations and Modern Management* (Amsterdam: North Holland Publishing Company), pp. 177–220.

Revans, R. W. (1959) "Operational Research and Personnel Management, Part 2", Institute of Personnel Management, Occasional Papers, 14, Part 2 (London: Institute of Personnel Management), (25 pages).

[*Note*: Part 1 was written by Stafford Beer.]

Revans, R. W. (1960) "The Hospital as an Organism: A study in communications and morale", in C. W. Churchman and M. Verhulst (eds.), *Management Sciences: Models and techniques, Volume 2, Proceedings of the Sixth International Meeting of The Institute of Management Sciences*, Conservatoire National [sic] des Arts [sic] and Métiers. Paris, 7–11 September, 1959. Pergamon Press: 17–24.

[*Note*: Republished in Revans, 1982. *The Origins*, pp. 123–32.]

Revans, R. W. (1960) "Can Management be Scientific?", *British Chemical Engineering*, 5(4), April, pp. 260–3.

[*Note*: See Revans, 1982."Management and the Scientific Method" republished in *The Origins*, pp. 95–110.]

Revans, R. W. (1960) "How Should a Hospital Be Judged?". Speech given at the Tenth Annual Conference of Chief Financial Officers in the Hospital Service in England and Wales on 10–11 November, 1960, and printed in *Hospital Service Finance*, 9(3), November–December, pp. 34–63.

[*Note*: This is a different speech from that with a similar name given in 1961.]

Revans, R. W. (1961) "How Should Hospitals Be Judged?", in Association of Hospital Management Committees Report of Annual General Meeting and Conference held at Southsea on 15 and 16 June, 1961, pp. 54–68.

[*Note*: This is a different speech from that with a similar name given in 1960.]

Revans, R. W. (1961) *The Measurement of Supervisory Attitudes* (Manchester: Manchester Statistical Society).

[*Note*: An extract from this address to the Society can be found in *The Lancet*, 1961, p. 1377.]

Revans, R. W. (1961) "What Management Expects of The Internal Auditor", *Internal Auditor*, 18(4), Winter, pp. 38–54.

[*Note*: Republished in Revans, 1982, *The Origins*, pp. 133–50.]

Revans, R. W. (1962) "The Hospital as a Human System", *Physics in Medicine and Biology*, 7, October.

[*Note*: This article was later republished in *Behavioral Science*, see 1990.]

Revans, R. W. (1962) "Hospital Attitudes and Communications", in Paul Halmos (ed.), *The Sociological Review Monograph*, 5, July, *Sociology and Medicine – Studies Within the Framework of the British National Health Service*. (Keele: University of Keele), pp. 117–44.

[*Note*: Revans, in addition to the degrees of B.Sc., Ph.D., is also credited with a M.Sc.Tech.) Master of Science (Technology), and M.I.Min.E. (as a Chartered Mining Engineer, from the Institute of Mining Engineers), also as Professor of Industrial Administration, The Manchester College of Science and Technology. The editor's preface to this monograph is of interest: "Hospitals have been the most accessible and inviting subjects of socio-medical investigation. As Professor Revans puts it in his outspoken and penetrating essay, the hospital service offers exceptional opportunities for clarifying some of the concepts of sociology: he could have added that sociological study, by exposing failures in communication and other defects, can point the way to continuous improvements in the service. Professor Revans' essay is an effective rejoinder to those who protest that sociological inquiries commonly display the obvious clothed in jargon. It is also instructive, if somewhat provocative guide to the theoretical and practical issues which have to be faced not only by those who administer hospitals but also by those who work professionally in them."]

Revans, R. W. (1962) "Industry and Technical Education", in A. M. Kean (ed.), *Researches and Studies*, 24, (Leeds, England: University of Leeds, Institute of Education), October, pp. 7–18.

[*Note*: Republished in Revans, 1982, *The Origins*, pp. 166–80.]

Revans, R. W. (1962) "Myths of Decentralization", *New Society*, 1(10), 6 December, pp. 17–19.

[*Note*: Republished in Revans, 1982, *The Origins*, pp. 181–9.]

Revans, R. W. (1962) "The Theory of Practice", *Universities Quarterly*, September.

[*Note*: Republished in *The Theory of Practice in Management*, 1966, pp. 53–69; and republished in Revans, 1982, *The Origins*, pp. 151–65 under the title "The Education of Managers".]

Revans, R. W. (1962) "Preface", in R. W. Rowbottom and H. A. Greenwood, *Understanding Management* (Manchester: Whitworth Press), pp. 9–11.

[*Note*: Writes of "the world of management being a vast tapestry of contradictions"; the importance of scientific research for management, and scientific method but integrating this with the "valid experience and practical wisdom of the business man"; management is about change and this takes a long time to carry out because fundamental questions have to be asked; also the oft repeated statement by Revans (paraphrasing Nietzsche he states) that no good idea "was ever adopted before it was ridiculed".]

Revans, R. W. (1962) "Preface", in D. N. Chorafas (ed.), *Programming Systems for Electronic Computers* (London: Butterworths), pp. vii–ix.

[*Note*: This book is dedicated to Reg Revans.]

Revans, R. W. (1963) "Communications as an Aid to Accident Prevention", Speech given at the Fifth National Safety Conference, Great Western Royal Hotel, London, 5–6 November, 1963, and published in *Proceedings. National Joint Industrial Council (N.J.I.C.) for the Rubber Manufacturing Industry*, pp. 81–100.

Revans, R. W. (1963) "Management, Morale and Productivity", in *Proceedings of the National Industrial Safety Conference*, The Spa, Scarborough, 2–5 May, 1963. Conference organized by the Industrial Safety Division of RoSPA (The Royal Society for the Prevention of Accidents), pp. 84–99.

Revans, R. W. (1963) "Where Professional Minds Meet", *Times Review of Industry and Technology*, 1(6), August, pp. 19–20.

Revans, R. W. (1964) *Standards for Morale: Causes and effect in hospitals* (London: Oxford University Press for the Nuffield Provincial Hospitals Trust).

[*Note*: Foreword by Lord Robert Platt.]

Revans, R. W. (1964) "The Morale and Effectiveness of General Hospitals", in Gordon McLachlan (ed.), *Problems and Progress in Medical Care: Essays on current research* (Published for the Nuffield Provincial Hospitals Trust by Oxford University Press).

[*Note*: This article is very similar, but not exact, to that of the same title in *New Society*, 68, pp. 6–8. No volume number; and the editor also published with John Revans, Reg Revans' brother.]

Revans, R. W. (1964) "The Pathology of Automation", *Advanced Management Journal*, Special Issue on Automation and Management, 29(2), April, pp. 12–21.

Revans, R. W. (1964) "Spotting a Company's Weak Points – I", *Accountants' Magazine*, 68(701), November, pp. 851–65.

Revans, R. W. (1964) "Spotting a Company's Weak Points – II", *Accountants' Magazine*, 68(702), December, pp. 968–76.

[*Note*: Not a duplicate, second part.]

Revans, R. W. (1964) "Morale and Effectiveness of Hospitals", *New Society*, 68, 16 January, pp. 6–8.

[*Note*: This article is very similar, but not exact, to that of the same title in Gordon McLachlan (ed.), 1964, *Problems and Progress in Medical Care: Essays on current research* (Published for the Nuffield Provincial Hospitals Trust by Oxford University Press.)]

Revans, R. W. (1964) "Hospital Cadet Schemes – A study in the Manchester region", *International Journal of Nursing Studies*, 1(2), May, pp. 65–74.

Revans, R. W. (1964) "The Design of Management Courses", *Management International*.

[*Note*: Republished in Revans, 1966, *The Theory of Practice in Management*, pp. 29–52.]

Revans, R. W. (1965) *The Development of Research into Management and Its Problems* (London: British Institute of Management).

[*Note*: Prepared for the BIM National Conference in Brighton, March, 1965; republished in Revans, 1966, *The Theory of Practice in Management*, pp. 152–67.]

Revans, R. W. (1965) *Science and the Manager* (London: Macdonald & Co).

[*Note*: See Chapter 6 for further details.]

Revans, R. W. (1965) *Measurement for Management* (London: Industrial and Commercial Techniques).

[*Note*: Reproduced from typescript.]

Revans, R. W. (1965) "Our Educational System and the Development of Qualified Personnel", *Management International*, 2(3), pp. 41–50.

Revans, R. W. (1965) "Involvement in School", *New Society*, 26 August, 6.

[*Note*: Republished in Revans, 1982, *The Origins*, pp. 217–25.]

Revans, R. W. (1965) "Bureaucracy in the Hospital Service", *Scientific Business*, 2(8), pp. 386–92.

Revans, R. W. (1965) "Managers, Men and the Art of Listening", *New Society*, 5(123), pp. 13–15.

[*Note*: This is virtually the same as the book chapter of the same name in S. H. Foulkes and G. S. Prince (eds.), 1969, *Psychiatry in a Changing Society*, pp. 93–8 (London: Tavistock Publications). Also republished in Revans, 1982, *The Origins*, pp. 210–25.]

Revans, R. W. (1966) *The Theory of Practice in Management* (London: Macdonald).

[*Note*: See Chapter 6 for further details.]

Revans, R. W. (1966) *What Makes You A Good Boss?: The effect of personality and leadership upon morale and efficiency* (London: Industrial and Commercial Techniques).

Revans, R. W. (1966) "Research into Hospital Management and Organization", *Milibank Memorial Fund Quarterly,* 44(3), part 2, pp. 207–45.

Revans, R. W. (1967) "Some Thoughts on Training in Managerial Action", CORSI Bulletin (Calcutta Branch of Operational Research Society of India) Annual, pp. 107–10.

Revans, R. W. (1967) "Recognizing and Solving Management Problems", *Journal of the Malaysian Institute of Management,* 2(1), July, pp. 8–18.

[*Note*: More extensive article than one with same title in *Management Decision,* 1(4), 1967.]

Revans, R. W. (1967, October 5) "Big Firms: The managerial gap", *New Society,* 10 (262), pp. 468–9.

[*Note*: See also Revans, 1982, *The Origins*, pp. 190–9, "Bigness and Change".]

Revans, R. W. (1967) "The Management Apprentice", *Management Decision,* 1(4), Winter, pp. 52–7.

[*Note*: On management education and universities; less detailed than one with same title in *Management International Review,* 1968.]

Revans, R. W. (1967) "Europe's Academic Supermarkets", *Management Today,* pp. 84–8.

Revans, R. W. (1967) *Studies in Institutional Learning* (Brussels: European Association of Management Training Centres).

Revans, R. W. (1968) "Management in an Automated Industry", *Journal of Dyers and Colourists,* 84, February.

Revans, R. W. (1968) "The Management Apprentice", *Management International Review,* 6, pp. 29–42.

[*Note*: More detailed than one with same title in *Management Decision,* 1967.]

Revans, R. W. (1968) "The Bible as Appointed to be read by Industry", *New Society,* 11(276), 11 January, pp. 43–6.

[*Note*: Republished in Revans, 1982, *The Origins*, pp. 200–9.]

Revans, R. W. (1969) "Managers, Men, and the Art of Listening", in S. H. Foulkes and G. S. Prince (eds.), *Psychiatry in a Changing Society* (London: Tavistock), pp. 93–8.

[*Note*: This is virtually the same article as that of same title in *New Society,* 5(156), 1965, except for the addition of introductory and final paragraphs in the other; republished in *The Origins*, pp. 210–16.]

Revans, R. W. (1969) "Alienation and Resistance to Change", *Management Decision,* 3(1), Spring, pp. 10–14.

[*Note*: See Revans, 1982, *The Origins*, pp. 303–19, under the title, "Alienation and Resistance".]

Revans, R. W. (1969) "The Structure of Disorder", in J. Rose (ed.), *A Survey of Cybernetics: A tribute to Norbert Wiener* (London: Illife), pp. 331–45.

[*Note*: Revans was very much engaged with the study of cybernetics and its leading figures, among them Stafford Beer (1926–2002), who was greatly involved in the field of management cybernetics and operational research.]

Revans, R. W. (1970) "Managers as Catalysts", *Personnel Management,* 2(10), pp. 28–32.

Revans, R. W. (1970) "The Managerial Alphabet", in G. Heald (ed.), *Approaches to the Study of Organizational Behaviour: Operational research and the behavioural sciences* (London: Tavistock Publications), pp. 141–61.
[*Note*: Revans' formulation of "Alpha, Beta, Gamma" Systems for a discussion about values and purpose, managerial decision-making and problem-solving, and personal development; also in Revans, 1982, *The Origins*, pp. 329–48.]
Revans, R. W. (1970) "Values and Enterprise as a Subject for Research", in M. Ivens (ed.), *Industry and Values: The objectives and responsibilities of business* (London: George G. Harrap), pp. 191–200.
[*Note*: Republished in Revans, 1982, *The Origins*, pp. 320–8.]
Revans, R. W. (1971) *Developing Effective Managers: A new approach to business education* (New York: Praeger).
[*Note*: Published in London, in 1971 by Longman. Description and analysis of Revans-designed and implemented Inter-University Advanced Management Program in Belgium, 1968–71, including the theory behind the experience, further developed from 1970, "The Managerial Alphabet".]
Revans, R. W. (1971) "Introduction [Background to the HIC Project]", in George Wieland (ed.), *Changing Hospitals: A Report on the Hospital Internal Communications Project*. (London: Tavistock Publications), pp. 3–24.
[*Note*: Highly recommended as it contains Revans ideas on what he already called the "learning organization", "change agents" and assumptions behind his thinking.]
Revans, R. W. (1971) "Anatomy of Achievement: Opening address to the 1971 Annual Conference of the Operational Research Society" (University of Lancaster. London: Operational Research Society).
Revans, R. W. (ed.) (1972) *Hospitals: Communication, choice and change. The Hospital Internal Communications Project Seen from Within*, Foreword by W. J. H. Butterfield (London: Tavistock).
Revans, R. W. and Ashmawy, S. (1972) "The Nile Project: An experiment in educational authotherapy". A monograph upon which the Fondation Industrie-Université contribution to the 1972 ATM [Association of Teachers of Management] Conference was based. Paris: The Development Centre, Organisation for Economic Co-operation and Development (OECD).
[*Note*: Ashmawy was the lead author and a former student of Revans', and the latter was a technical advisor to the 1971 project; republished in Revans, 1982, *The Origins*, pp. 372–425; also published, it seems, in 1973 as *The Nile Project: An experiment in educational autotherapy* (Southport: Action Learning Projects International.)]
Revans, R. W. (1972) (ed.) "The Emerging Attitudes and Motivations of Workers", Report on a management experts' meeting, Paris, 24–26 May, 1971. Labor/Management Program, Organization for Economic Cooperation and Development (OECD), Manpower and Social Affairs Directorate, Paris, France.
Revans, R. W. (1972) Action Learning – A management development program. *Personnel Review*, 1, Autumn, 4, pp. 36–44.
[*Note*: First time "action learning" as a term used by Revans in a publication; about the Egyptian "Nile" project and the Belgian experience, but more conceptual in nature by reflecting on these experiences; mention is made of a

book by Revans, *Childhood and Maturity* supposedly published in 1973 in London by Routledge but we could not find any further reference or copy. Was this perhaps Revans' unpublished memoir entitled, "Culture M"?; also listed as part 1 published by the International Foundation for Action Learning in 1973 but not found in our search.]

Revans, R. W. and Baquer, A. (1972, gestetnered) "I thought they were supposed to be doing that": A comparative study of co-ordination of services for the mentally handicapped in seven local authorities, June 1969 to September 1972. London: The Hospital Centre.

Revans, R. W. (1973) *Studies in Factory Communications* (Southport: Action Learning Projects International).

Revans, R. W. (1973) "The Response of the Manager to Change", *Management Education and Development*, 4(Part 2), pp. 61–76.

[*Note*: Very good explication of Revans' main ideas about learning, and action learning mentioned as well; mentions his father and his receptivity to learning.]

Revans, R. W. and Cortazzi, D. (1973) "Psychosocial Factors in Hospitals and Nurse Staffing", *International Journal of Nursing Studies*, 10(3), August, pp. 149–60.

Revans, R. W. and Baquer, A. Q. (1973) *"But Surely, That Is Their Job?": A study in practical cooperation through action learning* (Southport: Action Learning Projects International).

[*Note*: Baquer was the lead author and main researcher on this study on mental health care in the U.K.; apparently the study Revans felt most proud of up to 1972.]

Revans, R. W. (1974) *Participation in What?* (Southport: Action Learning Projects International).

Revans, R. W. (1974) "The Project Method: Learning by doing," in S. Mailick (ed.), *The Making of the Manager: A world view* (Garden City, NY: The United Nations Institute for Training and Research (UNITAR) and Anchor Press/Doubleday), pp. 132–61.

[*Note*: Contains an interesting description of Revans' work as a consultant in Nigeria, also on work with London hospitals, the Milwaukee Consortium, and mostly on the Belgian experience. This is an excellent collection of articles on the field of management education at this time. For background on the rise of business schools in the United Kingdom, see, for example, the article by John Morris.]

Revans, R. W. (1975) *General Principles of Action Learning* (Southport: Action Learning Projects International).

Revans, R. W. (1975) "Helping Each Other to Help the Helpless: An essay in self-organization, (Part I)", *Kybernetes*, 4, pp. 149–55.

[*Note*: Republished in Revans, 1982, *The Origins*, pp. 467–92.]

Revans, R. W. (1975) "Helping Each Other To Help the Helpless: An essay in self-organization, (Part II)", *Kybernetes*, 4, pp. 205–11.

[*Note*: Revans listed as being part of the Interuniversity College for Doctoral Studies in Management Sciences, Brussels. Part I appeared in the previous issue of the journal. "This essay, published in two parts, describes coordination in the British domiciliary services for the mentally handicapped, as seen by families helped and by field workers helping. Criteria of need and judgments of effectiveness are those of patients and field workers. Bias is minimised by the experimental design since five independent professions and parents interact between seven different areas over a sample of 212 cases. Part I suggests why and how this autonomous or self-study was made; Part II presents some findings and tells what was done about them". From the editor.]

Revans, R. W. (1975) "Preface", in D. Cortazzi and S. Roote, *Illuminative Incident Analysis*. (London: McGraw-Hill), pp. xi–xii.

[*Note*: The book is dedicated to Revans, and describes what would be called today "graphic capture".]

Revans, R. W., (ed.) (1976) *Action Learning in Hospitals: Diagnosis and therapy* (London: McGraw-Hill).

[*Note*: Part 1 of this book includes the republication of Revans' 1964 book, *Standards for Morale*; contains articles mostly about the London Hospital Internal Communications Project.]

Revans, R. W. (1976) "Progenitors and Progenies – Before and since the HIC project", in R. W. Revans, (ed.), *Action Learning in Hospitals: Diagnosis and therapy* (London: McGraw-Hill), pp. 169–80.

[*Note*: An important chapter tracing the chronology and evolution of Revans' eight major projects in all fields, not just in health care, up to that time.]

Revans, R. W. (1976) "Action Learning in a Developing Country", *Journal of the Malaysian Institute of Management*, 11(3), December, pp. 8–16.

Revans, R. W. (1976) "Management Education: Time for a rethink", *Personnel Management*, 8(7), July, pp. 20–4.

Revans, R. W. (1977) "An Action Learning Trust", *Journal of European Industrial Training*, 1(1), pp. 2–5.

[*Note*: Dated October, 1977; see Chapter 6 for further details.]

Revans, R. W. (1977) "Action Learning and the Nature of Knowledge", *Education and Training*, 19(10), November–December, pp. 318–22.

[*Note*: Republished in Revans, 1982, *The Origins*, pp. 652–64.]

Revans, R. W. (1977) "Action Learning: Its silver jubilee, 1952–1977: Inaugural Lecture", s.l. Yorkshire and Humberside Regional Management Centre.

Revans, R. W. (1977) "Action Learning: The business of learning about business", in D. Casey and D. Pearce, (eds.), *More than Management Mevelopment: Action learning at GEC* (Westmead, U.K.: Amacom), pp. 3–6.

[*Note*: A very comprehensive and valuable compilation including that of participants in the program that had its start in 1971 but its formal launch in 1972 in the General Electric Company, U.K. – no relation to General Electric in the U.S., see Chapter 6).]

Revans, R. W. (1977) "Hospital Performance and Length of Patient Stay", s.l.. Action Learning Trust.

Revans, R. W. (1978) "Action Learning and the Nature of Learning", *Education and Training*, January, pp. 8–11.

[*Note*: More on the theoretical thinking behind action learning; on the "mentally handicapped" project.]

Revans, R. W. (1978) "Action Learning – Or antiquity reborn", *Education and Training*, 20(4), April, pp. 121–4.

[*Note*: See Revans, 1982, *The Origins*, pp. 529–45, "The Immemorial Precursor: Action Learning Past and Present, on Buddha as the first action learner".]

Revans, R. W. (1978) "Fondation Industrie-Université: On the establishment of a Master's Programme in management studies", Paper from Irish Management Institute, Action Learning Workshop, May, 1978.

[*Note*: Location not given; republished in Revans, *The Origins*, pp. 455–66.]

Revans, R. W. (1978) "A Quest for Realism", *Education & Training*, 20(6), June, pp. 167–8.

Revans, R. W. (1978) "Action Learning Takes a Health Cure", *Education and Training*, November–December, pp. 295–9.

[*Note*: On the HIC Project, the international spread of action learning; and, action learning and worker participation.]

Revans, R. W. (1978) *The ABC of Action Learning: A Review of 25 Years of Experience*. Altrincham (8 Higher Downs, Greater Manchester): R. W. Revans.

[*Note*: Self-published 1st edn, apparently.]

Revans, R. W. (1978) *ABC of Action Learning* (London: Action Learning Trust).

[*Note*: 2nd edn; another source provides bibliographical details as having been published in Birmingham by F. H. Wakelin.]

Revans, R. W. (1979) "The Nature of Action Learning", *Management Education and Development*, 10(Part 1), Spring, pp. 3–23.

[*Note*: Republished in 1981, see below; and in Revans, 1982, *The Origins*, pp. 624–51.]

Revans, R. W. (1980) *Action Learning: New techniques for management* (London: Blond & Briggs).

[*Note*: See Chapter 6 for further details.]

Revans, R. W. (1980) "Productivity and Action Learning", Newsletter, 6. The Action Learning Trust, p. 3.

Revans, R. W. (1981) *Action Learning–att lära under risktagande och med ansvar i anslutning till handlingar* (Lund: Studentlitteratur).

[*Note*: 1st edn of four in Swedish of this work.]

Revans, R. W. (1981) "The Nature of Action Learning", *OMEGA: The International Journal of Management Science*, 9(1), pp. 9–24.

[*Note*: Republished from Revans, 1979, same title.]

Revans, R. W. (1981) "Management, Productivity and Risk – The way ahead", *OMEGA*, 9(2), pp. 127–41.

Revans, R. W. (1981) "Worker Participation as Action Learning: A note", *Economic and Industrial Democracy*, 2(4), pp. 521–41.

[*Note*: Republished in Revans, 1982, *The Origins*, pp. 546–65.]

Revans, R. W. (1981) "The Quest for Economic Leadership", *Management Education and Development*, 12(2), pp.102–12.

Revans. R. W. (1981) *Education for Change and Survival*. s.l.: IFAL.

Revans, R. W. (1982) *The Origins and Growth of Action Learning* (Bromley: Chartwell-Bratt).

[*Note*: See Chapter 6.]

Revans, R. W. (1982) "Action Learning and the Inner City: The lessons of Moss Side", *The Link 1982, Froebel Bicentenary edn* (London: Froebel Educational institute), pp. 40–4.

Revans, R. W. (1982) "What is Action Learning?", *Journal of Management Development*, 1(3), pp. 64–75.

Revans, R. W. (1982) "Action Learning: Its origins and nature", *Higher Education Review*, 15(1), Autumn, pp. 20–8.

Revans, R. W. (1982,) "Insufficient Education", Letter to the editor, *Management Today,* Book Review section: The Last Word on Action Learning, November.

Revans, R. W. (1982) "Management Skills and Abilities", in R. Wild (editor and compiler), *How to Manage: 123 world experts analyse the art of management* (London: Heinemann), pp. 39–43. [Note: Among other things Revans' discusses what he calls the "virtues of ignorance" and "the idolization of obsolescent technique".]

Revans, R. W. (1983) *The ABC of Action Learning* (Bromley: Chartwell-Bratt).

[*Note*: Perhaps the 3rd edn of this work from 1978; very good bibliography and republished in Reddy and Barker (eds.), 2005, pp. 11–20.]

Revans, R. W. (1983) ABC om Action Learning. Att lära under risktagande och med ansvar i anslutning till sina handlingar. Introduktion och efterord av Lennart Strandler (Översättning: Stig Andersson. Lund: Utbildningshuset).

[*Note*: 2nd edn (see 1981 for the 1st edn); translated from the 1978 edn, copyright by Revans, *The ABC of Action Learning: 25 years of action learning.* Contains an announcement that an Action Learning Society was formed in 1982 in Lund. Foreward to the Swedish edn by Lars O. Andersson, MiL, (Managementprogrammet i Lund). See Chapter 6 for further details.]

Revans, R. W. (1983) *L'ABC dell' "imparare facendo": non ci può essere apprendimento senza azione e neppure azione senza apprendimento* (Torino : Isper Edizioni).

[*Note*: English translation reads: The ABC of 'learning by doing': there can be no learning without action and no action without learning.]

Revans, R. W. (1983) *Studies in Action Learning* (Altrincham, 18 Higher Downs, Greater Manchester).

[*Note*: Revans self-published.]

Revans, R. W. (1983) "Action Learning: Its terms and character", *Management Decision,* 21(1), pp. 39–50.

[*Note*: Part of a series on the six stages of action learning projects and issues related to these stages; reprinted in Revans, R. W. (1984) *The Sequence of Managerial Achievement* (Bradford, England: MCB University Press).]

Revans, R. W. (1983) "Action Learning: The skills of diagnosis", *Management Decision,* 21(2), pp. 47–52.

[*Note*: Reprinted in Revans, R. W. (1984) *The Sequence of Managerial Achievement* (Bradford, England: MCB University Press).]

Revans, R. W. (1983) "Action Learning: The forces of achievement, or getting it done", *Management Decision,* 21(3), pp. 44–54.

[*Note*: Reprinted in Revans, R. W. (1984) *The Sequence of Managerial Achievement* (Bradford, England: MCB University Press).]

Revans, R. W. (1983) "Action Learning: The cure is started (at West Middlesex Hospital, Britain)", *Management Decision,* 21(4), pp. 11–16.

[*Note*: Reprinted in Revans, R. W. (1984) *The Sequence of Managerial Achievement* (Bradford, England: MCB University Press).]

Revans, R. W. (1983) "Action Learning: Kindling the touch paper", *Management Decision,* 21(6), pp. 3–10.

[*Note*: Part of a series on the six stages of action learning projects and issues related to these stages in this article about the role of senior executives; reprinted in Revans, R. W., 1984, *The Sequence of Managerial Achievement* (Bradford, England: MCB University Press).]

Revans, R. W. (1983) "'Ex Cathedra:' The validation of action learning programmes", *Management Education and Development*, 14(3), pp. 208–11.

Revans, R. W. (1983) "On the Paradox of Genuine Learning", in International Cerebral Palsy Society (ICPS) Bulletin, 29 September. Paper given at ICPS meeting entitled "What Happens Next? – Secondary Education and the Handicapped" (held at Sidney Sussex College, Cambridge, April, 1983. London: ICPS).

[*Note*: Editors' note says: Revans gave final paper without notes and was subsequently asked by the Editor to contribute to this edition of the bulletin. Much of what he said is contained in this paper, which also contains some additional material and is dated 29 September 1983.]

Revans, R. W. (1983) "The Validation of Action Learning Programs: Excerpts from a note by professor R. W. Revans", *Management Action*, 3, Autumn, pp. 3–4.

Revans, R. W. (1983) "What Mr. Butler Said", *Management Action*, 3, Autumn, pp. 4–5.

Revans, R. W. (1983) "Productivity is Not Enough", *Management Action*, 3, Autumn, p. 1.

Revans, R. W. (1983) "Action Learning at Work and in School – Part 1", *Education and Training*, 25(9), October, pp. 285–8.

Revans, R. W. (1983) "Action Learning at Work and in School – Part 2", *Education and Training*, 25(10), November–December, pp. 291–5.

Revans, R. W. (1983) "Action Learning Projects", in B. Taylor and G. Lippitt (eds.), *Management Development and Training Handbook* (London: McGraw-Hill Book Company (UK) Limited), pp. 266–79.

[*Note*: The essentials of Learning and students, the Belgian experience, key factors in designing an action learning program, the Nile experience in appendix and in the second appendix by Ronnie Lessem, on an action learning program with City University and other partners.]

Revans, R. W. (1983) "What is Action Learning?", *Journal of Management Development*, 1, pp. 64–75.

Revans, R. W. (1984) *The Universality of Action Learning*. s.l.: IFAL.

Revans, R. W. (1984) "Action Learning: Are we getting there?", *Management Decision*, 22(1), pp. 45–52.

Revans, R. W. (1984) *The Sequence of Managerial Achievement* (Bradford, England: MCB University Press).

[*Note*: Republished articles for the most part from the journal, Management Decision; the chapter listings include: Action Learning: Half a Lifetime Spent; [Action Learning] Its Terms and Character; The skills of Diagnosis; A Case Example [Foster Wheeler]; The Forces of Achievement, or Getting It Done; The Cure is Started; Kindling the Touch Paper; Are We Getting There?; Back to Square One.]

Revans, R. W. (1984) "On the Learning Equation in 1984", *Management Education and Development*, 15(3), pp. 209–20.

Revans, R. W. (1984) *Action Learning Past and Present*. s.l.: IFAL.

Revans, R. W. (1984) *Aksjons-Laeringens ABC* (Oslo: Bedriftsokonomens Forlag).

Revans, R. W. (1984) *Revans on Video* (Bradford: MCB University Press).

Revans, R. W. (1985) "Action Learning: An international contrast", *Business Education*, 6(3).

246   *Yury Boshyk and Robert L. Dilworth*

Revans, R. W. (1985) "Any More Unmeeting Twains?: Or Action Learning and its practitioners in the 1980s", *Industrial and Commercial Training*, 17(5), September–October, pp. 8–11.

Revans, R. W. (1985) "Action Learning and Its 'Practitioners' in the 1980s", IMD 85. *International Management Development*. Brussels: European Foundation for Management Development (EFMD), Winter, pp. 2–6.

Revans, R. W. (1985) *Confirming Cases* (Telford: Revans Action Learning International).

[*Note*: Republished in A. Barker and R. W. Revans, 2004, *Introduction to Genuine Action Learning*, (Oradea, Romania: Oradea University Press), pp. 267–318.]

Revans, R. W. (1986) *Action Learning, Past and Future* (Bekkestua: Bedriftsokonomisk Institut).

Revans, R. W. (1986) *Action Learning, Past and Future* (Bekkestua: Bedriftsokonomisk Institut), Report 2.

Revans, R. W. (1986) *Action Learning, Past and Future: Belgium and the Scandinavians* (Bekkestua: Bedriftsokonomisk Institut), Report 3.

Revans, R. W. (1986) "Action Learning Returns Home", University of Manchester, Institute for Development Policy and Management, Discussion paper series, 1 (Manchester: IDPM).

Revans, R. W. (1986) "Action Learning in Briefest Form", University of Manchester, Institute for Development Policy and Management, Discussion paper series, 2 (Manchester: IDPM).

Revans, R. W. (1986) "Action Learning in a Developing Country", *Management Decision*, 24(6), pp. 3–7.

Revans, R. W. (1986) "Action Learning, Past and Future", Institute of Management, Norwegian School of Management (BedriftsØkonomisk Institutt, Bekkestua, Norway).

Revans, R. W. (1986) "Education for Change and Survival, Part I", *Education and Training*, 28(2), February, pp. 62–4.

Revans, R. W. (1986) "Education for Change and Survival, Part II", *Education and Training*, 28(3), March, pp. 95–6.

Revans, R. W. (1986) "Action Learning and the Cowboys", *Organization Development Journal*, 4(3), Fall, pp. 71–80.

[*Note*: Reflection on the Harvard Business School, business education, education and learning.]

Revans, R. W. (1986) "Letter to the Editor", *Organization Development Journal*, 4(3), Fall, pp. 2–3.

Revans, R. W. (1986) "Letter to the Editor", *Organization Development Journal*, 4(1), Spring, p. 4.

Revans, R. W. (1986) "Action Learning Past and Present", *Bulletin of Educational Development and Research*, 31, Spring, pp. 4–19.

Revans, R. W. (1986/7) "Our Search for Identity", *Bulletin of Educational Development and Research*, 33, Winter, pp. 3–18.

Revans, R. W. (1987) "The Learning Equation: An introduction", in A. Mumford (ed.), (1987) *Action Learning, Journal of Management Development*, Special issue in honor of Reg Revans, 6(2), pp. 5–7.

Revans, R. W. (1987) "Action Learning and the Freshmen", An address to a Conference on Freshman Year Experience organised by Newcastle Polytechnic and the University of South Carolina held at the University of Southampton, July,

1987, Printed in *Meeting the Challenge of the 90s: Proceedings of the 1987 International Seminar on Staff/Faculty Development*, C. De Winter Hebron and A. B. Smith (eds.), International Seminar on Staff/Faculty Development (1987) [s.l.] : [s.n.], 1987.

[*Note*: Includes banquet speech 'Action Learning and the Freshman' by R. W. Revans: 11–29. Reprinted in Revans, 1988, *Golden Jubilee*.]

Revans, R. W. (1987) "The Learning Equation: An introduction", *Journal of Management Development*, 6(2).

[*Note*: Republished in Mumford, Alan, (ed.), *Action Learning at Work* (Aldershot: Gower, 1997), pp. xxi–xxii.]

Revans, R. W. (1987) *International Perspectives on Action Learning*. University of Manchester, Institute for Development Policy and Management, Manchester Training Handbooks, 9 (Manchester: IDPM Publications, University of Manchester).

Revans, R. W. (1987) "The Making of Managers: A comment by Prof. R. W. Revans", Newsletter, 6(3), *The International Foundation for Action Learning*, November, pp. 4–8.

Revans, R. W. (1987) "The Making of Managers", Newsletter 22, 12 September, IMCB Buckingham, pp. 13–19.

Revans, R. W. (1987) "Letter to the Editor", *Organization Development Journal*, 5(1), Spring, p. 1.

Revans, R. W. (1987) "Letter to the Editor", *Organization Development Journal*, 5(2), Summer, p. 1.

Revans, R. W. (1987) "Preface", in Nelson Coghill and Portia Holman (eds.), *Disruptive Behaviour in Schools!: Causes, treatment and prevention* (Bromley, U.K.: Chartwell-Bratt), p. iv.

[*Note*: Contains a thoughtful preface by Revans and a good bibliography of Revans' publications; Coghill worked with Revans on several health care related initiatives, and is also published in Revans, 1976, *Action Learning in Hospitals*. Coghill was also very instrumental in developing the International Foundation for Action Learning.]

Revans, R. W. (1988) *The Golden Jubilee of Action Learning: A collection of papers written during 1988* (Manchester Business School and Manchester Action Learning Exchange [MALEx]).

[*Note*: MALEx, University of Manchester, Manchester Business School, Booth St West, Manchester M15 6PB, England; see Chapter 6 for further details.]

Revans, R. W. (1988) "Action Learning – Its range and variety", in *The Golden Jubilee of Action Learning: A collection of papers written during 1988* (Manchester, England: Action Learning Exchange [MALEx], University of Manchester), pp. 37–79.

Revans, R. W. (1988) "Fifty years On", in *The Golden Jubilee of Action Learning: A collection of papers written during 1988* (Manchester, England: Action Learning Exchange [MALEx], University of Manchester), pp. 15–36.

Revans, R. W. (1988) "Action Learning and the Freshmen", *The Golden Jubilee of Action Learning: A collection of papers written during 1988* (Manchester, England: Action Learning Exchange [MALEx], University of Manchester), pp. 99–136.

Revans, R. W. (1988) "Action Learning in the Third World", *The Golden Jubilee of Action Learning: A collection of papers written during 1988* (Manchester, England: Action Learning Exchange [MALEx], University of Manchester), pp. 80–98.

248   *Yury Boshyk and Robert L. Dilworth*

Revans, R. W. (1988) "From Cleverness to Wisdom", *The Golden Jubilee of Action Learning: A collection of papers written during 1988* (Manchester, England: Action Learning Exchange [MALEx], University of Manchester), pp. 137–62.

Revans, R. W. (1988) "The Learning Equation: An introduction", in John Peters (ed.), *Customer First – The Independent Answer*, [Business Education Serial], 9(3/4) (Bradford, West Yorkshire, England: MCB University Press Limited), pp. 119–20.

Revans, R. W. (1988) "Management, Management Talent, and Society", Invited address, Manchester Business School, MALEx (Manchester Action Learning Exchange) delivered 13 January, 1988. Complete address printed, delivered under sponsorship of Prudential and BIM.

Revans, R. W. (1988) "Letter to the Editor", *Organization Development Journal*, 6(2), Summer, p. 2.

Revans, R. W. (1988) "The Last Days of October", *Organization Development Journal*, 6(4), Winter, pp. 33–40.

Revans, R. W. (1988) "Evidence of Learning: A study of manufacturing industry in Belgium where action learning was tried in 1968", Occasional paper, Manchester School of Management, 8807. Manchester: Manchester School of Management, University of Manchester Institute of Science and Technology.

Revans, R. W. and Mann, P. (1989) "Nepal Administrative Staff College: Promotion of Action Learning", University of Manchester Institute for Development Policy and Management, 18 March–8 April (Manchester: University of Manchester. Institute for Development Policy).

Revans, R. W. (1989) "Letter to the Editor", *OR Insight*, 2(2), April–June, p. 27.
[*Note*: *OR Insight* is a publication of the Operational Research Society.]

Revans, R. W. (1989) "Letter to the Editor", *Organization Development Journal*, 7(3), Fall, p. 96.

Revans, R. W. (1989) "Letter to the Editor", *Organization Development Journal*, 7(3), Fall, p. 97.
[*Note*: Not a duplicate; two letters in same issue.]

Revans, R. W. (1989) "Letter to the Editor", *OR Insight*, 2(1), January – March, pp. 22–3.
[*Note*: *OR Insight* is a publication of the Operational Research Society.]

Revans, R. W. (1989) "Integrity in the College Curriculum", *Higher Education Review*, 21(2), Spring, pp. 26–62.

Revans, R. W. (1990) "The Hospital as a Human System", *Behavioural Science*, 35(2), pp. 108–14.
[*Note*: Reprinted from Revans, 1962 with the same title.]

Revans, R. W. (1991) Reg Revans speaks about action learning, Interviewed by O. Zuber-Skerritt (Brisbane: TV Centre, University of Queensland).
[*Note*: Video.]

Revans, R. W. (1991) "Action Learning in the Third World", *International Journal of Human Resource Management*, 2, May, pp. 73–91.
[*Note*: From the article, Revans' comment: "In 1988 I accepted, after more than twenty years of refusal, an invitation to visit South Africa and to explain, to the best of my ability, the nature of action learning. I try, in this paper, to justify such acceptance and thereby the reasons for changing my mind."]

Revans, R. W. (1991) "Letter to the Editor entitled 'Keep away from gurus'", *Organization Development Journal*, 9(2), Summer, pp. 91–3.

Revans, R. W. (1992) "Improving Health Care: A social challenge?", *East European Medical Journal*, 1(1), pp. 5–8.

Revans, R. W. (1993) "Letter to the Editor", *Organization Development Journal*, 11(4), Winter, pp. 89.

Revans, R. W. (1993) "Address to the 2nd International Congress of Educating Cities", in *Farrington, Freire, Revans, Sapp: Four of the main speakers at the 2nd International Congress of Educating Cities*, 25–27 November, 1992, in Gothenburg, Sweden, edited by Torbjörn Stockfelt (Gothenburg: Gotheburg City Education Committee).

Revans, R. W. (1994) "Life History Interview [and] Action Learning and The Belgian Action Learning Program, Including an Address to the Faculty of the Defense Systems Management College at Fort Belvoir, Virginia", Interviews by Robert L. Dilworth et al., during Revans' visit to Virginia Commonwealth University as a Distinguished Scholar.

[*Note*: Videotaped, approximately three hours.]

Revans, R. W. (1994) "Action Learning or Partnership in Adversity. The Economic Effects of National Spontaneity", prepared by Albert E. Barker. s.l.

[*Note*: Mostly about national competitiveness, his work with the OECD, and the Belgian experience.]

Revans, R. W. (1996) "Past, Present and Future: Evidence of action learning", in *International Action Learning Seminar: Additional Papers*, Summer (Manchester: Revans Centre for Action Learning and Research, University of Salford).

[*Note*: Chapter 3 is on "Disclosing Doubts".]

Revans, R. W. (1997) "A Conversation with Reg Revans, 17 December, 1996", in M. Pedler (ed.), *Action Learning in Practice*, 3rd edn (Aldershot: Gower), pp. xi–xix.

Revans, R. W. (1997) "Action Learning: Its origins and nature", in M. Pedler (ed.), *Action Learning in Practice*, 3rd edn (Aldershot: Gower), pp. 3–14.

Revans, R. W. (1998) *The ABC of Action Learning* (London: Lemos & Crane. Mike Pedler Library).

[*Note*: Edited by Mike Pedler, with a good annotated bibliography.]

Revans, R. W. (1998) "Sketches of Action Learning", *Performance Improvement Quarterly*, 11(11), pp. 23–7.

Revans, R. W. (1999) "Action Learning: Wesen und Voraussetzungen", in *Action Learning: Ein Handbuch*, Otmar Donnenberg (ed.) (Stuttgart: Klett-Cotta), pp. 28–43.

Revans, R. W. (1999) "Foreword", in M. J. Marquardt, *Action Learning in Action: Transforming Problems and People for World-Class Organizational Learning* (Palo Alto: Davies-Black), p. ix–x.

[*Note*: Generic comment by Revans.]

Revans, R. W. (2001) *Essentials of Action Learning*, 1978, edited and revised by David Botham, 1998, in John Raven and John Stephenson (eds.), *Competence in the Learning Society* (New York: Peter Lang Publishing), pp. 333–7.

[*Note*: First published in *Link-Up with Action Learning*, 1(2), August–October, 1997, pp. 2–4.]

Revans, R. W. (2003) "Foreword", in Robert L. Dilworth and Verna J. Willis, *Action Learning: Images and pathways* (Malabar, Florida: Krieger), pp. vii–x.

[*Note*: The last published item by Revans authenticating the analysis done by the authors.]

Revans, R. W. (2004) "The ABC of Action Learning", in A. E. Barker and R. W. Revans, *An Introduction to Genuine Action Learning* (Oradea, Romania: Oradea University Press), pp. 212–64
[*Note*: Republication with some commentary by A. E. Barker.]
Revans (2004) "Confirming Cases", in A. E. Barker and R. W. Revans, *An Introduction to Genuine Action Learning* (Oradea, Romania: Oradea University Press), pp. 265–318.
[*Note*: Republication with some commentary by A. E. Barker.]

Archival and other primary sources

There is most likely going to be much more research into the history and evolution of action learning that will be based on primary sources such as archival materials and interviews. Below are just a few of the more available and critical materials.

(A) Institutional Collections

(1) United Kingdom

University of Manchester

The Archives and Books of Reg Revans
Reg Revan's Archival Materials (Manchester):
These materials were housed at Salford University at the Revans Institute but from 2009 they are in the process of being moved to the new Revans Academy at the Manchester Business School. The Revans Institute is no longer in existence.

http://www.mbs.ac.uk/research/revans_academy/revans-academy.aspx
Revans Academy website

http://www.revanscenter.com/
The Revans Centre, later to become the Revans Institute, was established at the University of Salford, England, 1994–2006. The new Revans Academy is now being established at the University of Manchester Business School, England.

There is a very useful link the Revans collection:
http://www.ils.salford.ac.uk/library/resources/special/

Lancaster University

International Foundation for Action Learning (IFAL)
www.ifal.org.uk/

Formed in 1977, the papers, publications and books of the IFAL are extensive and are in the process of being rehoused. For more information, please see the website. There is a link to the publications of both IFAL and the Action Learning Trust.

(2) Belgium

Archives of the Fondation Industrie-Université

These are housed in the Royal Library of Belgium.
www.kbr.be

Revans' work with the Fondation was described in his *Developing Effective Managers* (1971) and when he was involved in the Inter-University Advanced Management Program with industry and some universities. He was with the Fondation for about ten years.

The official list of archives list statutory publications (linked to legally binding activities such as the composition of Boards, accounts and publications in the State Journals). It continues with the official publications such as the Activity Reports, but also reference is made to letters, correspondence, lists of all management training organized by the Foundation and actual files relating to colloquia preceding the Revans' period. It seems that a great deal of preparatory work was done by top industrialists along with senior academic staff of the top universities in Belgium in workshops/colloquia mostly held in Knokke (the Nice of Belgium).

Those who wish to consult the content of these archives need to go through a lengthy request and approval process due to the fact they are stored in the State Archives. Part of these archives (referring to the items relating to individual personal data – could be assessments, interviews, applications) are by law only to be disclosed in 2011.

The Archives of the European Association of Management Training Centres (EAMTC) and the European Foundation for Management Development (EFMD)

Revans was President of the EAMTC and a research fellow in the 1960s and early 1970s. We have been informed that most of the materials of the EAMTC were not preserved.

(3) USA

Harvard University

The papers of George Lombard, supporter of Revans' approach to management education and action learning. He was a Professor at the

Harvard Business School from 1942 to 1977. There are several boxes of
Revans materials including correspondence between the two.

There is a guide to the collection available online:
http://oasis.lib.harvard.edu/oasis/deliver/~bak00036

(B) Private Collections

Original materials, correspondence, publications, video and sound
recordings are available to qualified researchers and in agreement with
the individuals listed below. There will no doubt be more individuals
who will volunteer to share their materials on action learning.

Professor Albert E. Barker
Email: prof.albertbarker@tiscali.co.uk

Dr. Yury Boshyk
Email: yury@gel-net.com

Dr. Donna Vick
Email: donnakvick@yahoo.com

Professor Verna J. Willis
Email: PADVJW@langate.gsu.edu

Selected publications relating to the history and evolution of action learning

Publications and articles by Reginald W. Revans when he is listed as the
first author are not included here, and are to be found in section (i) of
this chapter. For further details on some of these entries, see Chapter 6
in this volume.

Action Society Trust (1957) *Size and Morale, Part II: A Further Study of Attendance at Work in Large and Small Units* (London: The Acton Society Trust).
[*Note*: Part I was written by Revans but not this second part. See Revans, 1956, Revans' publications, chapter 8.]
Amdam, R. P. (ed.) (1996) *Management Education and Competitiveness: Europe, Japan and the United States* (London: Routledge).
Anderson, J. R. L. (1965) "Man at Work", *The Guardian*, 24 September.
[*Note*: Review of Revans' book, Science and the Manager.]
[Anonymous] (1987) Revans, Prof. Reginald William, in *Who's Who 1987: An Annual Biographical Dictionary*, 1468 (London: A & C Black).
[*Note*: Very accurate details about Reg Revans, including his brother John.]
[Anonymous] (1997) "A Prophet Is Not Without Honour, Save in His Own Country: The Story of Professor Reg Revans", *The Antidote*, 10.
Argyris, M. and Schön, D. (1974) *Theory in Practice. Increasing professional effectiveness* (San Francisco: Jossey-Bass).

[*Note*: Landmark statement of 'double-loop' learning' and distinction between espoused theory and theory-in-action.]

Argyris, C. and Schön D. (1978) *Organizational Learning: A Theory of Action Perspective* (Reading, MA: Addison-Wesley).

Argyris, C., Putnam R., and Smith D. M. (1985) *Action Science: Concepts, methods, and skills for research and intervention* (San Francisco: Jossey-Bass).

Ashmawy, S. and Revans, R. W. (1972) "The Nile Project: An experiment in educational authotherapy", A monograph upon which the Fondation Industrie-Université contribution to the 1972 ATM Conference was based. Paris: The Development Centre, Organisation for Economic Co-operation and Development (OECD).

[*Note*: First published in November, 1973 by ALP [Action Learning Projects] International. Revans was with The Foundation for Industry and the Universities, Brussels, and acted as technical adviser for the project. See Chapter 6 for further details.]

Ashmawy, S. (1972) "Consortium Revans", *Journal of European Training*, 1, Summer, pp. 54–6.

[*Note*: A description of the Egypt project (Nile Project) by its key organizer.]

Ashton, D. (1974) "Project-based Management Development", *Personnel Management*, 6(7), pp. 26–8, 36.

Attwood, M., Pedler, M., Pritchard, S., and Wilkinson, D. (2003) *Leading Change: A guide to whole systems working* (Bristol: Policy Press).

[*Note*: Change and action learning also discussed.]

Aubusson, P., Ewing, R., and Hoban, G. (2009) *Action Learning in Schools: Reframing school teachers' professional learning and development* (London: Routledge).

Bacon, C. J. (2005) "Winning against Difficult Issues: The power of action learning with systems thinking", in S. Reddy and A. E. Barker (eds.), (2005), *Genuine Action Learning: Following the spirit of Revans* (Hyderabad: ICFAI University Press), pp. 114–54.

Bailey, J. (1980) "Action Learning for Small Firms", *Training Officer*, 16(7), pp. 174–6.

Bakhshi, B. K. (1979) "Action Learning: An Indian experience", *Indian Journal of Training and Development*, July–August.

Baldassarre, S. (1995) "Action Learning for Italian Managers in a Changing Context", *Action Learning News: The Newsletter of IFAL*, 14(3), September, pp. 14–15.

Baquer, A. and Craig, J. (1973) "Action Learning: Staff training based on evaluation of the services by the providers", *Journal of European Training*, 2(1), pp. 43–55.

Baquer, A. Q. and Revans, R. W. (1973) *"But surely that is their job": A study in practical cooperation through action learning* (Southport: A.L.P. International Publications).

[*Note*: "Action learning" used in the title; on work with the "mentally handicapped", see also Revans and Baquer, 1972.]

Baquer, A. [Memoir] *Linkup 2 [2]. 2002–2003* (Manchester, Revans Institute for Action Learning and Research, University of Salford).

[*Note*: An exceptional memoir about Revans. The entire issue is devoted to memoirs about Revans on the occasion of his passing.]

Barker, A. E. (1998) "Profile of Action Learning's Principal Pioneer – Reginald W. Revans", *Perfomance Improvement Quarterly*, 11(1), pp. 9–22.

Barker, A. E. (1998) "Fundamental Aspects of Action Learning", in W. Gasparksi and D. Botham (eds.), *Action Learning* (New Brunswick, U.S.: Transaction Publishers), pp. 13–32.

Barker, A. E. and Revans, R. W. (2004) *An Introduction to Genuine Action Learning* (Oradea, Romania: Oradea University Press).

[*Note*: Very detailed background on the concepts of action learning and republication, with explanatory notes by Barker, of several of Revans' publications including *ABC of Action Learning* and *Confirming Cases*.]

Barker, A. E. (2004) "Elements of Action Learning", in A. E. Barker and R. W. Revans (eds.), *An Introduction to Genuine Action Learning* (Oradea, Romania: Oradea University Press), pp. 9–207.

Barker, A. E. (2005) "Action Learning – SETS – and Other Sensitivities, in S. Reddy, and A. E. Barker (eds.), *Genuine action learning: Following the spirit of Revans* (Hyderabad: The ICFAI University Press), pp. 29–87.

Barker, A. E. and Revans. R. W. (2004) *An Introduction to Genuine Action Learning* (Oradea, Romania: Oradea University Press).

[*Note*: Includes republication of Revans' *The ABC of Action Learning*, and *Confirming Cases*.]

Barker, A. E. (2004) "Professor R.W. Revans: The Founding Father of Action Learning – A short bio-summary", in A. E. Barker and R. W. Revans (eds.), *An Introduction to Genuine Action Learning* (Oradea, Romania: Oradea University Press), pp. 17–44.

[*Note*: Includes Revans' *Elegy to the Second World War.*]

Barrett, N. (2000) "'Learning the Hard 'Way': Creating an executive development opportunity for learning and reflection", in Boshyk (2000), pp. 227–37.

Beckhard, R. (1969) *Organization Development: Strategies and models* (Reading, MA: Addison-Wesley).

Beckhard, R. (2006) "What is Organization Development?", in J. V. Gallos (ed.), *Organization Development: A Jossey-Bass reader* (San Francisco: Jossey-Bass), pp. 3–12.

Beer, S. and Revans, R. W. (1959) *Operational Research and Personnel Management. Part 1 by S. Beer, Part 2 by R.W. Revans* (London: Institute of Personnel Management. Occasional Papers), p. 14.

[*Note*: Beer was a well known cyberneticist, systems thinker and practitioner, and a colleague of Revans' from the University of Manchester Business School. Both of them contributed chapters in honour of Weiner, the MIT pioneer in cybernetic. See Revans, 1969.]

Begley, S. (2007) *Train Your Mind, Change Your Brain: How a new science reveals our extraordinary potential to transform ourselves* (New York: Ballantine Books).

Bellah, R. N., Madsen, R., Sullivan, W. M., and Tipton, S. M. (1985) *Habits of the Heart: Individualism and Commitment in American Life* (New York: Harper & Row).

[*Note*: One of Revans' favourite books.]

Bellmann, M. (2000) "Siemens Management Learning: A highly integrated model to align learning processes with business needs", in Y. Boshyk, (ed.), *Business Driven Action Learning: Global best practices* (London/New York: Macmillan Business and St Martin's Press), pp. 140–51.

Bennis, W. G. (1969) *Organization Development: Its nature, origins, and prospects* (Reading, MA: Addison-Wesley).

Bertrams, K. (2001) "The Diffusion of US Management Models and the Role of the University: The Case of Belgium (1945–1970)", Article on the internet available at web.bi.no/forskning/ebha2001.nsf/23e5e39594c064ee852564ae0 04fa010/.../$FILE/C2%20-%20Bertrams.PDF

Bertrams, K. (2006) *Universités et enterprises: Milieux académiques et industriels en Belgique (1880–1970)* (Brussels: Le Cri).

[*Note*: Section on the Fondation Industrie-Université (FIU) in Brussels and photo of Gaston Deurinck, the Managing Director. Revans was a Fellow in the FIU.]

Bertsch, J. and Zürn P. (1997) *Führen und Gestalten: 100 Unternehmergespräche in Baden-Baden* (Berlin: Springer).

[Note: Includes an article by Hans Hellwig and a brief biography about him; Revans dedicated his 1971 book *Developing Effective Managers* to Hellwig. See Chapter 6 for further details.]

Bhandarker, Asha (2008) *Shaping Business Leaders: What B-schools don't do* (New Delhi: Sage).

[*Note*: Calls for more action learning in the curriculum in Indian business schools.]

Boddy, D. (1979) "Some Lessons Learned from an Action Learning Programme", *Journal of European Industrial Training*, 3(3), pp. 17–21.

Boddy, D. (1980) "An Action Learning Programme for Supervisors", *Journal of European Industrial Training*, 4(3), pp. 10–13.

Boddy, D. (1981) "Putting Action Learning into Action", *Journal of European Industrial Training*, 5(5), pp. 39–52.

[*Note*: Coghill, 1983, p. 277 provides different page numbers: 2–20.]

Boddy, D. (1983) "Supervisory Development", in M. Pedler (ed.), *Action Learning in Practice*, 1st edn (Aldershot: Gower), pp. 83–92.

Boisot, M. and Fiol, M. (1987) "Chinese Boxes and Learning Cubes: Action learning in a cross-cultural context", in A. Mumford (ed.), "Action Learning", *Journal of Management Development*, Special issue in honor of Reg Revans, 6(2), pp. 8–18.

Bolt, J. and Boshyk, Y. (2005) "Using Action Learning for Executive Development", in J. Bolt (ed.), *The Future of Executive Development*. s.l.: Executive Development Associates, pp. 86–99.

Boshyk, Y. (2000) "Beyond Knowledge Management: How companies mobilize experience", in D. Marchand, T. H. Davenport, and T. Dickson (eds.), *Mastering Information Management* (London: *Financial Times*/Prentice Hall), pp. 51–8.

Boshyk, Y. (ed.) (2000) *Business Driven Action Learning: Global best practices* (London/New York: Macmillan/St Martin's Press).

Boshyk, Y. (2000) "Business Driven Action Learning: The key elements", in Y. Boshyk, (ed.), *Business Driven Action Learning: Global best practices* (London/New York: Macmillan Business/St Martin's Press), pp. xi–xvii.

Boshyk, Y. (ed.) (2002) *Action Learning Worldwide: Experiences of leadership and organizational development* (Basingstoke, U.K./New York: Palgrave Macmillan).

[*Note*: Contains contributions from the various "approaches" to action learning and numerous examples from companies, the public service and non-governmental organizations; geographically, articles cover North and South America, South Africa, Europe, China, South Korea and Japan.]

256   *Yury Boshyk and Robert L. Dilworth*

Boshyk, Y. (2002) "Why Business Driven Action Learning?", in Y. Boshyk (ed.), *Action Learning Worldwide: Experiences of leadership and organizational development* (Basingstoke, U.K. and New York: Palgrave Macmillan), pp. 30–52.

Boshyk, Y. (2009) "The Development of Global Executives: Today and tomorrow", in D. Dotlich, P. Cairo, S. Rhinesmith and R. Meeks (eds.), (2009), *The 2009 Pfeiffer Annual: Leadership development* (San Francisco: Wiley), pp. 108–26.

Bossert, R. (2000) "Johnson & Johnson: Executive development and strategic business solutions through action learning", in Y. Boshyk (ed.), *Business Driven Action Learning: Global best practices* (London/New York: Macmillan Business/ St Martin's Press), pp. 91–103.

Botham, D. (1995) "Is Action Learning a Cult?", *Action Learning News: The Newsletter of IFAL*, 14(3), September, pp. 2–5.

Botham, D. (1998) "The Context of Action Learning: A short review of Revans' work", in W. Gasparski and D. Botham (eds.), *Action Learning* (New Brunswick: Transaction Books), pp. 33–61.

Botham, D. and Vick, D. (1998) "Action Learning and the Program at the Revans Centre", *Performance Improvement Quarterly*, 11(2), pp. 5–16.

Botham, D. (2001) *The Process of Action Learning and the Procedures of Research*. Salford: University of Salford, Revans Institute for Action Learning and Research (Seminar series: paper 3).

Botham, D. (2005) "The Revans Approach to Action learning: Learning to learn by doing", in S. Reddy, and A. E. Barker (eds.), *Genuine Action Learning: Following the spirit of Revans* (Hyderabad: ICFAI University Press), pp. 21–8.

Boulden, G. P. and Lowe, J. (1980) *Inplant Action Learning*. s.l.: Action Learning Associates.

Boulden, G. (1981) "How Action Learning Can Teach Firms", *Management Today*, February, pp. 33–6.

Boulden, G. and Lawlor, A. (eds.) (1987) *The Application of Action Learning*. (Geneva: ILO).

Boulden, G. P. and Safarikova, V. (1997) "Industrial Restructuring in the Czech Republic", in M. Pedler, (ed.), *Action Learning in Practice*, 3rd edn (Aldershot: Gower), pp. 107–16.

Bourner, T. (2000) *New Directions in Action Learning* (Salford: University of Salford, Revans Institute for Action Learning and Research, Seminar series).

Bowden, B. V. (1955) *Faster Than Thought: A symposium on digital computing machines* (London: Pitman and Sons).

[Note: Ahead of its time; Revans' friend from Cambridge University and head, Manchester College of Science and Technology at this time, recruiting Revans to this College in 1955.]

Bowden, Lord Vivien (1980) "Action Learning in the Lords", Newsletter 6 (The Action Learning Trust), pp. 6–7.

Boydell, T. (1976) "Experiential Learning", Manchester monograph 5 (Manchester: Department of Adult Education, University of Manchester).

Brassard, C. (2002) "Learning in Action: Accelerating the development of high-potential executives in the Canadian Public Service", in Y. Boshyk (ed.), *Action Learning Worldwide: Experiences of leadership and organizational development* (Basingstoke, U.K. and New York: Palgrave Macmillan), pp. 133–51.

Braun, W. (2000) "DaimlerChrysler: Global leadership development using action-oriented and distance-learning techniques", in Y. Boshyk (ed.), *Business*

Driven Action Learning: Global best practices (London/New York: Macmillan Business/St Martin's Press), pp. 3–13.

Brooks, A. K. (1988) "Educating Human Resource Development Leaders at the University of Texas at Austin: The use of action learning to facilitate university–workplace collaboration", *Performance Improvement Quarterly*, 11(2), pp. 48–58.

Brown, B. F. (1963) *The Non-Graded High School* (New York: Prentice-Hall).

[*Note*: Revans mentioned in private correspondence that the author was discussing "the learning equation almost at the very same time as I was into it".]

Brown, N. (1983) "Improving Management Morale and Efficiency", in M. Pedler (ed.), *Action Learning in Practice*, 1st edn (Aldershot: Gower), pp. 93–104.

Brummer, A. and Cowe, R. (1998) *Weinstock: The life and times of Britain's premier industrialist* (London: HarperCollins).

Burgoyne, J. G. (2001) "The Nature of Action Learning: What is learned about in action learning" (Salford: University of Salford, Revans Institute for Action Learning and Research, Seminar series).

Burke, W. W. (1978) *The Cutting Edge: Current theory and practice in organization development* (La Jolla, CA: University Associates).

Burke, W. W. (1987) *Organization Development: A normative view* (Reading, MA: Addison-Wesley).

[*Note*: Good on the origins of *OD*.]

Burke, W. W. (2006) "Where Did OD Come From?", in J. V. Gallos (ed.), *Organization Development: A Jossey-Bass Reader* (San Francisco: Jossey-Bass), pp. 13–38.

Burke, W. W. (2008) "A Contemporary View of Organization Development", in T. G. Cummings (ed.), *Handbook of Organization Development* (Los Angeles: Sage Publications), pp. 13–38.

Byrd, S. and Dorsey, L. (2002) "Getting to the Future First and the E-Business Leadership Challenge: Business driven action learning at Lilly", in Y. Boshyk (ed.), *Action Learning Worldwide*: Experiences of leadership and organizational development (Basingstoke, U.K./New York: Palgrave Macmillan), pp. 110–22.

Casey, D. (1975) "A Diagnostic Model for the OD Consultant", *Journal of European Training*, 4(1), pp. 33–41.

Casey, D. (1976) "The Emerging Role of Set Adviser in Action Learning Programmes", *Journal of European Training*, 5(3), pp. 3–14.

Casey, D. (1977) "Reflections of a Set Adviser", *ALT Newsletter*, 1.

[*Note*: No page numbers on the newsletter.]

Casey, D. (1978) "Project Training for Managers – The underlying paradox", *Journal of European Industrial Training*, 2(5).

Casey, D. (1980) "Transfer of Learning – There are two separate problems", in J. Beck and C. Cox (eds.), *Advances in Management Education* (Chichester: Wiley).

Casey, D. (1983) "Day Release for Chief Executives", *Personnel Management*, 15(6), July, pp. 30–3.

Casey, D. (1987) "Breaking the Shell that encloses Your Understanding", in A. Mumford (ed.), "Action Learning", *Journal of Management Development*, Special issue in honor of Reg Revans, 6(2), pp. 30–7.

Casey, D. (1993) *Managing Learning in Organisations* (Milton Keynes: Open University Press).

Casey, D. (1997) "The Role of the Set Advisor", in M. Pedler (ed.), *Action Learning in Practice, 3rd edn*, pp. 209–20.

[*Note*: Adapted from Casey (1976) and then republished in M. Pedler, 1983, 1st edn, *Action Learning in Practice*.]

Casey, D. (1997) "The Shell of Your Understanding", in M. Pedler (ed.), *Action Learning in Practice*, 3rd edn (Aldershot: Gower), pp. 221–8.

Casey, D. and Pearce, D. (eds.) (1977) *More than Management Development: Action learning at GEC* (New York: AMACOM).

[*Note*: An excellent example of Revans' approach to action learning in the business community with the General Electric Company, U.K.; for a review of this book see, *Education and Training*, 20(7), July/August, 1978.]

Caulkin, S. (1995) "A Past Master Passes Muster: Lord Weinstock and Sir Peter are fans of unsung UK management guru Reg Revans", *The Observer*, 30 April, p. 12.

Caulkin, S. (2003) "Reg Revans: Inspired management thinker of 'action learning'", *The Guardian*, 8 March.

[Obituary, accessed 11 November, 2009, available at http://www.guardian.co.uk/news/2003/mar/08/guardianobituaries.simoncaulkin]

Cell, E. (1984) *Learning to Learn from Experience* (Albany, NY: State University of New York Press).

Cederholm, L. (2002) "Tibetan Buddhism and the Action reflection Learning Philosophy", in Y. Boshyk (ed.), *Action Learning Worldwide: Experiences of leadership and organizational development* (Basingstoke, U.K./New York: Palgrave Macmillan), pp. 268–81.

Checkland, P. and Poulter, J. (2007) *Learning for Action: A short definitive account of soft systems methodology, and its use for practitioners, teachers and students* (Reading, MA: Wiley).

Chorafas, D. N. (1962) *Programming Systems for Electronic Computers* (London: Butterworths).

[*Note*: Dedicated to "Professor Revans"; Revans has a Preface: vii–ix.]

Clutterbuck, D. (1974) "An Egyptian Project for Swapping Managers", *International Management*, 29(11), November, pp. 28–34.

[*Note*: About Ashmawy's extension of the Nile project.]

Clutterbuck, D. (1976) "Whatever Happened to Action Learning? While the traditional massive projects continue, the future of the technique seems to lie in less ambitious undertakings", *International Management*, 31(11), November, pp. 47–9.

[*Note*: Very good article on the evolution of the "classic" principles and practices due to company demands and realities; also on the ALP team; future adaptability is inevitable says the author.]

Clutterbuck, D. and Crainer, S. (1990) *Makers of Management: Men and women who changed the business world* (London: Guild Publishing).

[*Note*: On Revans (pp. 124–7); described as "the bitterest of gurus" (p. 124); called by Igor Ansoff, 'an amazing and underestimated man' (p. 127).]

Coghill, N. F. (1983) "A Bibliography of Action Learning", in M. Pedler (ed.), *Action Learning in Practice* (Aldershot: Gower), pp. 277–83.

[*Note*: Very good bibliography.]

Coghill, N. F. and Stewart, J. S. (1998) *The NHS: Myth, Monster or Service? Action learning in hospital* (Salford, U.K.: Revans Centre for Action Learning and Research).

[*Note*: Nelson Coghill was a long time collaborator with Revans on health care projects.]

Cole, R. E. (1989) *Strategies for Learning: Small-group activities in American, Japanese and Swedish Industry* (Berkeley: University of California Press).

[*Note*: Well-written and researched analysis of the "Americanization" of small-group learning (similar to the "Americanization" of action learning) and of relevance to Revans' practice and ideas but Revans not mentioned.]

Comfort, W. W. (1968) *Just Among Friends: The Quaker way of life*, 5th and revised edn (Philadelphia: American Friends Service Committee).

Commemoration of the life of Lord Bowden of Chesterfield 1910–1989 (1989) (Manchester: University of Manchester, Institute of Science and Technology).

Commonwealth Fund (1990) *Directory of Commonwealth Fund Fellows and Harkness Fellows, 1925–1990* (New York: Commonwealth Fund).

[*Note*: Mention of Revans and includes his resume.]

Conference on the Education of the Young Worker (1949) *The Education of the Young Worker: Report of a Conference held at Oxford in 1948 under the auspices of the University Department of Education* (Oxford University Press for King George's Jubilee Trust).

Conference on the Education of the Young Worker (1950) *The Education of the Young Worker: Report of the Second Conference held at Oxford in July 1949 under the auspices of the University Department of Education* (Oxford University Press for King George's Jubilee Trust).

[*Note*: Revans has an introductory article, "Why we held our conference."]

Corfield, K. and Penney, M. (1983) "Action Learning in the Community", in M. Pedler, (ed.), *Action Learning in Practice*, 1st edn (Aldershot: Gower), pp. 119–26.

Cortazzi, D. and Baquer, A. (1972) *Action Learning: A guide to its use for hospital staff based on a pilot study in co-ordination in hospitals for the mentally handicapped*. S.l.[London]: King's Fund Hospital Centre.

[*Note*: The British Library catalogue indicates that this material had no place or date of publication. Coghill, 1983, p. 278, provided this information. If correct, besides Revans, 1972 and Nancy Fox, 1972, this would have been one of the first times "action learning" as term used in a publication, albeit an internal one.]

Crainer, S. (1996) Interview with Reg Revans, *Financial Times*, 12 April.

Cranwell, B. (1983) "Action Learning in the Community", in M. Pedler (ed.), *Action Learning in Practice*, 1st edn (Aldershot: Gower), pp. 127–40.

Cumming, J. and Hall, I. (2001) *Achieving Results through Action Learning: A Practitioner's Toolkit for Developing People* (Maidenhead, U.K.: Peter Honey Publications).

Cunningham, I. (1987) "When Is It Action Learning?", Newsletter 6(3), November, *International Foundation for Action Learning*, p. 18.

Cunningham, I., Dawes, G., and Bennett, B. (2004) *The Handbook of Work Based Learning* (Aldershot: Gower).

Davey, C. L., Powell, J. A. C., and Powell, J. E. (2004) "Innovation, Construction SMEs and Action Learning", *Engineering, Construction and Architectural Management*, 11(4), pp. 230–7.

Davids, B. N., Aspler, C., and McIvor, B. (2002) "General Electric's Action Learning Change Initiatives: Work-out and the change acceleration process", in Y. Boshyk (ed.), *Action Learning Worldwide: Experiences of leadership and organizational development* (Basingstoke, U.K. and New York: Palgrave Macmillan), pp. 76–89.

De Loo, I. and Verstegen, B (2001) "New Thoughts on Action Learning", *Journal of European Industrial Training*, 25(2,3,4), pp. 229–34.

Dennis, C., Cederholm, L., and Yorks, L. (1996) "Learning Your Way to a Global Organization: Grace Cocoa", in: Victoria J. Marsick and Karen. E. Watkins (eds.), in G. Deurinck, (1987), "University and Enterprise: Facing a new era", *IMD Journal*, 3, pp. 1–3.

Deutsche Vereiniging zur Forderung der Weiterbildung von Führungskraften (Wuppertaler Kreis) and the European Foundation for Management Development (EFMD) (1978) *Management Education in Europe: Towards a new deal, internal and external training* (Cologne: Hanstein).

Dierk, U. and Saslow, S. (2005) "Action Learning in Management Development Programs", *Chief Learning Officer*, May, pp. 20–5.

Dilworth, R. L. (1996) "Action Learning: Bridging academic and workplace domains", *Employee Counselling Today*, 8(6), pp. 48–56.

Dilworth, R. L. (1998) "Action Learning in a Nutshell", *Performace Improvement Quarterly*, 11(1), pp. 28–43.

Dilworth, R. L. (1998) "Action Learning at Virginia Commonwealth University: Blending action, reflection, critical incident methodologies, and portfolio assessment", *Performance Improvement Quarterly*, 11(2),pp. 17–33.

Dilworth, R. L. (ed.) (1998) *Performance Improvement Quarterly*, 11(1) and 11(2), Special issues on Action Learning.

Dilworth, R. L. (2005) "Creating Opportunities for Reflection in Action Learning: Nine important avenues", in S. Reddy and A. E. Barker (eds.), *Genuine Action Learning: Following the spirit of Revans*. Hyderabad: ICFAI University Press, pp. 88–113.

Dilworth, R. L. and Willis, V. J. (2003) *Action Learning: Images and pathways* (Malabar, FL: Krieger).

Dingle, H. (1954) *The Sources of Eddington's Philosophy* (Cambridge: Cambridge University Press).

Dixon, M. (1971) "David, Goliath and Dr. Revans: [European] Management Education Conference", *Financial Times*, 8 January, D15.

Dixon, N. M. (1997) "More Than Just a Task Force", in M. Pedler (ed.), *Action Learning in Practice*, 3rd edn (Aldershot: Gower), pp. 329–37.
[*Note*: Discusses what she terms the "modified or perhaps Americanized version of Action Learning".]

Dixon, N. M. (1999) *Organization Learning Cycle* (Aldershot: Gower).
[*Note*: "This book is dedicated to Reg Revans whose thinking has been so far ahead of his time, that after 50 years, the world is only just catching up."]

Dixon, N. M. (2000) "Talk, Authenticity and Action Learning in the Learning Organization: Dialogue at work", *The Learning Organization: An international journal*. 7(1), pp. 42–7.

Dobinson, C. H., (ed.) (1951) *Education in a Changing World: A symposium* (Oxford: Clarendon Press).
[*Note*: Includes an article by Revans.]

Donnenberg, O. (ed.) (1999) *Action Learning: Ein Handbuch* (Stuttgart: Klett-Cotta).

Dotlich, D. L. and Noel, J. (1998) *Action Learning: How the world's top companies are re-creating their leaders and themselves* (San Francisco: Jossey-Bass).
[*Note*: See Noel and Dotlich, 2008 for an "update" to this publication.]

Drieghe, L. (1990) *Action Learning: een biografie van Reginald William Revans: een overzicht van theorie en experimenten*. [s.l.] : [s.n.]. Licentiate Exordium.
[*Note*: Doctoral thesis in Flemish on the History of Action Learning. "Largely biographical description" of by a doctoral candidate from the University of Ghent (Gand) Belgium, stated Revans.]

Driehuis, M. (1997) *De lerende adviseur: een onderzoek naar intercollegiaal consult in organisatieadvisering* (Delft: Eburon).
[*Note*: *English translation reads,* The Learning Consultant: Research into Action Learning in Organization Consulting.]

Edmonstone, J. (2003) *The Action Learner's Toolkit* (Aldershot: Gower).

Eglin, R. (1977) "Reg Revans: Business schools come under fire from action man", *Industrial Management*, May, pp. 25–7.

Engwall, L. and Zamagni, V. (eds.) (1998) *Management Education in Historical Perspective* (Manchester: Manchester University Press).

European Foundation for Management Development (1996) *Training the Fire Brigade: Preparing for the Unimaginable* (Brussels: European Foundation for Management Development).
[*Note*: Some background history about the European Association of Management Training Centres with which Revans was associated as President and then Fellow.]

"Executive Swapping in Europe" (1971) *DUNS Review, International Business*, 97, March, p. 77.
[*Note*: On the Belgian experience.]

Foy, N. (1972) "The Maverick Mind of Reg Revans", *Management Today*, November, pp. 79, 81,163,168.
[*Note*: An excellent overview of Revans' work and thinking; also, the first time the term "action learning" is used in a published form by someone other than Revans (who himself introduced the term earlier in the same year).]

Foy, N. (1975) *The Sun Never Sets on IBM: The culture and folklore of IBM world trade* (New York: Morrow).
[*Note*: Included is a quote from Revans on IBM's use of the "penalty box" to punish executives for their mistakes.]

Foy, N. (1977) "Action Learning Comes to Industry", *Harvard Business Review*, 55(5), September–October, pp. 158–68.
[*Note*: The first time a largely U.S. and influential readership is introduced to Revans' action learning programs and approach in a major journal.]

Foy, N. (1977) "The Union Man Learns Action", *Management Today*, October, pp. 25–38.

Foy, N. (1979) "Management Education – Current Action and Future Needs: A summary of research into the requirements of british management education in the eighties", *Journal of European Industrial Training*, 3(2), pp. 1–28.
[*Note*: A very thoughtful and perceptive overview that is still relevant today.]

Foy, N. (1980) *The Yin and Yang of Organizations* (New York: William Morrow).
[*Note*: Reference to Revans as an "eccentric"; much on action learning and positive assessment of it as well.]

Foy, N. (1994) *Empowering People at Work* (Aldershot: Gower).
[*Note*: References to Revans.]

Freedman, N. J. (2000) "Philips and Action Learning Programs: From training to transformation", in Y. Boshyk (ed.), *Business Driven Action Learning: Global best practices* (London/New York: Macmillan Business/St Martin's Press), pp. 123–33.

Freire, P. (1970) *Pedagogy for the Oppressed* (New York: Continuum).

Garratt, R. (1976) *The Developing Use of Action Learning in Urban and Rural Development*. s.l.: ALP [Action Learning Projects] International.
[*Note*: Garratt was involved with Revans in Action Learning Projects International in 1974.]

Garratt, R. (1980) *Management Behavior: Individuals and groups. A primer on action learning sets, a basic guide for set advisers* (Rugby, England: Action Learning Associates).

Garratt, R. (1983) "The Role of the Learning Group Adviser: A process of phased redundancy?", *Management Education and Development*, 14(3), pp. 201–7.

Garratt, R. (1983) "The Power of Action Learning", in M. Pedler (ed.), *Action Learning in Practice*, 1st edn (Aldershot: Gower), pp. 23–38.
[*Note*: Reprinted in the 1997, 3rd edn of the book.]

Garratt, R. (1987) "Learning is the Core of Organisational Survival: Action learning is the key integrating process", in A. Mumford (ed.), "Action Learning", *Journal of Management Development,* Special issue in honor of Reg Revans, 6(2), pp. 38–44.

Garratt, R. (1987) *The Learning Organization: And the need for directors who think* (London: Fontana).

Gasparski, W. W. and Botham, D. (eds.) (1998) *Action Learning. Praxiology: The International Annual of Practical Philosophy and Methodology* (New Brunswick, NJ: Transaction Publishers).

Gay, P. (1983) "Action Learning and Organizational Change", in M. Pedler (ed.), *Action Learning in Practice*, 1st edn (Aldershot: Gower), pp. 153–64.

Gellerman, S. W. (1966) *The Management of Human Relations* (Hinsdale, IL: Dryden Press).
[*Note*: The author was part of the IBM World Trade Corporation. Discusses Revans' research with hospitals and stresses the applicability and the need for good communications within a firm and organization.]

Gilbert, R. V. (1979) "Action Learning Down Under Comes Out On Top", *Education and Training*, 21(10), pp. 315–16.

Gilbert, R. V. (1991) *Reglomania: The curse of organisational reform and how to cure it*. London: Prentice Hall.
[*Note*: Used action learning as chief executive in the Department of Housing, Victoria State Government in Australia; see his articles in Coghill's bibliography (1983).]

Gothenburg City Education Committee (1992) *Farrington, Freire, Revans, Sapp: Four of the main speakers at the 2nd International Conference of Educating Cities*, 25–27 November, 1992 in Gothenburg, Sweden (Gothenburg: Gothenburg City Education Committee).

Gourvish, T. R. and Tiratsoo, N. (eds.) (1998) *Missionaries and Managers: American influences on European management education, 1945–60* (Manchester: Manchester University Press).

Grayson, C. J. (1973) "Management Science and Business Practice", *Harvard Business Review*, July–August, pp. 41–9.

Gregg-Logan, A. (2002) "Business Driven Action Learning Catches on All Over the World". Accessed 11 November, 2009, [available at http://www.distance-educator.com/Article6809.phtml]

Greiner, L. E. (1977) "Reflections on OD American Style", in C. L. Cooper (ed.), *Organizational Development in the UK and USA* (London: Macmillan), pp. 65–82.

Greville, M. R. (2000) "Facilitating Leadership Development through High Performance Teamwork", in Yury Boshyk (ed.), *Business Driven Action Learning: Global best practices* (London/New York: Macmillan Business/St Martin's Press), pp. 191–9.

Guillon, P., Kasprzyk, R., and Sorge, J. (2000) "Dow: Sustaining Change and Accelerating Growth through Business Focused Learning", in Y. Boshyk (ed.), *Business Driven Action Learning: Global best practices* (London/New York: Macmillan Business/St Martin's Press), pp. 14–28.

Handy, C., Gordon, C., Gow, I., and Randlesome, C. (1988) *Making Managers: A report on management education, training and development in the USA, West Germany, France, Japan and the UK* (London: Pitman).
[*Note*: Highly complimentary of Revans.]

Hanika, F. de P. (1960) "The Role of Management Sciences in Training and Education for Management", Paper presented at Management Sciences. Models and Techniques, Proceedings of the Sixth International Meeting of the Institute of Management Sciences, at London.
[*Note*: Reference to Revans' management and scientific method 1958, including summary of his main points (p. 427).]

Hanson, K. H. (2000) "Motorola: Combining business projects with learning projects", in Y. Boshyk (ed.), *Business Driven Action Learning: Global best practices* (London/New York: Macmillan Business/St Martin's Press), pp. 104–22.

Harman, P. and Mitton S. (2002) *Cambridge Scientific Minds* (Cambridge: Cambridge University Press).

Harries, J. M. (1983) "Developing a Set Adviser", in M. Pedler (ed.), *Action Learning in Practice*, 1st edn (Aldershot: Gower), pp. 217–26.

Hauser, B. (2008) *Action Learning im Management Development: Eine vergleichende Analyse von Action-Learning Programmen zur Entwicklung von Führungskräften in drei verschiedenen Unternehmen* (Munich: Rainer Hampp Verlag).

Heald, G. (ed.) (1970) *Approaches to the Study of Organizational Behavior: Operational research and the behavioral sciences* (London: Tavistock).
[*Note*: Revans' article, "The Managerial Alphabet" is included.]

Hellwig, H. and Bertsch, J. (1997) "Usprung und Werden einer Erfolgsgeschichte", in J. Bertsch and P. Zürn (eds.), *Führen und Gestalten: 100 Unternehmergespräche in Baden-Baden* (Berlin: Springer), pp. 13–24.
[*Note*: Revans' book, Developing Effective Managers (1971) was dedicated to Hans Hellwig, a fellow member of the European Association of Management Training Centres. It then merged with another organization to form the European Foundation for Management Development in 1971. Includes a brief biography of Hellwig.]

Heron, J. (1999) *The Complete Facilitator's Handbook* (London: Kogan Page).

Hicks, S. (2002) "How Companies Plan and Design Action Learning Management Development Programmes in the United States: Lessons from practice", in Y. Boshyk (ed.), *Action Learning Worldwide: Experiences of leadership and organizational development* (Basingstoke, U.K./New York: Palgrave Macmillan), pp. 55–75.

Honjo Nakano M. (2002) "Business Driven Action Learning in Japan", in Y. Boshyk (ed.), *Action Learning Worldwide: Experiences of leadership and organizational development* (Basingstoke, U.K./New York: Palgrave Macmillan), pp. 260–7.

Horan, J. (2007) "Business Driven Action Learning: A powerful tool for building world-class entrepreneurial business leaders", *Organization Development Journal*, 25(3), pp. 75–80.

Holman, P. G. and Coghill, N. F. (1987) *Disruptive Behaviour in Schools! Causes, treatment and prevention* (Bromley, U.K.: Chartwell-Bratt).

[*Note*: Contains a section on action learning in Appendix 2; preface by Revans; with mention of Revans and Coghill's involvement with the International Foundation for Action Learning (IFAL).]

Honey, P. and Mumford, A. (1982) *Manual of Learning Styles*, 1st edn (Maidenhead: Peter Honey).

Honey, P and Mumford, A. (1986) *Using Your Learning Styles* (Maidenhead: Honey).

Hosta, R. (2000) "IBM: Using business driven action learning in a turnaround", in Y. Boshyk (ed.), *Business Driven Action Learning: Global best practices* (London/ New York: Macmillan Business/St Martin's Press), pp. 76–90.

Hughes, M. J. (1983) "The Mixed Set", in M. Pedler (ed.), *Action Learning in Practice*, 1st edn (Aldershot: Gower), pp. 73–82.

Inglis, Scott (1994) *Making the Most of Action Learning* (London: Gower).

Isaacson, B. (2002) "Action Learning Beyond Survival: A South African journey", in Y. Boshyk (ed.), *Action Learning Worldwide: Experiences of leadership and organizational development* (Basingstoke, U.K./New York: Palgrave Macmillan), pp. 229–45.

Isaacson, W. (2007) *Einstein: His Life and Universe* (New York: Simon & Schuster).

Keeble, S. P. (1992) *The Ability to Manage: A study of British management, 1890–1990* (Manchester: Manchester University Press).

Kensit, D. B. J. (1948) "European Voluntary Workers and their English", *Outlook*, July.

[*Note*: Report on Revans' project on teaching English to European volunteer miners using action learning. See Chapter 3 in this volume. This was the National Coal Board's training magazine.]

Kepner, C. H. and Tregoe, B. B. (1975) *The Rational Manager: A systematic approach to problem solving and decision making* (Princeton: Kepner-Tregoe, Inc).

[*Note*: Revans' potential partners for the Action Learning Trust and Revans Action Learning International.]

Khurana, Rakesh (2007) *From Higher Aims to Hired Hands. The social transformation of American business schools and the unfulfilled promise of management as a profession* (Princeton: Princeton University Press).

[*Note*: See especially chapter 5, "The Changing Institutional Field in the Postwar Era": 195–231.]

Kim, P. S., and Jin, J. (2008) "Action Learning and Its Applications in Government: The case of South Korea", *Public Administration Quarterly*, 1, July.

Kipping, Matthias, (1998) "The Hidden Business Schools: Management training in Germany since 1945", in Engwall and Zamagni, pp. 95–110.

Kissel, W. (2000) "Hoffman La Roche and Boehringer Mannheim: Mission Impossible? – Executive development during a takeover", in Yury Boshyk (ed.), *Business Driven Action Learning: Global best practices* (London/New York: Macmillan Business/St Martin's Press), pp. 65–75.

Kleiner, A. (1996) *The Age of Heretics: Heroes, Outlaws, and the Forerunners of Corporate Change* (New York: Currency).

Knowles, Malcolm S. (1998) *The Adult Learner* (Houston: Gulf Publishing).

Kolb, David A. (1984) *Experiential Learning: Experience as the source of learning and development* (Englewood Cliffs, NJ: Prentice-Hall).

Kynaston, D. (2007) *A World to Build: Austerity Britain, 1945–48* (London: Bloomsbury).

Lackie, G. L. (2000) "Heineken, Shell *et al*.: Twenty years of consortium action learning", in Yury Boshyk (ed.), *Business Driven Action Learning: Global best practices* (London/New York: Macmillan Business/St Martin's Press), pp. 55–64.

LaRue, B., Childs, P., and Larson, K. (2006) *Leading Organizations from the Inside-Out: Unleashing the collaborative genius of action-learning teams* (New York: Wiley).

Larsson, Peter (1985) *Chefer lär chefer: action learning fran ord till handling i chefs utbildningen* (Stockholm: Liber Förlag).

Lawlor, A. (1973) *Works Organisation* (London: Macmillan [for] the Institution of Works Managers [Macmillan handbooks in industrial management]).

Lawlor, A. (1983) The Components of Action Learning, in M. Pedler (ed.), *Action Learning in Practice*, 1st edn (Aldershot: Gower), pp. 191–204.
[*Note*: Republished in the 1997, 3rd edn of this book.]

Lawlor, A. (1985) *Productivity Improvement Manual* (Westport, CT: Quorum Books).
[*Note*: Boulden wrote most of the chapter on action learning; some materials by Action Learning Associates, of which Lawlor and Boulden and a few others were members, along with Revans, although at arms length.]

Lawrence, J. (1977) "ALP is Learning Too", in D. Casey and D. Pierce (eds.), *More Than Management Development: Action Learning at GEC* (NY: AMACOM), pp. 91–101.

Lawrence, J. (1994) "Action Learning – A Questioning Approach", in A. Mumford (ed.), *Handbook of Management Development*, 4th edn (Aldershot: Gower), pp. 209–35.

Lee, Taebok. (2002) "Action Learning in Korea", in Y. Boshyk (ed.), *Action Learning Worldwide: Experiences of leadership and organizational development* (Basingstoke, U.K. and New York: Palgrave Macmillan), pp. 249–59.

LeGros, V. M. and Topolosky, P. S. (2000) "DuPont: Business driven action learning to shift company direction", in Y. Boshyk (ed.), *Business Driven Action Learning: Global best practices* (London/New York: Macmillan Business/St Martin's Press), pp. 29–41.

Lennick, Doug and Kiel, Fred (2005) *Moral Intelligence: Enhancing business performance and leadership success* (Philadelphia: Wharton School Publishing).

Lessem, R. (1982) "A Biography of Action Learning", in R. W. Revans, (1982), *The Origins and Growth of Action Learning* (Bromley: Chartwell-Bratt), pp. 4–17.
[*Note*: A thoughtful essay on the major themes in Revans life and work.]

Lessem, R. (1983) "Building a Community of Action Learners", in M. Pedler (ed.), (1983), *Action Learning in Practice*, 1st edn (Aldershot: Gower), pp. 165–72.

Lessem, R. (1994) "The Emerging Businessphere", in R. Boot., J. Lawrence and J. Morris, *Managing the Unknown By Creating New Futures* (London: McGraw Hill), pp. 109–23.

[*Note*: Mention of Revans and the future of action learning.]

Levy, M. (2000) "Sage of Reason", *People Management*, pp. 24–6.

[*Note*: A good summary of Revans' life.]

Levy, P. (2000) "Organising the External Business Perspective: The role of the country coordinator in action learning programmes", in Yury Boshyk (ed.), *Business Driven Action Learning: Global best practices* (London/New York: Macmillan Business/St Martin's Press), pp. 206–26.

[*Note*: A detailed article on how to organize the "outside-in" component for business driven action learning programs.]

Lewis, A. (1983) "An In-Company Programme", in M. Pedler (ed.), *Action Learning in Practice*, 1st edn (Aldershot: Gower), pp. 105–18.

[*Note*: Also republished in the 1997, 3rd edn]

Lewis, A. and Marsh, W. (1987) Action Learning: The development of field managers in the Prudential Assurance Company, in A. Mumford (ed.), "Action Learning", *Journal of Management Development*, Special issue in honor of Reg Revans, 6(2), pp. 45–56.

Likert, R. (1961) *New Patterns of Management* (New York: McGraw Hill).

Link-up 2 [2]. (2002–2003) Manchester, Revans Institute for Action Learning and Research, Salford University.

[*Note*: "A publication created by and for individuals who desire to bring together research and practical experience". This issue contains many tributes to Revans upon his death. See especially the one by Baquer, includes photos of Revans.]

Lindeman. E. C. (1926) *The Meaning of Adult Education* (New York: New Republic).

McGill, I. and Beaty, L. (2001) *Action Learning: A guide for professional, management and educational development*, rev. 2nd edn (London: Kogan Page).

McGill, I. and Brockbank, A. (2004) *The Action Learning Handbook: Powerful techniques for education, professional development and training* (London: Routledge).

McGregor, D. (1961) *The Human Side of Enterprise* (New York: McGraw-Hill).

McNulty, N. G. (1983) "Action Learning around the World", in M. Pedler (ed.), *Action Learning in Practice*, 1st edn (Aldershot: Gower), pp. 173–87.

Mailick, S., (ed.) (1974) *The Making of the Manager: A world view* (Garden City, New York: United Nations Institute for Training and Research (UNITAR) and Anchor Press/Doubleday).

[*Note*: Contains an article by Revans.]

Maital, S., Cizin, S., Gilan, G., and Ramon, T. (2002) "Action Learning and National Competitive Strategy: A case study on the Technion Institute of Management in Israel", in Y. Boshyk (ed.), *Action Learning Worldwide: Experiences of leadership and organizational development* (Basingstoke, U.K. and New York: Palgrave Macmillan), pp. 208–28.

Malinen, A. (2000) *Towards the Essence of Adult Experiential Learning: A reading of the theories of Knowles, Kolb, Mezirow, Revans and Schön* (Jyväskylä, Finland: SoPhi, University of Jyväskylä).

Mansell, C. (1975) "How GEC Learns Action, *Management Today*, May, pp. 62, 134, 136, 138.

Mant, A. (1969) *The Experienced Manager: A major resource* (London: British Institute of Management).

Mant, A. (1977) *The Rise and Gall of the British Manager* (London: Macmillan). [*Note*: Positive references to Reg Revans citing the Belgian experience.]

Margerison, C. (1978) "Action Research and Action Learning in Management Education", *Journal of European Industrial Training*, 2(6), pp. 22–5.

Margerison, C. (2003) "Memories of Reg Revans, 1907–2003", *Organisations and People*, 10(3), August, pp. 2–7. [*Note*: On Revans and the International Management Centre; personal and interesting on the man and his style as well.]

Marquardt, M. J. (1999) *Action Learning in Action: Transforming problems and people for world-class organizational learning* (Palo Alto: Davies-Black).

Marquardt, M. J. (2004) *Optimizing the Power of Action Learning* (Palo Alto: Davies-Black).

Marquardt, M. J. (2004) "The Power of Learning in Action Learning: A conceptual analysis of how the five schools of adult learning theories are incorporated within the practice of action learning", *Action Learning: Research and Practice*, 1(2), pp. 185–202.

Marquardt, M. J., Skipton L. H., Freedman, A. M. and Hill, C. C. (2009) *Action Learning for Developing Leaders and Organizations: Principles, strategies, and cases* (Washington: American Psychological Association).

Marrow, A. J. (1969) *The Practical Theorist: The life and work of Kurt Lewin* (New York: Basic Books).

Marsick, V. J. and Cederholm L. (1988. Developing Leadership in International Managers: An Urgent Challenge! *The Columbia Journal of World Business* 23(4), pp. 3–11.

Marsick, V. J. (1990) "Action Learning and Reflection in the Workplace", in J. Mezirow *et al.* (eds.), *Fostering Critical Reflection in Adulthood: A guide to transformative and emancipatory learning* (San Francisco: Jossey-Bass, pp. 23–46).

Marsick, V. J., Cederholm, L., Turner, E., and Pearson, T. (1992) "Action-Reflection Learning", *Training and Development*, August, pp. 63–6.

Marsick, V. J. and Sauquet A. (2000) Learning Through Reflection, in M. Deutsch and P. Coleman (eds.), *Handbook of Conflict Resolution: Theory and practice*. San Francisco: Jossey-Bass: 382–99.

Marsick, V. J. and Watkins, Karen E. (1999) *Facilitating Learning Organizations: Making learning count* (Aldershot: Gower).

Marsick, V. J. (2002) "Exploring the Many Meanings of Action Learning and ARL", in L. Rohlin, K. Billing, A. Lindberg and M. Wickelgren (eds.), *Earning While Learning in Global Leadership* (Lund, Sweden: Studentlitteratur), pp. 297–314.

Maslow, A. H. (1970) *Motivation and Personality* (New York: Harper & Row).

Memorandum and Articles of Association of Action Learning Projects International Ltd. (Manchester: Hutton, Hartley & Co. Ltd, [c. 1974]).

Mercer, S. (2000) "General Electric's Executive Action Learning Programmes", in Y. Boshyk (ed.), *Business Driven Action Learning: Global best practices* (London/New York: Macmillan Business/St Martin's Press), pp. 42–54.

Mercer, S. (2000) "General Electric Executive Learning Programmes: Checklist and tools for action learning teams", in Y. Boshyk (ed.), *Business Driven Action Learning: Global best practices* (London/New York: Macmillan Business/St Martin's Press), pp. 179–90.

Mezirow, J. (1991) *Transformative Dimensions of Adult Learning* (San Francisco: Jossey-Bass).

Miles, D. H. (2003) *The 30-Second Encyclopedia of Learning and Performance: A trainer's guide to theory, technology and practice* (New York: American Management Association).

Miles, M. B. (1981) *Learning to Work in Groups: A practical guide for members and trainers*, 2nd edn (New York: Teacher's College, Columbia University).

[*Note*: Very good introduction on how project work in management programs evolved.]

Mintzberg, H. (2004) *Managers Not MBAs: A hard look at the soft practice of managing and management development* (San Francisco: Berrett-Koehler).

[*Note*: See especially chapter 10, on an action learning program for younger managers.]

Mollet, G. (2000) "Volkswagen: Action Learning and the Development of High Potentials", in Yury Boshyk (ed.), *Business Driven Action Learning: Global best practices* (London/New York: Macmillan Business/St Martin's Press), pp. 152–65.

Morris, J. (1974) "Experiences of the Newer Management Training Techniques in Britain", in S. Mailick, *The Making of the Manager: A world view* (New York: Anchor), pp. 93–118.

Morris, J. (1977) "Tacking down the Middle: Ten years of organizational development by a British business school", in Cary L. Cooper (ed.), *Organizational Development in the UK and the USA* (London: Macmillan), pp. 5–30.

[*Note*: Mention of Revans.]

Morris, J. (1975) "Reflections on Management Education in Britain", *Quarterly Journal of Administration*, Institute of Administration, University of Ife, Ile-Ife, Nigeria, October, pp. 13–23.

Morris, J. (1986) "The Learning Spiral", in A. Mumford (ed.), *Handbook of Management Development*, 2nd edn (Aldershot:Gower), pp. 183–96.

Morris, J. (1987) "Action Learning: Reflections on a process", in A. Mumford (ed.), "Action Learning", *Journal of Management Development*, Special issue in honor of Reg Revans, 6(2), pp. 57–70.

Morris, J. (1994) "Development Work and the Learning Spiral", in A. Mumford (ed.), *The Gower Handbook of Management Development*, 4th edn (Aldershot: Gower), pp. 127–38.

Muggeridge, M. (1940) *The Thirties, 1930–1940, in Great Britain* (London: Hamish Hamilton).

Mumford, A. (1979) "Self-development – Flavour of the month?", *Journal of European Industrial Training*, 3(3), pp. 13–15.

Mumford, A. (1980) *Making Experience Pay: Management success through effective learning* (London: McGraw-Hill).

Mumford, A. (1983) "Emphasis on the Learner: A new approach", *Industrial and Commercial Training*, 15(11), pp. 342–4.

Mumford, A. (ed.) (1984) *Insights into Action Learning* (Bradford: MCB University Press).

Mumford, A. (1989) *Management Development: Strategies for action* (London: Institute of Personnel Management).

Mumford, A. (1991) "Learning in Action", *Personnel Management*, 23(7), July, pp. 34–7.

[*Note*: Mumford's views on action learning.]

Mumford, A. (ed.) (1987) "Action Learning", *Journal of Management Development*, Special issue in honor of Reg Revans, 6(2).

Mumford, A. (1992) "New Ideas on Action Learning", in *Approaches to Action Learning: Papers delivered at a private seminar on Thursday 14th November 1991 at the King's Fund Centre* (London. Keele: Mercia Publications).

Mumford, A. (1994) *Gower Handbook of Management Development*, 4th edn (Aldershot: Gower).

Mumford, A. (1995) "Making the Most of Action Learning", *Journal of European Industrial Training*, 19(5), p. v.

Mumford, A. (1995) "Managers Developing Others Through Action Learning", *Industrial and Commercial Training*, 27(2), pp. 19–27.

Mumford, A. and Honey, P. (1986) *Manual of Learning Styles* (Maidenhead: Peter Honey Publications).

Mumford, A., (ed.) (1997) *Action Learning at Work* (Aldershot: Gower).

Mumford, A. (1997) "A Review of the Literature", in M. Pedler (ED.), *Action Learning in Practice*, 3rd edn (Aldershot: Gower), pp. 373–92.

[*Note*: Third literature review of the topic by the author since 1985; very good bibliography.]

Mumford, E. (1999) "Routinisation, Re-engineering, and Socio-technical Design. Changing ideas on the organisation of work", in W. L. Currie and B. Galliers (eds.), *Rethinking Management Information Systems* (Oxford: Oxford University Press), pp. 28–44.

[*Note*: Good background on the Tavistock Institute, small groups; the author was Emeritus Professor of Organizational Behaviour at Manchester Business School at the time of publication.]

Musschoot, F. (1973) *Action Learning in Small Enterprises: A consideration of action learning and the development of managers in small enterprises* (Ghent: for the University of Ghent by ALP [Action Learning Projects] International Publications).

Noel, J. L. and Charan, R. (1988) "Leadership Development at GE's Crotonville", *Human Resource Management*, 27(4), pp. 433–49.

Noel, J. L. and Charan, R. (1992) "GE brings Global Thinking to Light", *Training and Development*, 46(7), pp. 28–33.

[*Note*: The original manuscript read as "Action learning: How GE develops global business leaders" and included Stephen R. Mercer as a co-author.]

Noel, J. L. and Dotlich, D. L. (2008) "Action Learning: Creating leaders through work", in J. L. Noel and D. L. Dotlich (eds.), *The 2008 Pfeiffer Annual: Leadership development* (San Francisco: Wiley), pp. 239–47.

O'Neil, J., Arnell, E., and Turner, E. (1996) "Earning While Learning", in K. E. Watkins and V. J. Marsick (eds.), *In Action: Creating the learning organization* (Alexandria, VA: American Society for Training and Development), pp. 153–64.

O'Neil, J. and Lamm, S. L. (2000) "Working as a Learning Coach Team in Action Learning", *New Directions for Adult and Continuing Education*, Fall; 87, pp. 43–52.

O'Neil, J. and Marsick, V. J. (2007) *Understanding Action Learning: Theory into practice* (New York: AMACOM).

O'Neil, K. (1996) "Action Learning in Northern Ireland", in *Training the Fire Brigade*, edited by the EFMD, pp. 170–7.

Odebrecht, Norberto (1985) *Survival, Growth, and Perpetuity* (Salvador, Brazil: Emilio Odebrecht Foundation).

[*Note*: One of Brazil's executive leaders, owner of its largest engineering and construction company, outlines his learning philosophy as "Learning through work". First Portuguese edition published in 1983.]

Parker, P. (1989) *For Starters: The business of life* (London: Jonathan Cape).

[*Note*: Sir Peter Parker was a supporter of Revans; Parker advocated the creation of business schools and a better understanding by managers of the external environment; he led several institutions of which Revans was a part – for example, the British Institute of Management.]

Pearce, D. (1983) "The Role of the Personnel Specialist", in M. Pedler, (ed.), *Action Learning in Practice*, 1st edn (Aldershot: Gower), pp. 239–50.

Pearce, D. (1997) "Getting Started", in M. Pedler, (ed.), *Action Learning in Practice*, 3rd edn (Aldershot: Gower), pp. 355–71.

[*Note*: Also in the 1st edn, 1983.]

Pearce, D. and Williams, E. (2009) *Action Learning for Innovation and Change: Welsh farming families* (Aberystwyth: Menter a Busnes).

Pearson, R. (2002) "Strategic Change Management at Merck Hong Kong: Building a high performing executive team using action reflection learning", in Y. Boshyk (ed.), *Action Learning Worldwide: Experiences of leadership and organizational development* (Basingstoke, U.K./New York: Palgrave Macmillan), pp. 282–91.

Pedler, M. J. (1973) "Industrial Relations Training on the Shop Floor", *Journal of European Training*, 2(3), pp. 214–27.

Pedler, M. (1974) "An Action Research Approach to Training Interventions", *Management Learning*, 5, pp. 54–67.

Pedler, M. (1974) "Learning in Management Education", *Journal of European Training*, 3(3), pp. 182–94.

Pedler, M., Lawlor, A. et al. (1977) "Report of the Sheffield Action Learning Clinic". s.l.: Yorkshire and Humberside Regional Management Centre, in association with the Institution of Works Managers.

Pedler, M. (1980) "Group Learning Set – Midlands textile training group", Newsletter 6. The Action Learning Trust, pp. 8–13.

Pedler. M. (1980) "Book review of *Action Learning: New Techniques for Action Learning* by R.W. Revans", *Management Education and Development*, 11, pp. 219–23.

[*Note*: A very insightful article on Revans the man and his work.]

Pedler, M. (1981) "The Diffusion of Action Learning", Occasional Paper. 2, A joint project by the Departments of Management Studies of Sheffield City Polytechnic and Teeside Polytechnic funded by the Training Services Division of the Manpower Services Commission.

Pedler, M. (1983) "Transatlantic Virus threatens British Ethical Standards", *Management Education and Development*, 14(3), pp. 197–200.

Pedler, M. (ed.) (1983) *Action Learning Practice*, 1st edn (Aldershot: Gower).

[*Note*: A very useful compendium of articles, many contributed by those who worked directly with Revans. Subsequent editions of this work did not include about half of these articles.]

Pedler, M. (1983) "On the Difference between P and Q", in M. Pedler (ed.), *Action Learning in Practice*, 1st edn (Aldershot: Gower), pp. 55–61.

Pedler, M. (1983) "Another View at Set Advising", in M. Pedler (ed.), *Action Learning in Practice*, 1st edn (Aldershot: Gower), pp. 227–38.

Pedler, M. (1984) "Management Self-development", in B. Taylor and G. Lippitt (eds.), *Management Development and Training Handbook*, 2nd edn (London: McGraw-Hill), pp. 336–49.

Pedler, M. and Boutall, J. (1992) *Action Learning for Change: A resource book for managers and other professionals*. National Health Service Training Directorate (NHSTD) (Bristol: NHSTD), pp. 36.

Pedler, M., Burgoyne, J., and Boydell, T. (1997) *The Learning Company: A Strategy for Sustainable Development* (London: McGraw-Hill).

Pedler, M. (ed.) (1997) *Action Learning in Practice*. 3rd and revised edn (Aldershot: Gower).

[*Note*: A very valuable source with some articles written by those who worked with Revans. Note that the 1st edn in 1983 has many articles not included in the 1997 edn and they are a rich source on action learning.]

Pedler, M. (1997) "Managing as Moral Art", in M. Pedler (ed.), *Action Learning in Practice*. 3rd edn (Aldershot: Gower), pp. 31–40.

Pedler, Mike. (1999) "Eine Begegnung mit Reginald Revans", in O. Donnenberg (ed.), *Action Learning: Ein Hanbuch* (Stuttgart: Klett-Cotta), pp. 16–27.

Pedler, Mike. (2003) "A Tribute to Reg Revans", *Linkup*, 2(2), p. 5.

Pedler, M., Burgoyne, J., and Bodell, T. (1978) *A Manager's Guide to Self-Development* (London: McGraw-Hill).

Pedler, M., Burgoyne, J., and Brook C. (2005) "What Has Action Learning Learned to Become?", *Action Learning: Research and Practice*, 2(1), pp. 49–68.

[*Note*: An opinionated and somewhat misleading article on what constitutes "true" action learning. Nevertheless, worth reading.]

Pedler, M. (2008) *Action Learning for Managers*, 2nd edn (Aldershot: Gower).

"People and Organisations in Action Learning" (1983), in M. Pedler (ed.), *Action Learning in Practice*, 1st edn (Aldershot: Gower), pp. 283–7.

Pettigrew, A. (1975) "Strategic Aspects of the Management Specialists Activity", *Personnel Review*, 4(1), pp. 160–75.

Piaget, J. (1977) *Psychology and Epistemology: Towards a theory of knowledge*. (London: Penguin).

[*Note*: Revans comments on this work and the one below, in Revans (1982).]

Piaget, Je. (1977) *Science and Education and the Psychology of the Child* (London: Penguin).

Pike, J. (1983) "Action Learning on an Academic Course", in M. Pedler (ed.), *Action Learning in Practice*, 1st edn (Aldershot: Gower), pp. 141–52.

Platt, Robert (1972) *Private and Controversial* (London: Cassell).

Prestoungrange, G., [Willis, G.,] and Margerison, C. (1999) *Multinational Action Learning at Work* (Buckingham: Action Learning Institute for the Association of International Management Centres).

Raelin, Joseph A. (2008) *Work-Based Learning: Bridging knowledge and action in the workplace* (San Francisco: Jossey-Bass).

Raiser, K. and Gould, R. M. (2002) "Changing the Rules of the World Council of Churches: Action learning as large-scale system change", in Y. Boshyk (ed.), *Action Learning Worldwide: Experiences of leadership and organizational development* (Basingstoke, U.K./New York: Palgrave Macmillan), pp. 184–99.

Reddy, S. and Barker, A. E. (eds.) (2005) *Genuine Action Learning: Following the spirit of Revans* (Hyderabad: ICFAI University Press).

Reinholdsson, A. (2002) "Northern Light: A survey of action learning in the Nordic region of Europe", in Y. Boshyk (ed.), *Action Learning Worldwide: Experiences of leadership and organizational development* (Basingstoke, U.K./New York: Palgrave Macmillan), pp. 163–72.

Rice, A. K. (1965) *Learning for Leadership: Interpersonal and intergroup relations* (London: Tavistock).

Rigg, C. (2006) "Developing Public Service: The context for action learning", in C. Rigg and S. Richards (eds.), *Action Learning, Leadership and Organizational Development in Public Services* (London: Routledge), pp. 1–11.

Rigg, C. (2006) "Understanding the Organizational Potential of Action Learning", in C. Rigg, and S. Richards (eds.), *Action Learning, Leadership and Organizational Development in Public Services* (London: Routledge), pp. 41–51.

Rigg, C. and Richards, S. (eds.) (2006) *Action Learning, Leadership and Organizational Development in Public Services* (London: Routledge).

Rimanoczy, I. (2002) "Action Refection Learning in Latin America", in Y. Boshyk (ed.), *Action Learning Worldwide: Experiences of leadership and organizational development* (Basingstoke, U.K./New York: Palgrave Macmillan), pp. 152–60.

Rimanoczy, I. and Turner, E. (2008) *Action Reflection Learning: Solving real business problems by connecting learning with earning* (Mountain View, CA: Davies-Black).

Rohlin, L., Skarvad, P.H., and Nilsson, S. A. (1998) *Strategic Leadership in the Learning Society* (Vasbyholm: MiL Publishers).

Rohlin, L., Billing, K., Lindberg, A., and Wickelgren, M. (eds.) (2002) *Earning While Learning in Global Leadership: The Volvo MiL partnership* (Lund: MiL Publishers).

Rohlin, L. (2002) "The Story of MiL", in L. Rohlin et al., pp. 17–22.

Rolland, N. (2002) "Strategic Executive Learning and Development in French Multinationals", in Y. Boshyk (ed.), *Action Learning Worldwide: Experiences of leadership and organizational development* (Basingstoke, U.K. and New York: Palgrave Macmillan), pp. 173–83.

Rothwell, W. J. (1999) *The Action Learning Guidebook: A real-time strategy for problem solving, training design, and employee development* (San Francisco: Jossey-Bass). [Note: No relationship to Revans, and clearly in the category of the "modified and perhaps Americanized version of action learning". Useful checklists of program items used in this approach to action learning.]

Rowbottom, R. W. and Greenwald, H. A. (1962) *Understanding Management*, with a Preface by Reginald W. Revans (Manchester: Whitworth Press).

Sankaran, S. Dick B., Passfield, R., and Swepson, P. (eds.) (2001) *Effective Change Management Using Action Learning and Action Research: Concepts, frameworks, processes, applications* (Lismore, Australia: Southern Cross University Press).

Sargent, J. (ed.) (1955) *Education and Society: Some studies of education systems in Europe and America* (London: Batchworth Press).

[*Note*: Sargent's writings in the 1930s made an impact on Revans. For extracts of these writings and Revans' comments, see Revans, 1982, *The Origins*, pp. 18–22.]

Sasaki, N. (1981) *Management and Industrial Structure in Japan* (Oxford: Pergamon).
[*Note*: Mention of Revans in the introduction.]

Schein, Edgar H. (2008) "From Brainwashing to Organization Therapy: The evolution to organization therapy: The evolution of a model of change dynamics", in T. G. Cummings (ed.), *Handbook of Organization Development* (San Francisco: Jossey-Bass), pp. 39–52.

Schön, D. A. (1983) *The Reflective Practitioner: How professionals think in action* (Aldershot: Ashgate).

Schön, D. A. (1987) *Educating the Reflective Practitioner: Toward a new design for teaching and learning in the professions* (San Fransisco: Jossey-Bass).

Schumacher, E. F. (1973) *Small is Beautiful: Economics as if people mattered* (London: Blond & Briggs).

Senge, P. (1990) *The Fifth Discipline: The art and practice of the learning organization* (New York: Currency Doubleday).
[*Note*: Popularization of the "learning organization" influenced by the practice and writings of Argyris and Schön, discusses "action science".]

Senge, P. (1990) *The Fifth Discipline: The art and practice of the learning organization*. (New York: Currency Doubleday).

Senge, P., Kleiner, A., Roberts, C., Ross, R., Roth, G., and Smith, B. (1999) *The Dance of Change: The challenges of sustaining momentum in learning organizations* (New York: Currency Doubleday).

Simon, H. A. (1997) *Administrative Behaviour: A study of decision-making processes in administrative organizations*, 4th edn (New York: Free Press).
[*Note*: Revans made reference to Simon's criticism of the "case method". Updated with extensive new commentaries by the author.]

Smith, P. A. C. and O'Neil, J. (2003) "A Review of Action Learning 1994–2000, Part 1 – Bibliography and comments", *Journal of Workplace Learning*, 15(2).

Smith, P. A. C. and O'Neil, J. (2003) "A Review of Action Learning 1994–2000, Part 2 – Signposts into the literature", *Journal of Workplace Learning*, 15(4).
[*Note*: A detailed listing of papers, reports but not books by categories. Available in electronic form at: http://www.tlainc.com/ifalclib.htm]

Snyder, W. M. and Wenger, E. (2004) "Our World as a Learning System: A communities-of-practice approach", in M. L. Conner and J. G. Clawson (eds.), *Creating a Learning Culture: Strategy, technology, and practice* (Cambridge: Cambridge University Press).

Stenger, M. M. (2008) *Action Learning in der Führungskräfteentwicklung: Allgemeine Grundlagen und Erfolge bei der Anwendung* (Berlin: Verlag Dr. Müller).

Strandler, L. (1988) Läroplan 2000 *Hommage a Huldebetoon aan Gaston Deurinck* (Stockholm: Svenska arbetsgivarefören (SAF)).

Strebel, P. and Keys, T. (eds.) (2005) "Mastering Executive Education: How to combine content with context and emotion", *The IMD Guide* (Harlow, England: *Financial Times*/Prentice Hall).

Sutton, D. (1976) "Teaching and Learning in Management", *Management Education and Development*, 17, part 1, April.

Sutton, D. (1977) "Improving Services for the Mentally Handicapped", *ALT [Action Learning Trust] Newsletter,* 1.
[*Note*: No page numbers on the newsletter; perhaps the first issue of the *ALT Newsletter.*]
Sutton, D. (1977) "The Assumptions of Action Learning", Manuscript – 2 pages, IFAL Reference 566.
Sutton, D. (1983) "A Range of Applications", in M. Pedler (ed.), *Action Learning in Practice,* 1st edn (Aldershot: Gower), pp. 65–72.
[*Note*: Describes six programs in both the public and private sectors.]
Sutton, D. (1984) "Management Development in the Small Business", *Journal of European Industrial Training,* 8(3), pp. 23–8.
Sutton, D. (1989) "Further Thoughts on Action Learning", *Journal of European Industrial Training,* 13(3).
Sutton, D. (1990) "Action Learning: In search of P", *Industrial and Commercial Training,* 22(1), pp. 9–12.
Sutton, David (1997) "In Search of 'P'", in A. Mumford (ed.), *Action Learning at Work* (Aldershot: Gower), pp. 55–61.
[*Note*: One of the early collaborators with Revans; originally published in Industrial and Commercial Training, 22(1), 1990.]
Swepson, P., Dick, B., Zuber-Skerrit, O., Passfield, R., Carroll, A. M., and Wadsworth, Y. (2003) "A History of the Action Learning, Action Research, and Process Management Association (ALARPM): From Brisbane (Australia) to the World through inclusion and networks", *Systemic Practice and Action Research,* 16(4), pp. 237–81.
Taylor, B. and Lippitt, G. (eds.) (1983) *Management Development and Training Handbook* (Maidenhead, U.K.: McGraw-Hill).
[*Note*: With an article by Revans.]
Taylor, J., Marais, D., and Kaplan, A. (1997) *Action Learning for Development. Use your experience to improve your effectiveness* (Capetown: Juta & Co).
Taylor, J., Marais, D., and Heyns, S. (1998) *The Action-Learning Field Kit. Case studies of development issues and problems faced by development workers in South Africa, the Caribbean, Latin and North America* (Capetown: Juta & Co).
Tichy, N. M. (1978) "Demise, Absorption, or Renewal for the Future of Organization Development", in W. Warner Burke (ed.), *The Cutting Edge: Current theory and practice in organization development* (La Jolla, CA: University Associates), pp. 70–87.
Tichy, N. M. and Sherman, S. (1993) *Control Your Destiny or Someone Else Will: How Jack Welch is making General Electric the world's most competitive company* (New York: Currency-Doubleday).
Tichy, N. M. (2001) "No Ordinary Boot Camp". *Harvard Business Review,* 79(4), pp. 63–9.
[*Note*: Mention of "compact action learning" and company example.]
Tichy, N. M. and DeRose, C. (2003) "The Death and Rebirth of Organizational Development", in S. Chowdhury (ed.), *Organization 21C: Someday all organizations will lead this way* (Upper Saddle River, N.J: *Financial Times*/Prentice Hall), pp. 155–73.
TimesOnline (2003) "Reginald Revans: Management guru who taught executives to value experience over theory and put their people first", *The Times,*

21February. Accessed 11 November, 2009, available at http://www.times-online.co.uk/tol/comment/obituaries/article884986.ece

Tiratsoo, Nick (1998) "Management Education in Postwar Britain", in L. Engwall, L., and V. Zamagni, V. (eds.), *Management Education in Historical Perspective* (Manchester: Manchester University Press), pp. 111–26.

Tourloukis, P. (2002) "Using Action Learning to Develop Human Resource Executives at General Electric", in Y. Boshyk (ed.), *Action Learning Worldwide: Experiences of leadership and organizational development* (Basingstoke, U.K./New York: Palgrave Macmillan), pp. 90–109.

Trist, E. (1969) "On Socio-Technical Systems", in W. G. Bennis, K. D. Benne and R. Chin (eds.), *The Planning of Change* (New York: Holt, Rinehart & Winston), pp. 269–82.

Trist, E. and Bamforth, K. W. (1951) "Some Social and Psychological Consequences of the Longwall Method of Coal Getting", *Human Relations*, 4. pp. 3–38.

Trist, E. and Murray H. (1993) *The Social Engagement of Social Science: A Tavistock anthology. Volume II: The Socio-Technical Perspective* (Philadelphia: University of Pennsylvannia).

Tregoe, B. T. (1983) "Questioning: The key to effective problem solving and decision making", in B. Taylor and G. Lippitt (1983).

Ulrich, D., Kerr, S., and Ashkenas, R. (2002) *The GE Workout: How to implement GE's revolutionary method for busting bureaucracy and attacking organizational problems – fast!* (New York: McGraw-Hill).
[Note: No reference to action learning but to employee empowerment and, fight struggle against bureaucracy.]

Valpola, A. (ed.) (1988) *Resultat genom action learning, Foreningen Action Learning: rapport fran konferensen i Stockholm 1987* (Lund: Foreningen Action Learning).

Watkins, K. E. and Marsick, V. J. (eds.) (1996), in *Action: Creating the learning organization* (Alexandria, VA: American Society for Training and Development).

Weidemanis, M. and Boshyk, Y. (2000) Scancem: "'What Did We Earn and Learn?' Emerging markets and business driven action learning", in Y. Boshyk (ed.) *Business Driven Action Learning: Global best practices* (London/New York: Macmillan Business/St Martin's Press), pp. 134–9.

Weinstein, K. (1998) "Action Learning: A practical guide", 2nd edn (Aldershot: Gower).

Weinstein, K. (2002) "Action Learning: The classic approach", in Y. Boshyk (ed.), *Action Learning Worldwide: Experiences of leadership and organizational development* (Basingstoke, U.K. and New York: Palgrave Macmillan), pp. 3–18.

Weisbord, M. W. (1987) *Productive Workplaces: Organizing and managing for dignity, meaning, and community* (San Francisco: Jossey-Bass).

Weisbord, M. R. (1992) *Discovering Common Ground: How future search conferences bring people together to achieve breakthrough innovation, empowerment, shared vision, and collaborative action* (San Francisco: Berret-Koehler).

Wieland, G. F. and Leigh, H. (eds.) (1971) *Changing Hospitals: A report on the Hospital Internal Communications Project* (London: Tavistock Publications).
[Note: Generally negative view of the project according to Revans but note the more positive assessment by Wieland in 1981.]

Wieland, G. F. (ed.) (1981) *Improving Health Care Management: Organization development and organization change* (Ann Arbor: Health Administration Press).

Wiener, N. (1950) *The Human Use of Human Beings: Cybernetics and society* (London: Eyre & Spottiswoode).

Willis, J. L. (2004) "Inspecting Cases against Revans' 'Gold Standard' of Action Learning", *Action Learning: Research and practice*, 1(1), April, pp. 11–27.

Willis, V. J. (2005) "Spontaneity and Self-Organising in Action Learning", in S. Reddy and A. E. Barker (eds.), *Genuine Action Learning: Following the spirit of Revans* (Hyderabad: ICFAI University Press), pp. 155–82.

Wills, G., and Oliver, C. (1996) "Measuring the ROI from Management Action Learning", *Management Development Review*, 9(1), pp. 17–21.

Wills, G. (1999) "The Origins and Philosophy of International Management Centres", in A. Mumford (ed.), *Action Learning at Work* (Aldershot: Gower), pp. 30–41.

Wilson, J. F. (1992) *The Manchester Experiment: A history of Manchester Business School, 1965–1990* (London: Paul Chapman Publishing).

[*Note*: Very good source on the climate of the debate in and outside industry regarding business schools linked with universities; much on the Revans period and on Professor J. Morris, Revans' colleague and friend; the Manchester Experiment was very much a partnership with industry; published for Manchester Business School.]

Wilson, J. F. (1996) "Management Education in Britain: A compromise between culture and necessity", in R. P. Amdam (ed.), *Management, Education and Competitiveness: Europe, Japan and the United States* (London: Routledge), pp. 133–49.

Yiu, L. and Saner, R. (2002), in Y. Boshyk (ed.), *Action Learning Worldwide: Experiences of leadership and organizational development* (Basingstoke, U.K./New York: Palgrave Macmillan), pp. 293–310.

Yorks, L. (2000) "The Emergence of Action Learning", *Training & Development*, 54(1), January, p. 56.

Yorks, L., O'Neil, J., and Marsick, V. J. (eds.) (1999) *Action Learning: Successful strategies for individual, team, and organzational development*. Number 2 in the series *Advances in Developing Human Resources*, R. A. Swanson, Editor-in-Chief (Baton Rouge/San Francisco: Academy of Human Resource Development and Berrett-Koehler).

Yorks, L., O'Neil, J., and Marsick, V. J. (1999) "Action Learning: Theoretical bases and varieties of practice", in L. Yorks, J. O'Neil and V. J. Marsick (eds.), *Action Learning: Successful strategies for individual, team, and organizational development* (Baton Rouge, LA/San Francisco: Berret-Koehler), pp. 1–18.

Yorks, L., Lamm, S., and O'Neil, J. (1999) "Transfer of Learning from Action Learning Programs to the Organizational Setting", in L. Yorks, J. O'Neil, and V. J. Marsick (eds.), *Action Learning: Successful strategies for individual, team, and organizational development* (Baton Rouge, LA: Berrett-Koehler), pp. 56–74.

Yorks, L., Marsick, V., and O'Neil, J. (1999) "Lessons for Implementing Action Learning", in L. Yorks, J. O'Neil, and V. J. Marsick (eds.), *Action Learning: Successful strategies for individual, team, and organizational development* (Baton Rouge, LA/San Francisco: Berrett-Koehler), pp. 96–113.

Yorks, L., O'Neil, J., and Marsick, V. (2002) "Action Reflection Learning and Critical Reflection Approaches", in Y. Boshyk (ed.), *Action Learning Worldwide: Experiences of leadership and organizational development* (Basingstoke, U.K./New York: Palgrave Macmillan), pp. 19–29.

[*Note*: A very good overview of the history and evolution of "action reflection learning".]

Zuber-Skerritt, O. (2001) "Action Learning and Action Research: Paradigm, praxis and programs", in S. Sankaran et al. (eds.), *Effective Change Management Using Action Learning and Action Research: Concepts, frameworks, processes, applications* (Lismore, Australia: Southern Cross University Press), pp. 1–20.

Zulch, B. (1988) "Action Learning: A solution to SA's problems?", *Productivity SA*, August–September, pp. 4, 6.

[*Note*: A good summary of Revans' thinking about Action Learning, especially on explaining the task/setting matrix.]

Action learning networks and communities of practice

The following is a listing of the most active networks and communities of practice that are both global and regional.

Action Learning and Action Research Association (ALARA)

Formed in 1991 in Australia as the Action Learning Action Research and Process Management Association, and renamed ALARA in 2007. Holds worldwide conferences and produces articles in the Association's journal, with a part-time professional administration, focusing primarily on action research.

http://www.alara.net.au

Global networks and communities of practice

Global Forum on Executive Development and Business Driven Action Learning

www.GlobalForumActionLearning.com

The Global Forum is a by-invitation-only community of practice, involving practitioners from major companies and organizations from around the world who explore issues of concern and best practices in executive development and action learning. Since 1996, it organizes an annual meeting in various parts of the world, carries our research and publishes periodically.

International Action Learning Conference

Organized by the editors and supporters of the journal *Action Learning: Research and Practice* based at Henley Management College, University of Reading in the U.K. Two conferences, primarily for academics, have been held. For further information, contact: helen.james@henley.reading.ac.uk

International Foundation for Action Learning
http://www.ifal.org.uk/

IFAL exists to identify and encourage a network of enthusiasts who support and develop the work of action learning in the U.K. and worldwide, and was founded in parallel with the Revans-created Action Learning Trust in 1977 by some of his close colleagues. Its original purpose was to support philanthropic action learning work with organizations in the public and civil sector on the basis of profits that were to be generated from work with the private sector by the ALT, but this never materialized. IFAL is a membership-based organization with membership fees, newsletters (since 1981), meetings and a helpful website. There are regional affiliates in several parts of the world and their websites are linked on the IFAL U.K. site.

Regional networks and communities of practice

Dutch Action Learning Society
http://www.actionlearning.nl/

The Action Learning Association (ALA) was founded in 1994 and has grown into a network which is interested in, and works with the principles of, Action Learning. The association aims to promote a better understanding of Action Learning and its use in practice. Each year, the ALA organizes a number of activities for members, such as open discussions, a work conference, and a conference whose theme focuses on reflection. These activities are also open for non-members. In addition, members maintain contact with each other through workgroups.

The Korean Action Learning Association
http://www.kala.or.kr

Holds an annual meeting every year since its formation in 2005, and has several other activities throughout the year.

The MiL Institute, Sweden
http://www.milinstitute.se

With an annual meeting and various publications, MiL, a consultancy, has been in existence for 30 years working with companies and organizations in Sweden and in cooperation with other institutions outside Sweden. "Action Reflection Learning® is its trademark", states MiL. Affiliated with another consultancy, LIM, in the United States.

Nordic Forum on Business Driven Action Learning
http://www.novare.se/eng/Home/NovareAct/tabid/747/Default.aspx

A grouping of company representatives, at this stage primarily from Sweden (and initiated by the consultancy Novare Act, but with no fee for participation), this forum started its activity in 2009 with its first meeting, the purpose being to bring together practitioners who would like to share their experiences with action learning. The intention is to continue to organize an annual meeting and hold smaller workshops throughout the year.

South African Regional Forum
http://www.gibs.co.za
Organized every second year by the Gordon Institute of Business Science, University of Pretoria, but based in Sandton near Johannesburg. Representatives from organizations from neighboring countries also take part.

Photo 1   Reg Revans in the BBC television studio in London, November 1973

After his resignation from his chair at the University of Manchester, Revans spent 1965–1975 working in Brussels with frequent trips back to the U.K. and elsewhere. Here he is pictured at the BBC Sound and T.V. Studio, London, England, November 1973 where he was interviewed about his "Belgian Experiment", the Inter-University Program for Advanced Management (1968–) with the Fondation Industrie-Université. He was accompanied by an executive and participant from the program. This T.V. broadcast, seen by Sir Arnold Weinstock, Managing Director of the General Electric Company (later Marconi), led to one of the most important executive learning and program initiatives for GEC and Revans in the U.K. A detailed description and discussion is to be found in David Casey and David Pearce, eds., (1977), *More Than Management Development: Action Learning at GEC.*

Photo courtesy of Donna Wick.

Photo 2 Reg Revans as a Visiting Professor and Distinguished Scholar in the U.S., February, 1994.

From left to right: Dean John Oehler, Reg Revans, and Robert L. Dilworth taken during Revans' time as Distinguished Visiting Professor in the School of Education, Virginia Commonwealth University, February, 1994. Still very active at the age of eight-seven, Revans attended eighteen separate events during the week he was at the university.

Photo courtesy of Robert L. Dilworth.

Photo 3   Dedication of the Revans Centre for Action Learning and Research, 1 December, 1995.

Revans (left) and David Botham, dedication of the Revans Centre for Action Learning and Research, at the University of Salford, Manchester, on 1 December, 1995. Botham was made the Director of the Centre, later to be renamed the Revans Institute for Action Learning and Research. As of 2009, the Centre, now renamed the Revans Academy for Action Learning and Research is housed at the Manchester Business School at the University of Manchester.

Photo courtesy of David Botham.

Photo 4 Lennart Rohlin, President of the MiL Institute Facilitating a Session during the annual MiL Days , Lund, Sweden, 2004

Since 1980, the MiL Institute has arranged yearly MiL Days for its member corporations and faculty members at the MiL Campus. In 2004, one seminar was with the management team of SvT (Swedish Television) with its President, Christina Jutterström, and its VP HR, Kickan Söderberg Falck (right) in attendance. Revans took part in previous MiL Days on several occasions.

Photo courtesy of Lennart Rohlin.

Photo 5   Attendees to the 13th annual Global Forum on Executive Development and Business Driven Action Learning, Seoul, South Korea, June, 2008

Co-hosted with the Korean Action Learning Association and the Hyundai Oilbank. Since its formation in 1996 the Global Forum, a community of practice, has been open to all action learning practitioners throughout the world. www.GlobalForumActionLearning.com

Photo courtesy of Karl-Georg Degenhardt

Glossary

Robert L. Dilworth

Introduction

This glossary contains some of the more commonly used terminology and singular initiatives associated with the evolution of action learning. Rather than refer to "sets" as Revans did, we refer to teams in order to be clear. There was no known differentiation between sets and teams by Revans. It was simply his preferred way of referring to teams engaged in action learning.

Action. The centerpiece of action learning is action, in that the experience is to lead to action. As Reg Revans states, there is no learning without action and no action without learning. The action to be taken/project serves as the engine that drives the process, promoting learning and critical reflection.

Action Learning. Action learning is a process of reflecting on one's work and beliefs in a supportive/confrontational environment of one's peers for the purpose of gaining new insights and resolving real business and community problems in real time. (, Dilworth and Willis, 2003; Willis's definition, p. 11)

Action Learning Set or Team. A group of four to eight individuals, what Revans called a "set", selected to participate in an action learning experience. There is no assigned leader within the team. All members of the team enjoy equal status. Revans considered five to be the ideal team size. (Revans, R. (1983), p. 7–8)

Action Learning Team Process Questionnaire (ALTPQ). An instrument developed by John Bing of ITAP International and Lex Dilworth of Virginia Commonwealth University to monitor the internal action learning team group dynamics, as seen through the eyes of its members (i.e., their perceptions). It is administered on line, with member responses kept anonymous. Both quantitative (Likert scale based) and qualitative responses are involved. Results are reported back to team members as a profile of what is occurring in the team across a field of 32 indicators (e.g., equalization of work load within the team, quality of internal communications and team effectiveness). Positives and negatives related to the action learning experience are also plotted. Dealing with the group dynamics, using the ALTPQ as a reference point, becomes part of the learning experience for the team.

Action Reflection Learning (ARL). This is a form of action learning that places special emphasis on critical reflection and transformative learning, with a learning coach to help participants strike a better balance between work on their project and learning from doing that work. The Management Institute of Lund (Sweden) was a pioneer of this approach. "Different from Revans, MIL developed a focus on learning coaches, working with participants in a co-learner relationship, but taking accountability for assertively catalyzing learning in the process"(Yorks, L., Oneil, J., and Marsick, 2002), pp. 19–29)

Belgian Experiment. An action learning program conducted in Belgium in the 1960's with governmental sponsorship, involving a consortium of the five leading Belgian universities and major companies. Developed and orchestrated by Reg Revans, action learning's principal pioneer, it involved action learning teams of five senior corporate executives, each dealing with an unfamiliar problem of great complexity that was centered in an industry other than their own, as they shared with their set colleagues concerns and insights on the learning taking place, "learning from and with each other" (Revans, 1980, pp. 39–48).

Business Driven Action Learning. This is a term used to describe a results-focused orientation to individual leadership development and organizational learning and change. It can be summarized as emphasizing both business results and the integration of individual development, team effectiveness and organizational strategy. (Boshyk, 2002, PP. 36–52)

Traditional (also called Classic) Approach to action learning. It centers on the philosophy and teachings of Reg Revans, principal pioneer of action learning. Some of its most basic precepts are outlined in Dilworth 2010 as part of Explaining Traditional Action Learning: Its Basic Concepts and Beliefs. (See also Weinstein, K., pp. 3–18) 2002]

Coal Board and Collieries. Revans was for a time associated with the Coal Board in England, and as part of that involvement he elected to spend a great deal of time underground with the miners at the coalface. He studied the group dynamics, concluding that "small is dutiful" (similar to the "small is beautiful" terminology coined by E.M. Schumacher). Revans found that when small teams were empowered and allowed to become involved in planning their own work, that the teams were significantly more productive than teams managed in an autocratic way. The safety records were also considerably better. He proposed that a "staff college" be created where there could be open discussion of ideas between management and workers. In the end, Revans' proposal was not supported, largely in his view because the senior manages did want to dilute their control over the enterprise. Revans was influenced by the work of Likert re: use of small teams, what Revans came to call action learning sets.

Client. The person or persons who will be relating to the action learning team or individual members (depending on the action learning model being used) in refining the problem statement in the client organization and receiving the results of the action learning effort.

Critical Reflection. This involves a purposeful effort to reflect on one's experiences in depth in order to reveal the underlying assumptions that govern our lives and perceptions of the world. This goes beyond mere reflection. As Gregory Bateson has indicated, it is "Level Three Learning". "You look for the why behind the why". Edger Schien has referred to it as "Triple Loop Learning". You end up both exposing and "unfreezing" underlying assumptions, some of them carried with us indiscriminately since early childhood, and testing them against the realities that we now face. In action learning, critical reflection can occur both individually and in collective dialogue within the action learning set.

Everyone Bring One (EBO) Model. This is an action learning team in which each member brings a different problem to the table, usually from that member's workplace.

Four Squares. A model used by Revans to demonstrate that problems we confront in our lives are either familiar or unfamiliar, and they occur in a familiar or unfamiliar setting. He designed a simple display with four quadrants to show the four alternative situations (e.g., familiar problem in an unfamiliar setting). Revans argues that the greatest learning occurs when we find ourselves confronting an unfamiliar problem in an unfamiliar setting. He viewed that as the personification of a learning organization. Revans believed that when we find ourselves confronting the unfamiliar, we are then inclined to ask fresh questions and challenge our long-held assumptions.

Future Search Conferences. This modality was pioneered by Marvin Weisbord and Sandra Janoff, Co-Founders and Directors of the Future Search Network. It has been used extensively around the world in dealing with difficult problems, with the goal of arriving at Common Ground as a foundation for action. A Future Search Conference usually involves bringing a diverse group of 64 to 72 participants together to address a major issue. (Weisbord & Janoff, 2000)

The large group is subdivided into Regular Stakeholder Groups of roughly eight, composed of functional groups (e.g., business people, press, clergy, government officials, people from financial institutions, human resource professionals). During the Future Search Conference, which usually lasts about 16 hours over three days, participants will be further assigned to Mixed Stakeholder Groups, each containing members from the Regular Stakeholder Groups. Each mixed group in effect becomes a microcosm of the whole.

Weisbord considers this a form of action learning. However, as is true of the GE Work-Outs, which are similarly short in duration, the time for reflection can be limited.

GE Work-Out/Change Acceleration Program (CAP). This is an organization development (OD) strategy that was inaugurated throughout General Electric (GE), beginning in 1989. It was driven by the belief that the values emphasized at GE's corporate university at Crotonville, New York, were being lost when managers returned to their workplace. (Ashkenas et al., 2002; Ulrich et al., 2002) The Work-Out was an effort, considered highly successful by the company, to embed these values in the everyday work life of GE. It is considered by GE to be a form of action learning. In its typical form, a group (e.g., 32) is brought together and then subdivided into teams of eight. Covering as few as three days, both the overall group and the teams are a part of the process as it unfolds. Teams are empowered to present recommendations to top management in face-to-face meetings, with an expectation of immediate decisions.

Hospital Internal Communications (HIC) Project. In the 1960's Revans became involved with what came to be called the Hospital Internal Communication (HIC) Project/Study. It involved the ten largest hospitals in London. The impetus for the initiative was the fact that the hospitals were experiencing staff morale problems, patient morbidity rates that were considered excessive, hospital stays that were too long, and attrition rates that were exceptionally high (as much as 67 percent for nurses). Small groups were sent from one hospital to another, where they observed familiar problems but in an unfamiliar setting. The groups did not operate as action learning teams. Nonetheless, each small group (it might only be three) would discuss their findings, and then the overall group would meet to discuss what needed to be done across the hospitals. It led to a number of initiatives. Results showed, when compared with nonparticipating hospitals (a quasi control group), that patient morbidity rates had gone down, staff turnover reduced, hospital stays shortened, and staff morale improved. The overall conclusion drawn was that lack of effective intercommunication between doctors and patients, nurses and doctors, and between all parties, had been ineffective, and that when intercommunication improved, positive results began to become evident. (Revans, 1980, pp. 29–38).

Hybrid Set. This is a term used when members of multiple teams are mixed together to form hybrid sets for the purpose of broadening the exchange of views on learning that is taking place. By bringing a cross-section of teams together, the intense project orientation tends to be temporarily diffused, elevating the likelihood that reflection on learning can occur.

Joint Project Model. This is an action learning team where all members are dealing with a common problem, usually one of great complexity. Revans would refer to such an experience as "partners in adversity", since all team members were confronting a common and vexing challenge.

Learning Coach. Also referred to as an advisor, facilitator, or mentor. The role varies in relation to the application of action learning involved, but the learning coach usually helps guide the action learning process, to include assistance in determining the appropriate project and arriving at team composition. The learning coach role can range from omnipresence in team meetings (e.g., Action Reflection Learning) to interruptive involvement based on need and invitation of the team membership. Reg Revans believed in minimal facilitation and intervention of the learning coach, believing that the team members themselves were the best facilitators, and that managing the team dynamics was part of the learning yield.

Learning Equation. Revans suggests that learning equals programmed knowledge, what he refers to as P, plus questioning insight, or the Q factor $L = P + Q$). He espouses the belief that while both the P and the Q are necessary for learning to occur, the P (formal and accrued learning) needs to be preceded by the Q and its free-ranging address of what is happening and needs to occur. In other words, the Q drives the P. (Revans, 1983, p. 28)

Nile Project. This was a project, spawned by the Belgian Experiment, described elsewhere in the glossary. It involved thirteen Egyptian companies and used a very similar methodology. (Revans, 1982, pp. 372–425)

Programmed Knowledge. This encompasses all the forms of formal/instrumental learning we are commonly exposed to, including lectures, textbooks, case studies, simulations and puzzles. Revans states that all forms of programmed knowledge travel out of what has occurred in the past, and therefore represent imperfect formulations in dealing with problems that we either are facing now or might expect to face in the future.

Questioning Insight (Q). The Q factor hinges on asking the right questions. Revans indicates that we need an added infusion of the Q factor in dealing with the fast paced times in which we live, since our capacity to learn is now often outstripped by the velocity of the change forces around us. Through questioning insight we are able to test the adequacy of the available P and determine if it is flawed or a bad match with what we need. In some cases, we will find it necessary to discount existing P and create new P. If we had started with the existing P rather than Q, we might have been inclined to accept P that would have led us in the wrong direction.

"Structure d'acceuil". A term used by Revans to describe an internal "client group" inside a company or organization that either assists an outside action learner or action learning team (set) to help examine an issue and then implement recommendations for change, and/or to take on the responsibility themselves for implementing the recommended changes. Revans (1980, p. 45)

System Alpha. This is the first of three interlinked systems of thought and action in Revan's concept of action learning. It features iterative, evolving analysis of a real problem situation in an organizational context. During the process, unexpected roots and ramifications are discovered. Novel attacks on problems can be mounted when action learners continually ask themselves the questions: What is happening? What ought to be happening? How can it be made to happen? The same questions will apply at different points throughout the inquiry. These questions are pivotal in arriving at an initial problem statement and tracking the migration of the problem over time as new insights are gained. (Revans, 1982, pp. 333–48)

System Beta. This system resembles the use of the scientific method in the physical and life sciences. Revans calls it "intelligent trial and error" Beta elaborates on what is derived from System Alpha, applying fact finding and assumption-testing procedures to check what is being learned. System Beta includes research, data collection and interpretation, and other discovery methods. Survey and/ or observation, trial hypothesis or theory, experiment (test), audit (evaluation), and review, ratification, or rejection of results are all necessary Beta processes. System Beta uses whatever is revealed to pursue new avenues of inquiry that might yield a better solution. (Revans, 1982, pp. 336–45)

System Gamma. This system, grounded in critical reflection, is embedded in all the action learning processes. Revans called it "symbiotic" with Alpha and Beta. It demands an honest search for understanding of the realities and value systems of self and others, since it is these realities and values that guide what people say and do. Revans insists that greater self-knowledge leads to greater interpersonal competence and more sensitive organizational skills. System Gamma, with the transformational change opportunities it offers, is at the very core of action learning and the energy source for its powerful effects. (Revans, 1982, pp. 345–48)

Transformative Learning. We are transformed to the extent we are able to either modify or jettison assumptions that are revealed as no longer having meaning, replacing them with new and more fully differentiated points of view and frames of reference. (Mezirow et al., 2000)). Learning in and of itself contains the seeds of transformation. When we learn, we are transformed.

Virtual Organization/Virtuality. Action learning in a virtual mode involves doing most, if not all, of the set business/interaction by teleconference, email or other electronic means, as opposed to face-to-face interaction. This provides special challenges to a modality predicated on intimate, direct, and regular face-to-face contact where all the senses are engaged. The challenge is further magnified when dealing cross-culturally with global teams. This is relatively unexplored ground with respect to action learning.

References

Ashkenas, R., Ulrich, D., Jick, T. and Kerr, S. (2002) *The Boundaryless Organization: Breaking the Chains of Organizational Structure* (San Francisco: Jossey-Bass).

Boshyk, Y. (2002) "Why Business Driven Action Learning?" in Boshyk, Y., (ed.) in *Action learning worldwide* (New York: Palgrave Macmillan), pp. 30–52.

Dilworth, R.L. (2010) "Explaining Traditional Action Learning: Concepts and Beliefs", in Boshyk, Y. and Dilworth, R.L. (eds), *Action Learning: History and Evolution* (Basingstoke, U.K./New York: Palgrave Macmillan).

Dilworth, R. and Willis, V. (2003) *Action Learning: Images and pathways* (Malabar, FL: Krieger Publishing Company).

Mezirow, J. and Associates (2000) *Learning as Transformation* (San Francisco: Jossey-Bass).

Revans, R. (1983) *The ABC of Action Learning* (Kent, England: Chartwell-Bratt).

Revans, R. (1982) *The Origins and Growth of Action Learning* (Sweden: Chartwell-Bratt).

Revans, R. (1980) *Action learning* (London: Blond & Briggs).

Tichy, N. and Sherman, S. (1993) *Control Your Destiny Or Someone Else Will* (New York: Currency-Doubleday).

Ulrich, D., Kerr, S. and Ashkenas, R. (2002) *The GE Workout: How to implement GE's Revolutionary Method for Busting Bureaucracy and Attacking Organizational Problems – Fast!* (New York: McGraw-Hill).

Yorks, L., O'Neil, J., and Marsick (2002) (eds.) "Action Reflection Learning and Critical Reflection Approaches", in Boshyk, Y. (ed.), *Action Learning Worldwide* (New York: Palgrave Macmillan), pp. 19–29.

Weinstein, K. (2002). "Action Learning: The classic approach", in Boshyk, Y. (ed.), *Action Learning Worldwide* (New York: Palgrave Macmillan), pp. 3–18.

Weisbord, M. and Janoff, S. (2000) (2nd edn) *Future Search: An action guide to finding common ground in organizations and communities* (San Francisco: Berrett-Koehler Publishers).

Index